The Dandy

The DANDY I'm sure.

1. "The DANDY I'm sure" (1816)

The Dandy

BRUMMELL TO BEERBOHM

by
Ellen Moers

University of
Nebraska Press
LINCOLN AND LONDON

First Bison Book printing: 1978

Most recent printing indicated by first digit below:

1   2   3   4   5   6   7   8   9   10

Library of Congress Cataloging in Publication Data

Moers, Ellen, 1928–
  The dandy.

    Reprint of the ed. published by Viking Press, New York.
    Includes bibliographical references and index.
    1. Dandies. I. Title.
  [CT9985.M6   1978]   909   78–8915
  ISBN 0–8032–3052–4
  ISBN 0–8032–8101–3 pbk.

Reprinted by arrangement with the author

Manufactured in the United States of America

To Martin, with thanks

Contents

Illustrations

Introduction

La rébellion humaine finit en révolution métaphysique. Elle marche du paraître au faire, du dandy au révolutionnaire.

—Albert Camus

AS we use it today, for a species of well-dressed man about town, *Dandy* derives from the cant of the Brummell period—the first years of the nineteenth century. Dictionaries trace it back no farther than the seventeen-eighties, as a term of vague significance in Scottish border songs, and offer as a source merely the local diminutive for Andrew (or the English "Jack-a-Dandy"). Yet even earlier than that, and far from its native soil, the word appeared in a setting which suggests that from the beginning *dandy* had the power to fascinate, to puzzle, to travel, to persist and to figure in an ambiguous social situation in a revolutionary climate. At least as early as the seventeen-seventies the word was being sung throughout the American colonies in the phrase *Yankee Doodle Dandy.*

The oldest stanzas of "Yankee Doodle" bear directly on the origins of dandyism. The most popular (which may go back to the French and Indian War but more probably dates from the 'sixties) was written by an Englishman to make fun of the appearance of the American troops:

> *Yankee Doodle came to town,*
> *Riding on a pony,*
> *Stuck a feather in his hat*
> *And called it Macaroni!*

The colonial soldiery wore "variegated, ill-fitting and incomplete" uniforms; the Macaronis were that circle of affected, oddly-dressed, cosmopolitan Londoners who can be identified as the nearest ancestors of the Regency dandies; the anonymous satirist amused himself by comparing the two. The reference to the Macaronis probably places a limit on the antiquity of the verse, for the famous Macaroni Club was not founded until 1764.

In the chorus *Dandy* has the sound (to American ears) of patriotic nonsense:

> *Yankee Doodle keep it up,*
> *Yankee Doodle Dandy,*
> *Mind the music and the step*
> *And with the girls be handy.*

Yet *dandy* here must at first have been an insult, for the chorus was a favourite with British troops in the 'seventies until they lost the song as well as the battle to the Americans at Concord. The Americans then added several stanzas of their own social satire, but directed up rather than down. Their new version (beginning "Father and I went down to camp . . .") describes Washington's visit to the Provincial Camp at Cambridge, Massachusetts:

> *And there was Captain Washington,*
> *And gentlefolks about him;*
> *They say he's grown so tarnal proud*
> *He will not ride without 'em.*

Washington has "got him on his meeting clothes" and wears "flaming ribbons in his hat". He moves apart from the troops "upon a slapping stallion".

There could have been no more fitting introduction for the word *dandy* than a song written to ridicule provincialism and vulgarity *as revealed by costume*, then expanded to ridicule aristocratic pretensions, again *as revealed by costume*. The time was right, the circumstances favourable—for dandyism was a product of the revolutionary upheavals of the late eighteenth century. When such solid values as wealth and birth are upset, ephemera such as style and pose are called upon to justify the stratification of society.

Simple foppery (or affectation in male costume) is as old as time: some wags have traced it to the Old Testament. But dandyism as a social, even political phenomenon, with repercussions in the world of ideas, was the invention of the Regency, when aristocracy and monarchy were more widely despised (hence more nastily exclusive) than ever before or since in English history. What the utilitarian middle class most hated in the nobility was what the court most worshipped in the dandy—a creature perfect in externals and careless of anything below the surface, a man dedicated solely to his own perfection through a ritual of taste. The epitome of selfish irresponsibility, he was ideally free of all human commitments that conflict with taste: passions, moralities, ambitions, politics or occupations. The first great modern war was moving toward climax; those who stayed at home created a supernumerary supreme being: a Hero so evidently at the centre of the stage that he need do nothing to prove his heroism—need never, in fact, do anything at all.

Throughout the nineteenth century the rising majority called for equality, responsibility, energy; the dandy stood for superiority, irresponsibility, inactivity. Inexcusably, in all his ghostly elegance, he haunted the Victorian imagination. Carlyle could deride him as a thing made by a tailor; the Victorians could denounce him as Not-a-Gentleman; but the novelists could not avoid the dandy. Though it might be necessary for a man to have a function, a function was obviously not in itself a man. Finding it impossible to imagine either heroism without dandyism or a truly heroic dandy, Thackeray invented the Novel-without-a-Hero. And Dickens, disappointed in his success, expressed the tragedy of failure in the form of the dandy —the man who had failed to find a function, but was important nonetheless by the shape of his existence.

Distressingly personal in England, the dandy ideal in France could become an abstraction, a refinement of intellectual rebellion. Because the dandy was foreign, the French could idealize him for what he was *not*: not middle-class and drab, not philistine and stupid, not buried in the tedious, undistinguished existence of those who merely lived out their time in the bourgeois century. The ambiguous symbol of the dandy brought together ideas and attitudes of the most unlikely contemporaries in the two countries.

Politically, the dandy appealed to both the reactionary and the revolutionary, as man of the past or man of the future. Brummell, the one thorough exemplar of the type, had sprung up from almost nowhere—but only through the acceptance of a Prince. Because the dandy asserted himself, Stendhal and Disraeli could see him as ambitious; because he took no action, Baudelaire and Dickens could see him as the observer of evil in modern life; because he upheld no ready-made morality, Barbey d'Aurevilly could claim him as a Catholic; and Oscar Wilde, as an aesthete.

The persistence of the dandy ideal explains much about the bourgeois spirit of the time. Behind the dourness, the prudery, the heavy earnestness of the Victorian pose lay a tentative nostalgia for anti-bourgeois virtues. The decorative surface, the blind assurance, the wrongheaded (but inescapable) *rightness* of the dandy figure remained somehow attractive, even to those outraged at the thought of squandering talent, energy and money on such achievements.

Dandyism could return to the surface of English thought, clarified by the conceptualizing of the French, only when its time was past. The 'nineties made something at once bloodless and commercial out of what Holbrook Jackson called their New Dandyism. As the social age of dandyism ended with Brummell's flight to Calais, the age of intellectual dandyism ended with Beerbohm's self-exile from the twentieth century.

We are today legatees of the Victorian ambivalence. In our dissatisfaction with utopia we marvel at the *possibility* of ignoring progress, despising community and adoring self. We are tired of rubbing shoulders with humanity. But the dandy, who made a success (however despicable and trivial) of absolute selfishness, is now merely a nostalgic catchword in the poet's lexicon.

> Encore un livre; ô nostalgies. . . .

> Encore un de mes pierrots mort;
> Mort d'un chronique orphelinisme;
> C'était un cœur plein de dandysme
> Lunaire, en un drôle de corps.

Part One

ENGLAND

CHAPTER I

Brummell

THE definition of the dandy begins with a particular point in time, a special milieu and a man by the name of George Bryan Brummell. His personality, variously understood, established the canons of that vague agglomeration of affectations, aspirations and negations the nineteenth century called Dandyism or *le dandysme*. Brummell was a very small man, but he was perfection in his smallness.

The dandy made his first, impeccable bow in the uneasy atmosphere of shifting perspectives and sinking values that followed on the French Revolution. The closing years of the eighteenth century had shaken Monarchy and rattled the foundations of Aristocracy; the new century inevitably felt the need to justify the rights and redefine the manners of the essential superior being. To the question—*What is a gentleman?*—which was to obsess poets and philosophers, novelists and divines, radicals and conservatives, the dandy made the most frivolous answer conceivable. He *was* a gentleman—it was a visible fact—by virtue of a "certain something", a "je-ne-sais-quoi" which could not be defined—or denied.

That Albert Camus should be able to find in the dandy an archetype of the human being in revolt against society (a revolt which, Camus says, has moved "du paraître au faire, du dandy au révolutionnaire") is the first irony of Brummell's definition. His arrogant superiority was an affirmation of the aristocratic principle, his way of life an exaltation of aristocratic society; but his terrible independence proclaimed a subversive disregard for the essentials of aristocracy. The dandy, as Brummell made him, stands on an isolated pedestal of self. He has no coat of arms on his carriage (indeed, Brummell kept no carriage), no ancestral portraits along his halls (and no ancestral halls), no decorations on his uniform (he had rejected the uniform), and no title but Mr Brummell, *arbiter elegantiarum* or, in the language of Brummell's day, "top of the male *ton*".

The dandy has neither obligations nor attachments: wife or child would be unthinkable, and other relatives are unfortunate accidents. When Brummell first came up to London he disposed of his brother and sister by cutting them, and disowned his ancestors by alluding to his origins as baser than they were. "Who ever heard of George B.'s father," he would say, "and who would ever have heard of George B. himself, if he had been anything but what he is?"

The dandy has no occupation, and no obvious source of support. Money does not strike him as a subject worthy of his attention. A beggar once asked Brummell for alms—"if only a halfpenny". "Poor fellow," Brummell replied. "I have heard of such a coin, but I never possessed one"; and gave him a shilling.

The dandy's achievement is simply to be himself. In his terms, however, this phrase does not mean to relax, to sprawl, or (in an expression quintessentially anti-dandy) to unbutton; it means to tighten, to control, to attain perfection in all the accessories of life, to resist whatever may be suitable for the vulgar but is improper for the dandy. To the dandy the self is not an animal, but a gentleman. Instinctual reactions, passions and enthusiasms are animal, and thus abominable. Here the dandy temperament diverges most widely from the romantic, which dominated the major literature of Brummell's time. Brummell's first biographer tells the illustrative story:

> An acquaintance having, in a morning call, bored [Brummell] dreadfully about some tour he had made in the north of England, inquired with great pertinacity of his impatient listener which of the lakes he preferred; when Brummell, quite tired of the man's tedious raptures, turned his head imploringly toward his valet . . .
> "Robinson."
> "Sir."
> "Which of the lakes do I admire?"
> "Windermere, sir," replied that distinguished individual.
> "Ah yes,—Windermere," repeated Brummell, "so it is,—Windermere."

The dandy does not preserve his integrity by living in retirement, but goes purposefully among the romantics, pedants, athletes, bailiffs and other bores of this world to remind them of his superiority. To call him heroic would be too emphatic, and would imply more effort and activity than his pose allows: it would be better to say, if S. Potter's phrase may be borrowed without offence, that the dandy is permanently *one-up*. He maintains his position by the use of a wit which transcends verbal flourishes to involve all the resources of his being. The dandy's wit has reference always to a *situation*: it triumphs over an actual risk. Brummell's ability to dominate a difficult situation without uttering a word was documented by an anonymous contemporary, who had observed him in action one night at the opera, shortly after his break with the Prince Regent:

> I was standing near the stove of the lower waiting-room . . . The Prince of Wales, who always came out rather before the performance concluded, was also standing there, and waiting for his carriage . . . Presently, Brummell came out, talking eagerly to some friends, and not seeing the prince or his party, he took up his position near the check-taker's bar. As the crowd flowed out, Brummell was gradually pressed backwards, until he was all but driven against the regent, who distinctly saw him, but who of course would not move. In order to stop him, therefore, and prevent actual collision, one of the prince's suite tapped him on the back, when Brummell immediately turned sharply around, and saw that there was not much more than a foot between his nose and the Prince of Wales's.
>
> I watched him with intense curiosity, and observed that his countenance did not change in the slightest degree, nor did his head move; they looked straight into each other's eyes; the prince evidently amazed and annoyed. Brummell, however, did not quail, or show the least embarrassment. He receded quite quietly, and backed slowly step by step, till the crowd closed between them, never once taking his eyes off those of the prince.
>
> It is impossible to describe the impression made by this scene on the bystanders. There was in his manner nothing insolent, nothing offensive; by retiring with his face to the regent he recognized his rank, but he offered no apology for his inadvertence . . .; as man to man, his bearing was adverse and uncompromising.

The perfection of this episode lies in the fact that it was wordless. In Brummell's wit, words were a useful implement, not an

end in themselves; meaning lay in the tone of voice, the manner,
the glance and the situation that was to be mastered. Writing
only a decade after Brummell had fled England, William Hazlitt
—who had not known the dandy but knew about him—proclaimed
the Beau "the greatest of small wits".

> He has arrived at the very *minimum* of wit, and reduced it, "by
> happiness or pains", to an almost invisible point. All his *bons-mots*
> turn upon a single circumstance, the exaggerating of the merest
> trifles into matters of importance, or treating everything else with
> the utmost *nonchalance* and indifference, as if whatever pretended to
> pass beyond those limits was a *bore*, and disturbed the serene air of
> high life.

To Hazlitt Brummell's greatest witticism was the dry line:
"Do you call that *thing* a coat?" In Hazlitt's day an imaginative
man could summon in support of the words Brummell's shrug and
intonation, his raised eyebrow or glancing eye, and the essential
situation. Here is a nobleman with pretentions to elegance asking
Brummell's opinion of a new coat, *before at least one other gentleman*
of the same set; there is Brummell's answer. Hazlitt observes "a
distinction . . . as nice as it is startling. It seems all at once a vulgar prejudice to suppose that a coat is a coat, the commonest of all
common things,—it is here lifted into an ineffable essence, so
that a coat is no longer a *thing* . . . What a cut upon the Duke!
The beau becomes an emperor among such insects!"

Refinement in wit, as in all things subject to the rule of taste, was
the essence of Brummell's dandyism; his pose gave the word many
and subtle meanings, describing a temperament rather than a
social gloss, a gift (or penalty) from birth rather than an accomplishment. *Refinement* comprised shadings of sensitivity, delicacy,
exclusivism and effeminacy. *Fine*, a favourite adjective of the
Brummell period, came to be vaguely synonymous with dandified.
An imitation Brummell in a contemporary novel is described by
a dowager to her daughter as "very fine, and every thing of that
sort". "Yes mamma," says the young girl, "but in what way
fine?" "Oh, gives himself airs, and is very conceited, and a great
dandy, and every thing of that sort."

In the social sphere the dandy's refinement is exclusivism; in
the purely physical it is hyper-sensitivity. His nerves are set jang-
ling more easily than those of ordinary men, his teeth are more

commonly on edge, his skin prickles and his eyes widen upon less provocation—and he boasts of his delicacy. Brummell once explained a cold caught in a country inn with the complaint that he had been put into a room "with a damp stranger". He protested that certain foods were too coarse for his palate: asked if he never tasted vegetables, "Madam," he answered, "I once ate a pea." ("This," said Hazlitt, "was reducing the quantity of offensive grossness to the smallest assignable fraction: anything beyond *that* his imagination was oppressed with.") In the same way he required a silver basin among his toilet articles, for "it was impossible to spit in clay". Country gentlemen aroused all Brummell's organs of disgust, particularly his nose, and he would defend their exclusion from the fashionable clubs on the grounds that "their boots stunk of horse-dung and bad blacking".

This *fineness* was proclaimed in all the accessories of Brummell's existence: in his small but elegant London home, his impeccable dinners, his beautifully groomed horses, his elaborately phrased letters, his precious Buhl and Sèvres, and—perhaps his greatest extravagance—his magnificent collection of snuff-boxes. (One turned up at the sale of his effects with a note inside designating it as a gift intended for the Regent—"if he had conducted himself with more propriety toward me.") "In fact," said Gronow, "the superior taste of a Brummell was discernable in everything that belonged to him." But the ultimate expression of Brummell's fineness was his personal appearance.

Beerbohm has sufficiently chastised the biographers who glorify Beau Brummell by glossing over his devotion to costume; by reducing "to a mere phase that which was indeed the very core of his existence". "To analyse the temperament of a great artist," Beerbohm goes on to say, "and then to declare that his art was but a part—a little part—of his temperament, is a foolish proceeding." The ideal of the dandy is cut in cloth. The dandy's independence is expressed in his rejection of any visible distinction but elegance; his self-worship in self-adornment; his superiority to useful work in his tireless application to costume. His independence, assurance, originality, self-control and refinement should all be visible in the cut of his clothes.

Asked how it was done, Brummell listed the essentials: "Fine linen, plenty of it, and country washing."

2

Captain William Jesse, Brummell's first and still most valuable biographer, launched upon his task with an invocation to greatness. "I will now enter," he wrote, "upon the life of him who Lord Byron said was one of the great men of the nineteenth century, placing himself third, Napoleon second, and Brummell first." This statement has often been repeated as proof of Byron's fatuity, but there is one sense, at least, in which the coupling of these names is justified: all three men were figures of legend, almost of myth, well before they died.

Brummell's legend was made up largely of anecdotes which expanded in the telling. Like Byron and Napoleon, he had a voice in its final version. Many of the most outrageous stories Brummell told for the first time himself, and during his years of exile in France he was able to weed out the uncharacteristic items. Each of the distinguished tourists from England who stopped to see Brummell in Calais or Caen had a question about some aspect of his history. Had Brummell, for example, ordered the Prince to summon a servant, with the insolent words: "Wales, ring the bell"? Brummell's emphatic denial of this rather vulgar story became itself part of his legend:

> "I was on such intimate terms with the prince, that if we had been alone I could have asked him to ring the bell without offence; but with a third person in the room I should never have done so, I knew the regent too well."

Captain Jesse's search after material for his biography illustrates the making of the myth. Jesse knew almost nothing at first hand. He had spent most of his life serving in the army outside England, and when he first met Brummell the Beau had been sixteen years in exile. Jesse questioned Brummell in Caen and collected his brilliantly uninformative letters. He consulted a few —very few—printed records: three brief magazine articles, a sketchy book of memoirs by one of Brummell's acquaintances, and Byron's letters and papers. After Brummell's death Jesse pestered everyone who might have known him. He hunted up Brummell's landlord in Calais, people who had entertained Brummell in Caen, and the nuns who had nursed him through his last illness. He wrote importunate letters—to Leigh Hunt, to the son of the poet George Crabbe, to members of Brummell's clubs and the Beau's contemporaries at school. Finding himself seated next to the high sheriff of a southern county, who let fall that he had been at Eton during Brummell's time there, Jesse broke in with his eternal queries. "I knew him well, sir," the old fox-hunter said; "he was never flogged; and a man, sir, is not worth a d—n who was never flogged through the school."

The principal source on which Jesse drew, however, was the ephemeral literature of the day: fashionable novels, salon verses, lampoons, burlesques and miscellaneous sketches. These trifles are still the fountainhead of Brummelliana, for the dandy's oddi-ties of pose and manner were inspiration to an army of contempo-rary scribblers—few of whom could have hoped to gain admission to his exclusive company. Many of the Regency fashionable novels owed all their interest to a retelling of the Brummell story; almost all made at least passing reference to his fame.

Thomas Henry Lister's *Granby*, published in 1826, contains the best fictional portrait of Brummell in the character of Mr Trebeck. Lister was an inside observer of London society with aristocratic and political connections* but he had not known Brummell: he was only sixteen when the Beau left England for good. Brummell's friends, however, remarked the accuracy of the portrait. Jesse used Trebeck as a prime source for his account of Brummell's temperament; Barbey d'Aurevilly, who later worked over the Brummell history with great care, praised Lister's characteriza-tion of the dandy in his own biography:

> The portrait of Trebeck seems to have been drawn from life; such strange nuances, half-natural and half-social, are not invented, and one feels that the real presence must have animated the brush that traced them.

Brummell himself, who read the novel in exile, approved its accuracy in the superb phrase: "Lister must have known those who were intimate with me."

Only a dandy could have approved such a portrait, for Trebeck

* Lister's career (1800–42) included education at Westminster and Cambridge, the positions of commissioner for Ireland and Scotland and registrar-general of England and Wales, a high-born wife and an early death in "the mansion of his relative, the Earl of Morley". "*Granby*", wrote Lady Holland grudgingly when it came out, "is evidently by a man who has seen London society, tho' he talks of a person as *gentlemanly*."

repels as much as he fascinates. Trebeck is self-centred, morally thick-skinned, arrogant; he pursues women for their money and abandons them when he learns they have no money; he cuts his friends, tricks his rivals, patronizes his enemies. "There was," Lister concludes, "a heartlessness in his character, a spirit of gay misanthropy, a cynical, depreciating view of society, an absence of high-minded generous sentiment, a treacherous versatility, and deep powers of deceit . . ." Harsh as the judgment seems, Lister refuses to take it seriously: whatever his moral failings, Trebeck is admirable for being himself. From the start, the novelist was grateful for the dandy.

3

George Bryan Brummell was born in 1778 and died in 1840. Legend had it, in his day, that he was of plebeian birth, but his father was actually a respected and influential civil servant, acting for many years as secretary to Lord North, the prime minister, and growing exceedingly prosperous from sinecures (such as "Receiver of the Duties on Uninhabited Houses in London and Middlesex") in the gift of his patron. Brummell's mother was a well-bred lady* whose family boasted several generations of gentility. His brother and sister, while not fashionable people, prospered, married well and married off their children to people of rank and title. Behind Brummell's father, however, lies uncertainty. It is known only that the Beau's grandfather—alternately referred to as a confectioner, a treasury porter, an army tailor, a steward or (most likely) a valet—ended his days as the owner of a lodging-house with Members of Parliament among his tenants.

Thus Brummell was descended from the upper-servant class, an origin perhaps less odious to the society in which he moved than the new, monied upper-middle class. Brummell made no secret of his humble grandfather, and forestalled gibes at his birth by minimizing the status of his parents. "My *father*," he would say of the respected civil servant, "was a very superior valet, and kept his place all his life."

Young Brummell learned early to bear himself well in exacting company. Fox, Sheridan and other of the Whig wits from Down-

---

* Her sister married a Mr Samuel Brawne; so that Brummell, who never knew it, was a near cousin of Keats' Fanny.

ing Street were frequently entertained at The Grove, the Brummell estate in Berkshire. The boy's reputation for fashion and eccentricity began at Eton and grew at Oxford, which he left after a few months when his father's death brought him an inheritance variously estimated at fifteen to sixty-five thousand pounds. He had already, probably at Eton, caught the eye of the Prince of Wales, who, like his father George III, often honoured the school with royal visits of inspection and occasionally invited favoured young scholars to Windsor. When Brummell left Oxford, at the age of sixteen, a place was made for him in the Tenth Hussars, the "Prince's own command" in more ways than one : it was the most idle and fashionable regiment of the day, hand-picked for elegance, charm and—ordinarily—birth. The Elegant Extracts, as they were called, followed their royal colonel on pleasure trips up and down the country from London to Windsor to Brighton, where the minarets of the Prince's pavilion were rising by the sea.

Within two years Brummell had risen easily from cornet to captain and had solidified his intimacy with the Prince. He was a member of the escort which brought Caroline of Brunswick from Greenwich to London; he was present, in personal attendance upon the Prince, at their wedding; and it is even said that he accompanied the Royal couple on their honeymoon at Windsor. Backed by the Prince's approval, Brummell was already well known in the fashionable world when he resigned from his regiment in 1798 and took a house in London.

He was immediately made a member of White's and Brooks's, the two most exclusive clubs of the day. He was invited to spend his summers and weekends at ducal houses in the country and his evenings at all the great entertainments of the season. (Accounts of these routs in the morning papers listed Brummell's name first among the untitled guests.) He repaid hospitality graciously but not ostentatiously, serving small, perfect dinners in his tastefully furnished house in Chesterfield Street. He lived rather better than the size of his inheritance warranted (and he had no other known source of income)—how, no one knew or, at this time, cared, least of all his tailors and wine-merchants and greengrocers. They could scarcely question an intimate of the Prince of Wales; and Brummell was soon to be a power in his own right.

That power had its roots in the principle of Exclusivism which then dominated all social behaviour. Brummell's world considered itself the only human aggregate worth knowing or being; and this world deferred to Brummell, simply at his insistence on his own superiority. To specify his role among his contemporaries requires the words *fashion, ton, exclusive* and *the world* used in the exact sense and with all the intensity the Regency gave them. Brummell had only to look upon or speak to or walk with a man to make him fashionable, and only to cut another to make him a pariah. At least Brummell's impudence would have it so, and his impudence was virtually unanswerable. The Duchess of R—— offended. "She shall suffer for it," Brummell told Tom Moore; "I'll chase her from society; she shall not be another fortnight in existence." Further, the exercise of Brummell's power lay in his making rules, setting tastes, establishing standards for the management of those things that the superior world considered superior to all else. His dictates were obeyed in all the great issues of existence: the curve of a brim, the blend of a snuff, the turn of a phrase, the ways to pass those long boring years when wars were being fought, laws were being debated, history was being made—elsewhere. "All feared, many admired, none hated him," Disraeli wrote of a Brummell-figure in one of his novels. "He was too powerful not to dread, too dexterous not to admire, too superior to hate."

Or, as Mrs Gore wrote in a less charitable mood, the dandy was "a nobody, who had made himself somebody, and gave the law to everybody."

The extent to which Brummell had made himself an independent somebody was demonstrated at the start of the second decade of the century when the Prince suddenly withdrew his favour—why, nobody knew but everybody delighted in explaining. The break came, it was said, because Brummell ordered the Prince to ring the bell; because he commented once too often on the Prince's increasing corpulence; because he took the part of Mrs Fitzherbert, the Prince's wife in all but constitutional right, against the Prince, thus arousing the gentleman's antagonism; or because he took the part of the Prince against Mrs Fitzherbert, thus arousing the lady's antagonism. Whatever episode provided the excuse, however, the underlying cause was a matter of greater historic importance. In 1811 Brummell's old friend was constituted Prince Regent of England and given the responsibilities, if not all the rights, of the throne. Many old intimacies had to be abandoned; that with Brummell was merely the most embarrassing.

Brummell had five years left in England. Deprived of the Prince's favour, he lost much of his commercial credit and many of his sources of entertainment. His habits changed. He became more of a club man and more of a gambler, particularly at Watier's, a new Regency institution where play was unusually, and literally, deep. (Each pack of cards was used for only one deal, and the discarded packs were thrown on the floor after each hand. By morning, Brummell told a friend, the players were "nearly knee-deep in cards".) The story goes—Brummell's own story—that he broke an initial run of bad luck with a crooked sixpence which he picked up from the pavement at five o'clock one summer morning after a night of play, and wore for years hanging from his watch chain. When final disaster reached him, Brummell had an answer for those who asked about the lucky sixpence: he had given it by mistake to a hackney-coachman, had advertised in vain for its return, and "no doubt that rascal Rothschild, or some of his set, got hold of it."

But the loss of the Prince's favour made Brummell a greater, not a lesser dandy. Instead of taking the Regent's displeasure with humility, Brummell turned abandonment into triumph. "The ridiculous part of the story," wrote Thomas Raikes in his *Journal*, "is that Brummell took the matter up in a high tone, and waged open war against his royal enemy, assailing him with ridicule in all quarters, and affecting to say that *he* had cut the connection." Tom Moore, in a rhymed parody of the Royal epistolary style, had the Regent protest that he harboured no resentments against any man:

> nor wish there should come ill,
> To mortal—except (now I think on't) BEAU BR-MM-L,
> Who threaten'd, last year, in a superfine passion,
> To cut *me*, and bring the old K-NG into fashion.

Two of Brummell's impertinences became legendary. The most famous of all Brummell anecdotes, told in many versions, has it that the Prince came down the street one day in company with Lord A——, and met Brummell and Lord B—— strolling in the opposite direction. The Prince stopped to chat with Lord B——, ignoring Brummell; the Beau, who had taught a whole generation

how to cut, turned to Lord A—— and inquired loudly,"Who's
your fat friend?"

The other impertinence was merely a phrase. "I made him
what he is," Brummell would say of the Prince Regent, "and I
can unmake him."

By such bold gestures Brummell kept the story alive, and furthered the impression that he and the Prince were social powers
of equal importance, now posed one against the other in open
rivalry. The Regent held court at Carlton House; Brummell
ruled from his seat behind the Bow-window newly installed at
White's Club. Henry Luttrell, another fashionable versifier,
made a wretched pun out of the "critic arrow . . . shot from yon
Heavenly Bow, at White's," which alighted with deadly accuracy

> On some unconscious passer-by
> Whose cape's an inch too low or high;
> Whose doctrines are unsound in hat,
> In boots, in trowsers or cravat . . .

All society talked of Brummell's audacity. When Byron was presented to "our gracious Regent" in June of 1812, he attended to
the Prince's conversation (about poetry) with only half a mind:
the other half was on Brummell.

So the Beau's London seasons passed, apparently unchanged,
until the evening of May 16, 1816, when, it has been recorded,
Brummell dined much as usual off cold fowl and bottle of claret
and stopped in, again much as usual, at the opera. But he left
rather earlier than usual, to step out into a waiting chaise "which
had been procured for him by a noble friend"; transferred to another carriage on the road, and drove his four horses post-haste
to Dover. The following day he reached Calais, where he was to
spend the next fifteen years. The conventional curtain to this
drama of Vanity Fair was rung down a few days later, when his
disappointed creditors auctioned off

> The genuine property of
> A MAN OF FASHION
> Gone to the Continent . . .

Thomas Raikes, who had long admired Brummell from a little
distance, "never was more surprised" than when he learned that

Brummell's debts had forced him to leave the country. But others closer to the Beau had known the truth for some time. Scrope Davies, soon to go into exile himself for the same reason, had had occasion to deny Brummell a loan requested *in extremitatis.* "MY DEAR GEORGE," he wrote, "'Tis very unfortunate; but all my money is in the three per cents. Yours, S. DAVIES."

A year earlier Davies had whispered to John Cam Hobhouse that Brummell was, in a delightful expression of the day, " £40,000 worse than nothing." And Lord Alvanley, referring to the press of money-lenders at Brummell's heels, punned off his friend's exile as "Solomon's judgment". Harriette Wilson voiced sophisticated opinion when she wrote to her sister Fanny that everybody was "puzzled to guess how he has gone on so long!" Byron's friend Hobhouse found a parallel in the greater world. Brummell, he wrote, "after beginning on £15,000 lived for twenty years on about £8,000 a year, and had to run away owing about £50,000—in its way as great a fall as Napoleon's. He is as tranquil."

Those friends most closely affected by Brummell's downfall stood by him cheerfully and loyally. Alvanley, Robert and Charles Manners, Scrope Davies, Worcester, the Duke and Duchess of York kept secret anything disreputable they might have known about Brummell, sent him letters and money when they could, and visited him without fail whenever they passed through Calais. Indeed, a visit to Brummell was almost obligatory, whether from compassion or curiosity, for every member of the set in which he had once been all-powerful. He became one of the notable tourist attractions of the Continent. "I could hardly believe my eyes," wrote Hobhouse in 1816, "seeing Brummell in a great coat drinking punch in a little room with us . . ."

The story of Brummell's last twenty-four years, in exile, occupies more than half of Captain Jesse's biography and of Virginia Woolf's sketch of the dandy. Jesse derived a complicated satisfaction from unearthing the unpleasant details of his hero's decay, and Bloomsbury found the "curious process of disintegration" pertinent to its melancholy concern with the decadence of aristocratic civilization. But the disturbing story of Brummell's decline is separate entirely from the dandy legend, and played only an oblique part in its dissemination. The Victorian assumption that Brummell's collapse was a divine judgment on his career helped

to keep his name in circulation in England; and the lurid finale
of Brummell's story satisfied his mid-century French admirers in
their exploration of decadence.

Brummell's first years in Calais were bearable: he lived within
a certain measure of his former ease and comfort, and he saw
many of his old friends. (Not, however, the Prince, crowned King
in 1820, who passed through the city on a state visit in 1821 and
at his departure was heard to remark, with what accents of relief,
triumph or regret has not been recorded: "I leave Calais, and
have not seen Brummell.") At last in 1830, through the good
offices of Charles Greville, the Duke of Wellington and William IV
(this tolerant monarch having just succeeded his unrelenting
brother), Brummell was appointed English consul in Caen. He
left Calais immediately (narrowly escaping his creditors) and
passed briefly through Paris in the autumn of that year. But, from
the beginning, Brummell's affairs in Caen went badly. The dandy
who had always been able to calculate to a nicety the practical
limits of impudence wrote to Lord Palmerston that the consul at
Caen had no important functions to perform. And found himself,
in 1832, not with a better post as he must certainly have expected,
but without any post at all.

Thereafter he lost, one by one, the qualities that had made him
a dandy: dignity, elegance, refinement, self-control, pride and
lucidity. Charity came to him sporadically and was doled out to
him by an agent. Creditors no longer treated him with respect,
and in 1835 the police seized him with an unnecessary show of
force and carried him off to prison. The one-time master of deportment became conscious of a paralytic stroke one evening at
the *table d'hôte* of his hotel, when he found that soup was trickling
down his chin instead of into his mouth. The one-time master of
the art of dress wore clothes that were, literally, in rags. The one-
time master of the anecdote grew prematurely senile, and tire-
somely repeated his favourite stories to reluctant listeners. The
one-time master of arrogant independence was put into the care
of an old woman hired to look after him; neighbours heard him
scream at her. The one-time master, professor and preacher of the
virtues of cleanliness suffered a final stroke inhibiting his intes-
tinal functions, and his room became a sty. At sixty-one, an imbecile, disgusting old man, forgotten and unwanted by everyone but
the Sisters of Charity, Brummell was carried off to a sanatorium

on the outskirts of Caen, "screaming and shouting at the very top
of his voice, 'You are taking me to prison—loose me, scoundrels!
I owe nothing!' " A few months later, on March 30, 1840, he was
dead.

Brummell himself had said all that was proper about the end of
his story. Shortly before his death an anonymous military gentleman stopping at Caen recognized the Beau in the shabby old man
at the door of the Hôtel d'Angleterre. Brummell acknowledged
his greetings and expressions of sympathy without complaint.
"On est bien changé," he said, *"voilà tout !"*

4

"A dandy is a Clothes-wearing Man," wrote Carlyle, "a Man
whose trade, office, and existence consists in the wearing of
Clothes." Carlyle's definition, though meant for other purposes,
actually defines: this is all that need be said about the dandy-
species, if not about the dandy-ideal. Certainly Brummell was
nicknamed Beau for his style of dress, not for his physical beauty.
But legend is confused about the nature of that style. The popular
version has always been that he dressed too obviously well, with
fantastic colours and frills, exotic jewels and perfumes. The accurate (and important) report declares that he dressed in a style
more austere, manly and dignified than any before or since.

Fashionable fiction, light verse and engraved caricature, those
eager purveyors of Regency legend, made much of Brummell's
reputedly laborious toilette, and they worked with witticisms
Brummell gave them. Asked for the secret of his highly polished
boots he replied that for blacking he never used anything but the
froth of champagne. A versifier of the day expanded the conceit:

> My boot-tops—those unerring marks of a *blade*,
> With *champaigne* are polish'd, and *peach marmalade*.

He enjoyed mystifying anxious imitators who inquired about his
relations with tailors and suppliers, and about the time and credit
he devoted to the minutiae of costume. All wanted to know how
the famous cravat was tied, and how much time the Beau gave to
the performance. The story circulated that Brummell's valet was
seen one morning coming down the stairs with an armful of white

linen cloth. "These," he said solemnly in answer to the curious, "these are our failures." This also was recorded in rhyme:

> My neckcloth, of course, forms my principal care,
> For by that we criterions of elegance *swear*,
> And costs me, each morning, some hours of flurry,
> To make it *appear* to be tied in a *hurry*.

Stories of Brummell's sartorial preparations expanded into fantasy. Bulwer's version of the Beau, the Mr Russelton in *Pelham*, boasted that he employed three tradesmen to make his gloves— "one for the hand, a second for the fingers, and a *third for the thumb*!"

In fact, Brummell did not usually emerge from his dressing-room until the mid-afternoon, partly because he kept late hours ("I always like to have the morning well-aired before I get up," he would say), but also because of a genuinely time-consuming toilette. A few people were privileged to watch the process. The Prince, in his first years of intimacy with the Beau, went in the morning to watch Brummell dress and sat so late that at last he sent away his horses and asked Brummell to give him a quiet dinner; but the Prince left no record of the scene. Other intimates wrote down snatches of observation. Jesse, for example, waited for Brummell one morning in his antechamber, and, the bedroom door standing slightly ajar to permit conversation, learned some secrets from a reflection of Brummell caught in a mirror over the mantel. From these accounts it can be established that Brummell spent well over two hours every morning on his appearance. But the ritual involved no application of perfume, which Brummell abjured, no mysterious preparations or salves. On the contrary, what took the time was getting clean.

Indeed, Brummell's major contribution to history was his highly original advocacy of cleanliness. It was a matter of pride with him that he did not need perfume: he did not smell. His laborious toilette commenced with a furious scrubbing of the teeth, accompanied by the following monologue addressed to the assembled noblemen gaping at the process:

"Well, what do you want? don't you see I am brushing my teeth?" (all the while slowly moving his brush backward and forward across his mouth, and hawking and spitting): then he would cry,—"Oh!

2. Robert Dighton: Beau Brummell (1805)

3. George Cruikshank: "The Dandies *Coat* of *Arms*" (1819)

there's a spot—ah! it's nothing but a little coffee. Well, this is an excellent powder, but I won't let any of you have the receipt for it."

Then he would shave with extreme care (Brummell never grew whiskers of any kind), wash and scrub and wash again with plenty of good soap and hot water, then scratch his face with a stiff flesh-brush till "he looked very much like a man in the scarlet fever." His last painful chore before dressing was to stand with magnifying mirror in one hand and tweezer in the other, and pluck out one by one from cheek and chin each hair that had survived shaving and scrubbing.

For the clothes which Brummell then put on with elaborate care, Beerbohm has awarded him the title of "Father of Modern Costume". The Brummell style established the limits of male costume from his time to our own. It can be criticized as drab, dull and monotonous—or admired, as Beerbohm admired it, for being

so quiet, so reasonable, and, I say emphatically, so beautiful; free from folly or affectation, yet susceptible to exquisite ordering; plastic, austere, economical . . . I doubt even if any soever gradual evolution will lead us astray from the general precepts of Mr Brummell's code. At every step in the process of democracy those precepts will be strengthened.

Beerbohm's irony is quite in point: Brummell's costume was suitable for all classes and occupations. Hardly altered in essentials, it would clothe democracy.

In the generation immediately preceding Brummell's the Macaronis had sponsored a cult of slovenliness and disarray to counter their reputation for affectation and effeminacy in dress. Brummell established a mean of taste appropriate to this last Georgian age, which took pride in its application of the principles of restraint, naturalness and simplicity to the modest spheres of interior decoration and personal appearance. The chaotic history of male costume, alternating between the too fine and the too coarse, came to a close on "that bright morning," in Beerbohm's words, "when Mr Brummell, at his mirror, conceived the notion of trousers and simple coats."

Brummell's costume consisted of a coat buttoning tight over the waist, tails cut off just above the knee, lapels (perhaps lightly boned) rising to the ears and revealing a line of waistcoat and the folds of a cravat. Below the waist, form-following (rather than form-fitting) pantaloons tucked into Hessian boots cut almost to the knee. He used only two colours: blue for the coat, buff for the waistcoat and buckskins, these set off by the whitest white of his linen and the blackest black of his boots. The only ornaments he permitted himself were brass buttons on his coat, a plain ring and a heavy gold watchchain of which only two links were allowed to show. (In Caen he was also seen with a tightly furled umbrella, its head carved into an unflattering likeness of George IV.) For daytime wear Brummell abjured silks and satins, laces and ruffles. Wool, leather and linen were his materials. In the evening he wore a blue coat, a white waistcoat, black pantaloons buttoning tight to the ankles, striped silk stockings and oval-toed pumps. That was all. "His chief aim," Jesse recorded, "was to avoid anything marked." "One of his general maxims was," according to Raikes, "that the severest mortification which a gentleman could incur, was to attract observation in the street by his outward appearance."

Within these narrow, self-imposed limits Brummell was, as Beerbohm maintains, an artist: "no poet nor cook nor sculptor, ever bore that title more worthily than he." "In certain congruities of dark cloth, in the rigid perfection of his linen, in the symmetry of his glove with his hand, lay the secret of Mr Brummell's miracles." Here also lay a multitude of small but momentous decisions in which Brummell would guide, merely by the cold irony of his glance, the contemporary world of fashion. His first and most important disciple was the Prince of Wales, who had begun his own sartorial career by inventing a shoe-buckle one inch wide and five inches broad, which made walking rather difficult; and who had appeared at his first court ball wearing a pink silk coat with white cuffs, a waistcoat embroidered with coloured foil and myriad bits of French paste and a hat weighed down with five thousand steel beads. The enormous change Brummell wrought (momentarily) in the Regent's appearance is most delightfully evident in the Cruikshank etching, half caricature and half portrait, of the Prince standing before Brighton Pavilion. He is far too stout to be flattered by the natural, unadorned lines Brummell had ordered into fashion. Yet he stands aloof, dignified, serene in the very sparseness of his costume, not a bespangled monarch but, prouder yet, first gentleman of Europe.

Tailors guided the taste of lesser patrons by following Brummell's decisions. They would appraise a cloth:

". . . the prince wears superfine, and Mr Brummell the Bath coating; but it is immaterial which you choose, Sir John, you must be right; suppose, sir, we say Bath coating,—I think Mr Brummell has a trifle the preference."

Brummell imposed on his generation the practice of starching linen neckcloths, in order to produce a cravat folded with exactitude. (But *light* starching was his principle; when abuse set in and London dandies suffered from immovable stiff necks, he satirized the exaggeration. At Watier's one night Brummell proposed a glass of wine with the heavily starched Marquis of Worcester, who sat two chairs down the table, by leaning back in his seat and calling the waiter:

"Is Lord Worcester here?"
"Yes, Sir."
"Tell his Lordship I shall be happy to drink a glass of wine with him."
"Yes, Sir."
". . . Is his Lordship ready?"
"Yes, Sir."
"Then, tell him I drink his health!")

Brummell blacked the soles of his boots to match their brilliant tops. And, to keep his buckskins fitting with the proper natural grace, he invented a style of pantaloon which opened at the bottom of the leg and was closed by buttons and a strap reaching under the foot.

His was a costume, then, which relied for its effect on the manner and bearing of its wearer. Long hours of concentration and preparation, of finicky attention to detail, were required to produce its dignified simplicity. The end result was a general appearance "similar to that of every other gentleman". The dandy's distinction was to be apparent only to the initiate. ("He was not a fop as many now think he was," said an admiring contemporary; "he was better dressed than any man of his day, and we should all have dressed like him if we could have accomplished it.") By making simplicity the fashion, Brummell established a style suitable for any man, king or commoner, who aspired after the distinction of gentleman. Without sacrificing elegance or grace, he invented a costume that was indubitably masculine.

5

That Brummell's affectations yielded utilitarian fruit was an irony to amuse Beerbohm, but not Beerbohm's predecessors in the dandy tradition. "Un Dandy ne fait rien," said Baudelaire, decisively; and again, "Etre un homme utile m'a paru toujours quelque chose de bien hideux." In Brummell's lifetime it was the affectation alone that made him legendary.

How affected was he? The question bemused Brummell's contemporaries and returned to plague the *fin de siècle*, when it became clear what company dandyism was keeping. Had there been something sexually uncommon about George Brummell?

In a period abounding in gossips and memoir-writers no one drew up a list of Brummell's feminine conquests, or noted with conviction the name of even one lady favoured by the Beau. The omission is extraordinary. "I never knew him engaged in what is called a *liaison* in society," wrote Raikes, who did not keep secrets; and Harriette Wilson, the voluble courtesan who was not above blackmail, used every means to blacken Brummell's reputation except the accusation of debauch. (It was suggested that her dislike for the Beau sprang from the fact that he was virtually the only man of the fashionable set with whom she did not have so much as a respectable flirtation.) Once, to stigmatize the bad manners of some young Frenchmen, she called them "as indifferent as even Brummell himself, to every woman turned of twenty."

Contemporary opinion, so far as it was recorded, did not accuse Brummell of effeminacy—as the Macaronis had been accused, and as many of Brummell's disciples would later be accused. Opinion pronounced him cold, freezingly cold, and so self-committed as to avoid personal entanglements of any kind. The fictional dandy figures drawn after Brummell were portrayed as *indifferent* to the female sex, like Lister's Mr Trebeck, the heiress-hunter, who protests that he is not exactly a woman hater:

. . . unfortunately, the word "indifference" is much more applicable to my case. It is in fact, my fault—I *am* indifferent . . . I can talk, laugh, and philander, and keep up a silly *persiflage*, with the thousand pretty nonentities that one meets in society; but it is mere habit, or mere idleness; they excite no interest, and they seem to know it . . .

Contemporary satire let the cold fop speak for himself. *Pursuits of Fashion*, a privately-printed verse satire, brought forth *"The Fine Man*, or Buck of the First Set"* to say:

As for love—I conceive it a *mere empty bubble*,
And the fruits of success never worth *half* the trouble;
Yet as Fashion decrees it, I bear the *fatigue*,
That the world may suppose me *"a man of intrigue."*

Careful sifting of opinion, and studying of his subject, led Brummell's biographer, Captain Jesse, to say what must be the last word: that Brummell "had too much self-love ever to be really in love."

Others wondered how considerable an intelligence lay behind Brummell's affectations. A few among his contemporaries put him down as a mere impudent fool, tolerated for the amusement derived from his absurdities. His admirers, however, found in Brummell powers of minute observation and a brilliantly discriminating tact. They never thought him guilty of introspection (a romantic, not a dandy failing); they hardly judged the quality of his mind from anything he said (though so clear-headed an observer as George Crabbe delighted in Brummell's conversation). Instead they detected a *visible* manifestation of intelligence in the dandy's "small gray scrutinizing eye, which", as one contemporary put it, "instantly surveyed and summed up all the peculiarities of features, dress, and manners of those who approached him, so that the weak point was instantly hit." The dandy's intelligence, as everything else about him, is on the surface. Even Hazlitt, analysing Brummell's verbal wit, finds the dandy mind in his *discriminating eye.*

. . . We may say of Mr Brummell's jests, that they are of a meaning so attenuated that "nothing lives 'twixt them and nonsense":—they hover on the very brink of vacancy . . . It is impossible for anyone to go beyond him without falling flat into insignificance and insipidity: he has touched the *ne plus ultra* that divides the dandy from the dunce. But what a fine eye to discriminate: what a sure hand to hit this last and thinnest of all intellectual partitions!

Those who were most impressed by the dandy's intelligence were often most disturbed by his apparent lack of direction. They

further wondered whether Brummell had achieved his extraordinary position effortlessly, through the logic of a personality
entitled to supremacy—or whether a conscious ambition had
shaped every affectation and absurdity. In either case, was dandyism the limit of his ambition? Mr Beaumont, a Brummell-figure
in one of the novels, states decisively that it is finer to be "prime-
dandy" than "prime-minister" (a preference that Disraeli's
dandy heroes in the next generation would exactly reverse). And
Beaumont gives the dandy definition of ambition: "it is the passion of those whose hard fate it is to languish on top storeys
without a change of linen."

The search for a familiar motive behind Brummell's pose has
marked the entire history of literary dandyism. Albert Camus,
like so many other Frenchmen, likens the dandy to the revolutionary, devoted perhaps to some fashionable revolution designed
to humble the mighty, to reform the vulgar, and to glorify the
independent man of genius. Indeed, a recent film made the Beau
a conscious fighter in the democratic cause, his destiny cramped
at the outset by inability to finance passage to America. But even
the coolest attempts to dissect Beau Brummell, to crack the hard
shell of the dandy self, have led to absurdities. There remains an
irreducible firmness to the Brummell figure, something compounded of assurance, self-sufficiency, misanthropy, nastiness,
even cruelty, that made him feared in his lifetime and will never
be explained away. It lends authenticity to the reply he is reported
to have made to Lady Hester Stanhope when she, too, wished to
know why he "did not devote his talents to a higher purpose."
"To which Brummell replied that he knew human nature well,
and that he had adopted the only course which could place him in
a prominent light, and would enable him to separate himself from
the society of the ordinary herd of men, whom he held in
considerable contempt."

CHAPTER II

The Regency 1800–30

Goddess of arts, of pleasure, and of dress,
Of courts and clubs, the palace and the press,
Fond of the passing moment—till it's past—
And deeming each more lovely than the last;
Inconstant, charming, false, delightful queen,
In fancy restless, yet in form serene,
Bewitching Fashion!

Disraeli: *The Dunciad of To-day*

THE time of Brummell's ascendancy, 1800 to 1816, was the first half of that peculiar era of English history, loosely called the Regency. Actually, the fourth George served as Regent for his ailing father only during the second decade of the nineteenth century. In the first he was the erratic and troublesome Prince of Wales; in the third, the unsatisfactory and unpopular King George IV. Yet the word Regency, with its connotations of instability and irresponsibility, does describe the atmosphere of the entire thirty years. Warning signs of the mental illness that would eventually destroy George III had appeared as early as the seventeen-eighties and 'nineties, when Regency bills were debated in Parliament and the young Prince strained anxiously after power. By 1801, though the King had recovered from his most serious attack of insanity, it became obvious that the comfortable, conservative Georgian court was passing into history with the old century, and that the Prince was about to succeed, as Regent or heir.

Brummell's years were war years almost to the end. And the second, or post-Brummell, half of the Regency era was a post-war period, with all the restlessness and the disequilibrium that the phrase implies. The alarms of the Napoleonic wars echo only faintly through the story of Brummell's career, but the world of the dandies was founded on that fear of boredom which afflicts stay-at-homes in a time of great events. War's end intensified the fears, and *ennui*, as the Regency called it, became the monster god of the 'twenties generation. "It was dull . . . last season," wrote the young Benjamin Disraeli in 1826, "very dull; I think the game cannot be kept going another year. If it wasn't for the General Election, we really must have a war for variety's sake. Peace gets quite a bore. Everybody you dine with commands a good *cuisine*, and gives you twelve different wines, all perfect . . ."

2

Early in 1811 George III passed finally into the blind, deaf and mad limbo of his old age. His son, the fourth George, celebrated his ascent to the Regency by removing a bust of Charles James Fox from his sitting-room in Carlton House to a prominent position in the Council Chamber, where it glared alarmingly at the Tory ministers. It was an act symbolic of George's political partiality for the Whigs (whom he failed, however, to return to power), and also of his predilection for wit and for his own circle.

The Tories were not the only ones to be dismayed at the establishment of the Regency. The Prince of Wales had gradually lost his early popularity with the citizenry, who resented the extra taxes necessitated by his eternal indebtedness and disapproved of his open immorality. England had watched the great Revolution in progress across the Channel, Jacobinism was in the air, and the angry words of pamphleteers spoke a lesson to the irresponsible Prince: "To hate Republicans let us first learn to love our Princes; let Jacobinical vices be opposed by Royal virtues." The factory workers were even more terse and more explicit. They would march through the smoky towns of the north with placards reading, "NO REGENT!"

One class of English society, however, counted George's accession to the Regency as a personal triumph, a confirmation of their own supremacy. The fashionable world of London was invited to George's private celebration at Carlton House. They drove past the Horse Guards stationed at the four corners of the fashionable world (Pall Mall, St James's Street, Piccadilly and St James's Square) to admire the florid decorations of the palace (the crimson velvet, gold tassels, white ostrich plumes, ebony and gleaming bronze endlessly reflected in the tall pier-glasses) and to applaud the Regent as one of their own. To this society

George's tastes for gambling, racing, eating and dressing were congenial; his distaste for domesticity was not only conventional but fashionable; and his preference for a narrow circle of his own, his resolve to turn his back on the country at large and follow the edicts of *ton*, was highly reassuring. At a time when high society bowed to the all-powerful principle of Exclusivism, it was fitting that the Regent of England should be an exclusive.

It is the nature of High Society to exclude undesirables. What marks Regency society as unique is the determined way it went about exclusion, the innumerable hedges against intruders, the explicit, almost codified rules for membership, and the elaborate sub-rules for the behaviour of members. In no other society has the mechanism of exclusion been so prominent, elaborate and efficient. It was the universal, often the only, interest. Regency Society called itself exclusive, its members the exclusives, and its ruling principle exclusivism. A whole language, expressing the subtleties of the mechanism, grew up around the central words.

Chateaubriand was puzzled by this language when he sampled London society in the 'twenties as the Ambassador of Louis XVIII. "Les modes des mots, les affectations de langage et de prononciation, changeant dans la haute société de Londres presque à chaque session parlementaire," he complained, "un honnête homme est tout ébahi de ne plus savoir l'anglais, qu'il croyait savoir six mois auparavant." A Frenchman of all men, however, should not have been confused, for most of the cant words favoured by the Exclusives were fashionably French. The following, a fair sample of phrases found in every fashionable novel of the period, is culled from the affected language of only one, entitled *The Exclusives*:

> the society of *ton*; the dynasty of *ton*; the court of *ton*; the empire of *ton*; devotees of *ton*; the élite of *ton*; the polished ultras of *Ton*; ultra-*ton*ism; The *Ton*; the world of fashion; the fashionable multitude; the *canaille* of the fashionable world;
>
> a *société choisie*; a *société distinguée*; a select *coterie*;
>
> a *race à part*; young men *de la première volée*; a *haut grade* in society; the more *recherché* amusements; the *corps élite*; The *Elite*.

The Exclusives referred to themselves not merely as the great world, but *the world*, not merely as high society, but *society*. The world's place was London, its span the length of the yearly season.

(The end of the social season brought a kind of death in the midst of life, when city streets seemed unpleasantly hot, dusty and deserted, and when owners of the fashionable country houses and followers of the Prince at Brighton tried to fabricate a season out-of-season.) Its members had the sense of belonging to a very real social organization (so much a club, it could be said that either you were *in* or you were *out*) with its headquarters in St James's Street, where the institutions of exclusivism lived and issued their decisive edicts.

St James's Street was (and is) the great club street, and in Regency society, which was ruled by masculine tastes, the clubs were all-important. They were more than a gathering place for single men (or married men who wished to behave as if they were single), and the services they offered were more than the elegant dinners prepared in the French manner or the endless gambling for inordinately high stakes. They were most of all efficient servants of exclusivism, whose little black balls defended society against intrusion.

The most important of the Regency clubs, because the most difficult of entry, was White's. If you *made* White's, you were *in* with finality. A contemporary analyst of English society described it as "*the* club from which people have died of exclusion, . . . killed on the spot by a black ball; *the* club where, in dandy existence, 'either you must live or have no life.' " Disraeli is said to have called admission to White's a supreme human distinction (he was never admitted) comparable only to the Garter. White's had been established in the preceding century as a Tory institution, but during the Regency its political character was subordinate to its social importance: Brummell, a nominal Whig, was a member. At about the time George became Regent, a talented organizer by the name of George Raggett took over White's and spread the legend that he was growing rich from the sweepings of the gambling table. Under Raggett's management the façade was remodelled to include the famous bow window from which Brummell and his chosen disciples passed judgment on the fashionable world. The few who sat behind that window formed a club within a club, with their own special privileges and prerogatives. It was said that "an ordinary frequenter of White's would as soon have thought of taking his seat on the throne in the House of Lords as of appropriating one of the chairs in the bow

window." The club's semi-parliamentary, semi-regal position as
social arbiter was publicly celebrated in 1814, the triumphal year
of the Regency, when the victorious Allied sovereigns, and later
the Duke of Wellington, were honoured by magnificent fêtes at
White's.

Just under White's in importance, and across from it in St
James's Street, was Brooks's. In the small world of the Regency
the little stretch of pavement between them was significant:
Brummell once repaid a debt by giving his arm to a creditor from
Brooks's to White's. The great Whig club of the eighteenth
century, Brooks's also included a club within a club, dedicated
to the memory of Charles James Fox. But by the height of the
Regency Brooks's was known more for gambling than for politics,
and dandies like "Apollo" Raikes and "Poodle" Byng were among
its members.

A Regency addition to the clubs was Watier's, founded, according to legend, when members of White's and Brooks's complained to the Regent about the eternal sameness of club food.
Without pausing to commiserate, the Prince rang the bell for his
own cook, a Frenchman by the name of Watier, and proposed that
he assume the management of a new club. Byron, one of Watier's
most satisfied members, boasted that he was one of the very few
literary men admitted to the club. In 1827, toward the close of the
era of Regency Society, when the D'Orsay variety of dandyism
was superseding Brummell's, Crockford's was added to the clubs
in St. James's Street to express the slightly shifting balance of
values. The new club was wholly non-political. Called "The New
Pandemonium", Crockford's featured gambling at the modern
and dangerous game of hazard. The club's manager, affectionately known as "Crockey", was said to have won by one means
or another the whole of the ready money of his generation.

Any of the business of exclusivism not concluded in the clubs
was carried on behind the doors of Almack's, just off St James's
Street in King Street. The famous Assembly Rooms had been
established in the preceding century by a Scotsman named
MacCall or Macall (who concealed the stigma of his origin by
juggling the letters of his name) with the aim of providing a
wholly secure rendezvous for society. By 1810 Almack's was the
inner temple of exclusivism, called by its contemporaries "the
seventh heaven of the fashionable world." What Almack's offered

was superficially unexciting: a weekly ball, held every Wednesday evening throughout the season, a modest décor, and positively meagre refreshments: weak bohea, weak lemonade for variety, thin slices of brown bread and butter, biscuits and stale cake. But the ostentatious simplicity of Almack's entertainment was a typical Regency deception. The dull backdrop merely set off the cabals, intrigues, heartbreaks and feuds surrounding Almack's primary offering: the business and pleasure of exclusivism. "There shall be no ostentation of wealth, no suppers," says an imaginary patroness of Almack's in Bulwer's *Godolphin*. "It will be everything if these entertainments, being perfectly distinct from those of rich bankers, rich bankers cannot affect to vie with us."

Admission was by ticket only (called "vouchers of admission") and subscriptions were harder to secure than a peerage. You could not buy your way into Almack's (indeed, the tickets were inexpensive); you had to be scrutinized, dissected, genealogized and finally accepted by a half dozen or so lady patronesses whose word was law. In 1814 the patronesses included Lady Castlereagh, Lady Jersey, Lady Cowper (later Lady Palmerston), Lady Sefton, Mrs Drummond Burrell (later Lady Gwydyr and still later Lady Willoughby de Eresby) and two interesting cosmopolitans, Princess Esterhazy and Countess Lieven. The patronesses were commonly compared to the Venetian Council of Ten, the tyrants of ancient Rome and the gods on Mount Olympus. Young ladies, who reckoned their age and standing in society by the number of seasons they had danced at Almack's sobbed or fainted away when refused admission. Mothers with daughters to marry sacrificed pride and morality in a desperate scramble for the carefully guarded tickets. Captain Gronow tells the story of a Captain in the Guards who challenged Lord Jersey to a duel: his wife had refused the guardsman a ticket to Almack's.

When Lord Melbourne was Chief-Secretary for Ireland he watched the Orange gentry draw in each distinguished visitor simply "by assuming that their set was the only one worth associating with", and he recalled the exclusive frenzy of the Wednesday balls. "You, who know Almacks," he wrote a colleague, "know that this is one of the strongest, if not the very strongest passions of the human mind."

Wealth was no guarantee of admission, for defences were up

against the *nouveaux riches*, the vulgar *roturiers*. Birth was no guarantee, for three quarters of the nobility were said to knock on the sacred doors in vain; yet the patronesses were "as exacting concerning the sixteen quarterings of an aspirant, as a Herald of the Empire examining the claims of a pretendant to some German Chapter of the Golden Fleece." Beauty, talent, achievement, distinction—none of these meant anything unless qualified by that elusive term: *ton*. It was decided, for example, that a carefree, penniless Irish poet, who lived in St James's Street and sang prettily at evening parties, had *ton*—and Tom Moore was duly admitted. In 1819 he noted proudly in his diary: "Went to Almack's (the regular Assembly) and staid till three in the morning. Lord Morpeth said to me: 'You and I live at Almack's'."

A novel was of course written about Almack's and called, simply, *Almack's*. It was published in 1827 with the following dedication:

To that Most Distinguished and Despotic
CONCLAVE,
Composed of their High Mightinesses
The Lady Patronesses of the Balls at
ALMACK'S,
The Rulers of Fashion, the Arbiters of Taste,
The Leaders of Ton, and the Makers of Manners,
whose sovereign sway over "the world" of London has
long been established on the firmest basis,
whose Decrees are Laws, and from whose judgment there
is no appeal . . .

The evening costume Brummell brought to perfection was the required uniform for Almack's. If any man was so foolhardy as to arrive without the regulation knee breeches,* white cravat and *chapeau bras* (a bicorne shaped like a slice of lemon, made to be folded flat and carried under the arm), he would be denied admission despite his hard-won ticket to the ball. Decorum,

---

* "Knee-breeches" is not to be taken literally. The more common and equally acceptable costume was the form-fitting, black tights showing a modest amount of striped silk stocking, a trim ankle and a dainty foot in a flat black dancing slipper—in the manner of Brummell. What was prohibited was the full-length, informal trouser or pantaloon, a garment satirized in the period as resembling two Continental towns: *Too-long* and *Too-loose*.

including, of course, the dances to be danced, was rigidly supervised. The acceptance of a new dance from the Continent was a
subject of grave importance, to be debated and recorded in poetry
and fiction; for the decision would set a fashion. So the quadrille
was not danced at Almack's until Lady Jersey herself studied it
in Paris and was ready to demonstrate it personally to London.
And the introduction of the waltz (the dance which stimulated
impassioned argument, even from Byron, who found it alternately indecent or "the only dance which teaches girls to think")
was a major event requiring the personal patronage of Countess
Lieven.

Dancing went on far into the early Thursday mornings, but the
deadline for admission to Almack's balls was despotically, many
thought cruelly, prescribed: 11 p.m., and not a minute later.
George Ticknor, the American publisher and cosmopolite, overheard the following dialogue at Almack's and never forgot it:

> "Lady Jersey, the Duke of Wellington is at the door, and desires
> to be admitted."
> "What o'clock is it?"
> "Seven minutes after eleven, your ladyship." [—*brief pause, and
> then, emphatically and distinctly*—]
> "Give my compliments,—give Lady Jersey's compliments to the
> Duke of Wellington, and say she is very glad that the first enforce-
> ment of the rule of exclusion is such that hereafter no one can complain
> of its application. He cannot be admitted."

Power was given to the rulers of Almack's because the clubs,
far as they went in catering to Regency masculinity, could not
perform one necessary function. Almack's was, as the clubs were
not, a stable for both sexes, an institution which could supervise
the breeding (licit and illicit) of exclusives, much as the Jockey
Club supervised the perpetuation of thoroughbreds. Edward
Bulwer, who moved in and out of fashionable Regency life as
critic and participant, had many harsh words to say for Almack's:
"How unintellectual, how uncivilized, such a scene, and such
actors! What a remnant of barbarous times, when people danced
because they had nothing to say!" But, as a student of Mill and
Bentham, Bulwer could see Almack's utility. "We have some
excuse," he added; "we go to these assemblies to sell our
daughters, or corrupt our neighbours' wives. A ballroom is
nothing more or less than a great market-place of beauty."

3

Within the exclusive world it was necessary to tread the curlicue line of fashion, and there were fashions in all things. First, of all, it was fashionable to be idle, and most unfashionable to work. (Though keeping up with the fashions was no task for a lazy man: "La mode chez eux," wrote Stendhal, "n'est pas un plaisir, mais un devoir.") Many exclusives had a share in the great affairs of their day (like Wellington in the prosecution of war and the administration of peace, like Byron in the revitalizing of English poetry), but on the floor of Almack's or behind the bow-window at White's they boasted of their place in the ranks of the elegantly idle. So Lord Wellington, who, as one of his acquaintances said, "always placed first and foremost, far above his military and social honours, his position as an English gentleman," went to dance at Almack's and found time to philander with the courtesan Harriette Wilson. She noted his limitations in her scandalous (but very fashionable) *Memoirs*. Byron at his ease would scorn hard-working literary men, "the would-be wits and can't be gentlemen." "One hates an author that's *all author*," he wrote in *Beppo*, adding:

> Of coxcombry's worst coxcombs e'en the pink
> Are preferable to these shreds of paper,
> These unquench'd snuffings of the midnight taper.

And he took care to say that he "liked the Dandies; they were all very civil to *me* . . ."

It was, of course, fashionable to be a lord—but not a lord who lived on the family estate, distributed hot broth and warm clothes to his tenants, and supervised the management of the land. Indeed, it was unfashionable to know exactly the extent of one's resources. The fashionable way to describe a gentleman's dependence on the land was to say—with the abstraction of a Russian nobleman counting his "souls"—that he had a rent-roll of so many thousands, or hundreds of thousands, pounds a year. It was also fashionable and neatly convenient to have part of one's money "in the funds". And it was highly fashionable to go hopelessly into debt, for which the fashionable remedy was a discreet removal to the Continent.

There were even "fashionable and patronized money-lenders":

in 1814, for example, "the Israelitish establishment" of Howard
and Gibbs. Some members of this useful class went so far as to
imitate their dandy patrons. Gronow left an admiring portrait of
the most successful money-lender of the day, "Jew" King:

> King was a man of some talent, and had good taste in the fine arts; he
> had made the peerage a complete study, knew the exact position of
> every one who was connected with a coronet, the value of their
> property, how deeply the estates were mortgaged, and what incum-
> brances weighed upon them . . . He gave excellent dinners, at which
> many of the highest personages of the realm were present; and when
> they fancied that they were about to meet individuals whom it would
> be upon their conscience to recognize elsewhere, were not a little
> amused to find clients quite as highly placed as themselves, and with
> purses quite as empty.
>
> King had a well-appointed house in Clarges Street; but it was in a
> villa on the banks of the Thames, which had been beautifully fitted
> up by Walsh Porter in the Oriental style . . . that his hospitalities
> were most lavishly and luxuriously exercised . . .
>
> King kept a . . . splendid equipage, which he made to serve as
> an advertisement of his calling. A yellow carriage, with panels
> emblazoned with a well-executed shield and armorial bearings,
> and drawn by two richly-caparisoned steeds . . . daily made its
> appearance in the Park from four to seven in the height of the
> season.

It was considered more necessary than fashionable to raise a
family, and highly unfashionable to raise a large one or to discuss
the subject. A son's independence of parental ties was established
at an early age, when he was sent off to Eton. Brother cut brother
dead in the street, as Brummell did because his brother came to
town in country clothes. "Such intimations of fraternal coolness,"
noted one Regency novelist, "are by no means uncommon in that
model country of the domestic affections, Great Britain." Within
each family the exclusive hierarchy prevailed: Trelawny's *Adventures* begins, "I came into the world, branded and denounced as a
vagrant, for I was a younger son . . ."

Though there were a few fashionable churches, church weddings were not fashionable (a *"baroque* fancy", one of the characters in *The Exclusives* called them. "In church! *quelle idée, vraiment on mourra de froid."*) Husbands and wives went their
separate ways into society, and when, as often happened, they

4. George Cruikshank: "His Most Gracious Majesty
George the Fourth" (1821)

5. Richard Dighton: "A Welch Castle"
(Lord Gwydyr) (1818)

finally could not abide the sight of each other's face, the fashionable solution was a separation. In domestic affairs the Regent set the fashion, banishing the Princess Caroline from his sight as soon as his daughter was born (almost nine months to the day after they were married) and sending her the following classic of Regency prose: "MADAM", George wrote,

> . . . Our inclinations are not in our power, nor should either of us be held answerable to the other, because nature has not made us suitable to each other. Tranquil and comfortable society is however in our power; let our intercourse therefore be restricted to that, and I will distinctly subscribe to the condition . . . that even in the event of any accident happening to my daughter, which I trust Providence in its mercy will avert, I shall not infringe the terms of the restriction by proposing at any period, a connection of a more particular nature. I shall now finally close this disagreeable correspondence, trusting that, as we have completely explained ourselves to each other, the rest of our lives will be passed in uninterrupted tranquillity.

> I am, Madam,

> With great truth,
> Very sincerely yours,
> GEORGE P.

This magnificent letter was fortunately accessible to lesser exclusives as a model for their own epistolary style. When George later attempted to divorce his wife, Caroline included it in her testimony before the commission of peers investigating the Prince's charge that she was an adulteress. The complete record of the commission was printed under the title *An INQUIRY, or DELICATE INVESTIGATION into THE CONDUCT of Her Royal Highness THE PRINCESS OF WALES*. But it was so widely read that it became known simply as, *The Book*.

When, as in the case of the unfortunate GEORGE P., a separation did not bring uninterrupted tranquillity, the prosecution of a divorce was perhaps disagreeable but certainly not unfashionable. Again, the Regent set the pattern. Although unsuccessful in his attempt to divorce the Princess Caroline, he did bar her from his Coronation. Six prize-fighters were stationed for that purpose at the entrances to the Abbey.

Such domestic irregularities were no more popular with the people of Britain at that time than today. Indeed, the people of

London showed their appreciation of George's bachelor coronation by shouting to his face "God Save the Queen!" What disturbed George, however, was not the roar of popular disapproval but a distant grumble of fashionable distaste for the *vulgarity* of his treatment of Caroline. He anxiously summoned Lord Gwydyr (acting Lord Great Chamberlain of the Coronation, husband of a patroness of Almack's and one of Brummell's successors as dandy-in-ordinary to the Prince). "I care nothing for the mob," the Regent said, "but I do for the dandies!" At Gwydyr's suggestion a special breakfast was held in the neighbourhood of the Abbey on the morning of the Coronation and the gentlemen were pacified.

Retreating further and further from the concerns and the company of the people over whom he ruled, George at the last became an example of the excesses of fashion. For Regency fashion, as Bulwer pointed out, was simply "the public opinion of the lords of the social system", and to the exclusives the most natural opinion in the world was that which saw an inevitable antagonism of class to class, of coterie to coterie. In the case of the ageing Regent, hated by the populace and hating them with equal fervour, exclusivism came to be indistinguishable from the Hanoverian distemper; it became a mania. His public appearances grew more and more infrequent; his very emergence from Carlton House became an exclusive event to be remarked, a tableau with a peculiarly Regency flavour:

> At four o'clock the gates of Carlton House were opened daily [writes Thomas Raikes] and the plain *vis-à-vis* with the gray liveries, and the purple blinds down, was to be seen wending its way through the crowd to its usual destination, unremarked by any but the experienced eye, which knew the royal incognito, and the superb bay horses unequalled in London.

4

In such circumstances it became a matter of some moment whether a given book or journal was or was not fashionable: a stratified society produced a literature stratified along class lines. The early years of the nineteenth century were marked by the gradual extension of literacy to the lower classes, and the achievement of wealth, leisure and self-confidence by the middle classes;

the aristocracy fought to avoid contamination by the vulgar in its reading as in all its other social pursuits. For the mechanics and artisans of young industrial England, avid for education, there were the Penny Periodicals, and the "family libraries" which had, as one of the more thoughtful aristocrats put it, "the captivating profession of teaching all things useful—bound in cloth, for the sum of five shillings a month!" For the middle classes there were the powerful daily press and the distinguished reviews and magazines which provided not only an organ but in many cases a living for the Romantic generation of poets and essayists. (The Romantics were almost all of them middle class or less in origin; in the class-conscious Regency era many of them were grouped under the label of the "Cockney School".*)

For the aristocracy of *ton* there was a literature of *ton*, which for the most part had little but its *ton* to recommend it: the "aristocratic" journals, scandal-sheets like the *Age* (which Bulwer said were "supported alone by the excrescences of aristocracy, by gambling-houses, demireps, and valets"); the fancy London magazines, treasured for their elegant fashion plates or their devotion to the history of the Regent's relations with Caroline, with evocative titles: *La Belle Assemblée; or Bell's Court and Fashionable Magazine* and *The New Bon Ton Magazine*. There were the snob-ridden Annuals, like those edited by Lady Blessington, which Thackeray judged drawn up according to the best of all possible plans ". . . if it be desired to make the worst painters, the worst poets, and to create the worst taste in the public." There were fluent and frivolous salon verses, like "The Butterfly's Funeral" legendarily attributed to Brummell, and

---

* The world of Brummell and the world of the Romantics were contemporaneous but mutually exclusive. Reviewing the *Oxford Book of Regency Verse*, Desmond MacCarthy noted "how completely a suitable title may mislead one . . . I expected, of course, to find Byron in such an anthology, but chiefly poems marked by characteristics associated with the word 'Regency'. On opening the book I discovered . . . very many very familiar poems, such as 'The Ancient Mariner', 'Intimations of Immortality', 'The Lotus Eaters', 'The Ode to the West Wind', the 'Ode to a Nightingale' . . . etc., etc. Coleridge, Wordsworth, Blake, Shelley, Landor were, of course, writing during this period, but somehow I had never thought of them as 'Regency Poets' . . ."

Byron, the great exception that proved the rule, was as Lady Blessington quipped "a poet among lords and a lord among poets".

Henry Luttrell's "Advice to Julia", of which the table of contents alone clearly evokes the Regency literature of *ton*:

> Hyde Park—The Ride—The Promenade—The Opera—New-market—News of the Day—Sketch of a Small-talker—The Park on Sundays—A Submissive Lover—The Mysteries of Dress—Importance of the Cravat—An Apostate Beau—A modern Dinner—The Ball-room at Almack's—Waltzing—Quadrilling—Cautions to younger Brothers—End of the London Season—A Water-party—Brighton—Debts and Doubts of a Man of Fashion—etc., etc.

And, after 1825, there were the fashionable novels.

This remarkable form was the creature, if not the creation, of Henry Colburn, a publisher who amassed a fortune by brilliantly judging the tastes of his age. It was Colburn's genius to see that a literature written about the exclusives, by the exclusives (or those who knew them well) and for the exclusives would be royally supported by those who were not but wanted desperately to become exclusives: the *nouveaux riches* of post-war England. From Colburn's novels the "new people" could learn all they wanted of the "old people", as Disraeli pointed out in his satire of the rise of the fashionable novel, in *Popanilla*:

> so that when the delighted students had eaten some fifty or sixty imaginary dinners in my Lord's dining-room, and whirled some fifty or sixty imaginary waltzes in my lady's dancing-room, there was scarcely a brute left among the whole Millionaires.

Colburn's first great success was Lady Morgan's *France*, published in 1817, an exclusive's travel book with literary repercussions.* The first of the truly fashionable novels—Robert Plumer Ward's *Tremaine*—appeared under Colburn's imprint in 1825. He was Bulwer's publisher and Disraeli's, Lister's and Theodore Hook's, Lady Charlotte Bury's and Lord Normanby's; and it was he, more than any of his authors, who established the formula the new genre would follow.

The principal ingredients in Colburn's formula were balls, gambling scenes, social climbers, political gossip, Almack's, the clubs, younger sons looking for heiresses, dowagers protecting

---

* See Chapter V. Colburn also brought out the famous editions of the Evelyn (1818) and Pepys (1825) journals.

their daughters from younger sons. Most of the novels produced on this pattern were mere handbooks of exclusive manners, pseudo-literary gossip journalism concerned with neither characterization nor plot, but with the illusion of authenticity. In better hands, the fashionable novel also drew elements from the manners and sentimental novel of the eighteenth century, the didactic and domestic novel of 1800, and the German apprenticeship novel. Bulwer and Disraeli used the form as a vehicle for political theory —reportedly with Colburn's encouragement. For Colburn did not scruple to tell his authors what to write or how to write it; he prohibited excessive satire lest the exclusives be offended, he selected titles and disguised authors. He purchased books eagerly, he commissioned books freely, he paid his authors liberally.

It was as a publicist rather than as an editor, however, that Colburn left his mark on the history of publishing. He worked to create the impression that each of his novels was written by a tip-top exclusive, and in his work used with daring and imagination every fraudulent device known to his trade. He was a master of the preliminary puff; the tantalizing Key to Fashionable Persons Figuring in the Novel, ordinarily inaccurate; the subsidized adulatory review, usually written by one of Colburn's authors, preferably the author of the novel in question; and the carefully planted bits of gossip that the true author of the book was too great a personage and too little a professional writer to reveal his identity. At one time or another Colburn owned at least a piece of the *New Monthly Magazine*, the *Literary Gazette*, the *Athenaeum*, the *Court Journal* and several other periodicals; his advertising facilities were limitless. Ironically, out of Colburn's deliberate mystifications grew the legend, almost entirely unfounded, that the authors of fashionable novels were persons of no account who had never danced at a ball or entered a club, and whose information about the great world derived from service below stairs. Thence sprang Yellowplush.

In fact, many of Colburn's authors (Disraeli being a notorious exception) knew rather well whereof they spoke, and the first success of the fashionable novels was amongst the exclusives, who drew from them the pleasure of recognition. Today the best of the genre can still give the pleasure of genuine wit, and can evoke the coterie setting of the period. "I am not a difficult person to please," protests Trebeck, the Brummell-figure of Lister's *Granby*:

—I flatter myself that I mix well with people in general— . . . being a sort of unsophisticated person, ready to join in with all the odd humours of every class, both high and low . . . Of course . . . there *are* persons one wishes to avoid—a man, for instance, who commits a forgery, or a pun—or asks twice for soup—or goes to private balls in Town on a Wednesday. These are offenders one should be sorry to associate with; but as to the quiet, decent, orderly mass, who have no such crimes as these to answer for, nobody is more ready to exchange a nod, or a 'howd'ye do,' or give them two fingers to shake than myself.

(*"Private balls in Town on a Wednesday"*: on Wednesdays the coterie danced only at Almack's).

Such delicately accurate shots were also the great appeal of Ward's *Tremaine; or, The Man of Refinement*, which launched Colburn on his career as a publisher of fashionable novels. Robert Plumer Ward was sixty when *Tremaine*, his first novel, was published, and his roots were firmly in the eighteenth century. His novel was ostensibly didactic, telling the story of a jaded man of the world redeemed by pure love, pure religion and pure country air. But Ward's hero was something more than a man of the world; he was a dandy. And though the book ends with an entire volume devoted to Tremaine's religious conversion, the heart of the novel is a recapitulation of a dandy's life in London at the height of the Regency. In this sense, Ward's novel is the source from which sprang Disraeli and Bulwer, even Mrs Gore and Thackeray. "I love a dear, elegant votary of artificial life from my soul," Ward wrote: "There is something so heroically insolent in an exclusive; such a noble conviction of his or her superiority over all the rest of the human race; such a philosophic independence of everything which people of mere nature look to for happiness . . ."

A man of wealth and aristocratic connections, Ward had moved easily and constantly among exclusives, though not in the innermost circle. He had entered political life as a protégé of Pitt and Mulgrave (his wife's brother-in-law) and won prominence as a lawyer, member of parliament, under-secretary in the foreign office and acknowledged author of several political and legal treatises. (*Tremaine*, of course, was published anonymously.

Later, when Ward's authorship of fiction was known, Canning quipped that his "law books were as pleasant as novels, and his novels as dull as law books.") Ward put a good deal of himself into the character of Tremaine, who had tried and rejected travel, the ministry, law, politics, even "the court life"—but found satisfaction in the rule of fashion. Tremaine, wrote lawyer Ward, "sat sufficiently often in the window at White's, to conceive almost as high an idea of its power as a judge has of the dignity of the bench."

> His detractors . . . went, indeed, so far as to say, the only man for whom he ever shewed any real deference was a certain beau, who, spite of all his want of birth, fortune, and connexion, had, by the force of a masterly genius, acquired such an ascendancy over the dandies, as to be called their sovereign.

Nor does this Brummell-figure spare Tremaine—or Ward. Tremaine, he says, "with all his claims to reputation . . . had yet an original defect in his education, in having studied the law."

For Ward the central *humour* of the dandy temper, its curse as well as its distinction, is *refinement*, that Regency word with overtones of fastidiousness and sensitivity. Tremaine cannot condescend to an occupation, and he cannot live apart from "the highest circle" of the great world: "a sort of natural or early-acquired fastidiousness, having, even as a younger brother, forbidden much mixture with any other." This fineness dictates Tremaine's first deference: to himself.

> To be quizzed, much more to be called what is called *cut* by any one, never, indeed, entered his contemplation; but had it so happened, though by a duke, or royalty itself, it would have been a crime *laesae majestatis*, never to be forgiven.

The major consequence of Tremaine's *refinement* is his inability to love, a failing which Ward (who took three wives in the course of a long life) treats satirically, yet with a certain sympathy. Like the occupations, the ladies are one after another rejected as insufficiently *fine*: one for a want of sentiment, one for an excess, one for reading *Tom Jones*, one for eating peas with a knife, and so on.* That Tremaine, "with much susceptibility," Ward

---

* This conceit, like so much else in *Tremaine* and other dandy novels, derived from Brummell, who once protested he had broken with a lady because she ate cabbage. Mrs Gore and Thackeray would also make use of it.

writes, "was still a bachelor, though approaching the middle of life—that he should even have seemed to take his leave of the sex—is not at all inconsistent. His fastidiousness . . . coloured, indeed, all his pursuits." The dandy was fit only for "amourettes", being, as his enemies said, "too fine for an amour."

Through the book, Ward's dandy remains an attractive man. Surmounting an initial prejudice, he wins the heart of Georgina, the genteel country girl, and the respect of her father, the country rector. His elegance and distinction of manner, his easy conversation and his *"air noble"* all convince Georgina that Tremaine is "not only the finest gentleman, but the most interesting person she had ever seen." It is Georgina who makes an eager defence for *the Man of Refinement: "He hates* nobody—only dislikes impertinent people . . ." Parts of *Tremaine* are reminiscent of an earlier novel about the descent of a London gentleman upon the critical country gentry: *Pride and Prejudice.* The snobbish Mr Darcy, with his "satirical eye" and "distant civility" has been replaced by Tremaine, the fastidious dandy; and the concern with pride has given way to concern with a narrower, if more fashionably styled humour: exclusivism.*

The appearance of *Tremaine* was an event in the social season of 1825 and the exclusive community was immensely curious about the author's identity. But Ward had guarded his incognito carefully. He had dealt with Colburn solely through his solicitor Benjamin Austen, and Austen's wife Sarah; and his hand-writing was nowhere to be seen on the final manuscript, which had been copied by his daughters. Comments filtered back to Ward through Colburn via the Austens, however, and he was gratified to learn that Southey and the aged Henry Mackenzie (author of *The Man of Feeling,* a novel distantly responsible for the form of *Tremaine*) had approved his work. He kept their letters. But what gave him the greatest delight were the comments of his

---

* Jane Austen's books were known to the exclusives; indeed the Regent, who was a man of taste as well as an exclusive, loved them. (The story of her dedication of *Emma* to the Regent is one of the most amusing in the annals of literary patronage, and further illustrates the exclusiveness of the literary scene.) But her works were not popular with the coterie. A young exclusive in *Granby* voiced fashionable opinion when she said, "I hope you like nothing of . . . Miss Austen's. They are full of commonplace people, that one recognizes at once."

fashionable acquaintances, which he transcribed into his frequent letters to Mrs Austen.

"He had ever mixed in a society where he could note down the refinements, as well as the follies, of the great and fashionable," wrote Ward's biographer; into that society Ward went nightly, thriving on the role of anonymous author, eavesdropping on comments about *Tremaine*, delightedly participating in speculations about its authorship. He knew that it was "often a subject at White's"; that Lord Althorpe queried friends while riding in the Park; that Lord Binning brought up the subject "at the dinner at the Ch. of the Exchequer"; that Lady Holland was pumping Lady Bathurst; and that Lady Spencer had written Colburn begging to be told the author's name. "My incognito makes all this quite entertaining," Ward wrote Mrs Austen—as he gleefully spread the rumour that Sydney Smith had written *Tremaine*. He overheard young ladies mooning over Tremaine's charms, and concluding that "he was not a bit too old, and that they could not have refused him like Georgina, but would have married him first for the sake of converting him afterwards." He took efficient vengeance on a critical exclusive.

I heard in the morning that a determined "exclusive", an earl's daughter, had said [*Tremaine*] was vulgar . . . This was too contemptible, so in return I told her aunt (who had told me) that I had heard she had sat for *Lady Gertrude* [an outrageous exclusive in the novel], which of course will be told her again . . .

Once his identity was out, however, Ward bowed again to fashion. When he wrote his second novel, the less successful *De Vere*, he sent the manuscript to the Countess of Mulgrave, and she wrote back that he had been too harsh on Almack's, and that his harshness might be taken as a sign that the exclusives had slighted him. He at once resolved to correct "the abuse of the abuses of Almack's," and humbly stated his defence: "Certainly neither myself nor the girls [Ward's industrious daughters] can have any personal feelings to gratify in what I have painted, for I never was refused, and they never had an opportunity, even if they had had a wish, to apply. But people who don't know this might think as you say, which one would wish to avoid, and I will alter accordingly . . ."

In 1842, at the ripe age of seventy-seven, Robert Plumer Ward informed Ben Austen that he was retiring to the country. He could look back on a successful life as a respected politician, as the husband of three wives, each of whom had brought him happiness (and money besides) and as the author of three novels, each of which had advanced his reputation. He had won an estimable place in a society to which his personal distinction more than his antecedents had given him entrée. Now the parting was difficult. "Not that my passion for woods and fields, and a degree of solitude, is not as great as ever," he wrote, "and I always feel better and happier (perhaps wiser) for them. But then the *society* of London!"

5

To those in a position to watch them, the Regency dandies provided almost unlimited material for fiction or reflection. In a time obsessed with fears of boredom, they were the ones who created liveliness out of fashionable nonchalance. They were individuals; they cultivated a neat, amusing, tame eccentricity that could never be called vulgar or jar against the basic laws of exclusive society. Disraeli put his finger on the values given and received in *The Young Duke*:

> The miracles of creation have long agreed that body without soul will not do; and even a coxcomb in these days must be original, or he is a bore. No longer is such a character the mere creation of his tailor and his perfumer. He must dress, certainly; assuredly he must scent. But he must also let the world hourly feel by that delicate eccentricity, which infuses a graceful variety into the monotony of life, that he is entitled to invent a button, or to bathe in violets.

Most of the Regency dandies have come down to us intact with nickname, the label of their individual eccentricities. There was "Beau" Brummell himself; "King" Allen, a pompous gentleman who confined his daily exercise to a promenade between Crockford's and White's; "Silent" Hare, notorious for his loquacity; "Pea-Green" Hayne and "Blue Hanger" Lord Coleraine, who wore clothes of one colour; "Teapot" Crawfurd, named for an old black pot he treasured as a memento of Eton days; "Romeo" Coates, a mad pseudo-dandy who gained the attention of society by acting Shakespeare; "Long" Wellesley Pole, for obvious reasons; "Poodle" Byng, who derived his name from his curly head of hair and a joke Brummell made about it; "Apollo"

Raikes, one of the few dandies with business in the city, who therefore rose in the East and set in the West; "Kangaroo" Cooke, a military dandy, who complained to the Duke of York that he could find no food in the Peninsula but kangaroo; "Monk" Lewis, one of the few literary men who travelled with the dandies, for ever labelled by them with the title of his celebrated novel; and "Golden" Ball Hughes, one of the many dandies who inspired literary men—his fabulous wealth and matching extravagance figured in *The Young Duke* by Disraeli. "Red Herrings" Lord Hertford, the third Marquess, had personal eccentricities and progeny (legitimate, illegitimate and literary), which were to perpetuate dandyism into the hostile or uncomprehending future. He himself sprang in direct descent from two Plantagenets; his mother was one of the Regent's elderly mistresses; his wife's son, though certainly not his own, founded the Jockey-Club in France and demonstrated the dandy pose to the Jockey-Club dandies. Another illegitimate Hertford descendant of even more uncertain paternity was Sir Richard Wallace, who founded the Wallace collection with his inheritance of the Hertford art treasures. Hertford's own "open and unblushing depravity" waited for portrayal until the rise of a later, angry generation: Disraeli would put him into *Coningsby* as Lord Monmouth, Thackeray into *Vanity Fair* as Lord Steyne.

For most of these gentlemen and their fellows the dandy life rolled on, day, week and season round, in a pattern of fashionable nullity. Every Wednesday night, of course, there was the ritual appearance at Almack's. On other evenings of the week the dandy could go to his club for hour after hour of gambling, playing on into the next morning, often the next afternoon, and perhaps the evening after. Or there were evening parties, discreet, epicurean dinners at the homes of male acquaintances; elaborate affairs or modest *conversazioni* at the great houses of the Regency hostesses. The most typically *Regency* of these ladies had their own eccentricities: the flamboyant Lady Cork, called "Corky", a rumoured kleptomaniac, hideously old and shrill, dressed in white, highly rouged; the redoubtable Lady Holland, proud, domineering and a scourge of immorality despite her own past as a divorcée who had borne Lord Holland's son before she was Lady Holland. Visits could be paid to the famous Regency "blues" (very light blues they were in that fashionable age) like Lady Morgan, author of

The Wild Irish Girl and other best-selling novels and travel books; and Lady Blessington, who supported the dandyism of Count D'Orsay with her fashionable pen. The ladies maintained what Regency society legitimately called *salons*, for French customs in entertaining then prevailed. The exclusive world ignored the British tradition of sending the women out to chatter after dinner while the men sat alone to trade club stories or political gossip over their brandy. Perhaps there was less talk about politics in those days; perhaps Regency women did not mind obscenities.

One evening of the week was reserved for the opera at His Majesty's Theatre in the Haymarket, where for five extraordinary years at the height of the Regency the patronesses of Almack's made all allocations of boxes and tickets for the pit. The extension of exclusive despotism beyond the assembly rooms was considered necessary because the select company retired to the concert room for a supper and a ball after the opera. (Indeed the fashionable time to arrive at the opera was just as it was ending.) The theatre, on the other hand, was *not* a fashionable rendezvous, undoubtedly because tickets were readily available. A contemporary critic recommended to the distraught managers that they adopt the seasonal box scheme of the opera and follow the pattern of Almack's. "While money can procure admission," he wrote, "no entertainment in London can be select . . . Let the theatre be got up upon the same exclusive system [as Almack's] and you shall have . . . the most gorgeous audiences."

Since evening entertainments lasted on into the early morning, dandy days began late. "SATURDAY.—" the dandy would note in his diary; "—Rose at twelve, with a d——d headache. *Mem.* Not to drink the *Regent's Punch* after supper.—The green tea keeps one awake." The entry (in a contemporary spoof dated September, 1818) proceeds:

Breakfasted at one.—Read the *Morning Post*—the best Paper after all—always full of *wit, fine writing*, and *good* news.

Sent for the tailor and staymaker—ordered a morning *demi surtout* of the latest Parisian cut . . . —a pair of *Petersham Pantaloons* . . . (etc.).

Three o'clock.—Drove out in the *Dennet*.—Took a few turns in Pall Mall, St James's Street, and Piccadilly . . .

Five to seven.—Dressed for the evening—dined at half-past eight

. . . a neat dinner, in *Long's best style,* viz., a tureen of turtle, a small turbot, a dish of Carlton House Cutlets . . . (etc.).

Drank two tumblers of the Regent's Punch, iced, and a pint of Madeira.—Went to the Opera in high spirits—just over . . .

Supped at the Clarendon with the Dandy Club—cold collation—played a few rounds of Chicken Hazard, and went to bed quite cool.

SUNDAY.—Breakfasted at three . . .

The dandy day began with a breakfast cup of chocolate and an idle hour of lounging in an embroidered dressing-gown, reading the morning paper for its society news (the all-important, carefully prepared lists of who had been where the night before); or the magazines, the burlesques, the salon verses devoted to exclusivism—and, at the end of the era, the newest fashionable novel.

After the late breakfast and the leisurely recuperation came the great ritual of the dandy day: the long, portentous drama of the *toilette.* No society ever gave more time, more thought, more pages to male dress than the Regency. Minimal variations on the basic style, modest innovations in the cut of a lapel or the tilt of a hat made and broke dandy reputations. Listing the factors that made a man someone in the Regency, Byron wrote of wealth, talent, family and

> Fashion, which indeed's the best
> Recommendation; and to be well drest
> Will very often supersede the rest.

Foppery in the worst sense was involved; so was pride, in the best. Looking back from a crotchety old age in uncongenial Victorian surroundings, Alexander Cochrane (Lord Lamington), dandy and friend of D'Orsay, wrote simply: "Men took great pains with themselves; they did not slouch and moon through life."

Regency clothes made slouching, possibly even bending, impossible. The age abounds in unsympathetic portraits, such as the caricatures of George Cruikshank, who drew the dandies as monstrous insects (and labelled his etchings, "Montrosities, or London Dandies") with spindle legs, pointed toes, puffed bosoms and elongated necks. Less unflattering views of the dandies can be found in the work of Richard Dighton, son of the Dighton who painted the one reliable full-length portrait of Brummell and brother of the Dighton who did water colours for the Regent. Richard Dighton was the unofficial portraitist of the dandy world. His eye for posture and silhouette, his persistent sense of the relation between anatomy and dress, and his inclination to admire as much as to spoof, give his innumerable portraits of the famous dandies a manly distinction and apparent verisimilitude.

Some of Brummell's principles of dress were preserved through the 'teens and 'twenties when Dighton was at work: well-fitting clothes, designed to show off a trim, manly figure and demanding an erect posture; high standards of neatness, crispness and freshness; an elegance to be derived from the effect of the whole, not from a profusion of details. But Brummell had also aimed at a *natural* style. He had maintained respect for the real outlines of the figure and tolerance for the minimal exertions required by fashionable life: walking, entering and leaving a carriage, sitting. Brummell's successors of the 'twenties abandoned nature for the tortures and refinements of art. Even Dighton's dandies, drawn striding in profile, are ridiculously stiff.

Soon after the great Beau's departure from England in 1816, Brummell's tall, straight, close-fitting collar gave way to the collar *à la guillotine*, held two inches away from the neck and climbing up over the ears with the help of whale-bone. The crisp but manageable, lightly starched folds of Brummell's cravat became a formidable jagged range: ridges of stiff white cloth which choked the neck or, like a medieval visor, concealed the dandy face up to the nose. Shirt collars, which in Brummell's style had shown only a modest triangle above the lower jaw, came to stand high over the ears or to press up against the cheek—and they displayed a line of un-Brummellian embroidery. Coats became more high-waisted than ever, stiff with padding and even boning, stiff enough to keep their shape without being buttoned. The bosomy look was in evidence: an angular billow of dark cloth cutting out and away from the brilliant whiteness of the cravat. Coat-tails, which Brummell wore barely to the knee, dropped stiffly to a point almost at the ankle, and the new angularity of the 'twenties was heightened by a vogue for sharply contrasting black and white.

Once buckled, laced, strapped, polished and brushed into their daytime costumes, the dandies were ready for the day's amusements: a stroll down St James's Street, a ride up Piccadilly, an afternoon visit to the clubs, where gambling could be had at any hour of the day. (It was possible to enjoy one's club without being much of a gambler, but at Crockford's, according to

Lamington, there was an unwritten rule that a non-gambling member with a fondness for Francatelli's famous suppers should at the end of the season saunter through the "long suite of magnificent apartments" to the playing room, and throw a ten-pound note casually on the table. "That was really conscience money," Lamington adds; "no one inquired, asked for it, or perhaps even noticed it.") If the dandy did gamble he could be sure of being fleeced, even cheated, by the most select company. No one in the Regency was squeamish about cheating; its existence was an accepted fact in this gambling society. One anonymous cynic of that period, when asked what he would do if he saw a man cheating at cards, answered, "bet on him, to be sure." It was a later generation which closed down Crockford's for its low standard of gambling morality. Lord Lamington, who sat on the Gambling Committee of the House of Commons, fought valiantly against the decision.

Next to a pack of cards the dandy relied on his horses for amusement, with opera-girls, ballet-dancers and professional courtesans a poor third, though these ladies had often the fashionable preference over high-society mistresses. ("His amours," wrote Bulwer of a supposedly typical nobleman in *Godolphin*, "had been among opera-dancers, 'Because,' as he was wont to say, 'there was no d——d bore with them'.") There was a horsey set which spent its afternoons at Tattersall's, the fashionable market-place for the best in horseflesh. Pierce Egan's famous *Life in London* (or, *The Day and Night Scenes of Jerry Hawthorn, Esq., and his elegant friend Corinthian Tom in their Rambles and Sprees through the Metropolis*), published in 1821, describes Tattersall's in fond detail and, in the ebullient Tom and Jerry, attempts to portray the sport-mad buck who flourished in the Regency alongside the dandy. These athletic eccentrics were particularly fond of driving a pair or more of horses at breakneck speed, considering a day behind the reins of the public coach the height of amusement. The most famous of their number was the brainless Tommy Onslow of the jingle:

> What can Tommy Onslow do?
> Why, drive a Phaeton and Two!!
> Can Tommy Onslow do no more?
> Yes, drive a Phaeton and Four!!!!

For these gentlemen there were specialized clubs: the Whip, the Four-in-Hand, the Barouche, the Defiance and the Tandem.

The true dandies, however, were less energetic sportsmen. Though Egan was himself a favourite of George IV (to whom his book was dedicated), and though he claimed that Corinthian Tom was "the GO among the Goes, in the very centre of fashion in London," his raffish young bloods were hardly exclusives. For the real dandy the horse was merely to be admired, to be attached to the most fashionable little phaeton or *vis-à-vis*, to be leisurely ridden or driven through the city streets, or to be bet on at the races.

By the time of the Regency racing was firmly established in England as an aristocratic sport. When the Jockey Club was founded in the middle of the eighteenth century, its aim was not, as is commonly believed, to reform the turf or improve the horses, but "to enable its members [as one of them has said] to hold their own against the rabble . . . without more intrusion than was absolutely unavoidable on the part of the profane vulgar." Prince George was a member of this exclusive organisation almost as soon as he came of age. He was active on the turf in the 'eighties, though forced to withdraw because of mounting debts; and active again in the 'nineties until a famous scandal—known as "the Escape affair" after the horse which may have been tampered with—led the arrogant members of the Jockey Club virtually to warn their Prince off the track. From 1800 on, George was once again the fashionable patron of the turf. He spent lavishly on his own horses (though he won the Derby only once) and he sponsored several splendid innovations: the second meeting at Ascot; the gorgeous processions to the track; the annual dinner for members of the club. By the time of George's accession to the throne, in 1820, the members of the Jockey Club were the patrons of racing as clearly as the Ladies of Almack's were the patronesses of dancing. Members of the club, virtually all of them wealthy aristocrats, owned the horses, laid down the rules, and bought up virtually all the racing turf on Newmarket Heath. Their pronouncements on breeding and decorum were made known through the semi-official pages of the *Racing Calendar* and the *Stud-Book*—one of the few modern survivals of Regency exclusivism.

The conclusion to the dandy day, and the prelude to the dandy evening, was a ritual, public rendezvous of the two sexes. Late afternoons in the Regency were set aside for driving or riding through Hyde Park, casual flirtations, whispered gossip, the display and appraisal of beauties of form, dress and carriage. The dandies (a "line of men [according to one of the novels] drawn up in battle array, and with impertinent nonchalance, passing judgment on the women who drive before them") came to see the ladies but even more, it would appear, to let themselves be seen. One dandy character protests that the women come only to see the men. "And what do *you* come for?" he is asked. "Oh, to show ourselves, certainly: to *be* admired."

6

Though accessible via Piccadilly and Oxford Street, in the early nineteenth century Hyde Park was still rural. Under its green trees grazed cows and deer. On its green lawns gathered the dandies, dressed for riding according to Brummell, and their ladies, the "carriage company", seated in a *vis-à-vis* for two decked out with "the hammer-cloth, rich in heraldic designs, the powdered footmen in smart liveries, and a coachman who assumed all the gaiety and appearance of a wigged archbishop . . ." This was the most splendid scene of the day, the spectacle most peculiarly "Regency", which caught the eye of artists and fashionable novelists alike. Disraeli, who was always lyrical on the subject of the beautiful London of his youth, did justice to the scene:

> Is there a more gay and graceful spectacle in the world than Hyde Park, at the end of a long sunny morning in the merry month of May or June? Where can we see such beautiful women, such gallant cavaliers, such fine horses, and such brilliant equipages? The scene, too, is worthy of such agreeable accessories: the groves, the gleaming waters, and the triumphal arches. In the distance, the misty heights of Surrey, and the bowery glades of Kensington . . .

And such delights were as exclusive as the clubs. "In those days," wrote Gronow nostalgically, " 'pretty horse-breakers' would not have dared to shew themselves in Hyde Park; nor did you see any of the lower or middle classes of London intruding themselves in the regions which, with a sort of tacit understanding, were then given up exclusively to persons of rank and fashion."

Much of the rest of Regency London was equally set aside, by the same "tacit understanding", as select; and these sections, too, were beautiful and livable. Regency architects (unlike their Georgian predecessors, who had thought of taste in terms of country house and grounds) were challenged by their stubbornly urban patrons to refurbish aristocratic London and bring the country to the town. In that peculiarly Regency development, the lavish "housing estate" in the form of square or terrace, the essential charms of rural living were preserved: open space, fresh air, genuine gardens, pleasing vistas and green everywhere. Architects of a high calibre, men like John Nash, Decimus Burton and Humphry Repton, laid out or improved Regent's Park, St James's Park, Cumberland Terrace, Brunswick Square—each an oasis of exclusive elegance, "turning its back on its neighbours." The dandies could walk along the few aristocratic thoroughfares from square to park without fear of mud (Macadam as much as metropolitan exclusivism had made walking fashionable*) or embarrassing company. But outside the select West End of town the dandy dreaded to stray. Brummell, for example, made a great show of his ignorance of the barbarous outlying areas of London. He apologized to Sheridan for being found as far "east" as Charing Cross, and when invited to dine in Bloomsbury he loudly asked if he would have to change post-horses en route.

"As I consider the architecture of a nation is one of the most visible types of its prevalent character," wrote Bulwer, "so in that department all with us is comfortable and nothing vast." Comfort was the goal of Regency wealth at home, as pleasure was its target abroad, and a necessary ingredient of both was elegance. Gardens were gardens, not picturesque vistas, and rooms were not baronial halls but rooms, fit for subdued conversation and select dinners. The typical Regency salon had high ceilings and a wall of windows (some of them opened like doors into the garden: the so-called "french" window was a Regency innovation) reflected in a wall of mirrors. What wall space remained was given over to books and portraits, or other paintings of a comfortable size, like the Dutch interiors George IV made fashionable. The

---

* The cleanliness of London streets was the envy and despair of foreign tourists. One of them, a Parisian, wrote in 1830: "Paris est le purgatoire des gens qui n'ont pas perdu l'odorat . . . Par contre, quelle propreté règne à Londres! Avec quelle liberté on y respire un air pur . . ."

prevailing taste in interior design was Greek, not barbarous and gloomy Gothic, and it was reflected in that characteristic Regency piece, the low, flat chaise or sofa, curving gracefully upward at one end, on which Regency ladies languidly reclined. If, in deference to the spirit of the Pavilion, the ladies wished a fashionable orientalism, the couch of gilded wood could be given four clawed legs and curved upward into the head of an exotic but barely fierce little dragon.

The Regency coolly accepted the products of industrialism, as an aid to domestic comfort, knowing nothing of the monster that was waxing great in the Midlands. Regency householders watched the first gas-lamps illuminate the streets of London in 1807. They brought "gasoliers" into their homes and public buildings. They absorbed the produce of the iron-mills, turning that stern metal into airy, elegant wrought-iron traceries for balcony and garden; they employed the newly-improved produce of the glass manufacturers in clear, generous windows and huge mirrors; they even tried the novelties of central heating, rudimentary "air-conditioning" and fire-fighting sprinkler systems.

This was a confident age, serene in its pretension to good taste and the Greek ideals. "The true impressions of cheerfulness, elegance and refinement, are so well understood and so happily united in our modern domestic dwellings," boasted one Regency architect, "that I hesitate not to say we are rapidly advancing to a state of perfection." This was also a modern age in a modern city, but its comfortable modernity did not preclude elegance or even a certain mysterious, romantic charm. Disraeli, for whom all Regency London was like a fairyland, caught this charm in his description of Hyde Park. Cecil, the delightful fictional dandy created by Mrs Gore, sensed it as he left a night of play at Watier's in the hazy minutes just before dawn, and went reluctantly home to bed "by that peculiar, greenish, aqua-marine light, through which one never sees anything moving in London but dandies and watchmen going their rounds, and squares . . ."

CHAPTER III

Bulwer

I have drawn for the hero of my Work, such a person as seemed to me best fitted to retail the opinions and customs of the class and age to which he belongs; a personal combination of antitheses—a fop and a philosopher, a voluptuary and a moralist—a trifler in appearance, but rather one to whom trifles are instructive, than one to whom trifles are natural . . . Such a character I have found it more difficult to portray than to conceive . . . because I have with it nothing in common . . .
—Bulwer: Preface to *Pelham*, 1828

THE socially dominant dandy side of the Regency, the little World of fashion, wit, elegance and irresponsibility, produced one literary monument of unquestionable, though uneven, value: Edward Bulwer's *Pelham*. Celebrated in England as the "hornbook of dandyism", it taught the rules of the game to many an aspiring dandy, notably to Benjamin Disraeli. It titillated Exclusive society and—greatest proof of coterie success—actually set a new fashion in gentlemen's dress. Hailed in France as *"le manuel du dandysme le plus pur et le plus parfait"*, *Pelham* was a prime agent in the spread of the dandy gospel to the anglomaniac generation of the 'thirties.

But *Pelham* had a future which would have astonished and appalled the exclusive world. Simply because it was the most brilliant and outrageous of the fashionable novels, *Pelham* became a warning beacon to the early Victorians, a light marking dangerous shoals, attitudes to be rejected and for ever avoided. The little Carlyle read of *Pelham* made a lot of difference in *Sartor Resartus*. And because Bulwer had probed more deeply into the psychological springs of the dandy pose than any other novelist, *Pelham* in mid-century France became one of the solvents in the new blending of dandyism with aestheticism. Barbey d'Aurevilly read *Pelham* and understood it; Baudelaire read Barbey and fashioned an intellectual dandyism that might have delighted the author of *Pelham*—except that Bulwer by then had grown into a middle-aged peer and prop of the realm. Even today, Edward Bulwer is remembered not as the author of a dandy novel, his best work, but as one of the dullest and most serious of Victorians.

Pelham was brought out by Colburn in 1828 with all the folderol of anonymity and suggestive puffs. Under its full title, *Pelham; or, the Adventures of a Gentleman*, it appeared in the elegant, gentlemanly format typical of Regency publishing: three slim pocket-size volumes, each one, though over three hundred pages in length, no more than an hour's reading. The chapters are short and on each page are only twenty-two lines of a graceful type-face boxed in lavish margins and enlivened frequently by italic print. It is in such a format that this breezy, light-weight novel reads best—and indeed it is only in the pages of the first few editions that the true *Pelham* can be read at all. Frightened by what he had read in *Fraser's Magazine*, particularly by Carlyle's *Sartor Resartus*, Bulwer would edit out of his novel all of what was wicked, most of what was naughty and a great deal of what was amusing. Between 1828 and 1835 Bulwer had witnessed the destruction of a world he had been brought up to take for granted. Since 1836, *Pelham* has never been reprinted in its entirety.

Edward George Earle Lytton Bulwer Bulwer-Lytton, Lord Lytton was born in 1803 with the relatively simple name of Edward George Earle Lytton Bulwer and the status of a commoner. But from both sides of his family he inherited a tradition of wealth and privilege. Had his father lived long enough he would undoubtedly have attained the long-coveted title of Lord South Erpingham; as it was, young Bulwer saved the ridiculous name for the character of the phlegmatic, amorous, unwanted husband in one of his fashionable novels, and won an early baronetage for himself. Bulwer's pretensions to exclusivism began with his name; so did his unhappy liability to blows and taunts from small boys. One of the small boys of the day who could not abide him dubbed the baronet *Sawedwadgeorgearllittnbulwig*; but that is part of Thackeray's story rather than Bulwer's.

The rising Lord died in his son's fourth year, and his widow presently suffixed her maiden name of Lytton to her son's name and to her own. Mrs Bulwer-Lytton was an ambitious and intelligent woman who (like many other formidable Regency mothers) was anxious and able to dominate her son's youth and early manhood. She managed his début in the fashionable world. Some years after her death Bulwer was still writing of her in terms of considerable awe:

> She was . . . a woman of that high spirit which fully enjoys the blessings of liberty and independence. She drove, with her own fair hands (I mention this as emblematic of her whole character), a tall phaeton and pair; and in this equipage transported herself, as she listed, from London to Bath, and from Bath to London. So great was her confidence in herself, that one dark evening, having to return from some excursion across Hounslow Heath—at that time infested by highwaymen—she laughed to scorn the warnings she received on the road and the terrors of her two men-servants, and in the very centre of the heath was stopped by three foot-pads. She held one a moment in parley, and threw him off his guard, flicked the other in the eye, drove gallantly over the third, and arrived in London with spirits sufficiently composed to dress for a party, and relate her adventure, in illustration of the truth that a woman with her wits about her, and the whip-hand disengaged, is a match for three men any day in the year.

As a child, Bulwer was spoiled and petted—his two older brothers were either at school or in the hands of some relative— and crammed with reading by a scholarly grandfather. Early attempts to send him off to school were disastrous. His reminiscence of the tortures which an English school inflicts on the sensitive child has a familiar sound: "Oh, that first night, when my mother was gone, the last kiss given, the door closed, and I alone with the little mocking fiends to whom my anguish was such glee! . . . My utter ignorance of their low, gross slang, the disgust with which their language, their habits, their very looks inspired me—all this was excellent sport to them." He refused to go to Eton, but spent instead two happy, fruitful years in the home of a tutor. These crucial years (between the ages of sixteen and eighteen) were an education in the ways of society as well as in books. From his tutor's home in a London suburb Bulwer frequently went up to town, learning to fence and to dance: "Mr Bulwer," the tutor wrote Mrs Bulwer-Lytton in 1820, "regularly attends Mr Macfarren twice a week, and practises, before me, the quadrille steps; which I trust he does from the best motive, knowing that it is your wish . . ." He sampled the "dinners, routs, and balls" of a world which had lost Brummell only a few years before, flirted with young ladies, flattered dowagers and became precociously bored with it all. "At the age of twenty-two I hated balls as much as they are hated by most men of twenty-eight. For experience, which *is* time, had advanced me six years in the progress to satiety."

The next few years were crowded with the sort of experience that makes a self-conscious, prolific and superficial novelist. Bulwer reread his Byron, and had a serious flirtation with Caroline Lamb. He reread his Goethe, and fell madly in love with a young beauty whose cruel parents opposed their union, and who would perish of a broken heart, adjuring her lover to make a pilgrimage to her grave. He discovered the Utilitarians, and made a more sober pilgrimage to Robert Owen. He stored up enough melodrama to last a dozen novels by putting his life in the hands of a supposed murderer and by living with the gipsies. Most of all, he polished his dandyism. At Cambridge he had the example of his older brother Henry, who travelled with the "fastest" set and had "the handsomest stud, perhaps, Cambridge ever saw." He visited a fashionable watering-place and admired the carriage and dress of gentlemen who still followed Brummell:

> The style of dress worn of an evening by gentlemen contributed, perhaps, to forbid slovenliness of step and maintain a certain stateliness and grace. Tight pantaloons or knee-breeches with the chapeau bras . . . was then almost universal; and a fine shape, with correspondent elegance of movement, was more admired than even a handsome face. Fast talk and slang came in with trousers and turned-down collars.

Bulwer's own style, however, was more that of the "butterfly dandy" which D'Orsay would bring to perfection: a head of "beautiful curls" and a dress so extravagant that it made Macaulay (a fellow M.P. a few years later) mutter, "I suppose Bulwer is making money . . . for his dress must cost as much as that of any five other members of parliament."

In addition he had eight useful months in Paris, where he "became intimate at some of the most brilliant houses of the old *noblesse* domiciled in the Faubourg St Germain, and was received with marked courtesy at the select *soirées.*" There Bulwer listened to the worldly-wise advice of an older woman who commented on his dress, laughed at his attempts to flirt and called him her "Childe Harold". This lady, Paris society, London society and the fast men at Cambridge were all grist for *Pelham*'s mill, to say nothing of Bulwer's dandy image of himself. "*His writing-desk*," his grandson recorded, "*stood upon a console in front of a mirror . . .*"

2

Bulwer's literary apprenticeship for *Pelham* was hardly promising: three books of turgid verse and one wretched novel. *Falkland*, published the year before *Pelham*, though both books were begun during Bulwer's last year at Cambridge, is interesting only in the contrast it provides to the later novel. An unfortunate pastiche of Byron and the Gothic school, *Falkland* deals with the scion of a decadent race who inhabits "a ruin rather than a house", who falls into "gloomy reflections" because he has "feasted upon the passions", and who proclaims to the young woman he seduces: "I will not deceive you—it *is* guilt to which I tempt you!" Bulwer became disgusted with *Falkland* almost as soon as he saw it in print, and eight years later formally disavowed it as an early aberration. "I had rid my bosom of its 'perilous stuff'," he wrote, comparing himself with some flattery to the author of *Werther*.

Bulwer's relations with women, his family background and his day-to-day marital life were all in the same fashionable mould. His own parents were an ill-assorted couple and were on the point of separation when his father died; his mother's parents quarrelled and separated; his wife's parents quarrelled and separated; he and his wife would fight and separate. In 1826 he met Rosina Wheeler and courted her over the protests of his mother; in 1827, without his mother's consent, he married her. Years after the marriage had broken up he made a private memorandum to the effect that he had done so only because Rosina had previously become his mistress. It was to this young lady, his future wife, that Bulwer wrote the following calculated defence of *Falkland*:

> If *Falkland* succeeds at all . . . it may from its singularity gain that reading for itself which its stupidity might otherwise deprive it of . . . The book, after all, is only a trial. It has cost me little trouble, and yet much more than any other book of the sort ever would again.

One wonders whether it was also to his mistress that Bulwer addressed the lurid denunciation of adultery in the middle of

Falkland. "Whoever turns to these pages for an apology for sin will be mistaken," he wrote. "They contain the burning records of its sufferings, its repentance, and its doom . . ."

Rosina Wheeler was an Irish girl a few months older than Bulwer and with experience to match his. Showily beautiful and showily clever, fond of extravagance and fashionable life, she had been ill-prepared for marriage by a disrupted childhood. Life with Bulwer would develop almost to mania her tendencies to selfishness, deceit and temper. Mrs Bulwer-Lytton had been quite right about her; but, in fact, Bulwer was as little inclined to domesticity as his wife. They were a Regency couple. An intimate friend of the family observed that "Mr Bulwer always break- fasted alone in his library . . . He never dined at home unless there was company." From the first months of his marriage he took to running up to town from his country home—to hire servants, to buy furniture, to see his publisher, to look after "that place at the Palace" which he hoped would secure him a title and, most of all, to keep in touch with the world of easy masculine sociability. Rosina had more than once the occasion to remark in a letter: "Edward went to town on Wednesday to go to Almack's and has stayed for two or three parties . . ."

Within a few years Rosina's unruly temper and Bulwer's stiff- necked independence had brought discord and misery. Their two children were ignored, even mistreated; Bulwer wrote a friend two months before the birth of his first child: "Don't frighten me with your predictions of a numerous tribe. Nothing is so hideously uninteresting as an author with a large family." Rosina made ill- tempered jokes about her pregnancies and lavished affection on her dogs. Commenting on Bulwer's frequent disappearances to London, she wrote, "he has my leave, for in a place like this [Tunbridge Wells], where every second woman you see looks as if she was going to have twins, it is rather a relief . . . to get rid of one's darling precious husband for a short time." Quarrels, scenes, infidelities and jealousy led to a final separation in 1836. Rosina's hatred pursued her husband with insult and calumny until his death, and Bulwer took refuge in an over-active career and a series of mistresses.

Pelham came before the disaster. Although a few chapters had been written while Bulwer was at college, the novel was largely the product of his honeymoon. And it has the mark of being written during the one period of Bulwer's life when he was happy, serene and wholly self-confident. In spite of his mother's displeasure, which deprived him of his allowance, Bulwer took a large country house, furnished it extravagantly in the lavish Regency manner and flourished in the Regency style of "living on nothing a year"—the trick of Vanity Fair that most enraged Thackeray and probably accounted in large part for his dislike of Bulwer. The author of *Pelham* had the habits and manner of a dandy, the political opinions of a Radical, the taste for melodrama and melancholy of a Romantic, the energy and ambition of a young man. He abandoned the Gothic morality and murky sensationalism of *Falkland* to produce in *Pelham* a cool and impudent exposition of the amorality of Regency society.

3

On the title page of *Pelham; or, the Adventures of a Gentleman* is an epigraph from Etherege, which defines in the language of Restoration comedy the Regency sense of the term *gentleman*:

> "A complete gentleman, who, according to Sir Fopling, ought to dress well, dance well, fence well, have a genius for love letters, and an agreeable voice for a chamber."

Bulwer was not the only writer of the period to turn to the Restoration for a literary tradition. Benjamin Disraeli (whose father had written affectionately of the Stuarts) compared the dandies to "the fine gentlemen of our old brilliant comedy—the Dorimants, the Bellairs, and the Mirabels"; and Mrs Gore believed that the fashionable novel at which she excelled rose "from the ashes of our long-extinguished high-life comedy." *Pelham* particularly was a return, after a hundred years, to the principle of Restoration comedy: a satirical approach to the ways of the great world, sharpened by intimate acquaintance with it and softened by appreciation of its curious values.

Bulwer's novel diverges from the fashionable pattern set by *Tremaine* and *Granby* in its first-person narration by its dandy hero, Henry Pelham. The "cold, grey scrutinizing eye" of the dandy fits Pelham for the role of observer; the dandy's cynical wit and impudent tongue give him a subtle and dangerous satirical style. "Careless and indifferent as I seem to all things," says Pelham, "nothing ever escapes me: the minutest *erreur* in a dish or a domestic, the most trifling peculiarity in a criticism or a coat, my glance detects in an instant, and transmits for ever to my recollection."

But the dandy as observer must find *himself* by far the most interesting subject of observation, and the dandy as satirist must find his own pose by far the most fertile field for satire. As a dandy he must do almost nothing, yet his narration must begin and end with himself. Bulwer was quite aware of the ambiguities in the dandy-narrated novel and used them consciously. The plot of *Pelham*—something to do with rape of another man's mistress, a tortuous revenge, murder of the villain and suspicion falling on the innocent—concerns Pelham only as a bystander. The burden of melodrama falls on Pelham's friend Sir Reginald Glanville, inserted in the novel as a foil to the dandy, and more to be pitied than admired. Bulwer kept a distillation of the "perilous stuff" of *Falkland* in his second novel to demonstrate the unpleasant alternative to dandyism; it is hardly accidental that, in the depths of his misery, Glanville finds a last resource in turning out a novel much like *Falkland*.

The avoidance of entanglements and heroics is the beginning of Pelham's dandyism. He says as much: "I have always had a great horror of being a hero in scenes, and a still greater antipathy to 'females in distress'." Frenzy and fury he counts vulgar, and their opposite appears the essence of aristocratic behaviour:

> I have observed that the distinguishing trait of people accustomed to good society, is a calm imperturbable quiet, which pervades all their actions and habits, from the greatest to the least; they eat in quiet, move in quiet, live in quiet, and lose their wife, or even their money in quiet; while low persons cannot take up either a spoon or an affront without making such an amazing noise about it.

Raptures over the English lakes had sent Brummell in disgust to his valet, and the moving spectacle of a sunset on the water ("breaking the waves into unnumbered sapphires, and tinging the dark firs that overspread the margin with a rich and golden light"), puts Pelham "excessively in mind of the Duke of ———'s livery." Pelham prefers good cheer to melancholy, good sense to genius, and keeps "the darker and stormier emotions"—when he has them—to himself. When Bulwer was most ashamed of *Pelham* (in the *mea culpa* of the 1840 preface) he said in its defence that it had the virtue of making the Byronic pose unfashionable, and substituting for it the dandy pose, which was "at least more harmless, and even more manly and noble."

The graveyards, mad-houses, thieves' hideouts, and lonely country roads of the Glanville plot set off the brilliant scenes of Pelham's story: the story of the making of a man by means of dandyism. Bulwer had read his *Wilhelm Meister*. In the ballrooms and crowded salons of the Regency world Pelham fights for power and control, but as an aristocrat he fights in quiet, and as a dandy he strives first for control over himself, confident that it will lead to power over others. Like Bulwer, Pelham has his eye on a political career, but he takes elaborate pains to conceal under a mask of affectations his manoeuvrings after influence, his manipulation of rivals and his secret storing-up of bookish wisdom, largely that of the Utilitarians. Pelham presents himself first to the reader as an outrageous puppy of a dandy. Only gradually does he reveal that his dandyism is a pose: not a "*mere*" pose, but an immensely difficult, conscious and effective pose. It is a training for power. Pelham's dandy maxim runs: "Manage *yourself* well, and you may manage all the world."

Fortunately, Bulwer was able to manage himself, for the duration of *Pelham*, like a dandy. He took pains to conceal the novel's serious purpose, an attack on the excesses of Exclusive society, with casual effrontery. Readers far less narrow-minded than Carlyle could not decide whether Bulwer was for his dandy hero or against him, whether Pelham was the author's self or the author's villain. The confusion was in the author's mind as well as in his novel. Bulwer saw the evils of the Regency; he predicted its political collapse and later he personally fought for the passage of the Reform Bill, which more than any other event brought an end to Regency ways. In Bulwer's novel Pelham speaks the Radical's criticism of social irresponsibility—but Pelham speaks as a dandy, the most irresponsible of beings. The political and social system is rotten; but it created me, and I am sublime.

Pelham tells the story of his life with an intimate and casual air, regarding it as Every (exclusive) Man's. Therefore he scorns to dwell on the details of an upbringing that must be familiar to Every (fashionable) Reader. He merely sketches in, with a light and elegant hand, the outlines of his career: his aristocratic, unpleasant family; his spoiled childhood and disastrous school years at Eton; his novitiate at Cambridge and excursion to Paris; his

introduction to the country homes and town houses of the aristocracy; his French amours and English affairs; his campaign for
a seat in Parliament; and at last (for this, though a dandy novel,
must have an ending to please the female public) his marriage to
the sister of an Eton school-fellow. When Pelham lingers it is not
over his own concerns, but over the vignettes of exclusive society
that attract the dandy eye. One sample will serve to show how
cleverly Pelham satirizes, and with what impudence he appears
to revel in what he attacks. Lady Frances Pelham, the narrator's
mother, has been pursuing a liaison with a Mr Seymour Conway,
who "had just caused two divorces . . . —judge then of the pride
which Lady Frances felt at his addresses";

> The end of the season was unusually dull, and my mother, after
> having looked over her list of engagements, and ascertained that she
> had none remaining worth staying for, agreed to elope with her new
> lover.
>
> The carriage was at the end of the square. My mother, for the first
> time in her life, got up at six o'clock. Her foot was on the step, and
> her hand next to Mr Conway's heart, when she remembered that her
> favourite china monster and her French dog were left behind. She
> insisted on returning—re-entered the house, and was coming down
> stairs with one under each arm, when she was met by my father and
> two servants. My father's valet had discovered the flight (I forget
> how), and awakened his master.
>
> When my father was convinced of his loss, he called for his dressing
> gown—searched the garret and the kitchen—looked in the maids'
> drawers and the cellaret—and finally declared he was distracted. I
> have heard that the servants were quite melted by his grief, and I do
> not doubt it in the least, for he was always celebrated for his skill in
> private theatricals. He was just retiring to vent his grief in his dress-
> ing-room, when he met my mother. It must altogether have been
> an awkward *rencontre*, and, indeed, for my father, a remarkably
> unfortunate occurrence; for Seymour Conway was immensely rich,
> and the damages would, no doubt, have been proportionately high.

This remarkable mother is Master Pelham's trusted guide and
mentor through the intricacies of fashionable life. Her letters
punctuate the novel like the shrill outpourings of an exclusive
chorus, with a mixture of rattle-brained gossip, idle chit-chat and
shrewd advice. "My Dear Henry," she begins one letter, "I was
very glad to hear you were rather better than you had been.
I trust you will take great care of yourself. I think flannel

waist-coats might be advisable; and, by-the-bye, they are very good for the complexion." And she ends with this succinct advice: "P.S. Never talk much to young men—remember that it is the women who make a reputation in society."

4

In every gesture of impudence, affectation and self-love, Pelham is a dandy, in the outrageous, post-Brummell butterfly style. He personified what Tremaine and Trebeck had merely suggested. His affectations outrage the reader, not least because he describes them with the most shameless relish. The heart of Pelham's dandyism is self-love—a subject on which Bulwer was, from all accounts, something of an authority. (Disraeli once described another contemporary as "the most conceited man I ever met, though," he added, "I have read Cicero and known Bulwer Lytton.") "On one point," Pelham boasts, "all—friends and foes —were alike agreed; viz. that I was a consummate puppy, and excessively well satisfied with myself. *A la vérité*, they were not much mistaken there."

Self-love is also the principle behind Pelham's method of narration. Though he himself figures only remotely in the main events of the story, he manages to arrange every scene with himself at the centre. He observes himself as observer. In every detail he meets Hazlitt's definition of the dandy figure: "Whatever is going on, he himself is the hero of the scene; the distress (however excruciating) derives its chief claim to attention from the singular circumstance of his being present; and he manages the whole like a piece of private theatricals with an air of the most absolute *nonchalance* and decorum." So we see Pelham adjusting "my best curl",(**) we see him "yawning, stretching, admiring my rings",(**) we see him arranging "myself and my whiskers —two very distinct affairs." We see him absorbed in the greatest of dandy concerns, his dress. So consumed is Pelham with this subject that he gives almost an entire chapter, the famous Chapter VII of Book II (which would become notorious as the result of Carlyle's denunciation*), to the enunciation of his rules for cor-

---

* See below, Chapter VIII. Bulwer cut this chapter in its entirety from the 1835 edition of *Pelham*—and from all subsequent editions. Passages above and hereafter marked (**) were cut or modified for that edition.

rect male attire : from the great principles of colour and cut down
to the minutiae of coat-tails, collars, rings and shoe-strings. Most
of all we see Pelham, once dressed, ornamented, scented and
arranged, admiring himself in a mirror:

"Good Heavens! what an unbecoming glass that is! placed just opposite to *me*, too! could it not be removed while I stay here? Oh! by the
by, Lady Roseville, do you patronize the Bohemian glasses? For my
part, I have one which I only look at when I am out of humour; it
throws such a lovely flush upon the complexion, that it revives my
spirits for the rest of the day. Alas! Lady Roseville, I am looking much
paler than when I saw you at Garrett Park . . ."(**)

Beginning where Brummell left off, Pelham draws a fine distinction between what is proper to the dandy and what is suitable
for ordinary men. "Shooting is a most barbarous amusement,"
he sighs, "only fit for majors in the army, and royal dukes, and
that sort of people; *the mere walking* is bad enough . . ." "Riding
is too severe an exercise for men," he complains on another occasion, "it is only fit for the robuster nerves of women. Will any
gentleman present lend me his essence bottle?"(**) The same
anathema applies, in theory at least, to violent exertion of any
sort, to bad smells, to coarse foods, to heavy drinking and to the
rowdy debauchery "of that old fashioned *roué* set". Pelham is
willing to take part in a duel or two, if he can maintain his dandy
air of casual self-possession, but his favourite occupations are the
arts of the salon: conversing, gossiping, flirting, and dancing so
lightly and so gracefully that "I might tread on a butterfly's wings
without brushing off a tint."

Pelham has an exclusive's scorn for the wrong people with the
wrong habits, like the horsey set he avoids at Cambridge. "To
say truth, the whole place reeked with vulgarity. The men drank
beer by the gallon, and ate cheese by the hundred weight—wore
jockey-cut coats, and talked slang—rode for wagers, and swore
when they lost—smoked in your face, and expectorated on the
floor . . ." The lower orders he describes (mostly from hearsay,
since he rarely meets them) as "low people", "*demi-barbares*",
atrocious plebeians", "*roturiers*", and—best of all—"the unknown vulgar". He is always conscious of the fact that few people

(**) Cut or modified in the 1835 edition.

can appreciate his superb refinement. A Parisian acquaintance asks Pelham if he has "got one of Brequet's watches yet?"

"Watch!" said I: "*do* you think *I* could ever wear a watch? I know nothing so plebeian; what can any one, but a man of business, who has nine hours for his counting-house and one for his dinner, ever possibly want to know the time for? an assignation, you will say, true; but (here I played with my best ringlet) if a man is worth having he is surely worth waiting for!"(**)

The most curious side of Pelham's dandyism (and the one most carefully edited out of the 1835 edition) is the tendency to sensualism, not the coarse, libertine sensuality of the "fast" set, but the effete, luxuriant sensualism of the aesthete. In Pelham this attitude goes beyond the limits set by Brummell and follows the later, more extreme dandy of the 'twenties and 'thirties, who was called an "exquisite" as often as a "butterfly dandy". Invited to dine with an epicure, Pelham carries with him a set of specially designed tools—a shallow spoon, a tiny fork, and a blunt knife —to guard against his most lamentable weakness: a tendency to eat with "*too great a rapidity*". "It is a most unhappy failing," he says, "for one often hurries over in *one* minute, what ought to have afforded the fullest delight for the period of *five*. It is, indeed, a vice which deadens enjoyment, as well as abbreviates it . . ." He is careful of his comfort to the point of delicacy, and ventures reluctantly into a strange home or a country inn in fear of the shock that high-strung nerves and refined senses may suffer from uncouth surroundings. He complains petulantly of a "comfortless sort of dressing-room, without a fire-place, where I found a yellow ware jug and basin, and a towel, of so coarse a huckaback, that I did not dare adventure its rough texture next my complexion—my skin is not made for such rude fellowship."

Pelham feels most safe at home, where all is conveniently arranged for so *fine* a person. Some of his conveniences are of the sort that still haunt the sybaritic imagination:

I was a luxurious personage in those days. I had had a bath made from my own design; across it were constructed two small frames—one for the journal of the day, and another to hold my breakfast apparatus; in this manner I was accustomed to lie for about an hour, engaging the triple happiness of reading, feeding and bathing.(**)

(**) Cut or modified in the 1835 edition.

He takes delight in the fantastic London apartment of Sir Reginald Glanville, whose Byronism does not preclude a certain taste. Glanville's rooms are ornamented with girandoles of mother-of-pearl, door-knobs of silver, soft cushions of dark green velvet in place of carpets and chairs and, for Pelham best of all, "a profusion of mirrors, which enchanted me to the heart."(**) Such a décor would have enchanted Des Esseintes. Again, Pelham is particularly taken with the bath room:

> The decorations of this room were of a delicate rose colour; the bath, which was of the most elaborate workmanship, represented, in the whitest marble, a shell, supported by two Tritons. There was, as Glanville afterwards explained to me, a machine in this room, which kept up a faint but perpetual breeze, and the light curtains waving to and fro, scattered about perfumes of the most exquisite odour.(**)

Pelham is an amateur of perfume, approving its use by women (he meets his future wife outside a perfumer's shop) and by men. He himself cannot concentrate until he has summoned a servant "for my poodle and some *eau de Cologne*"(**) and he recommends the serving of perfumes with dessert. "In confectionary (delicate invention of the Sylphs), we imitate the forms of the rose and the jessamine; why not their odours too? What is nature without its scents?"

Such tastes ask to be called effeminate and—in the first edition of the novel only—Bulwer was not afraid of the term. He used it over and over again to characterize Pelham's dandyism. Pelham, of course, has many flirtations and affairs, and for all his sneers at sentiment and married life settles down to wedded bliss at the end, like a proper hero. For all his dandyism, he can defend himself nicely with stick or boxing-gloves against a crowd of bullies, but he maintains his delicacy throughout the fight, and protests that at the very appearance of these "masculine looking youths . . . my gentler frame shuddered from head to foot."(**) Bulwer hastens to show that much of this was a pose, and much of the pose was laughable; nevertheless, enough effeminacy stuck to Pelham to make a Carlyle fume and a soberer Bulwer take up a nervous blue pencil.

(**) Cut or modified in the 1835 edition. Glanville's palace would be transformed into a saloon hung with masterpieces of Flemish and Italian art.

Even Brummell was displeased. Inevitably, Bulwer included in the novel a portrait of the great Beau, but he is shown as a dandy in decline: Pelham, on his way home from Paris to London (where he will outshine Brummell's reputation) meets this "Mr Russelton" in exile in Calais. Brummell found the portrait inaccurate and unflattering. And he disapproved of Bulwer's views on dress. Captain Jesse once presented himself to Brummell in a formal evening costume of black and white—a combination which now seems inevitable and eternal, but which became the fashion only as a result of *Pelham*. Brummell, who wore blue, saw fit to admonish Jesse "gently" on his appearance. "My dear Jesse," he protested, "I am sadly afraid you have been reading 'Pelham'; but excuse me, you look very much like a magpie."

5

Despite the peevishness of Brummell and the fulminations of Carlyle, young men imitated Pelham. Bulwer had succeeded in drawing a dandy who was always fascinating, if not quite respectable. He had put thought and sympathy and relish into the creation of Pelham, and if he was ill at ease about his hero's most flagrant extravagances, and insistent on the latent seriousness beneath the dandy pose, and ironic throughout his tributes to dandyism, these ambiguities only gave the novel added complexity. But Bulwer could walk the tight-rope and keep his balance so long and no longer.

The year that *Pelham* was published Bulwer began another novel in the same vein: *Greville: A Satire upon Fine Life*. He never finished it, but from the brilliant fragment that remains (Bulwer's son included eight chapters of the novel in his biography of his father) it is clear that *Greville* held the promise of a better novel even than *Pelham*. Its plot is neater, its wit sharper, and it contains an unanswerable denunciation of Exclusivism from the viewpoint of an intelligent dandy. Colburn, it is said, protested that the aristocracy would resent such effective criticism, and encouraged Bulwer to turn his talents to the turgid *Devereux*. In any case, Bulwer wrote no more satire, and no other novel so daring as *Pelham*.

But he was not through with dandyism. In 1830 he brought out *Paul Clifford*, a novelists' version of *The Beggar's Opera*, including elegant highwaymen and thinly disguised caricatures of the political villains of the period. It was a very popular novel because of its excursions into the life of crime; crime novels were the coming thing in the 'thirties. Today *Paul Clifford* is virtually unreadable, but it is an interesting curiosity for its original demonstration that criminals could be dandies and dandies criminals —a theme which would disturb Dickens, intrigue Wilde and give rise to Raffles.

By 1833 Bulwer had found his spiritual home in the salon of Lady Blessington and Count D'Orsay, and in that year he published a memento of his admiration for D'Orsay: *Godolphin*. But the sparkling effrontery of *Pelham* had gone for ever. *Godolphin* is a morbid, introspective study of an insecure dandyism. *England and the English*, a serious work of social criticism also published in 1833 and praised by John Stuart Mill, expressed Bulwer's thorough awareness of the weaknesses of the Regency system, a perception underlying *Pelham*'s satire and *Greville*'s weariness.

But if Bulwer could champion the Reform Bill in Parliament, and transform himself by gradual stages from a Pelham to a Victorian, he could also turn a melancholy and nostalgic eye on the departed world of his youth. In *The Last Days of Pompeii*, published in 1834, four years after the death of George IV, Bulwer saw a Regency London destroyed by sudden eruption, in decadent Pompeii. This time Brummell was pleased. "I have heard of him speak of this," wrote Jesse, "in raptures."

CHAPTER IV

Disraeli

Fling to the heady wind
The tattered scroll of cold philosophy,
That vaunts of human REASON: nobler far
The faculty divine mankind impels,
IMAGINATION on her airy throne . . .
            —Disraeli: *The Revolutionary Epick*

"Ah! Contarini, beware of your Imagination."
            —Disraeli: *Contarini Fleming*

ON April Fool's Day, 1826, Colburn had a puff preliminary inserted in his *New Monthly Magazine*: "A very singular novel of the satirical kind is on the eve of publication, to be called 'Vivian Grey'. It is said to be a sort of Don Juan in prose, detailing the adventures of an ambitious, dashing and talented young man of high life . . . We understand [that] nearly all the individuals at present figuring in fashionable society, are made to flourish, with different degrees of honour, in the pages of this new work." Colburn was at it again; and other puffs followed, prodigal with references to "high circles" and "lords and ladies".

On the twenty-second of the month Colburn brought out *Vivian Grey*—author unknown, and for a few months well hidden. All the reviews, even those not written to Colburn's orders, treated the novel as a work of some social importance. A long review appeared on the day of publication in the *Literary Gazette*, half-complimentary (Colburn had a half-interest in the *Gazette*), half-critical (William Jerdan, who wrote the review, owned the other half). More important than mere literary appreciation was the reviewer's opinion that the high-society characters in the novel seemed "to have more than 'the air' of being drawn from actual life: for that they are so drawn, and are even intended to be so considered, is pretty evident . . . They belong to a class of which we never can approve in literature—personal portraits and satirical caricatures."

London society agreed—that the novel was clever, entertaining and, especially, wickedly satirical of their world. Scarcely two weeks after the book appeared, Robert Plumer Ward, the author of *Tremaine*, was writing Mrs Austen, his solicitor's wife, whom he suspected of having some hand in the new novel, that "all are talking of 'Vivian Grey' . . . it is much spreading in London, excites curiosity, and also resentment." He quoted the gossip he had heard at "Sir Thomas Freemantle's, where are Sir G. and Lady Nugent" and at "Lord Maryborough's dinner on Monday, where were many public men and some fine ladies": rumours about the unknown author and speculations on the originals of his characters. A week later he had more of the same for Mrs Austen, gleaned from "a dinner at Lord Gifford's, and another at Sir Henry Hardinge's, at both of which there was much of the *beau monde*."

Interest in the novel was increased by the sixth issue of *The Star-Chamber*, a short-lived magazine founded three days before *Vivian Grey* appeared, and purporting to be edited from a voluptuous Pall Mall apartment hung with a purple and gold-starred paper and ornamented with marble busts and portraits, including one of George IV. The sixth number included a *Key* to *Vivian Grey*, identifying characters as portraits of political figures (Brougham, Canning, Lord Eldon, the Duke of Wellington) and society personages (the Duke of Norfolk, the Marquis of Metford, the Marchioness of Londonderry). "There is not a name in the whole work," the *Key* boasted, "which has not its real prototype affixed to it . . ."

Some time in June the news leaked out that the author was a nobody, and a Jew; by July it was definitely known that *Vivian Grey* was written by so small a personage as "Mr D'Israeli, junior". The reviewers' tone changed abruptly. They began to denounce Colburn's dishonesty and to ridicule the author's attempts to appear fashionable, his "low" tone and his ignorance of the smallest matters of etiquette. They even became personally abusive, stating that Mr D'Israeli had the "meanness" to deny *"upon his honour as a gentleman"* that he had written the novel, for fear of a whipping. Reviews hinted that the author had purloined Ward's private diary and made use of it in his novel ("the 'circumcised' must have strange notions of common honesty . . ."); and suggested that Colburn would soon be bringing out another fashionable novel called '*The Complete Picklock,*' *or how to gain access to the Private Diaries of your Friends. By Solomon Prig, Ishmaelite* . . . They also argued that it was Mr D'Israeli himself who had edited *The Star-Chamber* and prepared the *Key* to *Vivian Grey*; and in this they were almost certainly correct.

But the damage had been done: society had been fooled. A first novel by an anonymous nobody who had never been anywhere had been accepted as fashionable. The mystery was, as Ward wrote Mrs Austen when he knew the truth, how Disraeli had done it, where he had come by "the variety of knowledge displayed", "the close observation of manners and character". "I am lost in astonishment," Ward wrote, "not merely at the natural powers, but the *acquisitions* of one so young . . ."

2

"We are not aware that the infancy of Vivian Grey was distinguished by any extraordinary incident." That is the opening sentence of the novel; in its exaggerated archness, its nervous insincerity, it sets the tone of what follows. The one Regency novelist who had no knowledge at all of the exclusive world of which he wrote, and who viewed its habits and ideals with fear rather than amusement, Disraeli set about his deception with bluff and bluster. "You, exclusive reader," he means to say, "must know that this is the story of a young gentleman whose birth, childhood and education are as fashionable as your own; and you must further deduce from the author's cool assurance that he has a gentleman's right to talk about gentlemen."

Disraeli's background was hardly fashionable. He had been born into a Jewish home where the presence of ancestors immemorially Jewish—and only recently English—hovered over a genealogy-conscious boy, and where many of the regulations of Orthodox Jewry were ritually if not eagerly observed. He was sent to a school kept by an Independent Minister, where he stood back from the rest of the boys at prayer and received instruction in his own religion every Saturday from a visiting Rabbi. He went neither to public school nor to university, and outside of the private schools he attended (which were as slipshod as the generality of such establishments at that time) he picked up his education at home under the desultory guidance of his father. Isaac

D'Israeli was a distinguished scholar, but in the field of modern languages and literature, and there lay most of the boy's reading. In Latin he was only a moderate student, his Greek was at most "scanty"—and while most of the "gentlemen" of his day knew no more, Disraeli never cultivated the exclusive art of appearing educated in the Classics.

In the Orthodox tradition, the D'Israeli home was a patriarchy. (Benjamin's mother, apparently a kindly and placid woman, had so little importance for her son that many years later he could write a memoir of his father without mentioning her name.) There tradition stopped: Isaac D'Israeli was unorthodox both as a father and as a Jew. His own father, the first Benjamin, had immigrated to England from Italy in 1748 and amassed a comfortable fortune in the City; it had been his desire to make Isaac a prosperous merchant in his own image. But Isaac's mother was another sort of person altogether. A proud and handsome lady, she came from a distinguished family related to the majestic Villa Reals of Portugal (as Disraeli, who could learn a good deal about snobbery in his own home, was fond of pointing out) and she encouraged the nonconformist desires of her son. Isaac adored books and despised commerce, and when his maternal grandmother left him enough of a fortune to be independent at twenty-five, he settled down to the life of a dilettante: a comfortable home, a comfortable unobtrusive wife, mornings in his well-stocked library, afternoons in the British Museum Reading Room, and conversations with a small but carefully chosen circle of friends. This circle was young Ben's circle, and gave him most of what he knew of English society before *Vivian Grey*.

Thoroughly educated, as his son put it, "in the revolutionary philosophy of the Eighteenth Century," Isaac D'Israeli had little respect for authorized, organized religion of any kind, and his participation in the Portuguese Jewish community was limited to regular payment of dues to the synagogue. When that synagogue, through a puzzling misjudgment of his character, suddenly elected him to a position of leadership, he picked a quarrel which led to his request that he be withdrawn from membership. Once his own father had died Isaac could be persuaded to have his children baptized; thus Benjamin was given a new faith (and, more important to him, eligibility for a political career) when he was thirteen. But Isaac, in his casual, abstracted way, did not feel the need for his own conversion and continued to draw most of his friends from the intellectual, prosperous community of Sephardim. Some were distinguished figures, like Sharon Turner, the historian, and Francis Cohen, later Lord Palgrave.

The D'Israeli circle also included the fashionable novelist Robert Plumer Ward, though how closely is something of a question. Benjamin Austen, Ward's solicitor, was a good friend of D'Israeli; Austen's wife Sarah, who had acted as Ward's agent in transmitting the anonymous manuscript of *Tremaine* to Colburn, helped young Disraeli with the editing of *Vivian Grey*, to the point where Ward regarded her as part-author. The D'Israelis knew a great deal, directly or indirectly, about Ward's personal affairs, and their interest in this highly respected political figure, successful novelist and undoubted gentleman must have been heightened by the fact that he was half Jewish.*

* On his mother's side. Ward's father, John Ward, a wealthy "Spanish merchant" living in Gibraltar, married Rebecca Raphael, a Spanish Jew from a Genoese family. She died when her son was three, and the boy was educated in English schools

Virtually the only evidence on the D'Israeli–Ward relationship comes from Edmund Phipps' inadequate biography of Ward, which includes numerous letters from Ward to Sarah Austen, many of them mentioning the D'Israelis, though they give no final proof that Ward and D'Israeli even met. In 1825 the D'Israelis, via the Austens, rented Ward's country home, Hyde House, and at least during that period there was an intimate correspondence between the two families; unfortunately, none of it has been preserved. Ward mentioned, in a letter to Mr Austen, that he had received "a few pleasant obliging letters from D'Israeli", and that his daughter had heard from "Miss D." (Benjamin's sister Sarah). Ward, however, was not in on the secret of the authorship of *Vivian Grey*, though he knew that Mrs Austen was. A year after the publication of the novel, when it was a secret no more, he referred to the author as "a certain friend of ours". And around this time young Disraeli wrote Ward a self-important letter praising *De Vere*, Ward's second novel, to the skies, and excusing his failure to find a single fault by saying, "when a man has himself a little acquaintance with the art of writing, he begins to grow a very temperate critic." In the following year Disraeli dedicated *Popanilla* to Ward.

Mostly on the basis of this Ward–Austen correspondence, Michael Sadleir has deduced that "the relationship between Ward and the d'Israeli's was at this time very close". "Very close" is probably too strong, but it seems likely that Ward and Isaac D'Israeli were on friendly terms before the publication of *Vivian Grey* and that Ward met Benjamin shortly after the novel appeared.

Isaac was also a distinguished literary figure in his own right; his perceptive, scholarly and entertaining books on literary and historical subjects (like the popular *Curiosities of Literature*, and the ambitious *Commentaries on the Life and Reign of Charles I*) won him the admiration of Byron, an honorary degree at Oxford, and the friendship and society of John Murray, his publisher. Because of his precocity, Benjamin was early permitted to go with his father to Murray's dinner parties, where he met such literary celebrities as William Maginn and Tom Moore, where he had his first taste of Regency manners and conversation, and where he could ask questions about dandyism, particularly Byron's dandyism. At one of these parties Murray answered the young man's questions about Byron's dress in such interesting detail that Disraeli recorded the description verbatim in his diary, and transferred it almost verbatim into *Vivian Grey*.

Besides the scholars and intellectuals of his father's circle, and the literati of Murray's, Disraeli had access to another social class. After finishing school at the age of sixteen, and after a year of reading through his father's library, he was articled in 1821 to a prosperous firm of solicitors in Frederick's Place, Old Jewry. The partners took to inviting him to their homes for the evening, and there Disraeli observed the manners of the upper middle class. He also demanded that his hosts observe him, for he had already learned that eccentricity in dress was as good a way as any to impress himself on people's memory. Long after this time the wife of one of the partners could still remember his "rather conspicuous attire": "a black velvet suit with ruffles, and black stockings with red clocks."

From such material (a Jewish childhood, an uncomfortable schooling, an exaggerated personal dandyism and glimpses of the Jewish, the literary and the professional men of the middle class) Disraeli fabricated *Vivian Grey*. He brought to the dandy novel, for the first time, the tensions and frustrations of adolescence. Vivian himself is a shameless adolescent projection of Disraeli: "an elegant, lively lad, with just enough of dandyism to preserve him from committing *gaucheries*, and with a devil of a tongue." Vivian's father is an equally idealized portrait of Isaac: "from his distinguished literary abilities he had always found himself an honoured guest among the powerful and the great." (Mr Grey is of course not Jewish, but he is admittedly middle-class in origin; and Vivian curses the handicap of "a little rascal blood".)

Vivian is sent to somewhat the same sort of school as Disraeli had attended, but the Jewish boy's first rude contact with the Gentile world is transformed into a triumph of precocious dandyism. "In a very few days," writes Disraeli, "Vivian Grey was decidedly the most popular fellow in the school." He was "so dashing! so devilish good-tempered! so completely up to everything!" There is something pathetic in the boy's smooth ascent to leadership—and something disturbing in the meanness of his exclusivism toward those outside his own charmed circle:

> One of the first principles of the new theory introduced into the establishment of Burnsley Vicarage by Mr Vivian Grey, was, that the ushers were to be considered by the boys as a species of upper servants; were to be treated with civility, certainly, as all servants are by gentlemen; but that no further attention was to be paid them, and that any fellow voluntarily conversing with an usher, was to be *cut dead* by the whole school.

Vivian eludes a university education—which was closed to Jews in Disraeli's day—by choice: "The idea of Oxford to such an individual was an insult!" And he disdainfully rejects the profession of Disraeli's employers in Frederick's Place: "to succeed as an advocate, I must be a great lawyer, and, to be a great lawyer, I must give up my chance of being a great man."

3

One path to greatness remains, and that, unaccountably, is politics—or, as Vivian Grey puts it: "POLITICS". Vivian stumbles on the solution:

> And now everything was solved! the inexplicable longings of his soul, which had so often perplexed him, were at length explained. The *want*, the indefinable *want*, which he had so constantly experienced, was at length supplied; the grand object on which to bring the powers of his mind to bear and work was at last provided. He paced his chamber in an agitated spirit, and panted for the Senate.

Reading the novels of the young Disraeli, one reminds oneself constantly that he could not have known the coming events of his career. For the Prime Minister of 1867 the early political aspirations of Vivian Grey are quite suitable if flamboyant; for the scholar's son and lawyer's clerk of 1827, devoid of knowledge or experience of the political scene, they are astonishing.

Vivian plunges headlong into political intrigue. At his father's table he meets the Marquis of Carabas, a discontented, imbecile nobleman. Seducing this gentleman and his wife with impudent flattery, he organizes the Carabas Party, which (in spite of a total absence of platform) is to rock the country and, incidentally, manœuvre Vivian into power. He visits the Marquis's resplendent country estate and there successively charms, flatters, beguiles, cheats and betrays a covey of visiting lords, millionaires, widows and virgins. (The Carabas home is wistfully named Château Désir; one of the guests bears the title of Lord Beaconsfield.) Then Vivian sets out upon a great and difficult mission: the enlisting of Frederick Cleveland, a melancholy political genius in retirement, into the ranks of the new party. Cleveland and Vivian fall into a state of affection that is too tender to be called friendship and too tentative to be called love. Nevertheless, Vivian's scheme collapses, and Part I comes to a close with a defeated and chastened hero, betrayed by treachery and by his own over-confident, indecent machinations.

What real experience lay behind so extravagant a plot? At the time of writing *Vivian Grey* Disraeli had not even a passing acquaintance with practical politics. He knew no lords and no ministers and he had nothing on which to base these aspirations, so crudely yet so confidently put into fiction, to political greatness. But he had Imagination—and Imagination went to work on small events. Immersed in the prosaic affairs of the law office in Frederick's Place, he could imagine himself tangling and untangling mysterious affairs of state. An excerpt from his reminiscences of the period, though written more than half a century later, reveals with what splendid facility the young Disraeli dreamed:

> It would be a mistake to suppose that the two years and more that I was in the office . . . were wasted . . . My business was to be the private secretary of the busiest partner . . . He dictated to me every day his correspondence, which was as extensive as a Minister's, and when the clients arrived I did not leave the room . . . They were in general men of great importance—bank directors, East India

directors, merchants, bankers. Often extraordinary scenes when firms in the highest credit came to announce and prepare for their impending suspension; questions, too, where great amounts were at stake . . . It gave me great facility with my pen . . .

If Disraeli concocted preoccupied Ministers out of busy law-yers, he could with even greater ease envision high political adventure in a publisher's project. Two years before *Vivian Grey* he had become involved through some friends in the City with a speculation in South American finance. He dashed off some pamphlets; they were published by Murray; and their author soared to optimistic heights on an inflated bubble. Before the bubble burst, Disraeli had a chance to impress his abilities on Murray and to be trusted with an important if not world-shaking mission. The publisher was thinking of founding a newspaper and chose Disraeli to sound out John Lockhart's willingness to become its editor. No sooner had Murray broached the idea than Disraeli, apparently without encouragement, spun grandiose dreams: the paper would eclipse *The Times* and become the organ for a new political party Disraeli had invented; there would be the joys of intrigue, espionage, and eventually, power.

Disraeli went to Scotland and, in his own opinion, charmed Lockhart and Lockhart's father-in-law, Sir Walter Scott. (He thought it necessary to reassure Murray that Lockhart was a "perfect gentleman", but Scott apparently had some doubts about his youthful visitor, whom he described as "a sprig of the root of Aaron" and "a young coxcomb".) The situation seemed to Disraeli so pregnant with romance and mystery, to say nothing of awesome significance, that he wrote breathless, conspiratorial letters to Murray, making use of a code in which Lockhart was "M.", Scott "The Chevalier", Canning "X." and Murray "The Emperor".

". . . M. enters into our views with a facility and readiness which were capital. He thinks that nothing can be more magnificent and excellent . . . He is fully aware that he may end by making his situation as important as any in the empire . . .

He must see that, through Powles, all America and the Commercial Interest is at our beck; . . . that the Chevalier is firm; that the West India Interest will pledge themselves; that such men . . . are *distinctly in our power*; and, finally, that he is coming to London, not to be an Editor of a Newspaper, but the Director-General of an immense organ, and at the head of a band of high-bred gentlemen and important interests . . .

If this point could be arranged, I have no doubt that I shall be able to organise, in the interest with which I am now engaged, a most *immense party* . . .; but I pray you, if you have any real desire to establish a mighty engine, to exert yourself at this present moment, and assist me to your very utmost . . . I write this despatch in the most extreme haste.

Ever yours,
B.D.

Unfortunately, Disraeli's visions were not catching. The "mighty engine" collided with the limitations of his partners, and his own immaturity; he came out of the affair bankrupt, ill, and liable to Murray's accusations of treachery and incompetence. Wholly discouraged he was not, could never be. If publishing and speculation were not the road to glory, then he would try a novel. So the perplexing experiences and emotions of twenty-one years were jumbled into *Vivian Grey*. Disraeli cast himself as the dandy Vivian, Lockhart as the melting Cleveland and poor John Murray as the Marquis of Carabas.

Such straining and stretching after destiny left their mark on the novel, which is crude, confused, often obnoxious. It is perhaps unfair to quote against *Vivian Grey* the opinion of Disraeli's most humourless political opponent, who read the book for the first time in 1874; but Gladstone was close to the truth when he jotted down his verdict: "the first quarter extremely clever, the rest trash." Though the book sold by the thousands and received praise even from Goethe and Heine, Disraeli himself had no illusions. With a snort at "public taste", he commemorated the announcement of an 1833 edition with this confidence to his diary: *Vivian Grey* had "faults which even youth can scarcely excuse"; it was "in short, the most unequal, imperfect, irregular thing that indiscretion ever published."

Nevertheless indiscretion *had* published it, and indiscretion had permitted Disraeli to draw an adolescent self-portrait so embarrassing that, like Bulwer, he would feel it necessary to *live it down* throughout his early political career. That portrait continues to fascinate students of Victoria's cherished Disraeli. For students of dandyism the differences between Vivian Grey as a dandy and his fellow heroes of the Regency novel are the absorbing interest.

Those differences become clear when *Vivian Grey* is set beside its successor *Pelham*, which appeared the year after the second part of Disraeli's novel. Pelham is a dandy who conceals a serious moral purpose behind his affectations; Vivian is a dandy whose lust for power defies concealment, and whose dandyism is a pose to gild immoral means used for an immoral end.

> Power! Oh! what sleepless nights, what days of hot anxiety! what exertions of mind and body! what travel! what hatred! what fierce encounters! what dangers of all possible kinds, would I not endure with a joyous spirit to gain it!

Pelham's motto reads: "Manage *yourself* well, and you may manage all the world." Vivian Grey's credo runs: "A Smile for a friend, and a Sneer for the World, is the way to govern mankind." The title page of *Vivian Grey* bears, instead of a quotation from Etherege defining the complete gentleman, the lines:

> "Why then, the world's mine oyster,
> Which with my sword I'll open."

For Pelham is withal a gentleman, and Vivian is a scoundrel.

Pelham merely exaggerates the exclusivism sanctioned by his set; Vivian can carry exclusivism to meanness. Pelham's desire for an active career conflicts with his indolent sensuality; Vivian cannot pause for breath. Pelham is cold-blooded and gay; Vivian is hot-blooded and tense. Pelham is favourably contrasted to the Byronic Glanville and left with the promise of a brilliant future ahead; Vivian has to be punished for his genuine sins and made to exhibit the melancholy, antisocial remorse of a Byronic hero. (The second part of the novel takes a chastened Vivian to the Continent where he can repent at leisure. "It is my opinion," says the Vivian of Part II, "that no one who has dared to think, can look upon this world in any other than a mournful spirit.")

Pelham's wit is fresh, spontaneous, impudent; Vivian's is always calculated and often sinister.

> "What a pity, Miss Manvers, the fashion has gone out for selling oneself to the devil."
>
> "Good gracious, Mr Grey!"
>
> "On my honour, I am quite serious. It does appear to me to be a very great pity. What a capital plan for younger brothers! It's a kind of thing I've been trying to do all my life, and never could succeed . . ."

Pelham is a member of a well-defined social set, though his intelligent "dandy eye" leads him to stand apart as critical observer. Vivian must fight to belong and never wholly loses his sense of being a stranger in a hostile world. Pelham, then, escapes entanglement through consciousness of his superiority, while Vivian runs away, through fear.

> Vivian Grey often asked himself, "who is to be my enemy tomorrow?" He was too cunning a master of the human mind, not to be aware of the quicksands upon which all greenhorns strike;—he knew too well the danger of *unnecessary intimacy*.

Pelham is absorbed by dandyism; Vivian *uses* it. As a dandy Pelham is an effortless success, though his effeminacy and his sensualism are exaggerations Brummell would not have condoned. As a dandy Vivian works too hard at the pose (like Bulwer, Disraeli included a whole chapter of advice on dress—duly cut from later editions—but it is addressed *to* Vivian by a critical older woman). And as a dandy Vivian is a failure. At every turn his frenzied energy, his unbridled ambition and his lust for power conflict with his self-control. These qualities carry Disraeli's hero far from the ideals of Brummell and relate him to another adolescent parvenu in a dandy world: Stendhal's Julien Sorel.

4

Disraeli liked to pretend that he wrote the first part of *Vivian Grey* in a week; it probably took him three. In any case, he was exhausted when it was done, and for a year and a half his activities were curtailed by some mysterious malady which he described as "one of those tremendous disorganisations which happen to all men at some period of their lives, and which are perhaps equally necessary for the formation of both body and constitution." His anxious father, who heard diagnoses ranging from "chronic inflammation of the membranes of the brain" to epilepsy, found the case "uncertain" and "obscure". Matters were worsened by the insulting reviews that greeted disclosure of the authorship of the novel, and it was thought wise to send young Disraeli abroad with friends, the Austens. On this trip he wrote the second part of *Vivian Grey*, which appeared in 1827. The following year saw the publication of three satires in verse and prose, among them the witty *Popanilla*, which mocked the fashionable novel and was dedicated to Robert Plumer Ward. Eighteen-twenty-eight was also the year of *Pelham*.

In spite of insults and bad reviews, *Vivian Grey* served exactly the purpose for which it was intended. It was popular, it was controversial, and it brought its author to the attention of his contemporaries. Significantly, Edward Bulwer took notice. The author of *Pelham* and the author of *Vivian Grey* exchanged volumes and began a correspondence in 1829; by the beginning of 1830 they were friends. Though only a year older than Disraeli, Bulwer had by this time seen enough of society balls and routs to be dreadfully bored with it all; he had a beautiful wife and a lavish home in Hertford Street, which was already known as a meeting-place for wits and men about town. He was famous, successful and, to all outward appearances, rich. Disraeli went to a few of Bulwer's little dinner parties in Hertford Street and was impressed, so impressed that fifty years later he reworked one of them into a scene for his last society novel, *Endymion*. He studied Bulwer's dandyism, he studied *Pelham*, and he went to Bulwer for advice on writing fashionable novels.

The impact of Bulwer and *Pelham* on Disraeli is apparent in the letters he wrote home from his second tour abroad, to the Mediterranean and the Near East. Disraeli set out in May of 1830 to behold the cradle of his family, his race, his civilization; but his personal baggage was the glamour of the Regency. Native eccentricity and histrionics led him to play a part before the society he encountered (or to say he played it) that was sometimes a clever pastiche, sometimes a vulgar caricature of Pelham. He wore his hair in long, black glossy ringlets that were taken for a wig; and "felt obliged to let the women pull it to satisfy their curiosity." He transformed the already theatrical dress he had worn at Bulwer's parties (Henry Bulwer remembered him in "green velvet trousers, a canary-coloured waistcoat, low shoes, silver buckles, lace at his wrists") into the costume of an actor in a bad play. "You should see me," he wrote gleefully, "in the costume of a Greek pirate. A blood-red shirt, with silver studs as big as shillings, an immense scarf for girdle, full of pistols and daggers, red cap, red slippers, broad blue striped jacket and trousers." Even the Turks, whom Disraeli described as "mad on the subject of dress", were astounded; a little Greek doctor with a small

6. Daniel Maclise: Disraeli (1833)

7. Isaac Robert Cruikshank: "A Dandy fainting or—An Exquisite in Fits" (1818)

grasp of Italian asked: "*Questo vestito Inglese o di fantasia?*" and received the only possible reply: "*Inglese e fantastico.*"

In more elegant company Disraeli kept closer to the way of Pelham. Thrusting himself upon the Governor of Cadiz ("a singular brute") he talked a mixture of nonsense and impudence that "made him stare for half an hour in a most extraordinary manner"; in short, "I Pelhamized him." He tried out the affectations demonstrated in Bulwer's curiously practical novel and marked with delight the effects of awe and notoriety that followed, as if Bulwer had personally guaranteed the commodity.

> I have also the fame of being the first who ever passed the Straits with two canes, a morning and an evening cane. I change my cane as the gun fires, and hope to carry them both on to Cairo. It is wonderful the effect these magical wands produce. I owe to them even more attention than to being the supposed author of—what is it?— I forget!

"Affectation tells here even better than wit," he noted on the occasion of his imitating Pelham's languid effeminacy:

> Yesterday, at the racket court, sitting in the gallery among strangers, the ball entered, and lightly struck me and fell at my feet. I picked it up, and observing a young rifleman excessively stiff, I humbly requested him to forward its passage into the court, as I really had never thrown a ball in my life. This incident has been the general subject of conversation at all the messes to-day!

In the letters Disraeli wrote his family he bubbled over with youthful high spirits. Dandyism was for the young tourist something of a sport. Yet the author of *Vivian Grey* also insisted time and again that he played the dandy for great stakes.* ("To govern men," he moralized at the end of the tennis ball story, "you must either excel them in their accomplishments, or despise them.") But to Bulwer he wrote in quite another tone, adapting

---

* The *success* of Disraeli's posings was called into question by his travelling companion, James Clay, who remarked that people often protested at meeting "that damned bumptious Jew boy". And, Clay added, there was a marked difference between the public and private Disraeli: "It would not have been possible to have found a more agreeable, unaffected companion when they were by themselves; but when they got into society, his coxcombry was intolerable."

his temper to what (he supposed) was the mood of the author of
Pelham. He became a languid sybarite:

> I confess to you that my Turkish prejudices are very much confirmed
> by my residence in Turkey. The life of this people greatly accords
> with my taste, which is naturally somewhat indolent and melancholy.
> And I do not think it would disgust you. To repose on voluptuous
> ottomans and smoke superb pipes, daily to indulge in the luxuries of
> a bath which requires half a dozen attendants for its perfection; to
> court the air in a carved caïque, by shores which are a perpetual scene;
> and to find no exertion greater than a canter on a barb; this is, I think
> a far more sensible life than all the bustle of clubs, all the boring of
> drawing-rooms, and all the coarse vulgarity of our political
> controversies.

Imagination was racing ahead, once again. Certainly Disraeli
knew very little about the life of a Regency man about town—the
"bustle of clubs", the "boring of drawing-rooms" and the "vulgarity of political controversies"—and far too little to complain
to Bulwer that the life palled. It was only after his second return
to England, in the autumn of 1831, that Disraeli entered confidently into the life of Regency society—and again it was largely
through Bulwer.

Bulwer invited his young friend to more dinner parties, which
Disraeli liked to describe as "brilliant *réunions*" and "really brilliant *soirées*". At these dinners he met many useful "notables"—
diplomats like Lord Strangford, politicians like Lord William
Lennox, blues like Lady Morgan and Mrs Gore. At one of
Bulwer's parties he was introduced, "by particular desire," to a
Mrs Wyndham Lewis, who struck him as "a pretty little woman,
a flirt, and a rattle; indeed, gifted with a volubility I should think
unequalled, and of which I can convey no idea." A useful acquaintance nonetheless: she was the lady who gave Disraeli his first
essential push into Parliament, and who later married him. At
another he was introduced to Bulwer's good friend Count
D'Orsay, "the famous Parisian dandy", who was only too delighted to extend the gift of his facile friendship to the promising
young Disraeli. And it was a useful friendship: through D'Orsay
and his family connections Disraeli found access to Crockford's
and Almack's.*

* On July 7, 1834, Disraeli wrote his sister (after describing an elegant
yacht party—"I never knew a more agreeable day, and never drank so much

Thus, launched by Bulwer and whispered about as the author of the naughty *Vivian Grey*, Disraeli burst upon society. By 1833 he could boast to his sister Sarah that his table was "literally covered with invitations, and some from people I do not know." By 1834 Lady Cork, the terrifying *grande dame* of Regency Society, could (according to Benjamin) describe him as "the best *ton* in London! There is not a party that goes down without him." By 1837 he was so firmly established as a social lion that when the Tory Carlton Club mapped London into canvassing districts, Disraeli was assigned to May Fair. The social triumphs he dreamed for Vivian Grey had come true at last.

Disraeli's dandyism was successful in that it won him what he wanted: attention. No one could fail to notice or remember the young man who went about in a black velvet, satin-lined coat, purple trousers with a gold band down the seam, a figured scarlet waistcoat, lace ruffles falling to the tips of his fingers, a profusion of jewels and chains (including the famous rings worn on the outside of his white gloves) and long black ringlets framing his markedly Semitic features. No one could fail to be astonished at the languid young man who campaigned for election to Parliament in such a costume, his mouth curved in "a sort of half-smile, half-sneer", his eyebrows finely arched over piercing black eyes

champagne in my life") that "Ossulston" planned to nominate him to Crockford's. Disraeli was, however, sure he would be blackballed and in fact became a member only in 1840.

On July 11, 1834, he wrote again that he had made his "*début* at Almack's with a subscription from Lady Tankerville."

D'Orsay's connection with the Ossulston–Tankerville family, and therefore with Disraeli's social success, is this: his sister Ida married the Duc de Guiche, son of the Duc de Gramont. Armandine Sophie Léonie *Corisande* de Gramont, sister of the Duc de Guiche, married the future fifth Earl of Tankerville and became the Lady Tankerville who gave Disraeli his ticket to Almack's. Her son was the Baron Ossulston (a young dandy six years Disraeli's junior) who nominated Disraeli to Crockford's. D'Orsay was extremely intimate with his sister's relations and often passed on their friendship to his own friends.

It is pleasant to note that Disraeli must have derived the name of his most charming heroine, the lovely Corisande of *Lothair*, from his friendship with this family—and may also have found there something of his nostalgic idealization of family life among the English aristocracy. One of young Ossulston's sisters was named Corisande after her French mother, and the name remained in the family throughout the nineteenth century—indeed, according to *Burke's Peerage*, up to the present day.

which blazed alarmingly from his pale face—especially when he opened his mouth and poured forth a stream of impassioned eloquence that had nothing of the dandy about it. The entire effect was planned and staged with consummate theatricality, and deserved the attention it received. It did not, however, receive respect—or votes. Disraeli had to run five times for Parliament before he was elected, and then he succeeded only after submitting his proud independence to Tory discipline and after enlisting the aid of the powerful Wyndham Lewises. His dandyism was flashy and certainly not quite gentlemanly; he was called a dandy less often than a coxcomb or a popinjay or an exquisite.

So, presently, Disraeli learned that manners which just got by in the Regency would not do at all for the Victorians, and that youthful dandiacal extravagances would have to be edited out of life and fiction. He tried to apologize in the 1853 preface to an emasculated edition of the disreputable *Vivian Grey*:

> Books written by boys, which pretend to give a picture of manners and to deal in knowledge of human nature, must necessarily be founded on affectation. They can be, at the best, but the results of imagination, acting upon knowledge not acquired by experience. Of such circumstances exaggeration is a necessary consequence, and false taste accompanies exaggeration . . .

5

Disraeli never again put himself into a novel in the shape of the dandified, power-seeking hero of *Vivian Grey*. But he continued to fashion his heroes after other sides of himself. "Poetry is the safety valve of my passions," he confided to his diary, "—but I wish to *act* what I *write*. My works are the embodification of my feelings. In *Vivian Grey* I have portrayed my active and real ambition." He needed the novel (which he significantly called "poetry") as an outlet for his Byronism, his messianism, his race consciousness, his pride and his sense of destiny; these passions poured over into *Contarini Fleming* (1832), *Alroy* (1833) and *Venetia* (1837). Once in Parliament and absorbed with the revitalizing of Tory ideals, he used the novel as a projection of his political principles in the famous and influential trilogy of *Coningsby*, *Sybil* and *Tancred* (1844-7).

But if he was through with describing himself as a dandy,

Disraeli was not through with the dandies. The mysterious, incapacitating illness of 1827 and 1828, which Disraeli understood as a "tremendous disorganization" of his body and mind, would seem to have brought an end to his adolescence. Thereafter the tensions, the meannesses, the painful insecurity which had marred *Vivian Grey* disappeared from Disraeli's novels, as they probably disappeared from his personality. He was able to hold himself at a distance from the dandy world, to admire the dandies without suspicion or fear. He began to describe them as princes of a fantasy world.

The first novel in which Disraeli tried his new approach to dandyism was *The Young Duke*, a full-fledged society novel, far more detailed and far more glamorous than *Vivian Grey* in its picture of exclusive society. It was written while Disraeli was in semi-retirement at Bradenham, convalescing from his illness, and was brought down to London in the spring of 1830 for the critical advice of Bulwer and the judgment of Colburn, who at last paid five hundred pounds for the copyright, making possible Disraeli's long-cherished dream of a tour of the Levant. The novel appeared while he was still abroad, in 1831, and had been completed before Disraeli was familiar with the society he described so lavishly. " 'The Young Duke'!" Isaac D'Israeli is said to have exclaimed at the title. "What does Ben know of dukes?"

But lack of exact knowledge did not mar *The Young Duke* in quite the same way as it had *Vivian Grey*. Disraeli was older, soberer, and more self-confident; he was now a somebody, even if that somebody was only "the Author of *Vivian Grey*", to whom the authorship of the new novel was ascribed. He had also done a good deal of reading: society novels (especially *Pelham*), memoirs and newspapers. That accounts for the novel's great defect, and for its author's disaffection ("I don't care a jot about *The Young Duke*," he wrote to his sister; "I never staked any fame on it."). It reads too much like hack work (which it was); it is too much the conventional society novel. But in one way Disraeli turned his lack of concrete knowledge to good account, and brought a new quality to the fashionable novel. *The Young Duke* does not even pretend to realism: it is a fantasy, a modern tale out of an Anglicized *Arabian Nights*. And suggested here and there through the novel is Disraeli's amusement at the discrepancy between fact and fancy—the first appearance of that odd, wry, half-cynical, half-tender humour which distinguishes *Lothair* and *Endymion*, his last and finest novels.

Thus the hero of the novel is not Disraeli, but a Duke—and not only a Duke, but the youngest, handsomest, richest, freest, gayest little duke in all the world.

Estates, Irish province, London squares; rent-roll £200,000; half a million in the funds . . . and although perhaps in his two palaces, three castles, four halls, and lodges *ad libitum*, there were more fires burnt than in any other establishment in the Empire, this was of no consequence, because the coals were his own.

The Young Duke is not only a dandy, but the most conceited, most delightful, most successful, most effortless little dandy in all England. "An air of habitual calm, a look of kind condescension, and an inclination to a smile, which never burst into a beam, announced that the Duke of St James was perfectly satisfied with existence, and conscious that he was himself, of that existence, the most distinguished ornament. In fact, he was a sublime coxcomb . . ." He is certainly the best dressed, not in the strident colours Disraeli affected, but in the delicate pastels and mysterious scents of the butterfly dandy: white silk waistcoat lined in rose, buttoned with pink topaz, sprayed with essence of violet, and a coat "of a colour . . . stolen from the neck of Juno's peacock." His equipage is exotic (he rolls in to London "attended by a French cook, an Italian valet, a German jäger, and a Greek page") and his homes—his palaces, castles, halls and lodges—are a fairy-tale setting. Sweet music sounds "from an unseen source", and swinging censers give off heavy perfumes; the walls are hung with exotic jewel-inlaid weapons and pearl-embroidered saddles, which gleam mysteriously through the "subdued and quiet light"; footmen in scarlet and silver wait on tables set with gold, and decorated down the centre with a rivulet of rose-water through which swim "gold and silver fish"; "the bouquets were exchanged every half hour . . ."

The Duke of St James has only one problem: what to do with himself. He sets out to conquer society, but the conquest proves too easy.

He almost determined not again to mingle in society; but, like a monarch, merely to receive the world which worshipped him. The idea was sublime . . . In the midst of his splendour, he fell into a reverie, and mused on his magnificence. He could no longer resist the conviction that he was a superior essence, even to all around him. The world seemed created solely for his enjoyment. Nor man nor woman could withstand him.

He gives fêtes the like of which London never saw, but even masquerading as a courtier at the court of Charles I (and sprinkling a shower of diamonds to round out the character) begins to pall. He tries kidnapping a ballet-dancer and transporting her to a secluded harem (this episode was taken from the legend of the contemporary dandy "Golden" Ball Hughes, on which the Duke of St James was partially modelled), but the adventure proves as boring as daily life. Finally, Disraeli takes pity on his bewildered hero and artfully directs him to the exciting and absorbing interest of a cause: Catholic Emancipation, which, along with Jewish Emancipation, was one of the burning political issues of the 'twenties and 'thirties. It was an issue in which Disraeli himself took a profound interest.

Disraeli had a good deal of fun with all this, and he incidentally showed that he had taken up a confident and relaxed position toward the dandies. They were wonderful and admirable, if faintly amusing; they were the triumph of the most magnificent order of creation, the English aristocracy; and they could be turned to sublime uses by a masterly hand working behind the scenes. That would be the moral of *Coningsby* as well as the theme of Disraeli's romantic Toryism. His paean to dandyism in *The Young Duke* was involved with a hymn to England, for Disraeli had also taken up a position toward his country: he was a stranger cherishing his strangeness, a visitor with a divine mission, and his heart overflowed into grandiloquent rhapsodies:

Oh! England!—Oh! my country . . . My heart is thine, although my shadow falls upon a foreign strand; and although full many an Eastern clime and Southern race have given me something of their burning blood, it flows for thee! I rejoice that my flying fathers threw their ancient seed on the stern shores which they have not dishonoured:—I am proud to be thy child. Thy noble laws have fed with freedom a soul that ill can brook restraint . . .

6

The author of *Vivian Grey* knew nothing about society; the author of *The Young Duke* knew very little; the author of *Henrietta*

Temple (1836) knew a great deal. But the latter was less a society novel than a love story, a tender farewell to the three-year affair between Disraeli and Henrietta Lady Sykes. He had commemorated its beginning with a notation in his diary on September 1, 1833 : "one incident has indeed made this year the happiest of my life"; he commemorated its conclusion with a romantic novel decorated with portraits of society figures he now knew quite well—like Lady Cork, drawn with all her eccentricities as Lady Bellair, and Count D'Orsay, to whom the novel was affectionately dedicated. The portrait of D'Orsay is as affectionate as the dedication, and the tribute to his dandyism warm and uncritical.

In his novel of 1836 Disraeli was sufficiently sure of himself to poke malicious fun at a vulgar money-grabbing coal merchant by the name of Levison, and to pour forth an uncritical love for England : especially that segment of English society "superior in talents, intelligence, and accomplishments, in public spirit and in private virtues, to any in the world—the English nobility."

Disraeli concluded *Henrietta Temple* by sending a whole flock of his English noblemen off to Parliament, thereby proving their public spirit. The following year he was at last able to join them and many of his other heroes in the House of Commons. As cocksure as Vivian Grey, he had already told Lord Melbourne that he wanted to be Prime Minister. For a time fiction would be put aside to make way for the far more exciting and romantic world of action. "I am only truly great in action," he had written in 1833.

If ever I am placed in a truly eminent position I shall prove this. I could rule the House of Commons, although there would be a great prejudice against me at first. It is the most jealous assembly in the world. The fixed character of our aristocratic institutions, renders a career difficult. Poetry is the safety valve of my passions, but I wish to *act* what I *write*.

In 1837 Victoria ascended the throne; and Disraeli ascended to Parliament.

Part Two

FRANCE

CHAPTER V

Dandyism Goes to France 1815–30

My good sir, what could we do without our Paris? I came here first in 1815 (when the Duke and I were a good deal remarked by the inhabitants); I proposed but to stay a week; stopped three months, and have returned every year since. There is something fatal in the place—a wicked one very likely—but it acts on us all; and perpetually the old Paris man comes hieing back to his quarters again, and is to be found, as usual, sunning himself on the Rue de la Paix.
—Thackeray: *Memorials of Gourmandising*

THE rise of dandyism in France was a social phenomenon of the most frivolous nature, but its roots were in the great events of history. The fall of the Emperor, the return of Louis XVIII in 1814; the *Cent Jours*, the defeat at Waterloo, the second return of the House of Bourbon in 1815—these were the necessary preludes to the dandy occupation of Paris and the triumph of anglomania. Brummell's flight to France in 1816 signified not only the Beau's personal insolvency and the beginning of the end of Regency manners; it also demonstrated that Peace had returned to France at last, bringing with it the peculiar blessing of tourism.

In the year of Brummell's flight a Regency gentleman urged prudence on his touring countrymen in a gingerly treatise entitled:

BRIEF REMARKS ON ENGLISH MANNERS, and an attempt to account for some of our most striking peculiarities. In a series of letters to a friend in France. By an Englishman.

The anonymous author is aware that an occupied people, still proud and critical in defeat, will never be kindly disposed to the manners and attitudes of their conquerors. But how much more serious the case when these are dandy manners and exclusive attitudes! With the air of a man horrified to see displayed abroad what he has barely managed to accept at home, the anonymous moralist scrutinizes one by one, in the harsh light of international relations, the social "peculiarities" of the Regency: *Aristocratick Feeling; Reserve; Taciturnity; Exclusivism of the Great World; Superciliousness of High Life*; and so on. *Cutting* he describes as a "gothick custom", lamenting that its vogue has been "set by that class which in foreign countries is justly considered the pattern of politeness, though not always, I fear, entitled to the same character in this." He stigmatizes as both offensive and surprising the air of "insolent superiority too commonly assumed by persons of rank and fashion in this country . . . In foreign countries it is always considered the mark of a 'nouveau riche'."

Clearly, the worst was to be expected from the export of native English dandyism.

> Foreigners seldom take to us kindly at first . . . It is much to be regretted that we do not manage to make [our good qualities] float on the surface a little more than we are in the habit of doing, and by a prevailing civility and kindness of manner prove at once, even to strangers, that our hearts are good.

But this was 1816, not 1916 and certainly not 1946: the English dandies took Paris much as Wellington had taken Waterloo. *Dandysme* and *anglomanie* became the distinguishing marks on the surface of Paris life during the Restoration and the July monarchy.

Anglomania had been a significant factor in French life throughout the eighteenth century, but in the sense that the French were "mad for" English *ideas*. In the new century the fascination was with manners, and dandy manners were the English export. That they were for the French an import, that they were in fact alien to the native temper, was never doubted. Even when *le dandysme* had become part of the essential furniture of the intellectual community in France, men like Baudelaire and Barbey d'Aurevilly would find much of its charm in its exoticism.

When Lady Morgan, the Regency blue, toured France in 1816 and turned her observations into literary capital—a travel book (*France*) compounded of naïveté, shrewdness and pretension— she sententiously attributed the absence of native dandyism to the *studiousness* and *cultivation* of French youth. "I have seen," she noted, "the sudden appearance of a London '*dandy*' make as

great a sensation in a French assembly, by its novelty and incom-
prehensibility," as the arrival of a new species in the *Jardin des
Plantes.*

> I was one evening in the apartment of the Princesse de Volkonski . . .
> when one of these "fashion-mongering boys," . . . newly arrived in
> Paris, appeared at the door of the saloon, flushed with the conscious
> pride of the toilette, and reconnoitring the company through his
> glass. I had the honour to be recognized by him; he approached, and
> half yawned, half articulated some enquiries, which he did not wait
> to be answered, but drawled on to somebody else, whom he dis-
> tinguished with his notice. A very pleasant little French woman,
> the daughter of the Comte de L-s-ge, . . . stared at him with
> unsated curiosity and evident amusement; and when he had passed
> on asked, "*Mais qu'est-ce que cela veut dire?*" I answered, "*C'est un
> dandi!*"
>   "*Un dandi!*" she repeated, "*un dandi! c'est donc un genre parmi
> vous, qu'un dandi?*"

Lady Morgan's scene would be repeated again and again
throughout the 'teens and 'twenties. The first touring dandies
inspired amusement, distaste, horror—but primarily surprise.
They were not, however, wholly new to *all* the French. Though
revolution, imperialism and war had officially closed the Channel
to tourists through a quarter of a century (except for the abortive
Peace of Amiens in 1802), large numbers of the French aristocracy who fled the Revolution as *émigrés* had witnessed at first
hand the rise of the dandy in England. Many had sampled
Regency hospitality, like Philippe Egalité, the notorious Duc
d'Orléans, who was entertained by the Prince of Wales at
Brighton; many had intermarried with the English nobility, like
the Gramont family, whose English connections would smooth
D'Orsay's début in London. (The *émigrés* had also contributed,
of course, to the general Regency style: their *cuisine*, their *salon*
and, above all, their *mots.*)

And the Restoration brought the *émigrés* back to Paris, regarding Waterloo as a victory rather than a defeat, and applauding
the popular ballet—"L'Heureux Retour"—which celebrated the
return of the Bourbons to the French throne. A few had already
learned dandy ways and would, like D'Orsay's brother-in-law
the Duc de Guiche, play a part in furthering anglomania and *le
dandysme.* Many found the readjustment to French life extremely

difficult. On his return to France, Chateaubriand was startled to find himself half-English:

> Je nourissais toujours au fond de mon cœur les regrets et les souvenirs de l'Angleterre; j'avais vécu si longtemps dans ce pays que j'en avais pris les habitudes; je ne pouvais me faire à la saleté de nos maisons, de nos escaliers, de nos tables, à notre malpropreté, à notre bruit, à notre familiarité, à l'indiscretion de notre bavardage: j'étais Anglais de manière, de goûts et, jusqu'à un certain point, de pensées . . .

Joining the French returning to Paris from England were a band of Englishmen who had spent the previous decade in the French provinces. The treaty of Amiens had brought to France a flood of wealthy Englishmen impatient at being severed from the Continent, and those unfortunate enough to be still on French soil when hostilities broke out again in 1803 were consigned as hostages by Napoleon and sent to Verdun, the main depot for both civilian and military prisoners. Many of them noble and most of them prosperous, prisoners mainly in the sense that they were restricted to the boundaries of the city, the English colony of Verdun set about reproducing London society in miniature. They established their own clubs, even to a Jockey Club; they gave masked balls and formally celebrated the birthday of His Highness, the Prince of Wales; they kept French mistresses in the finest style; they organized steeple-chases and cock-fights. By day they hunted and fought duels; by night they applauded opera singers imported expressly for them from Metz, and played away fantastic sums of money at Balbi's, their personal gambling house. "Young Englishmen," commented one of their class, "are much the same whether prisoners or at home, playing, driving, and shooting each other . . . One might fancie oneself in London."

Freed by the war's end, the prisoners of Verdun hurried in large numbers to Paris, stopping before their trip home to join the *émigrés* in welcoming the victorious English, who descended on the city in and out of uniform. At the height of the tourist invasion the number of English in the capital was estimated at fourteen thousand. The unfortunate few who had to remain in London were singing a song called "All the World's in Paris", and in the occupied city the phrase heard everywhere was *"John Bull a pris possession!"*

Among the first military men to enter the city in 1815 was

Captain Gronow, most observant of the dandies. Gronow had participated in the great events of Waterloo on the 18th of June (and would remember, among other important details, that Wellington had directed a defensive engagement dressed in a grey great-coat with a cape, a white cravat, Hessian boots, leather pantaloons and a large cocked hat *à la Russe*). Gronow marched with his decimated regiment on the capital, dodged fire from the batteries of Montmartre, bivouacked in the Bois de Boulogne and on the 25th entered Paris by the Porte Maillot, passing by the half-completed Arc de Triomphe. He would be an almost constant resident of Paris for close on fifty years. Typical of Wellington's officers in that he was as much dandy as soldier, he could record the peculiarities of touring dandies (Hervey Aston, "Kangaroo" Cooke, Charles Standish, Lord Alvanley, the Duke of Devonshire, Lord Thanet, Lord Fife and so on) with the assurance of one of their set.

The great Duke himself had been nicknamed "the Dandy" by his troops in the Peninsular campaign; and he would convince historians of the difficulty of describing the strategy of Waterloo by pointing out that "the history of a battle is not unlike the history of a ball." Wellington was just forty-six, still handsome in face and trim in figure, and he enjoyed dressing up to his role as "Saviour of Europe". All Paris marvelled at his personal distinction, and at his peculiarly Regency blending of the austere and the eccentric. One image of the Duke remained long after he had left the city: a stiff figure riding through the streets mounted on a tiny horse, and followed at a respectful distance by his groom.

Wellington's army lived up to Wellington's manner—at least the officers did, and his was an officer's army. It was a time when commissioned officers went into battle literally without knowing how to drill, when no citations for bravery in the field were given below the rank of captain, and when, in the ranks, the term "gentlemen's sons" frequently passed as an equivalent for "Officers". (The gorgeously costumed "gentlemen's sons" of the Grenadier Guards were once reprimanded by Wellington for riding into battle on a rainy day with their umbrellas raised. "The Guards may in uniform, when on duty at St James's, carry them if they please;" he said, "but in the field it is not only ridiculous but unmilitary.") Even during the fighting, when there was much else to notice, the French had wondered at the dandy

manners of the English officers. Marshal Exelmans went on
record with his opinions about the English cavalry: they had the
best horses in the world, he said, but the officers had "nothing to
recommend them but their dash and sitting well in their saddles";
and they rode recklessly "over everything; as if the art of war
were precisely the same as that of fox-hunting." Most serious,
he added, their clothes fitted too tightly to permit effective use of
the sabre . . .

For the visiting dandies Paris refurbished pre-war pleasures
and invented new ones. There was the Opera, where Malibran
and Grisi sang and Vestris danced; there were ices at Tortoni's,
whither the dandies drove their mistresses when the curtain fell.
There was gambling at Frascati's or in the Palais-Royal, where
hells alternated with brothels. There were lounging in the
Tuileries, riding and duelling in the Bois and strolling on the
"Boulevart". Best of all there were the restaurants, charging
especially steep prices for the *milords*: Rocher de Cancale, Véry's,
Les Trois Frères Provençaux, the Café Hardy and the Café
Anglais. For the gourmets of St James's Street dining at the Paris
restaurants was a treat of a special nature: superb food combined
with the sensation of slumming. "A *dîner de restaurant*", explained the magnificent Lady Blessington, "is pleasant for its
novelty."

> The guests seem less ceremonious and more gay; the absence of the
> elegance that marks the dinner-table appointments in a *maison bien
> monté* gives a homeliness and heartiness to the repast; and even the
> attendance of two or three ill-dressed *garçons*, hurrying about, instead
> of half-a-dozen sedate servants in rich liveries . . . gives a zest to the
> dinner often wanted in more luxurious feasts.

In the first years of the Restoration such delights of Paris were
distinctly for the conquering English: few Frenchmen could
afford them. Impoverished and enervated by the emigration, the
native aristocracy felt the difference between a Restoration and a
Regency. Insecurity, both political and financial, forced on the
ultras of the Faubourg Saint-Germain a social life narrow and
austere in the extreme, under the rule of dowagers and Dauphine.
Visiting Englishmen, to whom hospitality was dutifully repaid
by the former *émigrés*, found that the Faubourg salon offered, as
return for the showiness, the glitter, the extravagance of the

8. Horace Vernet: *Incroyable* (1814)

L'Egoïsme personnifié

9. "L'Egoïsme personnifié" from *Le Bon Genre* (1814)

Regency world, an endless round of cards, family visits, cards, muted gossip, cards, simple meals, cards . . .

Few young men among the French aristocracy had the polish —or the money—to rival the English dandies, but one very young Frenchman made himself noticed. Alfred D'Orsay, a mere thirteen-year-old in 1814, emerged into the world of dandyism, which he would one day reorder, in the first year of the dandy occupation. Parvenu aristocrats and adventurers, with roots other than the Faubourg, the D'Orsays had shown a readiness to support the Bourbons, the Republic, the Empire or the English, depending on circumstances. Young Alfred himself, who was said to have learned to read from the *bulletins de la grande armée*, had easily transferred his youthful hero-worship from Napoleon to Napoleon's arch-enemy. Though only a boy D'Orsay was already enough of a dandy to be singled out by the Duke, and to be pressed into service as a guide for the young attachés at the English embassy.

The salon of Mme Craufurd, D'Orsay's grandmother, had much of the showy elegance of the Regency; Mme Craufurd's husband was a Briton; and D'Orsay himself was already half-anglicized in the sense that would come to matter most for the French: he had an English horse. He had in fact first caught Wellington's eye at a royal stag hunt in the Bois de Boulogne, astride a particularly fine mount: "high crest, short ears, straight legs, and passing strong". This admirable animal had been a gift from the Duc de Guiche, D'Orsay's friend and future brother-in-law, then living in England and a fine judge of horses.

2

Lady Morgan's first travel book about France made her money, scandal and something of a literary reputation. (Her *France in 1816* is sometimes said to have precipitated the *anciens-modernes* quarrel in France by its aggressively unfavourable comparison of Racine to Shakespeare.) She returned to try it again in 1829 and found a different country. The English were still there, the particularly French delights of the restaurants, the opera girls and the boulevard were still amusing the tourists, but now there were also English pleasures in embarrassing confusion. Anglomania, "cette sorte de folie d'imitation" (as the French called it), had met with an initial resistance in 1814 and 1815: "Redoutons l'anglomanie," sang Béranger, "elle a déjà gâté tout." But the fashion of mimicking all things English had strengthened through the 'twenties and was about to triumph in the 'thirties. Calais was Lady Morgan's first disappointment:

> How English! Not a sanded floor, nor a sullied parquet are now visible. Nothing but English carpets, and English cleanliness; English delf and English damask; not a rag of the old huckaback left . . . The *garçon* cries, "coming up;" and the tea and muffins are worthy of the Talbot at Shrewsbury . . . Not a jack-boot, not a *queue*, not a powdered *toupée* left; nothing to ridicule, nothing to blame . . . The age of tourists and of chivalry is alike over. What luck to have written *my* France, while France was still so French!

She found Paris even worse. "This was too much!" she protested. "Was it for this we left the snugness and oeconomical comfort of our Irish home, and encountered the expensive inconveniences of a foreign journey, in the hope of seeing nothing British . . . ?"

Anglomania in the 'twenties was a cheap commodity, compounded of fads and foolishness. The shops were full of it. Catering to the ever-present English tourist and to the increasingly English tastes of the French rich, Paris merchants hastily put up for sale English comforts and English products. The *patisserie* ticketed its good things as the *toasts*, the *muffling*, the *plom-cake* (or *plume-cake*), the *crompet*, the *apple-dumplin*; and the placard over the door read "HERE IS TO BE HAD ALL SORTS OF ENGLISH PASTRY." The *parfumerie* offered, instead of the classic *eaux*, *essences* and *extraits*, such things as *lavender-vatre*, *Vindsor* soap, the *Regent's vash-ball* and *Hunt's blacking*. Restaurants like LITTLE GARRAWAY—*Chez Mme Harriet-Dum* were serving roast-veal, roast-mutton, roast-beef, and potatoes with everything. The *bottier* called himself "Fournisseur to His Excellency prince Talleyrand", and the *pharmacien* "Apothecary to the duke of Northumberland".

Inevitably, poor sense, poor taste and poor spelling marked the first French imitation of the dandy pose, which had arrived in a package of *lavender-vatre* and *plume-cake*. Only the most superficial aspects of the pose interested the *anglomanes*, and they usually misinterpreted these. The sharp outlines of Brummell's dandyism, and the fine line he drew between what was proper for the dandy and what was not, had already been blurred by his English followers. Now they were to be erased. The French dandies could not even spell the great Beau's name: such abominations as *Brunmel* and *Blummel* gave way only to the conviction (still maintained in France) that *Brummel* was the one correct form.

The Paris generation of the 'twenties affected a pseudo-dandyism of loud English clothes (the *spencer* or the *redingote lord Novart*) and garish English colours (*fumée de Londres, vert anglais, bronze anglais*). The first French dandy called his French valet by an English name; he made bets, smoked cigars, patronized cock-fights, affected near-sightedness and—above all—bad manners. This last characteristic was the despair of those who remembered the pretty ways of the *Ancien Régime*, which the dowagers of the Faubourg had attempted to revive in the first years of the Restoration by sending their untutored young to school under the Court's dancing master, an old man with a long memory for outdated graces. The French journal *La Mode* protested bitterly against *cette épidémie britannique*, including such follies as saying *la fashion* instead of *la mode*, "comme on disait jadis quand on se contentait de parler français en France." But the grossness of such a sport as the cock-fight was for *La Mode* the last straw: "Voilà le gracieux passetemps de cette jeunesse fashionable . . .! Voilà où en est l'urbanité, le bon goût, l'élégance des manières dans le pays de François Ier, de Lauzun et de Richelieu!"

The first French dandies denied the native temperament and the native tradition in a blundering attempt to imitate the English. They cultivated a sullen silence instead of the art of conversation, insolence instead of the art of pleasing. Scorning to perform the mannered gestures and to whisper the formalities of the *salon*, they lolled on sofas and thrust their boots into the faces of the ladies. Yet the resulting pose was somehow more French than English. Thus, a new use was found for the dandy pretence of near-sightedness, a Regency affectation facilitating the art of the cut. Lister describes the phenomenon in *Granby*: Mr Trebeck, his Brummell-figure, can assume at will "that calm but wandering gaze, which veers, as if unconsciously, round the prescribed individual; neither fixing, nor to be fixed; not looking on vacancy, nor on any one object; neither occupied, nor abstracted; a look which perhaps excuses you to the person *cut*, and, at any rate, prevents him from accosting you." The French dandy found

another use for his *lorgnon*: to ogle the ladies. As a *lion* explains
it, in a contemporary document called the *Physiologie du lion*:

> —Vous voulez, je suppose, témoigner à une femme que vous la
> trouvez jolie . . .; le mouvement que vous faites pour saisir votre
> lorgnon avertit la dame de l'impression favorable que ses charmes
> ont produit. Son attention se concentre sur votre individu. Alors
> vous clignez les paupières. Rien qui donne l'air aussi provocateur.
> On dirait que vous appréciez chaque détail, et que vous suivez
> attentivement la ligne sous le vêtement.

Near-sightedness, like so much else, was cultivated by the
lions, the *incroyables*, the *merveilleux*, the *élégants*, the *fashionables*
(as the French alternatively called their dandies) because it was
la mode; and most of *la mode* was modish because it had already
been fashionable among the English. There was a fashionable
tailor, the celebrated Staub, who gained favour with the French
dandies through the patronage of Sir Henry Mildmay, Brummell's
old friend. (The prudent Staub married Lady Mildmay's *dame de
compagnie*.) There was a fashionable watch-maker, Breguet, who
counted among his patrons the Marquis of Londonderry, Lord
Chesterfield and, notably, the Duke of Wellington, who was enchanted by a watch that (on request) struck the hour *and the
minute*; it was rumoured to have cost the Duke three hundred
guineas. (Breguet's watches were so popular, among those who
could afford them, that Pelham, passing through Paris in the
'twenties, was particularly annoyed to be asked whether "he had
got one of Brequet's (*sic*) watches yet?") There was a fashionable
place to sit at the opera, *la loge infernale*; and a fashionable op-
tician, Chevalier, who supplied opera glasses to magnify the
fashionable dancers thirty-two times. There was a fashionable
outdoor shooting range, the famous *tir aux pigeons* in the Tivoli
gardens established by an expatriate Englishman "à l'instar de la
Red House, à Battersea, près de Londres."

It was fashionable to join a club, and since there had never been
clubs in Paris the Cercle Francais was founded in 1824 on English
models. Re-established in 1828 as the Cercle de l'Union, its permanent and famous name, the club bore the arms of the House of
France and the House of England as its insignia. Encouragement
of friendship between the two nations was the ostensible purpose
of the Cercle; sociability in the masculine English manner was
its actual contribution to French society. (Among its founders

were D'Orsay and the Duc de Guiche; among its most faithful members, Talleyrand and Palmerston.) When, in 1842, the need was felt for a more intimate club, the Petit Cercle was founded by such French dandies as Alfred de Musset and Roger de Beauvoir, and such English "old Paris men" (in Thackeray's phrase) as Captain Gronow.

3

Most fashionable of all was the horse. Worshipping the animal as "le sacré roi de la création", the anglomaniac dandy liked to fancy himself a centaur. It was more than fashionable, it was essential to ride a horse, drive a horse, own a horse, bet on a horse or, at the least (often at the most), talk horse all day and all night long. This attitude was the most foolish and the most colourful mistake in the history of anglomania: confusing the urbane dandy and the horsey buck. For Brummell and Pelham horses had been incidentals, hunting and racing vulgarly energetic; but the French dandy at least pretended that racing, driving and Jockey-Clubbing were his primary interests. D'Orsay, after all, had made his début on a horse.

The sport of driving (that is, the art of remaining alive in a carriage built for display rather than locomotion) returned to France with the Restoration. Aristocratic carriages had been ritually burned during the Revolution as "restes impurs de la tyrannie", and the new models that crowded the streets of Paris in the 'twenties were usually designed and named after English styles: the *tilbury*, the *landau*, the *gigue*, the *wiski*, the *carrick*, the *bokay* and so on. "Il faut que la mode soit un tyran bien despote," pronounced the *Almanach des Modes*, "pour avoir mis en vogue des équipages si fragiles, qu'un homme raisonnable n'y monte jamais sans réfléchir qu'il touche peut-être à sa dernière heure."

Racing as a society and a court sport was a revival rather than a new fashion. It had been imported from England before the Revolution, but had met then with strong resistance. "On ne la transportera pas ici," wrote one Frenchman; "elle est exotique et le climat ne lui est pas favorable." *L'Encyclopédie* in 1786 defined the sport coldly:

C'est un défi de plusieurs hommes à cheval à qui arrivera le premier, en courant de toute la vitesse de son cheval, à un but fixé. Les Anglais

font fréquemment de ces courses. Il y a quelques années qu'on en
faisait à Paris, mais cette mode est déjà passée.

During the Restoration, however, racing on the Champ de Mars
received the seal of authentic fashion: it was revived specifically
by Englishmen, notably Lord Henry Seymour, aided by *émigrés*,
notably D'Orsay's brother-in-law the Duc de Guiche. In 1829
De Guiche published the first of his scholarly essays (*"De
l'amélioration des races de chevaux en France"*) which were to establish the traditions of the thoroughbred in France and which
are still classics of the technical literature of the horse.

By the opening years of the July Monarchy the taste for racing
had become so fervent among the aristocracy that Louis-Philippe
was obliged to look on it with favour, and his son and heir, the
Duc d'Orléans, became the sport's official patron. He was a
founding member of that famous institution begun in 1833 as the
*Société d'encouragement pour l'amélioration des races de chevaux en
France*, but invariably known from its first years by its neo-
English title: *le Jockey-Club.*

The guiding spirit behind the new club and its first president
was Lord Henry Seymour, perhaps the most curious figure in the
history of anglomania. Related by blood, by family connections
and by temperament to all that was fashionable—and disreputable
—in Regency society, Seymour appears never to have set foot in
England. He was born in France; his mother, Lady Yarmouth,
born Maria Fagniani, was the daughter of a ballet-dancer and
either George Augustus Selwyn or "Old Q", the Duke of
Queensberry; the gentlemen wrangled over her paternity in court
and both left her a considerable fortune. Lady Yarmouth's husband
(*not* Seymour's father) was the Lord Yarmouth (third Marquis
of Hertford) who inspired Thackeray's Marquis of Steyne and
Disraeli's Lord Monmouth; Seymour was born during the period
of Yarmouth's detention as one of Napoleon's prisoners at
Verdun. Seymour's father, presumably, was the Comte de
Montrond, gambler, adventurer, wit, *fort beau garçon*, intimate
of Talleyrand and admiring friend of most of the English dandies.

Though Lord Henry had been brought up in France, his
peculiarities were English.* He was showily wealthy in the

---

* Seymour became a legendary figure partly because of his own eccentricities, partly because of confusion with those of another man, a certain

Regency style; his manner was cold and humourless (though Gronow protested he had a good heart); and he was passionately fond of cigars, maintaining a special sanctuary in his apartments for the selecting, curing, perfuming, arranging and rearranging of them. Most extraordinary for this period in France, Seymour was a genuine sportsman—that is, he actually rode, drove, fenced, boxed, even lifted weights. His huge biceps were notorious. Three times a week he received the friendly and the curious in his *salle d'armes et de boxe*, three large rooms set apart in his home on the Boulevard and alarmingly decorated with foils and boxing-gloves.

Seymour patronized the famous *tir aux pigeons* in the Tivoli gardens and helped to make it fashionable. He introduced the phaeton to Paris, and his own splendid pair of horses and elegant carriages set the standard for the dandies. Though he could lead the dandies to the Jockey-Club and the *tir aux pigeons*, however, he could not make Englishmen out of Frenchmen, even French dandies. When Lord Seymour disbanded his stable in 1842, at last convinced that the French would never understand the true principles of racing or share his zeal for sport, *La Mode* greeted the news with this gloomy admission: "Le sport repasse le détroit: il n'a jamais pu se naturaliser chez nous."

Whatever mark Lord Henry Seymour may have left on the Jockey-Club it was not single-minded devotion to sport. In this select atmosphere horses were a constant subject of conversation, but its *raison d'être* was simply leadership of the world of fashion. From its beginnings the Jockey-Club was as Proust described it:

"Charles la Battut", who shared with him the popular nickname of "milord Arsouille". The confusion is important as a possible source for the hero of Eugène Sue's *Mystères de Paris*. Battut was the son of a wealthy English chemist and an *émigrée*, born out of wedlock and brought up alternately in Paris and in England. He became renowned for his love of boxing and for his attraction to Paris low life. Upon inheriting a large fortune from his father, Battut set up an apartment on the Boulevard des Capucines and attempted to imitate the style of D'Orsay, his idol. But he was irresistibly drawn to the poorer quarters of the city, where he would dance at public balls and appear at carnival time in his elaborate six-horse carriage, scattering showers of gold over the heads of the crowd, which adored him. Lord Henry, to his intense irritation, was periodically mobbed by cheering partisans of "milord Arsouille".

the closest French equivalent to White's or even Almack's. Saturated with anglomania, in matters of speech, dress and deportment, the Club relied on rigorous limitation of membership to preserve its exclusive sanctity. Alfred de Musset, poet and aristocrat, the closest (quite conscious) imitation of Byron in Paris, tried to join but was refused. "C'est de tous les clubs de Paris le plus parfaitement aristocratique," wrote a contemporary observer of the dandies:

> Sans aucune couleur politique déterminée, le cercle des Jockeys n'a d'autre but que de réunir la fashion . . . On vous accepte, pourvu que vous ayez de bonnes manières, de la fortune, et que deux amis, membres de cette société éclectique, veuillent bien vous présenter. On reçoit les candidats au scrutin secret . . .
>
> La sévérité des membres du Jockey's-Club [sic] en fait d'admission n'a rien qui m'étonne; mais j'ai peine à concevoir qu'il y ait à Paris, dans un monde bien placé, un nombre suffisant d'amateurs de plum-pudding, de whist et de beefteak à l'anglaise, pour soutenir cette institution . . .

But there were more than enough prospective members. The club was an elegant oasis in a city fast becoming middle class. The Jockey-Club dandies never ceased to play at being sportsmen and at talking horse (in the proper English terms); but what inspired enthusiasm among them was the fashionable atmosphere of Longchamp, the clothes, the beautiful women and the splendid carriages. Janin enumerated the ingredients of this atmosphere:

> Les plus beaux chevaux et les plus rénommés de la ville, les plus élégants cavaliers et les plus jeunes et les plus jolies Parisiennes qui se soient jamais occupés de chevaux anglais . . .; les Anglais, les maîtres de la France dans ces sortes de plaisirs, le *Jockey-Club* qui donne le signal de ces fêtes; . . . ils étaient tous à ce rendez-vous rempli d'intérêt et d'émotion; sans compter ces calèches brillantes, ces coupés mystérieux, ces imprudents tilburys, ces berlines majestueuses, ces grands chars à bancs, les meneurs, les grooms, les courriers, les postillons à grandes guides, les quatre chevaux galopant à l'outrance . . .

"It is at Longchamp," wrote Lady Blessington of an unchanging institution, "that the Parisian spring fashions are first exhibited, and busy are the *modistes* for many weeks previously . . ."

4

Part of the confusion in French dandyism in the 'teens and 'twenties can be attributed to the coincidental arrival of another import: English Romanticism. Anglomania made the dandy and the romantic one and the same, though the two had scarcely met at home. It was not unusual for an *anglomane* to show his enthusiasm for the defeat of Napoleon by dressing one week as a dandy, and the next as a *chevalier* out of *Valtre-Scott*. Masquerade suited the temper of the times. Ever since the Revolution the French had been accustomed to express political opinions and literary tastes by means of costume and pose: from the start the republicans were the *sans-culottes*.

Now there was a style for every position. There were *ultras* in knee-breeches, fingering antique snuff-boxes; liberals flourishing their grey hats; bonapartists wearing the imperial frock coat with large gold buttons. There were feminists in men's clothes, *à la* George Sand; blues in turbans *à la* Mme de Stael. There were followers of Byron with artificially pale faces and wild hair. There were followers of Scott who wore tartans, dressed their children in kilts and bought their wives *les tissus Diana Vernon* and *les châles Lamermoor*. There were followers of Dumas with velvet capes and swords, *genre moyen-âge*; followers of Gautier and Hugo with *pourpoints à la Van Dyck, polonaises à brandebourg, redingotes hongroises, genre pittoresque*. The impetuous *Jeune-France* could be distinguished from his more subdued opponent, the classicist, by the famous *gilet rouge*: it was the *flamboyants* against the *grisâtres*. "Ces fantasies de costume sembleraient étranges maintenant," wrote Théophile Gautier forty years later, "mais alors on les trouvait naturelles: le mot 'artiste' excusait tout, et chacun suivait à peu près son caprice."

In the eighteen-thirties, however, dandyism outgrew the wardrobe of the masqueraders. As a pose and as an attitude it came to serve a social need. The Revolution of 1830 clearly destroyed for ever all chance of aristocratic rule under an absolute monarchy: the middle class had visibly asserted its power. Lady Morgan, who prided herself on her liberal opinions, remarked complacently, when she heard the news of the revolution, that "without a landed aristocracy, a king must be but the first citizen of a state,—a crowned president"; and events bore her out.

Certainly the new court was hardly a court at all, in the old sense. Louis-Philippe was the despair of poets, who found him wholly lacking in literary taste; and he and his family set few standards for the world of fashion. "There were young and handsome princesses, always well and tastefully dressed, but they were pronounced *rococo*," noted Gronow regretfully, "and no one ever dreamed of wearing any particular bonnet or cloak, because the beautiful Duchesse de Nemours, or the graceful Princesse de Joinville appeared in a similar one."

Cut off from court life by loyalty to the Bourbons, cut off from political power by the same reason, the old aristocracy saw itself outstripped in wealth, even in elegance, by the new monied aristocracy of the Bourse. Two alternatives remained: to hold aloof in the closed world of the Faubourg—and even there the rigid etiquette of the Restoration was fast losing ground—or to open the salons to the *nouveaux riches*. Whichever was chosen, dandyism would become a necessary badge of class for the dis-affected aristocrat (and for the bourgeois with pretentions to aristocratic society). As an attitude, it justified social superiority without reference to wealth and power. As a pose, for those who sincerely deplored the abandonment of aristocratic ideals before the bourgeois slogan "enrichessez-vous", it was a defence against vulgarity.

The mask for its own sake became an article of faith for those who despised "ce stupide dix-neuvième siècle". Dandy reserve and dandy scorn would in the 'thirties have sources other than anglomania. Surveying his era in 1835, Alfred de Vigny justified the apparent coldness of his contemporaries:

> Loin d'étaler sur ses traits et dans son langage l'excès de force que donnent les passions, chacun s'étudie à renfermer en soi les émotions violentes, les chagrins profonds ou les élans involontaires. Je ne pense point que la civilisation ait tout énervé, je vois qu'elle a tout masqué. J'avoue que c'est un bien, et j'aime le caractère contenu de notre époque. Dans cette froideur apparente il y a de la pudeur, et les sentiments vrais en ont besoin. Il y entre aussi du dédain, bonne monnaie pour payer les choses humaines. (*Servitude et Grandeur militaires.*)

At the same time, invaluable dandy documents became avail-able to the French reading public. The fashionable novels of the Regency passed into general circulation in France almost immediately after their appearance in England in the late 'twenties and early 'thirties. Theodore Hook's tales of fashionable life were translated in 1825, Lister's *Granby* in 1829, Ward's *Tremaine (ou les raffinements d'un homme blasé)* in 1830, along with *The Exclusives* and Lord Normanby's *Yes and No; a Tale of the Day.* (The latter was reprinted when Normanby became ambassador to France in 1846.) And translations were only part of the story. The fashionable novels were read widely in English, and French publishers brought them out as often in English as in French. *Pelham* was published in France, in the original, in 1828, the year of its appearance in England; it was first translated in 1832 and had run through seven editions by 1840.

Many fashionable novels were available in their London editions; in the Tauchnitz English-language editions; and in Baudry's popular English-language series for the French market (called "Standard Ancient and Modern British Novels and Romances", and including almost a complete Bulwer). All of these editions, moreover, were obtainable at the abundant lending libraries and reading-rooms of the period. During her stay in Paris, from 1828 to 1830, Lady Blessington had no difficulty finding copies of *Vivian Grey** and she noted that *Pelham*, the most important of the fashionable novels in France as in England, was making a great stir. "All Paris talk of it," she wrote. *Pelham* was praised for its literary merits, and even more for its value as a dandy document, as Gustave Planché noted in his review of the novel in the *Revue des deux mondes*: "Il fut cité dans les cafés et les salons comme le manuel du dandysme le plus parfait et le plus pur. Paris se trouva de même avis que Londres. Le succès de ce livre se progagea avec une rapidité merveilleuse."

The fact that aspiring French dandies drew many of their attitudes *from books* left its mark on the history of dandyism in France.

* There is no evidence of French publication of *Vivian Grey* or *The Young Duke* during this period, though the books were known. The stir Disraeli's novels made in England was common knowledge in France, he himself was referred to as "the author of *Vivian Grey*", and in 1844 E. Forcade, reviewing *Henrietta Temple* (which had its second French English-language edition in that year) in the *Revue des deux mondes*, wrote at length about *Vivian Grey*. He said, among other things, that "on y rencontre plus d'un trait frappé au bon coin de cette mordante impertinence, de cette tranchante ironie, de ce coupant si aimé des Anglais, qu'on pourrait appeler le sel britannique."

By the mid-century French dandyism would be an essentially literary doctrine, a pose for the intellectual in revolt. Ironically, the Victorian crusade to do away with everything belonging to the Regency would force dandyism to go underground at home for half a century; but in France the imported dandy tradition—subtler, slighter, less social than intellectual—would be unbroken. And the dandyism that came to the fore in England in the 'nineties was largely influenced by French ideas.

The year 1830 marked a turning-point in the history of dandyism in both France and England. Appropriately, the dandy's new role was demonstrated by the *doyen* of them all, Beau Brummell. Fat and over fifty, he passed through Paris on his way to the last stage of his exile in Caen, and showed the dandy manner in adversity. He was a frequent guest at the English embassy and at the home of the ambassador, Lord Stuart de Rothesay; he met and dined with social lions like Talleyrand, the Prince de Benevento, Mme de Bagration, Lamartine and Victor Hugo. He was not wholly pleased with his reception, concluding, upon his presentation to Hugo, that the poet, "I believe, was not sufficiently aware of who I was." But the decayed Beau made one gesture long remembered by the Parisians. Just before leaving the capital he scrutinized all the snuff-boxes for sale on the Rue de la Paix, pronounced them inadequate, and placed an order with Dabert for an enamelled gold box to cost 2500 francs; that was more than his year's income.

Once settled in Caen, Brummell of course went only to the salons of the legitimist nobility, avoiding the circles of the *juste milieu*. Partly on principle and partly out of pique (he had not been invited to the dinner which preceded it), he refused to attend a ball celebrating the accession of Louis-Philippe. The next day an acquaintance asked why he had not joined the festivities honouring the King. "What king?" asked Brummell, with feigned surprise.

"The French King to be sure: Louis-Philippe!"

"Oh! the Duke of Orléans, you mean; no, I did not go, but I sent my servant."

CHAPTER VI

The Dandy Goes to Press: France 1830

REGENCY dandyism created a literature of its own, the fashionable novel, which expressed directly—without self-consciousness and often without pretensions to literary quality—the preoccupations of a dandy society. French dandyism under Louis-Philippe, to its advantage and disadvantage, came to literature in another manner altogether. Professional authors, not exclusive blues or idle politicians, wrote it into a new literature of social realism, which took the whole of society as its subject, and as its audience.

There was no specifically dandy literature in France in the 'thirties and 'forties—except perhaps the periodical literature of the horse, with its anglomaniac titles: *Le Betting*; *Le Bulletin officiel des Steeple-chases*; *La Chronique du turf*; *L' Echo sportique*; *Le Jockey*, etc. But more descriptions, analyses, and criticisms of the dandies were published in this period in France than in all the society novels of the Regency, for the dandies were not the province of one class, but the amusement of all classes. They crowded into the novels, the poems, the songs, the letters, the sketches, the plays and the journals of the greatest and least of authors. Even in the solemnity of *l'outre-tombe*, the majestic Chateaubriand found time to record his memories of Almack's and the West-end, the London of 1822 when "rien ne réussissait comme l'insolence, témoin D'Orsay, frère de la duchesse de Guiche . . ."

Le *dandy* doit avoir un air conquérant, léger, insolent; il doit soigner sa toilette, porter des moustaches ou une barbe taillée au rond comme la fraise de la reine Elisabeth, ou comme le disque radieux du soleil; il décèle la fière indépendance de son caractère en gardant son chapeau sur la tête, en se roulant sur les sofas, en allongeant ses bottes au nez des ladies assisses en admiration sur des chaises devant lui; il monte à cheval avec une canne qu'il porte comme un cierge, indifférent au cheval qui est entre ses jambes par hasard . . .

The reign of Louis-Philippe was the golden age of the French press, and its members celebrated their new influence by calling themselves "journalists", and their trade, "journalism"—invented words which were promptly imported by the English. Journalists like Thiers had much of the credit for the July Revolution, the new régime appreciated their influence, and when the revolution was over an immense variety of periodicals was either newly established or newly converted to reach a wider audience than ever before: the *Journal des Débats*, the *Constitutionnel*, the *Courrier français*, the *Siècle*, the *Populaire*, and others. There were dailies, weeklies and monthlies expressing every shade of political opinion or ignoring politics to favour the arts or society chit-chat or simply caricature, like the famous *Charivari*. They reached wholly new sections of the population (like the original *Journal des enfants*) and they made money.

The prosperity of the press under Louis-Philippe was due largely to the efforts of one man, Emile de Girardin, and his revolutionary attitude to periodical publishing, which was simply this: that a newspaper or magazine was primarily a commercial enterprise and not necessarily an organ for its editors' political or literary prejudices. Girardin is best remembered as editor of the *Presse*, which he took over in 1836; but he began his career as the founder of three modest reviews: *Le Voleur* (openly dedicated to plagiarism) in 1828; *La Silhouette* (a magazine of.caricature) and *La Mode* in 1829. The most famous and lucrative of these, *La Mode*, was the leading society review, devoted to the amusements of Parisian life from the toilette to the horse; it was also the organ for the early works of Balzac, Eugène Sue, George Sand and Gavarni.

Under the leadership of Girardin, an extraordinary group of youthful, vivacious, talented and eccentric journalists created a popular press, wielded political power, made—and lost—fortunes, and incidentally formed a social clique of such sparkle that it is still remembered as the *jeunesse dorée*. They congregated at the fashionable restaurants, particularly the Café de Paris; they took possession of the *boulevart* and the *loge infernale* at the Opera; they had mistresses in the ballet; they were devoted gastronomes and tireless talkers of a private slang, a perpetual firework of epigrams and impromptu verses. Though most of them were bourgeois born, they invaded the salons, mingling with the nobility and copying many of its mannerisms.

As a group this golden inner circle of the press stood halfway, in manner and allegiance, between the dandy world of the Jockey-Club and the Bohemian world of letters: too irrepressible, busy and ambitious to be dandies, too sophisticated, social-minded and prosperous to be Bohemians. But they were all fascinated by dandyism in both its English and French versions, adopting parts of the attitude for their private use and filling the pages of their newspapers and magazines with its description. They developed the technique of writing caricatures in words (observant, minute, pseudo-scientific social studies often called *physiologies*) illustrated with caricatures drawn by the greatest draughtsmen in that golden age of caricature: Garvarni and Daumier.

Most of their names have been forgotten, though their portraits are still to be admired in the *Comédie humaine*. There was Dr. Véron, founder of the still flourishing *Revue de Paris*, who gave extravagant banquets for the entire *corps de ballet*, and wore so vast a neckcloth that his friends addressed their letters "à Monsieur Véron, dans sa cravate, à Paris". There was Armand Malitourne, wit, epigrammatist and professional idler, whose evening paper, *La Charte de 1830*, never came out until the morning, despite the efforts of Théophile Gautier and Gérard de Nerval. There was Lautour-Mézeray, who collaborated with Girardin on *Le Voleur* and *La Mode*, and whose elegant dress and splendid calèche dazzled Balzac. There was Nestor Roqueplan, graceful and perfumed, who said he could not sleep the night before trying on a new costume, and who predicted his destiny: "Mon rêve est de mourir insolvable et à la mode." There was the most dandified of them all, Roger de Beauvoir, whose gilded personality taught Baudelaire and Barbey d'Aurevilly most of what they knew about practical dandyism. Roger de Beauvoir made the inner circle, as few others did: he was a member of the Jockey-Club. He personified the new composite creature, man of letters, journalist and dandy, at Dr Véron's table at the Café de Paris. "Qui n'a pas vu le Café de Paris," he said, "n'a rien vu."

2

At the end of the year 1830 Honoré Balzac, an ambitious young man from the provinces, owed his tailor 904 francs, more than he had budgeted for a year's food and lodging. This was the year in which Balzac began to travel with the journalist set, to write articles on fashionable life for the fashionable magazines, to imitate as far as he was able the personal dandyism of his friend Lautour-Mézeray. Stimulated by the success of one novel, *Les Derniers Chouans*, published the year before, he was pressing a campaign to get into society. Balzac worked as hard at the dandyism of costume as Disraeli, for some of the same reasons and with even less taste. His affectations of dress—the monstrous cane, studded with turquoises, the elaborately carved gold buttons, the unending stream of new *gilets* and gloves (a different pair, in theory, for every day in the year)—were the subject of unending discussion, little of it flattering, among his friends. His cane, he noted with satisfaction, "fait jaser tout Paris"; and he laughingly described his extraordinary dress as "une réclame"—an invaluable advertisement for a young writer making his way in the world.

There was much that was ridiculous, vulgar and calculating about Balzac's attempts at dandyism; but there was also a passion for elegance and a conviction that clothes were important. "La toilette est l'expression de la société," he wrote in 1830; it was a maxim he faithfully illustrated throughout the ninety-odd volumes of *La Comédie humaine*. He crammed into his great social chronicles every variety of dandy he knew: the timid provincials adopting dandyism to get ahead, the self-indulgent journalists, the effortlessly elegant, coldly insolent noblemen of the Jockey-Club. Eugène de Rastignac, Lucien de Rubempré, Maxime de Trailles, Charles Grandet, Georges Marest, Amédée Soulas, Lousteau, Raphael Valentin, Henri de Marsay—all testify both to Balzac's powers of observation and to the dandification of Parisian society. His personal habits are signalized by the presence in his novels of tailors, bootmakers and glovemakers as well as their dandy customers. It is believed (on some evidence) that he inserted these purveyors of elegance into his work as a payment in lieu of cash, for he advertised them shamelessly: names, addresses and merits.

His own appearance, however, did little credit to their ministrations. Balzac's friends—Gavarni, Goxlan, Muret, Mme Ancelot—were continually dismayed at the appearance of the great chronicler of the dandy world : a fat little man with a broad, vulgar face, who would roam the streets one day in ragged, dirty disarray (when too absorbed by his latest novel or financial scheme to care about his appearance) and turn out the next showily *endimanché*. Captain Gronow was particularly surprised and disappointed :

> Balzac had nothing in his outward man that could in any way respond to the ideal his readers were likely to form of the enthusiastic admirer of beauty and elegance in all its forms and phases . . . The great enchanter was one of the oiliest and commonest looking mortals I ever beheld; being short and corpulent, with a broad florid face, a cascade of double chins, and straight greasy hair . . . Balzac had that unwashed appearance which seems generally to belong to French *litterati*, and dressed in the worst possible taste, wore sparkling jewels on a dirty shirt front, and diamond rings on unwashed fingers . . .

In 1830, however, Balzac had no reputation as chronicler of Parisian society to maintain. He was serving a journalist's apprenticeship for the major works ahead, as a contributor of *physiologies*, sketches, snatches of dialogue (most of them gleaned in his studious observation of the world of fashion) to Girardin's *Le Voleur*, *La Silhouette* and *La Mode*. His first piece for Girardin was an *"Etude de mœurs par les gants"*, and a long series* followed: *"Physiologie de la toilette"*, subtitled *"De la Cravate considérée en elle-même et dans ses rapports avec la société . . ."*; *"Nouvelle théorie du déjeuner"*, a study of the fashionable predilection for tea and *muflings*; *"Des mots à la mode"*; *"L'Oisif et le Travailleur"*, a comparison between the industrious writer and the lazy dandy; *"Physiologie gastronomique"*; *"Physiologie du cigare"*, in praise of the new fashion for smoking, with Lautour-Mézeray cited as authority; and *"De ce qui n'est pas à la mode"*, which contained a motto for the whole series :

* Most of these articles were signed *"le comte Alexandre de B. . . ."* It was around this time that Balzac began to call himself Honoré *de* Balzac, assuming the arms and antiquity of a noble provincial family of the same name.

Connaître ce qui est à la mode, c'est une science.
Cela s'étudie et s'apprend.
Savoir ce qui n'est pas à la mode, c'est un instinct.
Cela se devine et se sent.

The most ambitious of all these early studies was the *Traité de la vie élégante*, published in *La Mode* in the fall of 1830. It is an oddly serious treatise, proclaiming the necessity for a concern with costume in the new bourgeois society. To Balzac, the meaningful criteria of the new society are how the individual spends his time and how deeply he is devoted to *l'élégance* (the two are obviously related). Applying these criteria, he divides French society into three basic classes. At one social extreme Balzac places the worker, *le zéro social*, a creature devoid of individuality —and incapable of understanding even the word elegance. At the other extreme stands the idler, *l'oisif*, the traditional leader of *la vie élégante*. Somewhere between them Balzac sees the exceptional figure with whom, of course, he identifies himself: the artist, whose work is relaxation and whose relaxation is work, and who can properly dress with elegance or negligence, as he chooses.

The need for this new division of society has arisen from the revolutionary breakdown of traditional class barriers. Rank and privilege are disappearing; a new aristocracy of wealth threatens the old aristocracy of birth; "les nobles de 1804 ou de l'an MCXX," Balzac writes, "ne représentent plus rien." The old aristocracy cannot justify a reassertion of traditional privilege on the argument of birth; the aristocracy of the future—intellectuals and artists—will require something besides talent to win social supremacy. The new, necessary element is elegance, as expressed in the arts of dandyism.*

---

* Balzac avoids the terms dandyism or dandy throughout this essay; they carry for him, as for many of his contemporaries, a pejorative (and an eccentrically English) sense: as, fop and foppery. Balzac does use the very 1830 term "centaur" ("Pour la vie élégante il n'y a d'être complet que le *centaure*, l'homme en tilbury"), which commonly served at this time to suggest the dandy's attachment to his horse. By the eighteen-forties that term would also have a pejorative connotation, for Gautier found it necessary to defend the Jockey-Club from the accusation that it was nothing but "a society of young centaurs, fashionable above the waist and English horse below it . . ." (1847).

Alors, dans notre société, les différences ont disparu : il n'y a plus que des nuances. Aussi le savoir-vivre, l'élégance des manières, le *je ne sais quoi*, fruit d'une éducation complète, forment la seule barrière qui sépare l'oisif de l'homme occupé. S'il existe un privilège, il dérive de la supériorité morale.

"Moral superiority" : it is a new and unusually earnest claim for dandyism. Balzac buttresses it by an ambitious definition of the word elegance : "Ce tacte exquis, dont le constant exercice peut seul faire découvrir soudain les rapports, prévoir les conséquences, deviner la place ou la portée des objets, des mots, des idées et des personnes . . ." The argument is lightly presented, in epigrams rather than in formal logic :

Le but de la vie civilisée ou sauvage est le repos.
Le repos absolu produit le *spleen*.
La vie élégante est, dans une large acception du terme, l'art d'animer le repos.
L'homme habitué au travail ne peut comprendre la vie élégante.
Pour être fashionable, il faut jouir du repos sans avoir passé par le travail . . .

Having demonstrated in this manner the significance of *la vie élégante*, Balzac breaks off to report a conversation—certainly not wholly imaginary—between himself and his friends at *La Mode*. They are all agreed on the urgent need for a treatise on the subject but doubt whether a man can be found so egotistical and so intrepid as to undertake it.

En ce moment . . . un des plus élégants rédacteurs de la MODE se leva en jetant un regard de triomphe sur ses collaborateurs :
— Cet homme existe, dit-il.
Un rire general accueillit cet exorde, mais le silence de l'admiration y succéda bientôt quand il eut ajouté :
— BRUMMEL!

With breathtaking assurance, Balzac then details a pilgrimage to *Brummel* at Boulogne (where Brummell had never been) and a long colloquy with the "patriarche de la *fashion*", whom he had never met (and neither, in all likelihood, had any of his collaborators. Very few of Brummell's French admirers ever met him. His one visit to Paris probably lasted no more than a week, and

Calais and Caen were far off the fashionable path. But his achievements were a commonplace in the salons and the cafés, and the fact that he was in France, as everyone knew, made his legend more immediate.) Balzac proceeds to describe the Beau at length (inaccurately), to attribute to Brummell his own most un-Brummellian theory of society, to report Brummell's confidential remarks, and to cite Brummell as the authority for the concluding sections of the essay: the General Principles of elegance, and the specific rules governing *la toilette*.

It must be said that this final part would not have offended Brummell—indeed, that it follows his principles on the art of dress rather than Balzac's practice. The dandy rules are recorded here with almost as much nicety as in *Pelham*. Balzac does full justice to the cardinal principles of simplicity and unity; to the preponderance of manner over the clothes themselves; to the absolute necessity for cleanliness: "Une déchirure est un malheur, une tache est un vice." And to establish the elusive distinction between the truly elegant man, whose subtle variations on *la mode* mark him as a leader of fashion, and the simply eccentric dresser, he adroitly paraphrases something that Brummell actually said:

> Brummell a, du reste, laissé la maxime la plus admirable sur cette matière, et l'assentiment de l'Angleterre l'a consacrée:
> — Si le peuple vous regarde avec attention, vous n'êtes pas bien mis: vous êtes trop bien mis, trop empesé, ou trop recherché.

"D'après cette immortelle sentence," Balzac adds blithely, "tout fantassin doit passer inaperçu . . ."

3

In 1830 Eugène Sue was twenty-six, and was having far too good a time as an anglomaniac dandy, a *bon viveur* and a *jeune fashionable* to devote himself more than casually to literature. Instead he acted as liaison between the two separately dandified worlds of journalists and aristocrats. He was a faithful member of the circle of scribblers who gathered at the Café de Paris around his friend Dr Véron. He was a contributor of stories and sketches of fashionable life to *La Nouveauté*, *Le Voleur* and *La Mode*. He dazzled, then befriended the young Balzac, to whom he wrote superior and cynical letters about his complicated love affairs and his fondness for opium; one of them, a catalogue of Sue's perverse affectations, concluded "Ce qui me plaît le plus, c'est de chasser." Sue took personal responsibility for Balzac's introduction to the world of *filles de joie* and *courtisanes*, and had him invited to the salon of his own mistress, Olympe Pélissier (who is said to have rejected proposals from both Sue and Balzac before settling down as the wife of Rossini). When Balzac noted in his *Traité de la vie élégante* that he had been promised a chapter on Impertinence by one of his best friends—a man noted for originality, for exquisite taste, for a "merveilleuse entente de la vie"—he had Sue in mind.

At the same time, despite his bourgeois origins (his ancestors were all prosperous physicians) and his bourgeois features ("C'est ennuyeux!" he said, "j'ai le nez canaille!") Sue was intimately connected in the aristocratic world. Taken up by the Duchesse de Rauzan, he frequented the salons of Mme Sophie Gay, Mme de Cubières and Jules de Rességuier. He was, like Lord Henry Seymour, an assiduous patron of Thomas Bryon's *tir aux pigeons*; his horses and carriages were in the best English taste; and he dressed well enough to win the praise of so stern a critic as Captain Gronow. In all this he was guided by his admiration for D'Orsay; he was one of D'Orsay's oldest and most faithful friends. The two visited each other constantly on trips back and forth across the Channel; and among the most imposing and least marketable items to turn up for sale some years later at the auction of D'Orsay's possessions were thirty-seven handsomely bound and affectionately inscribed volumes of the works of Eugène Sue.

Legends proliferated about Sue's personal habits and particularly about his apartments, which would seem to have outdone in reality the merely imaginary settings for Bulwer's Pelham and Huysmans' Des Esseintes. Visitors could make out an incredible jumble of antique carvings, suits of armour, tropical plants, paintings of dogs and horses, Renaissance furniture, stuffed trophies of the hunt, bibelots and curiosities of all sorts—but they could not see anything very clearly, because sunlight penetrated Sue's rooms only through stained-glass windows obfuscated with vines and hanging flowers. As if in a state of nature, pheasants, wood-doves and two magnificent hunting dogs (the gift of *milord* Chesterfield) ornamented his fastidiously planted gardens.

Visitors took away, along with these confused impressions, a confusion of odours: exotic perfumes and plants, opium, rare bind-
ings of Russian leather. They spread the rumour that Sue's table
was served by male servants dressed in quasi-royal livery—or
by female servants not dressed at all. The master of this *temple de
volupté*, they said, would not accept a letter that was not presented
on a carved silver platter; would not pick it up without scented
straw-colour gloves; would not open it without solid gold
scissors. Among Sue's correspondence were many love letters;
those that seemed likely to be tedious he passed on, unopened,
to friends.

Sue made his way in the salons purely as a dandy, not as the
founder of the French maritime novel (his first books on the sea,
based on youthful experience, won him the title of "le Fénimore
Cooper français") though the French aristocracy, unlike the
English, never regarded talent as a fault. But in the late 'thirties
Sue began to turn out novels with increasing speed. His extravagances demanded more money than he had inherited from his
father and grandfather, and he had discovered among his possessions an astonishingly facile pen and a limitless supply of the
tricks of melodrama. He wrote a series of *romans mondains* in
which he drew recognizable portraits of his fashionable acquaintances, a habit which persisted through his later forays into
historical subjects. (His portrait of *Le Marquis de Létorière*, subtitled *l'art de plaire*, was said to be drawn from D'Orsay.) The
ingredients of melodrama, eroticism and Byronism, combined
with suggestive clues to the author's peculiar personal habits,
made these books a success with the only audience to which Sue
at this time aspired: the fashionable audience.

But toward the end of the 'thirties the entente between the
novelist and the Faubourg was broken. Derogatory stories circulated, bearing on his bourgeois origins and his bourgeois impertinence; but the real problem was money. By 1837 the elegant
young Sue, who boasted that he could not begin a chapter without
a fresh pair of gloves, had run through two inheritances *and* the
proceeds of his novels. He informed his closest friends, on perfumed note-paper, that he was leaving Paris, and shut himself up
in the country to write another novel.

Arthur is the closest Sue came to a self-portrait. His hero is a
dandy whose doubts (about himself, about the motives of others)

lead him to a coarse cynicism, and to a sadistic attitude toward love and friendship. An abortive association with an English dandy brings to the novel an odour—merely an odour—of homosexuality. The most effective parts of *Arthur* are background descriptions, raffish, highly coloured sketches of the anglomaniac Paris of the 'thirties. Sue's dandies spend their time talking horse, smoking cigars and eating English lunches; when rivals in love they meet (and die) in the steeple-chase, not in the duel. They use English phrases constantly, particularly the word *gentleman*, because it connotes, as Sue points out, a distinction of manner rather than the distinction of birth implicit in the word *gentilhomme*. Their world is beginning to revolve less about the salon than about the club, which satisfies their masculine preferences for English comfort, for smoking, and for betting. What drags *Arthur* down is the crude and confused analysis of its hero: Sue lacked the touch of genius that might have made his novel an illuminating psychological study of the French dandy.

Arthur paid Sue's debts and permitted him to resume a life of luxury and salon-going in Paris; indeed, he was to persist in dandy ways until his death. But his first experience with financial ruin had modified his sense of identification with the aristocracy, and he was now wholly dependent on the revenue from his novels. Five years later, he entered, in effect, upon a new career.

When *Les Mystères de Paris* appeared in serial form in 1842, a public quite different from the fashionable audience proclaimed it a literary event of major importance. Victor Considérant, the socialist editor of *La Démocratie Pacifique*, hailed Sue as the great "romancier populaire". "Je vois où va l'auteur," he wrote; "il entre dans une voie inexplorée." Considérant and his friends undoubtedly saw more clearly than Sue himself, who had begun the serial at his editor's suggestion that he do a French version of an illustrated English magazine entitled *The Mysteries of London*. He began it with little confidence, and with no suspicion that it would reach a wider audience than any novel ever before published in France. "C'est peut-être bête comme un chou," he had written a friend whose criticism he solicited. But it did not seem "stupid" to the readers of the *Journal des Débats*, in which the novel appeared; circulation spiralled upward. The serial stretched out to 147 instalments, for which Sue received 26,500 francs; originally planned as a two-volume novel, it grew to ten. A bitter

debate broke out in the Chamber of Deputies as to whether the
novel was dangerous and immoral, or whether it served the cause
of humanity; during the course of its publication Sue was awarded
the cross of the Legion of Honour. On the basis of *Les Mystères
de Paris*, and a continuing series of social tracts and novels
(notably *The Wandering Jew*), the dandy author became famous
—or notorious—as a champion of socialism and Friend of the
People. In 1850 the People elected him, by a huge majority, to
the Chamber of Deputies, where he took his seat at the extreme
left but never uttered a word, not even in the debate on the *roman-
feuilleton*. At last, after the December coup d'état, *Les Mystères
de Paris* brought down upon Sue the wrath of Louis-Napoléon,
and years of exile.

What propels *Les Mystères* onward and ever onward, however,
is melodrama rather than "socialist" theory. The novel contains
no consistent radical doctrine. Instead, there are sensible, enthusiastic sermons along the lines of the social humanitarianism
Dickens and other Victorian novelists would preach in England—
pleas for a better penal code, for better prisons, hospitals and
orphan asylums, for easier divorce; and for greater understanding
of the unavoidable vices of the poor, such as poverty, unemployment, criminal recidivism and prostitution. Knowing his fashionable past and his previous disregard for social issues, Sue's more
sophisticated contemporaries questioned his authority—and his
good faith. They noted that his championship of the proletariat
was extraordinarily lucrative and wondered if, having ceased to
please the fashionable public, Sue now proposed to shock it into
recognition of his talents. Sainte-Beuve, for example, tartly defined Sue's purpose as "faire un roman bien épicé, bien salé, à
l'usage du beau monde." The reader who attempts the book
today, however, questions Sue's literary rather than his social
morality; it must be said that Sue continued to expound his late-
acquired humanitarianism long after it had ceased to sell—indeed,
after it had brought about his involuntary exile.

In the character of the hero of *Les Mystères* Sue again revealed
his dandy habits of mind, and contributed something new and
disturbing to the literature of the century. "Monsieur Rodolphe",
the spokesman for Sue's humanitarianism, is hardly a well-
meaning social worker; he is an arrogant aristocrat (the ruler of
one of those conveniently inconspicuous German principalities)

who finds peculiar satisfactions in consorting with the wretched
and the criminal. Rodolphe has taken unto himself the mission of
showering money, justice and love upon the Parisian poor. In
part a fairy-tale prince, in part an elegant, anglophile dandy in
the manner of the 'thirties, equally at home in ball-room or hunting field, Rodolphe was undoubtedly to some degree modelled
on Lord Henry Seymour and the legend of "milord Arsouille".
The Prince, romantically disguised, nightly leaves his regal
mansion in the Faubourg to go among the criminal classes, armed
only with an extensive knowledge of criminal slang and an exceptional facility with his fists—acquired in lessons from a fashionable boxing master. A faithful attendant, an Englishman named
Murph (whose sterling qualities are pure *Valtre-Scott*), accom-
panies him on his nocturnal forays, and the entire ten-volume
novel is the story of their adventures.

Rodolphe is titillated by the contrast between the fashionable
milieu he inhabits and the lurid back-alleys he explores: the
prisons, the saloons, the criminal hangouts. (The Regency would
have called it the contrast between high and low life.) Titillation
is Rodolphe's necessary daily fare: he loves his masquerade, the
exposure to danger, the ravelling and unravelling of mysteries.
He is always explaining, with alarming frankness, that he has
taken to works of charity in part to expiate a childhood sin (the
temptation to patricide*) but in larger part to amuse himself;
and he advises his Society friends to revive their jaded appetite
for amusement in the same manner. Rodolphe's manner is that
of the sadist. No indiscriminate scatterer of blessings, he works
with deliberate ingenuity to deal rewards to the good and, far
more important (to him, to Sue, and to the reading public),
punishments to the wicked. The melodramatic high points of the
novel are Rodolphe's blinding of a homicidal bully and his drawn-
out, vindictive torture of a hypocritical, lustful villain (he
dangles a nymphomaniac quadroon before the villain's eyes). In
defence of Rodolphe (if not of Sue) it must be said that the novel's
numerous villains are themselves highly imaginative sadists.

It has been recorded that Sue actually took the trouble (if not
before the novel was begun, then during its serialization) to imitate his hero. He is said on occasion to have practised his slang

* The story of Sue's childhood is a long, almost farcical history of
floutings of paternal authority.

and his boxing; substituted the dress of the streets for his dandy
clothes (the glossy broad-brimmed hat, the tight, light-coloured
trousers, the scented gloves and the white camelia); turned his
back on the elegant little house in the Rue de la Pépinière (the
haunting perfumes, the sensuous lighting, the vast, elaborate
writing desk) and picked his way furtively to the sinister back
alleys of Paris. A servant followed, at a discreet distance.

4

In 1830, while Balzac was refining his technique as a novelist
in the pages of *La Mode* and Sue was delighting in the salons,
Stendhal published one of the greatest of all novels: *Le Rouge et
le Noir*. Stendhal was of a different generation, a contemporary
of Brummell, not of D'Orsay; the events of the Revolution echoed
through his childhood in Grenoble, and the campaigns of the
Emperor took him across Europe and into Russia. In the 'twenties, while Balzac was struggling with the financial perils of
publishing, Stendhal had been free to make a pilgrimage of
curiosity to England, even to visit Almack's.

Stendhal's reactions to dandyism were endlessly contradictory
and peculiarly personal. At many points the core of his personality
—that cluster of prejudices, principles and eccentricities that he
himself called *beylisme*—touched on what a later generation
would consider dandyism. But no one had harsher words for the
English dandies. Over and over again he stigmatized their affectation as superfluous, their manner as rude, their pride as insufferable, their coldness as ridiculous, their vanity as pitifully
inhibiting. On every count he found them inferior to his beloved
Milanese and even to the Parisians he affected strenuously to
despise. He read English avidly, wrote for English magazines,*
eulogized English literature and even used English words to
express his most personal ideas (he wrote, he said, for "the happy
few"); but that was the limit of his anglomania. "Rien ne peut
égaler mon amour pour leur littérature," he wrote dryly of the
English, "si ce n'est mon éloignement pour leurs personnes."

---

* Colburn was the first publisher, in France or England, to hire
Stendhal's services as a journalist. Stendhal wrote a *chronique littéraire* for
Colburn's *New Monthly Magazine* in the 'twenties. It has been suggested
that Stendhal's hostility to the contemporary French poets was the reason
for English ignorance of French Romanticism.

Despite his distaste for the English dandies, Stendhal shared their distinguishing trait: the exaggerated refinement which made Tremaine weak, the heightened sensitivity which made Pelham shrink from vulgarity. With definite satisfaction he analysed this quality in himself, describing it alternately as a disease and a distinction. His chronic spiritual ailment, Stendhal noted in his *Souvenirs d'égotisme*, was "une horreur presque hydrophobique à l'aspect de tout être grossier." He also had, as he said on other occasions, the thin skin of a woman, the excessive *nervous irritability* of a medical monster; he was mortally wounded by infinitesimal nuances.

This hypersensitivity influenced all Stendhal's attitudes. It confused his politics, and made his friends puzzle over the apparent contradiction between outspoken liberal opinions and aristocratic prejudices. (Stendhal, wrote Mérimée, "se piquait de libéralisme et était, au fond de l'âme, un aristocrat achevé.") Stendhal put the problem bluntly: "J'aime le peuple, je déteste les oppresseurs, mais ce serait pour moi un supplice de tous les instants de vivre avec le peuple." And his defence of the contradiction was dandyism of the most outrageous sort: to him the People were always filthy, and he had a horror of filth.

This same moral and physical exclusivism inspired Stendhal's love of mystification: "Je porterais un masque avec plaisir, je changerais de nom"—and indeed he did—"avec délices." He tried persistently to mask his feelings with an affectation of coldness, and to bely his deeply held convictions with a show of indifference. All his life he was on guard against being found out, against being made a fool. He demanded of himself inordinate self-control: "Je fais tous les efforts possibles pour être *sec*. Je veux imposer silence à mon cœur qui croit avoir beaucoup à dire . . ."

Stendhal was the first to criticize these qualities in others and to champion, on principle, the opposing qualities of energy, unselfconscious passion, freedom from inhibition. In 1830, the year in which Balzac set out to conquer a dandified, anglomaniac Paris, Stendhal turned his back on the languid and effete graces of the north and went to Italy in search of the Latin fire and spontaneity. But he always saw the split in his own temperament: he stood half-way between "la grossièreté énergique . . . et les grâces un peu lilliputiennes, un peu étroites."

In his novel of 1830 Stendhal presents a hero plagued by the same contradiction, and he sets Julien Sorel's dilemma against a background of the same dandified society which Balzac transcribed in *La Comédie humaine* and Sue portrayed in *Arthur*. Julien in Paris is from the first overwhelmed by the circle of young noblemen who gather at the feet of Mathilde de La Mole: Stendhal calls them the "jeunes gens à moustaches". Some of these bewhiskered aristocrats are out-and-out dandies in the 1830 manner (the moustache itself became fashionable around that date*), some are sober legitimists of the Faubourg practising only a minimal and partial dandyism, but all of them inhabit a dandy world: the Marquis de Croisenois, Mathilde's recognized suitor; the Comte de Caylus, impassioned horseman; Norbert de La Mole, Mathilde's elegant brother; the Vicomte de Luz, the ambitious young man Julien chooses as a husband for Mathilde; the Comte de Thaler, wealthy son of a Jewish banker, who affects the dandy passion for horses; the Chevalier de Beauvoisis, a wholly dandified young diplomat; and an anonymous circle of officers and men about town.

We learn that they dress elegantly and favour the clothes made by Staub; that they frequent the Opera and inspect each other "dans le vestibule à la sortie du beau monde"; that they spend their late evenings at Tortoni's (where the Marquis de Croisenois cuts Julien) or at a fashionable ball, where they go to be bored, to estimate the cost of the decorations, to crowd on the staircase, to dance a quadrille (according to the instructions of Coulon, who was also Pelham's dancing-master in Paris) and to pass judgment on the reigning beauties of the season. They are the "jolis cavaliers qui peuplent le bois de Boulogne". Absorbed in the fashionable sports of riding and driving, they spend much thought and large sums of money on the selection of their *fameux chevaux arabes*, as much as 5000 francs for a prize specimen. The Comte de Caylus, for example,

> avait ou feignait une grande passion pour les chevaux; il passait sa vie dans son écurie, et souvent y déjeunait. Cette grande passion,

---

* In the first edition of the novel the ridiculous illustration opening the second volume showed a young woman in a sumptuous boudoir (presumably Mathilde) contemplating the severed head of her lover (presumably Julien) on a marble pedestal: the head boasted a set of chic *moustaches à la* 1830.

jointe à l'habitude de ne jamais rire, lui donnait beaucoup de con-
sidération parmi ses amis : c'était l'aigle de ce petit cercle.

Mathilde regards the dandies as devoid of ideas; they dress,
converse, even make love and fight duels according to a rigid
ceremonial of *les convenances*; their greatest fears are of *l'imprévu,
le ridicule, le mauvais goût*. They are charming, graceful, polite
only when they wish to be, mystifying and insolent when they do
not. At their best, in the words of Mathilde's complaint, they are
too perfect.

But Julien is neither so ferocious nor so unwavering in his
attitude to the dandies. Initially he is so enchanted by the elegance
of Norbert de La Mole (Stendhal's word is *séduit*) that he forgets
to hate him for his wealth and his class. His joy at the conquest of
Mathilde is doubled when he sees it as a victory over the fascinating Marquis de Croisenois, with his moustaches, his pretty
uniform, his subtle wit. And before the thoroughly dandified
Chevalier de Beauvoisis, with whom, through an error, he fights
a duel, Julien revels in uncritical admiration. In his unusually
detailed description of Beauvoisis Stendhal brings out not only
what is ridiculous but also what is charming in the dandy manner.

[Julien] fut si frappé de la douceur des manières de M. de Beauvoisis,
de son air à la fois compassé, important et content de soi, de l'élégance
admirable de ce qui l'entourait, qu'il perdit en un clin d'œil toute
idée d'être insolent.

The more Julien sees of this dandy circle, the more he adopts
for himself, and for his own purposes, the dandy pose—it suits
his *humeur hautaine*, that sensitivity to refinement combined with
horror of vulgarity which also distinguished Stendhal. Driven to
some of his most daring actions by a fear of ridicule, Julien culti-
vates self-control. His manner is naturally cold and dignified and
he has "de la grâce sans le savoir". Even before he gets to Paris
he is warned by the scrupulous Jansenist, the Abbé Pirard, of his
crucial weakness: "trop de sensibilité aux vaines grâces de
l'extérieur."

The decisive moment in Julien's attitude to dandyism comes in
his trip to England, where he has the opportunity to observe, for
his own enlightenment, *la haute fatuité*.* Almost immediately

* Stendhal himself spent short periods of 1817, 1821 and 1826 in England.
Resolutely anglophobe, he refuses to give Julien English preceptors in the

after Julien's return from England Stendhal notes a metamorphosis in his hero: "Julien était un dandy maintenant, et comprenait l'art de vivre à Paris . . ." At the apogee of his career, the accepted suitor of Mathilde de La Mole, the newly christened "M. Julien de La Vernaye", lieutenant of the brilliant 15th Regiment of Hussars, Julien displays the impassive reserve, the dignity, the *sang-froid*, the cold but perfect politeness of the dandy officer. "Ses chevaux, ses uniformes, les livrées de ses gens étaient tenus avec une correction qui aurait fait honneur à la ponctualité d'un grand seigneur anglais." Into this glory and this happiness comes Mathilde's letter like a thunderbolt: "Tout est perdu . . ."

Julien's role in the novel is certainly not that of the idle dandy, but that of the young man in a hurry. In this respect he shows a similarity to the hero of a novel of quite a different quality, published four years before: *Vivian Grey*. But where Disraeli set out to draw the dandy and came up with the man of ambition, Stendhal set out to draw the man of ambition and came up with a character who finds guilty satisfactions in the dandy role. There is more Pelham in Stendhal's hero than in Disraeli's.

As a novel of 1830, *Le Rouge et le Noir* is in part, almost inevitably, a study in costume. For Stendhal, however, there were no treatises on the elegant life, no meticulous descriptions of dandy dress and furnishings. Instead, the unavoidable preoccupation with costume (last and subtlest of social demarcations) fits into the scheme of *Le Rouge et le Noir* by means of a dry, but effective symbolism: red for the uniform of the soldier, black for the soutane of the priest, the colours implying alternative paths up the ladder. The soutane and the uniform confront Julien at every turn of his career; awkwardness and ill-made clothes drag his steps and exacerbate his sensibilities.

It is particularly in his relationship with the Marquis de La Mole, the cunning manipulator of social situations, that Julien

---

arts of dandyism. Instead he chooses Prince Korasoff and his friends, the anglomaniac Russian dandies, who predict a great future for Julien in the achievement of *la haute fatuité*. "Vous êtes prédestiné, mon cher Sorel, lui disaient-ils, vous avez naturellement cette mine froide et à *mille lieues de la sensation présente,* que nous cherchons tant à nous donner." It is Korasoff who, later in Strasbourg, teaches Julien the superiority of the dandy pose to the Byronic.

learns to fear the symbolism of costume. His clothes are carefully prescribed for his first appearance before the Marquis: he is to wear black, not as a priest but as a man in mourning.* And their first interview is about clothes; Julien is "intimidé de voir un grand seigneur descendre à ces détails". Restricted to his room by an attack of gout, the Marquis demands that his new secretary keep him company, wearing black during working hours and blue for the evenings of sociability; a difference, literally, of night and day. It is, for Julien Sorel, a cruelly complex social and moral lesson.

> Julien ne comprenait trop de quoi il s'agissait; le soir même il essaya une visit en habit bleu. Le marquis le traita comme un égal. Julien avait un cœur digne de sentir la vraie politesse, mais il n'avait pas d'idée des nuances . . .

* Stendhal may be drawing here on a common reflection of his period: that the increasingly uniform blackness of male dress was the mark of a century in mourning. Alfred de Musset was one of many to make this point: "Ce vêtement noir que portent les hommes de notre temps est un symbole terrible; pour en venir là, il a fallu que les armures tombassent piece à piece et les broderies fleur à fleur. C'est la raison humaine qui a renversé toutes les illusions, mais elle en porte elle-même le deuil . . ."

Part Three

ENGLAND AND FRANCE

CHAPTER VII

Count D'Orsay

"Fancy a man ever being in low spirits . . . Life is too short for such bêtises . . . Existence is a pleasure, and the greatest. The world cannot rob us of that, and if it be better to live than to die, it is better to live in a good humour than a bad one . . . The sun shines on all; every man can go to sleep; if you cannot ride a fine horse, it is something to look upon one; if you have not a fine dinner, there is some amusement in a crust of bread and Gruyère. Feel slightly, think little, never plan, never brood. Every thing depends upon the circulation; take care of it. Take the world as you find it, enjoy every thing. Vive la bagatelle!"
—Count Alcibiades de Mirabel in Disraeli's *Henrietta Temple*

ALFRED Guillaume Gabriel Count D'Orsay, the graceful French lad of thirteen whom Wellington had singled out with his discriminating eye in 1814, was the child of Restoration anglomania and of the Regency, and the father of Victorian dandyism. His story belongs to none of these periods exclusively and to neither France nor England, for D'Orsay, who never stood alone in life, stands alone in the history of dandyism, straddling worlds of time and place and class. Trained to dandyism in the reign of George IV, but flourishing under William IV and Victoria, he was the essential link between two eras. Born into an Anglo-French borderland of émigrés and tourists, reigning in post-Regency England, dying in France under the hesitant patronage of his friend Napoleon III, he carried dandyism back and forth and back again across the Channel. Pride of the aristocracy but also friend of virtually every distinguished literary man in his period, he fathered the literary tradition of dandyism.

"As the arbiter elegantiarum," the *New Monthly Magazine* said of D'Orsay in 1845, "he has reigned supreme in matters of taste and fashion, confirming the attempts of others by his approbation, or gratifying them by his example." That was the role Brummell created, and of all those who briefly succeeded the Beau only D'Orsay is remembered. But he played the part with entirely different emphasis, and his dandyism was made from weaker stuff.

Brummell achieved power and used it with decision; D'Orsay neither had real power nor seemed to want it. His one desire was for enjoyment, for an easy, relaxed way of life free equally from anxiety and boredom. Where Brummell imposed his will on others, D'Orsay graciously accepted the tributes of those who offered themselves voluntarily to serve his beauty, his imperishable youth, his charm, his brilliant radiance. He was the last, late flowering of the Regency dandy, and with him a certain overpowering sweetness comes to dandyism. His was the age and he the prototype of what was called the "butterfly dandy".* As one contemporary wrote, D'Orsay was the dandy "whom Fortune had so cruelly spoiled".

D'Orsay left behind him innumerable personal relics—voluminous letters, dozens of examples of his own art-work—and few of his friends failed to jot down impressions of him in their journals or memoirs. But surprisingly little of his character remains. Brummell comes down to us clear and unmistakable (if impenetrable) in the handful of pointed anecdotes which were preserved for several decades by verbal tradition, but the bulk of written material on D'Orsay includes almost no anecdotes. There are merely various little tales illustrative of one or another of his qualities: his beauty, and his vanity on that score; his immense height, and the jokes he made about it; his athletic prowess; his fondness for puns; and his confidence in a benign, cruelly spoiling Fortune. Alongside the wonderfully dramatic story of Brummell's royal snub of the Regent can be placed only the legend that D'Orsay saw his name scribbled on the window of a Greenwich inn in "improper conjunction" with that of an opera girl, picked up an orange from the table, tossed it up in the air once or twice, and then, as if by accident, shot it through the offending pane.

Brummell is remembered as a real man moving into and out of a series of difficult situations. D'Orsay comes down to us as a flat image superimposed on a picturesque setting at a moment of easy triumph. So must Wellington have seen him at the royal stag hunt in the Bois de Boulogne. Lady Blessington captured a similar

---

* The butterfly dandy is memorialized once a year by the anniversary cover of *The New Yorker* magazine, showing a dandy dressed in the D'Orsay style and complete with butterfly.

lantern slide of D'Orsay: scene—Paris, time—winter, early in 1830.

> The prettiest sight imaginable was a party of our friends in sledges, who yesterday passed through the streets. This was the first time I had ever seen this mode of conveyance, and nothing can be more picturesque . . .
>
> Count A. d'Orsay's sledge presented the form of a dragon, and the accoutrements and horse were beautiful; the harness was of red morocco, embroidered with gold . . .
>
> The dragon . . . looked strangely fantastic at night. In the mouth, as well as the eyes, was a brilliant red light; and to a tiger-skin covering, that nearly concealed the cream-coloured horse, revealing only the white mane and tail, was attached a double line of silver-gilt bells, the jingle of which was very musical and cheerful.
>
> The shadows of the tall trees falling on an immense plain of snow, the light flashing in fitful gleams from the torches and lamps as we were hurried rapidly along, looked strange and unearthly, and re-minded me of some of the scenes described in those northern fictions perused in the happy days of childhood.

The charm of this scene—the brilliant colours, the glitter, the tinkling, the speed and the romance—was not for Lady Blessing-ton's delight alone for, as she feels it necessary to add, "the Parisians appeared to be highly delighted with the sight . . ." A few months later these same Parisians staged a revolution, and when D'Orsay ventured out into the streets (again according to Lady Blessington) he was roundly cheered. " '*Vive le Comte d'Orsay! Vive le Comte d'Orsay!*' and the cry [was] taken up by the mass . . ."

Lord Lamington, another of D'Orsay's admirers, recorded a companion piece to Lady Blessington's: scene—the road to Richmond, time—the early 'forties.

> I have frequently ridden down to Richmond with Count D'Orsay. A striking figure he was in his blue coat with gilt buttons, thrown well back to show the wide expanse of snowy shirt-front and buff waist-coat; his tight leathers and polished boots; his well-curled whiskers and handsome countenance; a wide-brimmed glossy hat, spotless white gloves. He was the very beau-ideal of a leader of fashion. As he rode through Kensington and Brompton he excited general attention.

Lord Lamington, like Lady Blessington, feels he must show how highly D'Orsay was appreciated by "the crowd, not only of the upper but the lower classes . . . I was greatly interested," he adds, "in noticing the admiration with which he was regarded. What sentiment such an appearance might excite at the present day [Lamington was writing in 1890] I cannot pretend to say, but at that time the effect produced was unmistakable: they stared at him as at a superior being . . ." Times had changed from Brummell's day. D'Orsay played for the crowd, and enjoyed it; while his friends applauded nervously in the background.

2

D'Orsay's path to success was easier than Brummell's. He did not come up out of nothing, but out of a mixture of a little of everything. By legal title he was a Count of France, the scion of a rich provincial bourgeois family which had purchased its nobility outright and ready-made in the mid-eighteenth century. That accounts for his D'Orsay grandparent; the others were a Flemish princess, an Italian dancer and lady of fortune, and a German duke. His father, Count Albert, was one of Napoleon's most handsome generals, and his beautiful mother was illegitimate.

Like Brummell, D'Orsay was schooled to social graces in a salon. An unusually exquisite child, he was paraded through the crowded rooms of the Hôtel de Craufurd, where his grandmother (the extraordinary Italian lady) entertained Parisian society for many years as the mistress of a Mr Quintin Craufurd, and for a few as his legal wife. Craufurd was a Scot who had made his fortune in India; as such, he provided a peculiarly suitable introduction to the English for a French boy who would triumph among Victoria's subjects.

In 1814 D'Orsay met the conquering English in Paris. In 1815, Napoleon's escape from Elba having sent his now legitimist family scurrying to London, he saw England for the first time. D'Orsay's formal introduction to Regency society came, later, in 1821. His beautiful sister Ida had married into one of the greatest noble families of France, which, like many others, emigrated to England during the Revolution and intermarried with the English nobility. With his sister and her husband, the young Duc de Guiche, D'Orsay was invited to England by de Guiche's father, the Duc de Gramont, who had been named Ambassador Extraordinary to the coronation of George IV. The social festivities of the coronation year were at once an education and a stage for the twenty-year-old D'Orsay. Within a few months he had visited the great houses, applauded the fireworks, danced at Almack's, charmed the Duke of Wellington once again, and impressed the dandies with his appearance and his horsemanship.

D'Orsay was accepted with astonishing speed—and even singled out as a leader—by the exclusive set. Shortly after his arrival he made a triumphal appearance at a ball given by Count Marcellus, Chateaubriand's *chargé d'affaires*, who remarked that "d'Orsay y amena son escorte habituelle de dandys." And he climaxed his social triumphs with an achievement that would change the course of his life : the seduction of one of the showiest of Regency couples, Lord and Lady Blessington, who were to cherish and support him for the rest of his life. Chateaubriand, then ambassador to England, observed D'Orsay's swift conquest and summarized it dryly :

> Il s'était mis à galoper dans Hyde-Park, à sauter des barrières, à jouer, à tutoyer sans façons les dandys : il avait un succès sans égal, et, pour y mettre le comble, il finit par enlever une famille entière, père, mère et enfants.

From this time forward the names of Blessington and D'Orsay were so firmly linked that a 'thirties caricature of the Countess of Blessington and the dandy D'Orsay could be titled simply, without possibility of confusion, "BLESS-'N-TON".

Undeniably members of the *ton*, the *élite*, the world of fashion, Lord and Lady Blessington had as little claim as D'Orsay to ancient aristocratic lineage. The Earl, born Baron Mountjoy, was a parvenu nobleman, immensely wealthy and giddily spendthrift. He spent his money where the fashionables could see and enjoy it : his hobby was buying, remodelling and lavishly furnishing one great house after another. His wife, the Countess Marguerite, had a scandalous Irish past behind her. By birth— twelve years before D'Orsay—she was Miss Margaret (Sally) Power, the daughter of a brutal, besotted Irish squire. Married off at fifteen to a soldier who shared her father's habits, she had left her unendurable husband after three months and some years later gone to live with a more amiable Captain Jenkins. In 1814 she met young Blessington, then a widower, charmed him into proposing and, it was persistently rumoured, buying her outright from Jenkins for ten thousand pounds. The facts of this illicit liaison and the stories about her youthful behaviour (she was said to have paraded naked on the public mess-table to the gratification and possible profit of Captain Jenkins) were to follow Lady Blessington all her life.

Still, she flourished. Certainly when D'Orsay met her in 1821 she was not walking on mess-tables but sitting at the head of a dinner table, directing with charm, intelligence and considerable cultivation the talk of wits and noblemen. Her novitiate in Blessington's first London house had been successful, despite the malice spent on her by rival Regency hostesses, Lady Cork and Lady Holland (whose history was little better than her own). Now, in St James's Square, she was one of the great ladies of Regency society.

As long as they lived, the Blessingtons gave D'Orsay all they had to give, and all he could ask: a home, a country, a fortune and a bride. First, in 1822, they carried him off to Italy, after arranging with his family that he should leave his regiment (with which he had been briefly leading in France the decorative military life of a Brummell) on the understanding that he need never be concerned for his financial future. The Blessington–D'Orsay ménage stayed abroad for seven years, outside of Regency England but not out of touch with Regency notables. (Their acquaintance included travelling men of letters like Byron and Landor, scholars like Sir William Gell, wits like Henry Luttrell, diplomats like Lord Normanby, youthful nobleman on the grand tour like Henry Fox, heir to Lord Holland, and assorted tourists and wealthy expatriates.) In 1829 they headed back to England, and on the journey Lord Blessington died, leaving a curious will which appointed D'Orsay his executor and major heir. To qualify for the bequest, however, D'Orsay was obliged by the will to marry one —either one—of Blessington's young daughters by a previous marriage.

Stopping in Paris only long enough to observe the July revolution, D'Orsay returned to England with his new bride, Blessington's fifteen-year-old daughter Lady Harriet Gardiner, and Lady Blessington, now his step-mother-in-law. George IV was dead, and William IV, another sort of monarch altogether, was on the throne, soon to be succeeded by a youthful Queen. D'Orsay did not rise to eminence as the personal friend of a reigning monarch

—the closest he came to Brummell's position was his friendship with a parvenu prince in exile, Louis-Napoleon. It was rumoured that Victoria would not have him presented at court and crossed his name off a list of invitations to a ball. Moreover, he did without the vantage-point of the bow-window at White's, for that backward-looking institution would not have him any more than his friend and disciple, the young Disraeli. Instead D'Orsay reigned at Crockford's, the raffish, late-Regency gambling club which became, for much of London, *the* fashionable club. For almost twenty years D'Orsay held his pre-eminent social position, first as idol of the dandies, and finally, to the delight and astonishment of the early Victorians, as last of the dandies.

D'Orsay's dandyism, like Brummell's, was centred in his dress, but the great Beau's austerity and manliness of style were foreign to D'Orsay's nature. While Brummell's dressing paraphernalia were solid silver, D'Orsay's were gold. For riding D'Orsay wore much what Brummell had made fashionable but the cut—and everything was in the cut—was different. His hat was taller, slimmer, glossier; the curve of its brim was more exaggerated and more dashing. The buttons of his blue coat were gilt, not Brummell's sturdy brass, and its lapels were very wide and arching.

Brummell had worn a coat with a firm and square line, buttoning trimly over the chest and showing only the cravat and a trifle of shirt-front; the dandies of the 'twenties had exaggerated this line to one of spiky angularity; D'Orsay in the 'thirties brought in the curve. His coat was rarely buttoned, but was thrown back recklessly over his shoulders to cover scarcely more than the upper arm. Inside the open curve of the coat lapels could be seen the curve of the waistcoat lapels, a curve accentuated in turn by a gold watch-chain which was looped through a buttonhole and curved across his chest. (Only two links of Brummell's had been visible.) Sometimes D'Orsay wore a white cravat, but as often a neck-cloth of shiny black satin (Brummell abhorred this style, and adopted it only when he was too poor to afford clean linen); and the neck-cloth was not starched and crisply folded into place by a movement of the chin, but rippled softly and glossily through the open curve of the waistcoat. The final triumph of the curve was in D'Orsay's bright auburn hair, worn in a mass of waves and ringlets; and in his beard, a charming ruff of curls circling his chin completely from ear to ear. (Brummell had been clean-shaven, his hair barely waved above his forehead.)

Shimmering pastel colours, soft velvets and silks, perfumes, jewels—all the fantasies of costume that Brummell disdained were part of the D'Orsay style. And while Brummell's costume had won a unanimous, quiet approval by its perfection, D'Orsay's inspired extended comment from the hostile and admiring alike. Benjamin Haydon revelled in a painter's admiration for the rainbow elegance of "such a dress—white greatcoat, blue satin cravat, hair oiled and curling, hat of the primest curve and purest water, gloves scented with eau de Cologne, or eau de jasmine, primrose in tint, skin in tightness." Jane Carlyle mocked and marvelled simultaneously at her first sight of "the fantastical finery of his dress: sky-blue satin cravat, yards of gold chain, white French gloves, light drab great-coat lined with velvet of the same colour, invisible inexpressibles, skin-coloured and fitting like a glove . . ." Entrenched in prejudice, Lady Holland acidly reported that D'Orsay was "laughed at for his dress, which is composed of sky-blue pantaloons of silk & other strange mixtures. He wears his shirt without a neckcloth, fastened with diamonds & coloured stones—in short a costume that *men* disapprove as effeminate and nondescript."

Like Brummell D'Orsay was impeccably groomed and trim in figure, but unlike Brummell he resembled a god more than a gentleman. Six-foot-three, with the pretty face of a woman and the magnificent body of an athlete (he was renowned in his day as fencer, boxer, swimmer, runner, shot, horseman, even cricket-player), D'Orsay reminded his contemporaries of Hercules, Jove or Apollo. "He is the divinity of dandies," wrote an adoring American, "in another age he would have passed into the court of the gods, and youths would have sacrificed to the God of fashion."

He had the Brummell talents and graces. He made innovations in dress (the wide lapel, the extravagantly tall hat, the wristband turned back over the cuff); he gambled nonchalantly and paid debts casually; he was a collector of *objets d'art* and a decorator of beautiful houses. (Though Brummell would have felt out of place in D'Orsay's bedroom which, a French lady said, was "a *tente* of blue *cachemire* embroidered in silver, where he receives, reposing like a second Achilles.") He was a gourmet and something of a wit, though his humour was gentler than Brummell's and his conversation and letters pleased more by their gaiety and gossip than by any cold exactitude. He spoke English fluently and accurately, with just enough of a French accent to remind the English that he was not one of them.

Less eccentric, less independent, less cold and less exclusive than Brummell, he had a superabundance of charm. Never bored, he made others feel that life was amusing. Never anxious, he made others forget their worries: to be in D'Orsay's company was happiness itself. In the infectious laugh, powerful handshake and warm *"A-ha! mon ami!"* of his invariable greeting; in the gay delight he took in any activity, from practical jokes to private theatricals; in his letters bubbling with protestations of friendship; in the fury he exhibited over an injustice or the enthusiasm he put into his taste for art; in his liberal politics; in his eagerness to make up with an enemy; in his gloriously self-confident high spirits—D'Orsay was an amiable man. Too amiable. The loving testimony of his friends is disturbing in its unanimity. Take Thackeray ("gracious and good natured beyond measure . . . He pleases I think by his unbounded good humour and generous sympathy with everybody"). Take Carlyle ("We did amazingly well, the Count and I"); Peter G. Patmore ("No man has ever been more popular in the upper circles, or has deserved to be so"), or Tennyson ("Count d'Orsay is a friend of mine"). Take Albany Fonblanque ("He can be wittier with kindness than the rest of the world with malice"), or Captain Gronow ("never betraying the slightest affectation or pretension"). Take Disraeli (*"a friend*, and the best and kindest of men"), Eugène Sue ("ce vaillant cœur, si chaud, si généreux pour ceux qu'il aime"), or Macready (". . . dear Count D'Orsay. No one who knew him and had affections could help loving him"). And take this posthumous tribute to D'Orsay in Dickens's *Household Words*, which completes the canonization of the dandy:

> Count D'Orsay, whose name is publicly synonymous with elegant and graceful accomplishment, and who, by those who knew him well, is affectionately remembered and regretted, as a man whose great abilities might have raised him to any distinction, and whose gentle heart even a world of fashion left unspoiled.

To delight men of wealth and aristocracy, like Lord Chesterfield, Lord Alvanley and Lord Combermere, and to be chosen as their favourite companion and leader at the club, the hunt and the track, D'Orsay needed no more than his dandyism. But to win the affection of men of talent of the 'thirties and 'forties, whose loyalties and standards were of another class altogether, D'Orsay needed evidences of a good heart and a frank spirit unspoiled "even" by the world of fashion. He also needed á good deal of the most undandified effort simply to make their acquaintance, and at least the flavour of an artist.

This too was not wanting. The Count, as his talented friends remarked complacently while he was among them and *The Globe* commented primly when he was dead, was more than a *mere* dandy: "It were unjust to class him with the mere Brummels, Mildmays, Alvanleys or Pierreponts of the Regency . . ." He could sketch portraits and he did—hundreds of them, moderately skilful, rather stilted sketches, most of the left profile only, a few revelatory of character. He could even, at the lowest point of his finances, charge money for his portraits and, ordinarily with the assistance of more professional artists, get them up into ambitious full-length oils or statues. ("At last I have been painted like a gentleman!" Wellington is said to have exclaimed. "I'll never sit to anyone else.")

And, standing behind D'Orsay, there was Lady Blessington, certainly not a "mere" Exclusive. She wrote voluminous fashionable novels and travel journals, edited modish annuals with titles like *Gems of Beauty* and *Flowers of Loveliness*, and was rumoured to earn as much as a thousand pounds a year with her pen. ("A name," growled Lady Holland, "will sell any trash.") She produced one work which escaped being "merely" fashionable: her justly famous *Conversations with Lord Byron*—in which, inevitably, she was careful to quote Byron's praise of the brilliant young D'Orsay.

The first literary notables to whom D'Orsay and Lady Blessington offered their glittering hospitality and warm friendship were the two masters of the Regency novel, Bulwer and Disraeli. Bulwer first, in the early 'thirties, found his spiritual home in their salon, and remained their most loyal admirer. He put his admiration (of D'Orsay's dandyism and Lady Blessington's intellectual exclusivism) into print with *Godolphin*, a novel of 1833 later affectionately dedicated to D'Orsay.

It was through Bulwer that Disraeli passed into the D'Orsay

orbit and, like Bulwer, he chose the Count as a model for his personal dandyism. Their friendship was a warm one, and socially valuable to the young novelist and aspiring politician. D'Orsay helped Disraeli out of some bad debts and offered him the most charmingly sound advice, phrased in his racy anglicized French. On one occasion he wrote Disraeli:

Je suis bien aise pour votre intérèt présent et futur que vous vous soyez décidé à avouer à votre père, l'étendue de votre scrape. Car les plasterings-over se démolissent toujours et vous en auriez été victime continuellement. Votre imagination vive et brillante, vous fait bâtir des châteaux en Espagne. Tout cela est bel et bon pour les Wonderful Tales of Alroy, mais pour la matérielle vie de l'Angleterre le positif bat l'imaginaire.

Disraeli's grateful tribute to D'Orsay, who also provided the passport to Almack's and the clubs, took the form of a careful portrait of the dandy as Count Alcibiades de Mirabel in *Henrietta Temple* (1836). A benign agent brought in toward the end of the novel to settle with effortless tact the misunderstandings of the love story, Mirabel is a *dandy ex machina* responsible for a happy ending. Incapable of boredom or anxiety, he deals with every problem by calling it a *bêtise* and defies gloom by crying *"Vive la bagatelle!"*

Care—he knew nothing about; Time he defied; Indisposition he could not comprehend. He had never been ill in his life, even for five minutes . . . There was something in Count Mirabel's very presence which put every body in good spirits. His lightheartedness was caught by all. Melancholy was a farce in the presence of his smile; and there was no possible combination of scrapes that could withstand his kind and brilliant raillery.

Elsewhere Disraeli shows his susceptibility to D'Orsay's taste, his beauty and especially his wholehearted admiration of his adopted country, a sentiment which by 1836 was music to Disraeli's ears. (Even the English climate, to Count Mirabel, "is the only good climate there is . . . To those who love variety, like myself, you are not sure of seeing the same sky every morning you rise, which, for my part, I think the greatest of all existing sources of ennui.")

Henrietta Temple also includes Disraeli's testimonial (delivered by a Mr Bond Sharpe, a former prize-fighter grown rich

from a gambling hell and a money-lending establishment) to the
D'Orsay who could be generous with his friendship to the
parvenu. "There is not a man in that room," says Mr Sharpe,

> who, if I were to break tomorrow, would walk down St James's Street
> to serve me. Yes! there is one—there is the Count. He has a great
> and generous soul. I believe Count Mirabel sympathizes with my
> situation. I believe he does not think, because a man has risen from
> an origin the most ignoble and obscure, to a very powerful position,
> by great courage and dexterity, and let me add also, by some pro-
> found thought, and by struggling too, be it remembered, with a class
> of society as little scrupulous though not as skilful as himself, that he
> is necessarily an infamous character . . .

3

That D'Orsay should have made friends with Regency novelists
is not surprising; that he should have had even more success with
the Victorians is no less than astounding. Yet the greatest
Blessington–D'Orsay salon was the last: Gore House, to which
they moved in 1836. The crimson damask curtains, the gilt
couches, the mirrors nine feet high, the portraits, the busts and
the bibelots were Regency décor, but the location was not. Flee-
ing the traffic noises (and perhaps the pressures) at the centre of
town, Lady Blessington set her final salon behind a high, protec-
tive garden wall in Kensington Road, an almost suburban spot.
(The preceding tenant had been William Wilberforce, the
philanthropist.) D'Orsay lived "nominally," as Lady Holland
reported, "in a small bijou, for such it is described, adjoining."

The visiting writers, artists, journalists, politicians, actors
and scholars viewed Gore House not as the centre of London but
as a delightful retreat. In addition to those whose praise of
D'Orsay has already been quoted, Gore House entertained
Ainsworth, Dickens, Marryat, William Jerdan, Landseer,
Macaulay, Landor, John Forster, William Maginn, Barry
Cornwall, Monckton Milnes, Henry Reeve, Dr Quin (the popu-
lar homeopathist), Edward Trelawny, Sheridan Knowles,
Theodore Hook, Henry Chorley, Maclise and Turner—the
great and the small among the early Victorian talents. In addition
D'Orsay went out of his way to catch the most distinguished
foreigners who passed through London: Countess Guiccioli,

sentimental over Byron but still full of female vitality; Franz Liszt, who "killed" the Gore House piano in the grand manner and supervised the buying of a new one; Longfellow, who was "delighted," D'Orsay wrote, "with my condescension towards him"; and Hans Christian Andersen, who came to make friends with Dickens. French tourists and political exiles passed through in abundance, and the list of D'Orsay's French friends (of men he knew either at Gore House or in Italy or in France) is as long, as distinguished and as pertinent as the English list. It includes Lamartine, Vigny, Talleyrand, Eugène Sue, Clésinger, Paul de Kock, Rachel, Alexandre Dumas, Arsène Houssaye, Horace de Viel-Castel, Antoine Frédérick-Lemaître, the Vicomte d'Arlincourt, Theodore Gudin, Auguste Romieu, the Comte Guy de la Tour du Pin, Emile Girardin, Eugène Lami and Louis Blanc.

Most prominent of D'Orsay's French friends was a gentleman who thought he would like to be an emperor: Prince Louis-Napoleon, very distantly related to the D'Orsay family and an intimate of Gore House during his years of exile in England. In 1852, when Napoleon III had achieved his object, and when D'Orsay had fled his creditors to Paris, the emperor paid part of his long-standing debt to the dandy by appointing him Director of Fine Arts for the Second Empire. A few months later D'Orsay was dead.

4

Much as D'Orsay's contemporaries valued his amiable qualities, they were often disturbed by his personification of the moral issues surrounding dandyism and the Regency itself. Beautiful to look upon and sweet to know, he seemed almost to justify the existence of a creature so irresponsible, so supernumerary, so expensive as a dandy—almost, but not quite. Beside the glorious vision of the butterfly dandy had to be set the facts of his existence, which were not nearly so pleasant.

Up to the moment of her death only three years before his own D'Orsay lived with Lady Blessington, who was twelve years older than he and seemed middle-aged beside what Disraeli called D'Orsay's "immortal youth". He was either in the same house, his bedroom on the same floor as hers, or in a cottage close by and accessible through a door cut in the garden wall. His claim to

Blessington hospitality, and to a close relationship with Lady Blessington, had been established by his marriage with Lord Blessington's daughter, whom he had agreed to take sight unseen. It had been stipulated, apparently at the insistence of Lady Blessington, that the marriage would not be consummated for four years. And according to almost all accounts, Lady Harriet, the virgin Countess D'Orsay, was miserable. Less than four years after her marriage she literally ran away, into the arms of sympathetic relatives. There is a little evidence and a good deal of gossip to the effect that D'Orsay consummated the marriage shortly after three years had passed, and shortly before Harriet left him.

From these facts the scandal-mongering journals of the period drew an obvious conclusion: Lord Blessington was the cuckold and the dupe, Lady Blessington the shameless wife and scheming mistress, D'Orsay the mercenary lover and Harriet the defenceless victim, a "modern Iphigenia", whose husband asserted his rights over her only to prevent a divorce and secure his income. But D'Orsay's closest intimates believed he was sincere when he mourned Lady Blessington as his "douce mère chérie" ("*In losing her I lost everything in this world—she was to me a mother! a dear, dear mother! a true, loving mother to me!*") Edward Bulwer, long a close friend of both parties, wrote the following judgment in his portfolio for posterity:

> To all appearance the affection between [Lady Blessington and Count D'Orsay] was that of a mother for a spoilt child. I feel a strong conviction that, at least after D'Orsay's marriage, there was never any criminal connection between them. Nor, indeed, any love of that kind, especially on her part. She was confessedly of a very cold temperament, though most affectionate to her friends.

Few contemporaries went so far in interpreting the D'Orsay–Blessington history as Horace de Viel-Castel, irascible and unreliable memorialist, who proclaimed that D'Orsay had had sexual relations with both Lord *and* Lady Blessington.* But vague and ugly rumours proliferated. D'Orsay, wrote a French

---

* Michael Sadleir has concluded from his detailed analysis of the story that only one explanation, and that an extreme one, suits the facts: that Lady Blessington's disastrous first marriage had shocked her into frigidity, that Lord Blessington's passion for D'Orsay was in part sexual, and that D'Orsay himself was impotent.

countess early in his dandy career, "never comes into the society of women; but he . . . has acquired immense influence with all the dandies and *aspirants* to that noble profession, so that the House is a den of corruption which promises to be the ruin of all the young men in Paris . . ." Women generally did not take to D'Orsay. They were disturbed by the sexual ambivalence not only of his relationship with Lady Blessington but also of his butterfly variety of dandyism. Like Lady Holland, many found his costume "effeminate". Camilla Toulmin, a silly English miss of a novelist (and a contributor to Lady Blessington's annuals), found D'Orsay "mannish rather than manly, and yet with a touch of effeminacy quite different from that woman-like tenderness which adds to the excellence of a man."* "At first sight," wrote Jane Carlyle, "his beauty is of that rather disgusting sort which seems to be . . . 'of no sex'."

Men were powerfully drawn to D'Orsay (Byron called him a *Cupidon déchaîné*) or occasionally repelled (Cobden called him a "fleshy, animal-looking creature"). Enchanted or offended, however, they all found his dandyism a daring blend of the masculine and the feminine graces. As R. R. Madden, Lady Blessington's deferential biographer, put the case with his usual politeness, D'Orsay presented a mingling of "the high bearing, proud spirit, and strong energy of a nobly constituted man . . . with the gentleness, the sensibility, self-devotion, and tenderness of a woman's nature."

But D'Orsay's superficial or essential effeminacy bothered the Victorians less than his parasitical way of life. Again, the facts of his existence called into question the moral values of the dandy. For almost thirty years D'Orsay lived on the bounty of the Blessingtons. Lord Blessington had left D'Orsay the bulk of his estate, thus depriving his own children of a large part of their inheritance; and D'Orsay was for a number of years involved in lawsuits over the will. He was not merely extravagant, he was wholly thoughtless about money matters, never calculating the relation between his income and his expenses. (His extravagances included thoughtless generosity.) And the resulting weight of debts imperilled not only D'Orsay (who hardly cared to notice) but Lady Blessington, altogether a more responsible

* Miss Toulmin also noted with surprise a flaw in D'Orsay's much-vaunted beauty, of which no one had spoken: bad teeth.

person. D'Orsay let her manage their affairs, let her worry about the apparent luxuriousness of Gore House and the very real financial ruin it implied, let her use her pen to pay for his trinkets and his gambling debts. Everyone knew that she spent each waking moment away from the salon writing against time and against the growing reluctance of her publishers, ruining her health and beauty while D'Orsay gambled, rode, visited the aristocratic houses to which she was not admitted, or toyed with his portraits in the elegant studio she had made for him in Gore House. (It was only when things were most desperate that D'Orsay realized he might earn some money by his talent.) Many knew, too, that she had long been willing to sell up Gore House and retire to the Continent, while the ever confident D'Orsay persisted in his faith in a special providence cruelly spoiling such as he.

Henry Chorley, one of D'Orsay's fondest admirers, jotted down a few notes about the dandy in his memoirs in order to evoke, he said, "the magnificent presence, and joyous, prosperous voice and charming temper." But something about D'Orsay's radiant optimism disturbed the *Athenaeum*'s eminent critic as much as it attracted him. In what was surely meant to be a wholly flattering reminiscence Chorley let slip a touch of pique. D'Orsay, he wrote, "was spoiled during most of his life by every one whom he came near";

and to one like myself, endowed with many luxurious tastes, but whom the discipline of poverty had compelled prematurely to weigh and to count, it was a curious sight to see, as I often did in the early days of our acquaintance, how he seemed to take it for granted that everybody had any conceivable quantity of five-pound notes. To this fancy the Lichfield, Beaufort, Chesterfield, Massey, Stanley set, among whom he was conversant, ministered largely. He spent their money for them royally, and made them fancy they were inventing all manner of sumptuous and original ways of spending it.

Even Disraeli came to find D'Orsay's irrepressible gaiety difficult to take. "Agreed to dine at Gore House today," he wrote on March 13, 1842, during a particularly low period in the Blessington–D'Orsay finances. "But I dislike going there, D'Orsay being in high spirits, quite unchanged, but Lady B. very altered—silent, subdued and broken. She told me another year would kill her, and complained bitterly . . ." Thackeray on the other hand, though he was to weep at the final destruction of Gore House, must have had his doubts and reservations from the start. After his first formal presentation to D'Orsay he carefully copied into his diary his friend Leech's opinion that the Count was not quite "a regular gentleman".

Certainly D'Orsay was a dandy, but was he a gentleman? And what was the difference between the two? That was the Victorian dilemma.

Part Four

ENGLAND: THE VICTORIAN REACTION

CHAPTER VIII

England in 1830 and the Anti-Dandiacals

. . . I could not help thinking that a gentleman was not the sort of a king for this country.—(Cheers.) *Do not mistake—I mean a gentleman of the tailor's making; for a gentleman of God's making is a different matter, and one of them we have upon the throne at present . . .*

—Oliver Yorke's toast to William IV
(*Fraser's Magazine*, September 1830)

IN England as well as in France, 1830 was the year for dandyism in the press; but in England it was the year for reaction. Dandyism was new to France, where journalists were popularizing a current fad, making a humorous obeisance to *milord Brummel*. But the dandies were an old and notorious story in England, and 1830 was the year to renounce the Regency and vilify the dandy class. It was the year George IV died and *Fraser's Magazine* was born.

The roots of the long, complex Victorian campaign against Regency thought and habits can be found in the closely printed, double-column pages of *Fraser's*, behind its drab, brown cover bearing an emblem of Scotch thistles. There Carlyle's *Sartor Resartus* first appeared, and Thackeray made his first reputation with Yellowplush, the below-stairs dandy. Well before Thackeray and Carlyle had taken their stand with the anti-dandiacals, however, *Fraser's* under the leadership of William Maginn, its first editor, had begun to express the resentment of the ill-paid and ill-respected man of talent against the tyranny of exclusivism, both literary and social. It aired the provincial (especially Irish and Scotch) suspicion of foreign affectations and domestic degeneracy. It voiced, with fresh and confident invective, the growing middle-class indignation at irresponsibility in high places. Alongside its sober commentary on politics, literature, philosophy (especially German thought and letters), theology and even science, the magazine made its own contribution to the new spirit. Coming in with William IV, *Fraser's* expressed the temper of a transitional reign. It was destructive, satirical, independent, opinionated, rambunctious, vulgar.

Girardin's journalists in France and Maginn's Fraserians in England provide an absolute contrast of literary types. The former have found their way to posterity in the *Comédie humaine*; the latter in Thackeray's gallery of penny-a-liners in *Pendennis*. Booming, glittering prosperity made it possible for the French periodical writers to style themselves journalists and to play on the boulevard, in the café and the salon the role of *jeunesse dorée*. In London, however, the press was still located on Grub Street, in what Carlyle glumly called "the valley of the shadow of Magazine Editors". There were fewer magazines in England than in France, and fewer fortunes to be made out of periodicals; and in England publishers were proprietors, while editors were merely anonymous employees.

Many of the French journalists came originally from the provinces, but once in Paris they prided themselves on being the most Parisian of the Parisians. London publishing offices were crowded with Irishmen and Scotsmen, easily distinguishable (and often caricatured) by their brogues and burrs, never completely assimilated Londoners. Maginn was an aggressive Irishman who had first written under the pungent pseudonym of "Sir Morgan O'Doherty", and his magazine sneered at the "Cockneys" and bragged about its numerous "provincial" contributors:

> In Ireland we are particularly formidable. Scores of Paddies . . . have started from the sod, like devils incarnate, at the touch of O'Doherty's wand . . . Look at [their] effusions. . . . They all smack of the brogue, broad, pure, and unadulterated, as on the green hills of Connaught; while the blarney that runs through them out-flavours the eloquence of Cicero . . . Nor are our thanks less due to the land of cakes, of *feelosophy*, and the SCOTCH FIDDLE . . .

The ostensible editor of *Fraser's* was a fictitious, composite figure called Oliver Yorke, a high-handed, heavy-drinking, proud-speaking fellow who dramatized the blustering spirit of the Fraserians. In the first seven years of the magazine Oliver Yorke was mostly Billy Maginn, and behind the bluster lay a private existence of humdrum middle-class respectability at best and sordid lower-class misery at worst. Maginn had been a schoolmaster and had thrown it up for the excitements of the literary capital. During his first years in London, with an Irish wife and an increasing family to support, he lived a precarious existence as contributor or editorial assistant to a variety of periodicals, from the most scurrilous newspaper to the most dignified magazine (he even had a hand in Disraeli's ill-fated project, the *Representative*, and in Thackeray's *Standard*). Maginn gained a reputation for versatility and originality, but his qualities never brought him the political patronage and literary fame he sought; as the years passed he became known, too, for drunkenness and irresponsibility. His literary career finished in a debtors' prison, and he died shortly after his release from imprisonment.

Maginn was more than a "mere" journalist: he was a brilliant and learned man, a formidable linguist fluent in all the major and most of the minor European languages, and so confident a classicist that some of his best parodies were written in Greek and Latin. A knowledgeable and discriminating literary critic, he was also an intelligent commentator on contemporary affairs. But his most salable qualities on the literary market-place were his Irish love of a quarrel and his mastery of the dubious arts of lampoon, satire and burlesque. These talents Maginn devoted whole-heartedly to *Fraser's* war on the dandy school, and his work for *Fraser's*—ill-mannered and cruel, but witty and effective—left its mark on the style of all the early Victorian satirists.

Much of what *Fraser's* published was a composite effort, written in casual collaboration by the staff as a whole. Editorial meetings were social occasions, held not at a reserved table in some elegant café, but at the famous Round Table "in the back room of the establishment of Mr James Fraser, at No. 215, Regent-street, the *birth-place of Regina* [as the magazine proudly called itself] and temple of true fun." There the Fraserians, with Maginn as chairman, would congregate until dawn, "a gathering of as many good fellows as chose to go, with a sufficient sprinkling of foolish frivolios to afford sport for the chosen few"—who included, at one time or another, Gleig, Churchill, Cornwall, Thackeray, Croker, Lockhart and Hook. They spent their time not appraising horseflesh, gossiping of ballet-girls or envying the Jockey Club but singing Irish songs, scribbling parodies and, above all, downing great quantities of whiskey punch. It was a proud badge of their trade to be always drinking and often drunk.

The war on literary and social exclusivism which came out of these Round Table meetings inevitably fell first on personalities and last on issues. It was declared early in 1830 under an ominous standard: "All criticism . . . must not be good-natured; for, if it were so, it would become no longer criticism." And it was prosecuted with the cry: "*Guerra a cuchillo!*" In its third number (April, 1830) *Fraser's* came forward with a summary of its intended victims: Lytton-Bulwerism, Colburn-and-Bentleyism, Pelhamites and Exclusivites,* all of them purveyors "of cant and humbug,—of fraud, folly, and foppery." The battle with Colburn-and-Bentleyism was central, and from this position *Fraser's* wheeled to attack the whole exclusive system of literary fame and finance. Maginn had come in contact with Colburn in the early 'twenties, when that eminently practical publisher ferreted out the well-hidden identity of "Sir Morgan O'Doherty", and tried to buy Maginn's services for his own side. Maginn came away with a distaste for West End publishing methods (which he satirized in a novel, *Whitehall*, in 1827) and a respect for Colburn's formidable powers, both these reactions implicit in his account of the meeting:

> He asked me to dine with him for to-morrow, which I declined: he shook hands at parting, quite cordial, and he whispered to me as I went away, "Thirty guineas a sheet." I laughed at him, and drove off.

The satirical keynote of *Fraser's* attack on Colburn was the word "puff", or as one Fraserian put it, "one grand, cabalistic word—Puff: ay—Puff—Puff—Puff." In the expansive metaphorical style later used with great effect by Carlyle, the Fraserians toyed endlessly and brilliantly with this word, leaving far behind its technical meaning (the adulatory self-review bought in large quantities by Colburn) and extending it to the school of *puffers* and the vice of *puffery*. The word came to suggest hot-air, sham, vanity, superficiality, affectation and irresponsibility, and to be applied liberally to publishers, authors, fashionables, and utilitarians alike. By 1833 *Fraser's* was congratulating itself for its defeat of Puff:

> The Puffers had poisoned the whole blood of our literature, extending their infection over author, bookseller, reader, critic. All was either corruption or mystification, quackery or deceit. Three

---

* Also included was "Jeremy-Benthamism"; *Fraser's* did not like radicalism, and some of its distaste for fashionable authors like Bulwer and Disraeli stemmed from the radical cast of their (early) political opinions.

years ago it appeared to be so deeply rooted, and so decidedly triumphant, that any opposition to it seemed hopeless; yet, like all systems of deception, it crumbled at a touch.

Colburn's advertising methods were not the only point of *Fraser's* attack: his major dereliction was trading on the fashionable. *Fraser's* defined fashion as a "mania", a "false varnish" applied to inferior goods, a "house of refuge for the poor in mind and thought; who, wanting taste, tact, courage, and character, are forced to take shelter under some fashionable folly or fantasy, in order to conceal the feebleness that prevents them from standing on their own ground." By financing authors from the exclusive set and capitalizing on their exclusive connections, Colburn furthered the exaltation of mediocre talent. In the case of Bulwer, Colburn's leading novelist, the process had been alarmingly simple:

> Mr Bulwer belongs to the higher classes of the social order in England; and having from some of the principals of that set received praises which have been echoed by men of smaller dimensions, Mr Bulwer stands confirmed in the public estimation as a first-rate novelist . . .

Far from being the best judge of literary ability, the exclusive aristocracy is the worst, said *Fraser's*, for "the thoughts, feeling, habits, mode of life, movements of all fashionable circles, are actuated and guided by certain fixed, invariable principles. Every thing with them is artificial and conventional." In short, the exclusives' only standard of taste is "that they are too well pleased to have one of their own order to write a book of any sort."

In the magazine world, Colburn's malign influence had the effect of transforming Thomas Campbell (then the editor of Colburn's *New Monthly Magazine*) from a genuine poet into a "merely fine gentleman", fit only for "the sickly and perfumed atmosphere of the drawing-rooms", and satisfied with "the effeminate pleasure of talking small literature to frowsy old spinsters, fusty demireps, and snuffy women of quality in boudoirs." And the *New Monthly* itself was castigated as "that elegant-ish, dandy-ish, washy-ish periodical", and compared for greater emphasis with a suit of clothes:

> . . . one of Stultze's coats without a man in it: super-super drapery, with nothing below; cut, and smoothed down, and stuffed out, and

needled, and squared, and rounded, to fit the fantastic shapings of fashion, until you are sick of looking at a *thing* so empty and so aimless.

This sample of *Fraser's* satirical writing at its most emphatic could hardly have been lost on Carlyle, who echoed its tone throughout *Sartor Resartus*; nor on Thackeray, who would return to the image of the empty suit of clothes in his denunciation of George IV.

Fraser's bewailed the decadence of English literature, proclaiming the contemporary poets mediocre, the novelists worse. And of all classes of novelists "the most execrable, the most abominable . . . is the pseudo-fashionable class. O that we might be preserved for ever from perusing this degenerate spawn . . ." It was not difficult for Maginn and his collaborators to tear apart the fashionable novel as a literary genre, but literary values were merely the beginning. The demolition of the fashionable novel was, above all, a moral crusade:

> Amusement should only be made the organ of instruction. In what are people edified by perusing the fashionable novels . . .? What noble faculties are addressed in such works? Are they calculated to make readers in general better or wiser?—to brace up manly energy, and promote heroic virtue? Or rather, have they not an evident tendency to effeminate and enfeeble the mind . . .?

The fashionable novelist's sin, in *Fraser's* eyes, is his aimless, even sickly curiosity about the exclusive world, his "one unvaried, eternal harping on high society." And of all classes of society, said *Fraser's*, the aristocracy is least worthy of curiosity. Worse, the very heroes of these novels are immoral. Maginn drew an easy parallel between the moral degradation of the dandies and the immorality of the dandy novel: "It is a libertine —whether because its heroes are notoriously such, deponent sayeth not. They are, however, moral libertines—the novel, it seems is an intellectual one."

Fraser's most searing denunciation of the dandy as dandy grew out of its personal war with Bulwer, an enlargement of Maginn's well-known but obscurely motivated dislike for the man. From the first, *Fraser's* was after Bulwer as a person rather than Bulwer as a novelist. The magazine's initial article on Bulwer's novels, early in its first year, was only moderately antagonistic, but after Bulwer had foolishly replied (in the Preface to *Paul Clifford*, where, in his most dandified manner, he characterized his critics as "the great unwashed"), Maginn struck out in earnest. In the twenty-five page leader of the June number ("Mr Edward Lytton Bulwer's Novels; and Remarks on Novel Writing") he seized on the dandy qualities in Bulwer's novels.

The worst of these qualities, in Maginn's eyes, was Bulwer's tendency to sneer at the middle class, a cliché of the Regency position and, like French phrases, a permanent feature of the fashionable novel. "It would appear," wrote Maginn, "that it was esteemed a mark of superior breeding with these vain young foplings, to express contempt of the middle classes of society." (The vain young foplings, of course, were merely copying their elders: no less than Robert Plumer Ward had voiced the exclusive's distaste for the rising bourgeoisie in his preface to *Tremaine*. About the upper and lower classes, he wrote, he was confident, but "I am not so sure about the middle. The wide spread of that luxury which is consequent to wealth, by extinguishing the modest style of living which once belonged to us, has undermined our independence, and left our virtue defenceless. All would be Statesmen, Philosophers, or people of fashion!") In *Paul Clifford*, Bulwer's rogue novel, Maginn detected a sinister consequence of the Regency scorn for the middle class: a sense of relationship between "high life" and "low life", a bond between the fashionable high and the criminal low.

> It is a favourite notion with our fashionable novelists, to sacrifice the middle classes equally to the lowest and highest . . . There is a sort of instinct in this. The one class esteem themselves above law, and the other are too frequently below it. They are attracted, then, by a sympathy with their mutual lawlessness. They recognize a likeness in their libertinism . . .

This insight was as shrewd as it was damaging. It had application to Ainsworth as well as Bulwer; it could be fastened to the fashionable Eugène Sue and his dubious *Mystères de Paris*; it has something to say about Dickens's last novels and the late Victorian crime novel.

It was Maginn's role to champion middle-class virtues against exclusive affectations,* and to denounce the *fop* and his *foppery*—

---

* In the June 1830 article on Bulwer's novels, Maginn dramatized his preference for the homely simplicity of middle-class life with a damning

words which Maginn hammered at Bulwer as he hammered *puff*
and *puffery* at Colburn. More important than Maginn's impassioned satire, however, was his proposal of an alternative to the
Regency dandy: the true gentleman. The endless Victorian preoccupation with the proper nature of the gentleman may be said
to have originated from Maginn's simple argument that the true
gentleman is known first *by his differences from the false*, and that
the virtues of the Regency dandy are merely the vices of the
Victorian gentleman. The starting-point of the whole discussion
was the epigraph to *Pelham*, which Bulwer took from Etherege
and which Maginn quotes in his article on Bulwer's novels:

> "A complete gentleman, who, according to Sir Fopling, ought to
> dress well, dance well, fence well, have a genius for love letters, and
> an agreeable voice for a chamber."

"There are," Maginn concludes, "*gentlemen* of two sorts; the
natural, and the tailor-made. Let the reader judge to which class
Pelham belongs." The reader is helped to judge with an extensive
quotation from *Pelham*: six very closely printed columns containing almost the whole of the famous chapter on clothes and
tailors. One result of this article was Carlyle's *Sartor Resartus*;
another was Bulwer's editing of *Pelham* to exclude this chapter in
its entirety, as well as many other traces of Regency dandyism.
And hereafter the opposition of dandies to gentlemen became
something of a point of honour with *Fraser's*.

Maginn was not done with Bulwer; in fact, the novelist's ordeal
was only beginning. From July 1830 to the middle of 1833 Bulwer
the dandy was ragged and burlesqued without surcease. He was
treated to insults and invective ("strutting and cocking of

comparison: between a humble middle-class household and an outrageous
dandy apartment. Both descriptions were quotations from Bulwer's
Disowned, the former given with some satire in the body of the novel and
the latter sketched in as the setting for the preface to the novel (first
edition only). This preface is in the form of a very long dialogue between
Bulwer and Pelham; Bulwer's whole point was to distinguish himself from
his character Pelham, which the critics refused to do, and for this purpose
he made the dandy even more outrageously effeminate than he was in
Pelham. The luxurious setting for the dialogue was, unquestionably,
Pelham's apartment, not Bulwer's. But Maginn, with full knowledge of his
mistake, calls it the author's own apartment; and Carlyle, who used the
same dandy setting satirically in *Sartor Resartus*, unwittingly repeated the
error.

plumes"—"swaggering and bullying air"); odious comparisons
(to "snorting, kicking, hee-hawing donkeys" and "snakes, rats,
and other vermin"); side attacks, as nasty as possible, on his
mother, brother, wife, and mother-in-law; humiliating dissec-
tions of his novels and issues of the *New Monthly* when he became
its editor ("dirty cringing for favour"—"rubbish"—politics of
the "sneaking kind"—"shabby little thoughts"); even snatches
of verse in praise of *Fraser's* virulence:

> She deigneth not to spit on
> The trash of Ned Lytton;

and insulting manipulations of his pretty, aristocratic name.
"Edward Liston Bulwer, Cad to Colburn," was *Fraser's*
favourite; Thackeray would improve on it.

"That magazine," said Bulwer sadly of *Fraser's*, ". . . long
continued to assail me, not in any form that can fairly be called
criticism, but with a kind of ribald impertinence offered, so far as
I can remember, to no other writer of my time." Speaking for
Fraser's at the end of its seventh volume, in June 1833, Maginn
was jubilant:

> We have, we flatter ourselves, done one literary good . . . our
> demolition of the Puffers . . . Where are all the great authors, whose
> praises rang from the *Literary Gazette* to the *New Monthly* . . .? All
> gone, and no memorial left. Who would now give a baubee for a bale
> of Bulwer, when we began our labours the topmost man of the
> province of Puff? Nobody . . . A monument should be erected to the
> glory of the feat . . .

Maginn's temperament and pungent style fitted him best for
the work of tearing away. It was for others, many of them his
pupils in satire, to round out the social issues involved in his
attack on dandyism and to expand his suggestion of the ideal of
the gentleman into a moral alternative. Maginn's own rudimentary and largely negative concept of gentlemanliness is revealed
in his humorous idealization of William IV as the gentlemanly
king. Oliver Yorke made frequent protestations of his affection
for the King, but refused to descend to the servile adulation more
proper to an exclusive court. "Whipt-cream", "froth", and
flowery "lingo" were out of date, he said: "among men, among
Englishmen, among brother sailors, ought it to be the order of

the day? No. The Duke of Clarence—I beg a thousand pardons
—his Majesty is a man above such stuff." His Majesty is a *Man*
—this was *Fraser's* way of saying he was a gentleman: a rough,
unassuming, old-fashioned, sturdy, manly Englishman, stupid
perhaps (it was a charm rather than a defect) but untainted by
foreign affectations or native effeminacies. The opposite of a Man
was a dandy, the non-man; throughout its attack on "Lytton
Bulwerism" *Fraser's* emphasized (by innuendo only) the vices
of effeminacy and penalties of emasculation.

About all of *Fraser's* principles there was a gruff Philistine tone
of no-nonsense and old-fashioned English common sense. "We
started Ultra-Tory," boasted *Fraser's*, "and so we continue,"
unalterably opposed to "abstract principles in politics," to
"mushroom doctrines" and to theories in general, resolved to
assist the public "in returning into the right path, and teaching
it to look with something more of respect on maxims and principles which, in all countries, but especially in this country, have
been the parents of wealth and power." The cornerstone of
Fraser's toryism was support of Church and King (and Reform
to secure them both, for *Fraser's* was not unintelligent), and
opposition to English interference in foreign politics. In the
accents of an unregenerated isolationism, *Fraser's* proclaimed
that "our creed is this—that if the Foreign Office were closed
altogether, it would be so much the better for the country; and that
the policy of England should be insular, as she is an island, and
colonial, as she is the queen of colonies, the nursing mother of
empires,"—this, note, in 1830. The specifically 'thirties quality
of *Fraser's* toryism lay in its antagonism to the House of Lords
(particularly over the Lords' resistance to the Reform Bill) as a
"congregation of snobs":

> Why hang them! I'm sure scarce a sprinkle remains
> Of their ancestor's blood in their spiritless veins.

A hearty distrust of a degenerate and effeminate aristocracy
was the Regency's legacy to the men of William IV's day, who
came to believe that England's salvation lay in a return to old-
fashioned English manliness. Even Maginn's perpetual boasting
about the quantities of wine and whiskey his Fraserians could
drink was a defence of his manliness—much as G. K. Chesterton,
after a later upsurge of English dandyism and radicalism, would

boast that "the rolling English drunkard made the rolling English road." Fraserians swallowed whole seas of port and madeira, "the most gentlemanly wine in existence . . . spite of what White's club-men say . . .," Maginn wrote, "—and in this we differ very materially from your fashionable parties, where the cloth is whipped off the table before you have gargled your throat with a few initiatory glasses of the vinous juice." Maginn's own epitaph on his virtues, which the Fraserians were fond of repeating, was a description of himself as

> A randy, bandy, brandy, no Dandy,
> Rollicking jig of an Irishman!

2

By the middle of 1830 Thomas Carlyle was ready to do a book, a *true* book cast in its own true form and expressing the true gospel of Thomas Carlyle. In 1829 he had written a literary friend: "I have some thoughts of beginning to prophesy next year, if I prosper; that seems the best style, could one strike it rightly." Though already thirty-five he had nothing to his credit but translations and articles for the magazines, a sort of work which he despised; "Magazine work," he said, "is below street-sweeping as a trade." All his first prophetic book waited on was a final inspiration, which would synthesize his thoughts into one proper form. Innumerable ideas were in the air: a metaphor from Swift, stylistic innovations from Jean Paul Richter, ponderings from his beloved Goethe. But it was the arrival of two packages in the mail to Craigenputtock that set Carlyle off. The first came in July: books and articles expounding the Saint-Simonian doctrine, routed from Paris via Edinburgh. They brought to Carlyle the suggestion of a new religion which would preach social reform without materialism and faith without orthodoxy. The second package came direct from London on the ninth of August, and was received less gladly: a bundle of *Fraser's Magazines*, which Carlyle found to contain a "hurly-burly of rhodomontade, punch, loyalty, and Saturnalian Toryism . . . a kind of wild popular Lower-Comedy." "Nevertheless," he added, "the thing has its meaning." The particular *things* which caught Carlyle's attention were the April and June articles denouncing Bulwer and the fashionable novels. They must have suggested to him, among other things, that it was time to put down the "clothes-wearing man", and by the middle of September the plan of his book had crystallized. "I am going to write—Nonsense," he wrote in his Journal. "It is on 'clothes'." And with a sense of the irreverent folly of the idea, he added: "Heaven be my comforter!"

Sartor Resartus, the book about clothes, was sent off to *Fraser's* in November 1830 and promptly rejected; revised and expanded by Carlyle and submitted in vain to all the London publishers; revised again into magazine articles and submitted to *Fraser's*, which brought it out serially from November 1833 to August 1834; printed in book form in America in 1836 and in England, by James Fraser, in 1838. This book, which took the whole of the reign of William IV in the making, was the foundation of the Victorian spirit, influencing with its peculiar style and unsettling content the work of Dickens, Thackeray, Ruskin, Morris, even the Bulwer and Disraeli of a later day. One section of it, the chapter entitled "The Dandiacal Body", served as the Victorian epitaph for Regency dandyism. It made a stir in fashionable circles from the day it appeared in *Fraser's*, and gained steadily in influence—chastising the mighty and working conversion among them—well into the mid-century, at which time the "moral consciousness of ultra-polite drawing rooms", in the words of W. H. Mallock, professional apologist for the Victorian aristocracy, was still "being stirred to its well-dressed depths, by [Carlyle's] attack on 'the dandies' in his book *Sartor Resartus*, which many earnest and ornamental persons were accepting as a new revelation."

Much has been written about the abstract double symbolism of Carlyle's clothes philosophy, with its implication of a spiritual universe and a changing society, but very little about the obvious practical timeliness of the subject of clothes themselves. In France, where dandyism was merely an import, the significance of costume as a social phenomenon preoccupied many writers in the early 'thirties; certainly in England, where a clothes-obsessed monarch had just completed his reign over a society of dandies, the subject was unavoidable. Younger than Bulwer and Disraeli, Carlyle was as much a Regency product as they, though he grew up under the reverse side of the Regency coin. Born into a Scotch family of hard-pressed farmers and artisans, he knew from experience what they had to learn from books and parliamentary reports: the rebellious discontent of the north country, industrial unemployment, agricultural depression, and the inequities of the Corn Laws. Workers' agitation had made the Edinburgh of his student days hum with forebodings of "radical" uprisings. Carlyle had gone deliberately to Manchester, the dirty city Brummell refused to visit when his regiment was ordered there to put down a rebellion ("Think, Sire," he said to George, "Manchester!" and sold out).

Carlyle had also seen enough of fashionable Londoners to justify his anger at their ways, and to resent the critics' attribution of his rough, north-country style to "insufficient acquaintance with good society" as De Quincey wrote of his *Wilhelm Meister* translation. He had done the translation in the home of Mr and Mrs Charles Buller, whose sons he was tutoring, and, while they were not part of the exclusive inner circle of London society, the Bullers were fashionable enough to irritate Carlyle. Charles Jr. had the reputation of being something of a dandy, his tastes "all given to Boxiana, Bond Street, and pleasures gathered out of the speculations and ambitions of Harrow School." Mr Buller Sr. seemed to Carlyle a typically idle, fox-hunting English gentleman; and the Buller's visitors, up from London for a week of hunting, impressed Carlyle most strongly with the boredom and inactivity of the aristocracy. "I see something of fashionable people here;" he wrote Jane Welsh, "and truly to my plebeian conception there is not a more futile class of persons on the face of God's earth."

> If I were doomed to exist as a man of fashion I do honestly believe I should swallow ratsbane or apply to hemp or steel before three months were over. There is something so *very* unsubstantial in their whole proceedings, such toiling and wrestling and so very little realized, that really I know not well how even stupid people can endure it. From day to day and year to year the problem is not how to use time, but how to waste it least painfully: they have their dinners and their routs, they move heaven and earth to get everything arranged and enacted properly, and when the whole is done, what is it? The uneasy destruction of half a dozen hours . . .

The dandy world of the Regency was real enough to Carlyle, poor and provincial though he was. What youthful contacts he had with his "betters" taught him, by their very brevity and inconclusiveness, to hate exclusivism with the class hatred then dangerously growing in Britain, especially among those who could describe themselves, in Carlyle's words, as "poor men, but nothing worse." During his student days in Edinburgh Carlyle had been too poor to dress for the fashionable afternoon promenade in Princes Street; he could only watch from a distance, glowering at the "dandies" on parade. He took a trip to Moffat and was struck by an English *"popinjay"* in the hotel monopolizing the newspaper; when asked the news, this gentleman could say only that "the Prince Regent was gone to Brighton." Well before his encounter with the Bullers he had tutored for a living, at one time reduced to teaching "two Dandies Mathematics", at another undergoing the irritation of listening to "the cant and slang of the coxcombs, the bloods, the bucks, the boobies, with which all earth is filled." When he got to London at last he sought out the literary men and was "astonished to learn on inquiry, that the Authors did not dwell [on Grub-street] now, but had all removed years ago to a sort of 'High Life below Stairs', far in the West." He could not see the men of letters for the "dandy wits" and when he hunted up the poet Thomas Campbell, an idol of his childhood, Carlyle was dismayed to find the editor of Colburn's *New Monthly Magazine* a conceited dandy with fashionable airs.

Then there was the disturbing example of Miss Jane Welsh, the girl he hoped to marry, who—understandably—put a value on good looks, fine clothes, grace, refinement and money. She was a victim of "gigmanity", Carlyle's word for snobbishness. Jane had a string of handsome suitors with fine clothes, and Carlyle at first could not measure up to them. His talent, intelligence, and "independence of soul" reminded her of her ideal hero, Rousseau's Saint-Preux. "But then—Ah, these *buts*!" she wrote. "St Preux never kicked the fire-irons, nor made puddings in his teacup. Want of Elegance! Want of Elegance, Rousseau says, is a defect which no woman can overlook." Jane flirted mercilessly with Captain Baillie of the Lancers, "the handsomest, most fascinating young man in England", who drove his four horses to Jane's door and glittered with jewels and bright colours—a gold pendant on his rose cap, ruby buckles on his slippers, and four rings on his fingers. Jane began to think she was "meant by nature to be a fine-lady", and Jane joined the crowds going to look at King George, while Carlyle pouted and growled "Scandalous flunkeys!" Jane bought her lover a fashionable hat, and when Carlyle got to London he bought a suit of fine clothes to match— but that was the end of Jane. In two years they were married, and her opinions had already changed. Captain Baillie still looked splendid, but Carlyle, she wrote, had no cause for jealousy. "When I compare this fine gentleman with the *man* I love, what is he after all? A mere painted butterfly, while he—my own—is like to the royal eagle, who soars." And Carlyle soon was ordering clothes from an Ecclefechan tailor.

In Carlyle's morality it was not enough to value the soul over the exterior (as Jane, at first, refused to do). True merit lay in the renunciation of surface adornment altogether. In the Third Book of *Sartor* he devotes a whole chapter to "the most remarkable incident in Modern History" : George Fox's initial renunciation of the world, implicit in his stitching together for himself "one perennial suit of leather!" "Stitch away, thou noble Fox :" cries Carlyle; "every prick of that little instrument is pricking into the heart of Slavery, and World-worship, and the Mammon-god." Now Carlyle belittles the suggestion that all mankind should dress, or rather undress, in the manner of Fox, in order to escape from "Vanity's Workhouse and Ragfair" (a phrase that may have come to Thackeray's mind when he was groping for a title for his anti-fashionable novel). But his animosity toward those who dressed for the sake of fine clothes is abundantly clear—so clear that Carlyle's definition of the Dandy, which opens the chapter on the Dandiacal Body, carries great ironic force: "A Dandy is a Clothes-wearing Man," he writes, "a Man whose trade, office, and existence consists in the wearing of Clothes."

This chapter, from its title to its prophetic conclusion, is one of the best things Carlyle ever did : a splendid example of sustained irony, taut and harsh, suggestive of a moral position without being narrowly explicit or clearly logical. The ugly phrase *dandiacal*, for example, is Carlyle's own invention : he turns a pretty, familiar noun into a clumsy, unfamiliar adjective, with a suggestion of the words maniacal and demoniacal. He demolishes the dandy position by malicious flattery. Thus the dandy, he says, is an inspired man (inspired with the all-importance of Clothes), a creative enthusiast (enthusiastic over clothes), a poet (of Cloth—

"in Macaronic verses"), a (Clothes-) prophet, and a (Clothes-) martyr. He goes further, finding Dandyism a veritable religion—an idea Carlyle throws out with some amusement, but which would be picked up by others with considerable seriousness. Carlyle's account of the "Dandiacal Sect" is devastating not through its exaggeration but by its accuracy. The Sect is devoted to the primeval Superstition of *Self-worship*, and its members,

> animated with the zeal of a new Sect, display courage and perse-verance, and what force there is in man's nature . . . They affect great purity and separatism; distinguish themselves by a particular cos-tume . . .; likewise, so far as possible, by a particular speech (ap-parently some broken *Lingua-franca*, or English-French); and, on the whole, strive to maintain a true Nazarene deportment, and keep themselves unspotted from the world.

Their temple is Almack's; they worship by night with secret rites; they have their High Priests (the Brummells and D'Orsays) and High Priestesses (of course, the lady patronesses); and they have their Sacred Books—the *Fashionable Novels*.

Carlyle then culls from *Pelham* (the "to me unknown indivi-dual named *Pelham*, who seems to be a Mystagogue, and leading Teacher and Preacher of the Sect") the "Articles of Faith" of the dandiacal body: seven rules, flatly stated and numbered in order, prescribing the cut and colour of trouser, waistcoat and coat, and establishing the importance of rings. These rules come from Chapter VIII of the second volume of *Pelham* (in the first edi-tion): Bulwer's famous disquisition on what he called "the greatest of all science—the science of dress".

Carlyle is not through with Bulwer. The next stage of the chapter is a comparison between the dandies and an opposing "religious" sect: the Irish "Poor-Slaves" or "Drudges", bound by vows of poverty and obedience, dressed in the peculiar costume of rags, subsisting on a prescribed diet of potatoes and living in squalor. He places a contemporary description of an actual "Poor-Slave Household" alongside Bulwer's description of a "Dandiacal Household", taken from the introduction to *The Disowned*. In the former a large Irish family are shown sharing a hovel with their cow and pig, and eating potatoes out of a trough-like table; " 'all the luxuries of meat and beer, bread, knives and dishes were dis-pensed with'." Bulwer's "Dandiacal Household" is an elegant bachelor's apartment, crowded with buhl, mirrors, mother-of-pearl, and all the other luxurious superfluities of the dandy existence.

Carlyle has often been criticized for misinterpreting Bulwer. A careful reading of the whole of *Pelham* shows that Bulwer was quite conscious of his impertinence, and had a serious purpose in his dissection of the dandy pose. Certainly a thorough reading of *The Disowned* would prove that Bulwer could preach good living and high thinking with the gloomiest resolution. Indeed, this dreadful novel is one of Bulwer's many productions to show the sobering influence of Carlyle's bible, Goethe's *Wilhelm Meister*. Carlyle did not know Bulwer and had no grudge against him personally; the passages he quotes merely served his purpose, of illustrating the dandy pose, as no others could.

Besides, there is no reason to believe Carlyle ever read the two novels in question. He nourished a distrust of fiction in general, formed by a family prejudice behind which lay a religious principle. ("Fiction, while the feigner of it knows that he is feigning," he once wrote, "partakes, more than we suspect, of the nature of *lying* . . .") It is difficult to imagine Carlyle reading through the whole of *Pelham* (and he would have had to read through half to arrive at the chapter on clothes) while in isolation at Craigenputtock farm, writing high-souled articles and talking philosophy with Jeffrey. It is even unlikely that the three elegant volumes of *Pelham* should have been sent to him through the tedious and expensive mails.

And for this chapter of *Sartor* he needed nothing more than the issues of *Fraser's* mailed to him in the summer of 1830. There, already transformed into ammunition for the anti-dandiacal campaign, were the clothes prescription from *Pelham* and the dandy apartment from *The Disowned*. Even the idea of juxtaposing a wealthy with a modest household—the device of the damning comparison—was in *Fraser's*. But where Maginn had been content to contrast dandy luxury with middle-class respectability. Carlyle opposed it to the abject misery of the very lowest class in Britain.

Carlyle appears, indeed, to have admitted his debt to *Fraser's*. His spokesman in *Sartor*, the myopic German professor Teufelsdröckh, says that he *tried* to read several sample fashionable novels; but, "seized with not so much what I can call a drumming in my ears, as a kind of infinite, insufferable, Jews' harping and scrannel-piping there," he fell asleep. Fortunately a book-package arrived in the mail, wrapped in interesting waste-paper: "the outcast fraction of some English periodical, such as they name *Magazine*, [with] something like a dissertation on this very subject of Fashionable Novels!" And, adds the professor, though the article is limited and "Secular", "nevertheless scattered lights do from time to time sparkle out, whereby 1 have endeavoured to profit."

Whatever Carlyle's sources, his point was made. All that remained was a prophecy of class war: two splendid pages conjuring forth, in Carlyle's most fervent biblical voice, a vision of doom for England. The two Sects, of Dandies and Drudges, are increasing, he writes, and shall some day oppose each other like "two bottomless boiling Whirlpools" or two spluttering, supercharged "Electrical Machines".

> If, indeed, there were to arise a *Communion of Drudges*, as there is already a Communion of Saints, what strangest effects would follow therefrom! Dandyism as yet affects to look-down on Drudgism: but perhaps the hour of trial, when it will be practically seen which ought to look down, and which up, is not so distant.

3

Carlyle's prophecy of revolution was being fulfilled even as he wrote it, though more peacefully than he suspected. The seven years of William IV were punctuated with social and political disorders reaching toward the edge of upheaval. It is extraordinary with what clarity the fashionables themselves remarked the piecemeal destruction of exclusivism which took place throughout the early 'thirties. With conviction, even with relief, they dated the ebb of Regency attitudes from the death, in 1830, of George IV, a monarch more quickly forgotten and less sincerely mourned, as *Fraser's* noted in its obituary, than any other.

Even the dandies did not stay to mourn, but seemed to age overnight into the "old bucks" of Mrs Gore's and Thackeray's novels. Bulwer drew such a dandy in *Godolphin*: Augustus Saville, a decadent gentleman who dies in 1830, explaining to young Godolphin that he cannot outlast his monarch. "The death of

George IV," wrote Bulwer only three years after the event, "was the birth of a new era . . . the English world began to breathe more freely, to look around, and to feel that the change, long coming, was come at last." George's funeral was an empty anticlimax. The real epitaph to his reign came later in 1830 with the auction of his wardrobe and personal effects, a sorry spectacle the Victorians neither forgot nor forgave. Indeed, it was almost all they could remember about the Regent, that he never gave away a suit of clothes, and that the sale of his wardrobe realized £15,000.

In the following year William IV had a coronation remarkable for its shabbiness. So many petty economies were made that the ceremony was dubbed "a half-crownation", and H. B.'s cartoon of the event showed King William and Queen Adelaide going to Westminster in a hackney coach, followed by William's illegitimate family in an omnibus and the peers and peeresses on foot. Carlyle was in London in 1831, and, walking to Jeffrey's house, he stumbled on the procession. The poor old King and Queen looked to him like "two foolish wax dolls", he wrote his wife, and he could not keep from bursting "into the heartiest fit of laughter I have had for some time." "Perhaps I ought rather to have cried;" he added, "for it was the ghost of the past, perhaps taking leave."

In 1831 Lord John Russell brought in the Reform Bill for the first time, and the Lords rejected it for the first time, and the people rioted at the Lords for neither the first nor the last time. The passage of the great Bill in 1832, though it brought about only a partial reform of the electoral system, signified at least as great an upheaval as the July Revolution two years before in France. No one knew better than the exclusives themselves that Reform was a death-blow to oligarchical politics in England, and thus by extension to the rickety institutions of exclusivism. Dandyism as a social force died with the Reform Bill. For the "Drudges" *Reform* seemed a password to Utopia. Rosina Bulwer up in the country was astonished by the "infatuation of the common people" over the bill, and their persuasion that it would "feed and clothe them for nothing. Poor geese!" Her husband made his major speech in Parliament in favour of what he considered "the most important act that for a century and a half had passed the National Assembly." Creevey had watched the gloomy anti-Reform faces at Crockford's and decided that "as sure as my name is Diddy Creevey, this sweeping plan of Reform . . . *must* and *will* be carried." After the battle Raikes concluded that Earl Grey had sealed the "future ruin" of the aristocracy by his Reform Bill, and Disraeli saw in it the destruction of the ARISTOCRATIC PRINCIPLE and the House of Lords. "The moment that they passed the Reform Act," he wrote, "that assembly was as completely abrogated and extinguished as if its members had torn off their robes and coronets, and flung them into the river . . ." While Mrs Gore's Cecil, with his eye on smaller things, commented that "Exclusivism, fashionable novelism, Nashism, and fifty other fribbleisms of the West-end, were utterly extinguished by the Reform Bill."

Portents of change flashed through the skies over the England of William IV. Rioting crowds in London, inspired by revolutionary France, carried the tricolour; the counties sweated under the terrorism of "Captain Swing", the anonymous author of threats to burn, riot and destroy. The first passenger railway line opened (and the railways, as Disraeli would remark, ended among other things the self-containment of the London season). Cholera broke out in 1831, with the salutary effect of arousing public concern over the dangerous condition of the poor. "One great good will be accomplished," Greville wrote in his journal, ". . . for much of the filth and misery of the town will be brought to light, and the condition of the poorer and more wretched of the inhabitants can hardly fail to be ameliorated." Cecil put in more dandified language this new concern of the aristocracy with the health of their neighbours:

> The rich became suddenly solicitous about the state of the poor;—not because rebuked by the approach of judgment to come, but because misery was supposed to be the nest-egg of this brood of death . . . The little blue noses we had thought only disgusting when the result of cold and hunger, became instruments of destruction when connected with the idea of the Cholera . . .

In 1834 fire swept the Houses of Parliament, and, with a significance that escaped no one, the House of Lords was far more seriously damaged than the Commons. Carlyle was in the crowd watching the fire and noted the air of festivity and satisfaction in the faces around him; he heard shouts, as the flames went higher,

of "There's a *flare-up* for the House of Lords!" and "There go
their *hacts*!"

And in this same year, 1834, a highly popular novel dramatized
an ancient spectacle of destruction with a pertinence to contemporary events that many readers must have found disturbing.
Bulwer's *Last Days of Pompeii* was, in any case, the most successful novel since *Waverley*. For once Bulwer had turned up a theme
suited to his stylized melancholy and his decorous paraphrasings.
Upon the ancient city recently uncovered from its layers of dust
and debris, Bulwer superimposed still another layer, the attitudes and interpretations of the Regency, with the result that the
tourists' Pompeii, even today, is a Regency Pompeii. Bulwer
lingered over his descriptions of the decadent pleasure-loving
dandy of Pompeii, wearing his tunic "in those loose and effeminate folds which proved him to be a gentleman and a coxcomb,"
gourmandising, gambling (with crooked dice), riding in the park
and taking perfumed baths. Bulwer's hero Glaucus, "the fastidious, the luxurious, the refined", was set in a jewel of a house in
Pompeii that would be, so Bulwer wrote, "a model at this day
for the house of 'a single man in Mayfair'." What a subject for
the author of *Pelham*! And what a vehicle for his opinion that
Regency England was already a dead civilization, buried swiftly
and irrevocably by the volcanic eruption of the Reform Bill. He
could even trot out those useful moralists, the Nazarenes, to
moan a direful prophecy.

> Woe! woe . . . Behold! the Lord descendeth to judgment! . . . Woe!
> woe! ye strong and mighty! Woe to ye of the fasces and the purple!
> Woe to the idolator and the worshipper of the beast! . . . Woe to the
> harlot of the sea!—woe! woe!

Brummell loved *Pompeii*. Lady Blessington, who had already
written Bulwer glowingly about his novel, passed the book on to
D'Orsay and wrote again to say that he "has read your *Pompeii*,
and says that no one ever before succeeded in giving the *beau ideal*
of a fine gentleman as you have done in Glaucus." And she added:
"*He* might have been such a character had he *not* been a Frenchman, or thrown into London fashionable society, that Dead Sea
which destroys the energy of all who float over it."

Cecil, in the 'forties, looked at London through Bulwer's eyes.
"Were Primrose Hill to send forth an eruption of cinders and

lava," he suggested, "and Herculaneanize or Pompeiify the west end of London, how greatly A.D. 3001 would wonder at the vulgarity of our taste, and the littleness of our productions . . . the thousand nameless trinkets invented to amuse the great babies of our enlightened times." In fact the monuments of Regency London would shortly be buried under the strata of another civilization.

That social paradise in Kensington, Lady Blessington's Gore House, was emptied of both Bless-'n-Ton in 1849, its "costly and elegant effects" auctioned off in May to the accompaniment of tears from Thackeray: "Ah it was a strange sad picture of Wanaty Fair." Two years later Gore House, Kensington, was opened as a restaurant by Alexis Soyer, the famous chef who fled France after the Revolution of 1830 to cook for London lords and clubs, and later proved himself a naturalized Victorian by volunteering to supervise the diet of famished Irishmen in Ireland and British soldiers in the Crimea. The restaurant was not a success, though such a distinguished body as the Metropolitan Sanitary Association met there in 1851 to hear a speech by Charles Dickens, who preached the moral of a new wave of cholera: "the air from Gin Lane will be carried, when the wind is Easterly, into May Fair, and . . . if you once have a vigorous pestilence raging furiously in Saint Giles's, no mortal list of Lady Patronesses can keep it out of Almack's." In the 'sixties Gore House came down to make way for a different memorial to a different society. Queen Victoria herself laid the foundation stone, on the site of Lady Blessington's mansion, for the Royal Albert Hall.

The Lady Patronesses continued their work at Almack's until 1863, although this Regency institution had begun its decline in the years of Reform Bill agitation, when society found itself for once seriously divided into Whigs and Tories, and could not meet together peacefully on Wednesday nights. For the Victorians Almack's was a thing of the past; the present was summed up by "Willis's Rooms", the Victorian name for the old Almack's building on King Street, famous now not for its balls but for its lecture series. Almack's rechristened was the scene, for example, of Charles Kemble's "Readings from Shakespeare" in the grand ballroom, of Dickens's address to the "Railway Benevolent Society", and of Thackeray's series on the English Humorists in the year of the Great Exhibition. As for the Regency clubs,

White's and Brooks's go on for ever, but Crockford's died as the result of a parliamentary investigation into gambling; and the great clubs of the Victorian period, clubs literary, political and professional rather than social (the Reform, the Garrick, the Carlton, the City of London, the Army and Navy), were established during the reign of William IV. The Athenaeum was born even earlier, but it had been founded in reaction to the exclusive tyranny of the Regency clubs, and its pre-eminence as an intellectual centre was solidified when the club settled in the 'thirties into its permanent quarters: an imposing building designed by Decimus Burton, ornamented with a statue of Athene, and located on what had once been the grounds of Carlton House.

By 1834 the work of obliteration of the Regency was so far advanced that *Fraser's* could look back on the vices of what it called the "tuft and tinsel-hunting generation" as if they were ancient history.

> The striving after fashionable notoriety led to extravagance; the best were forced, in consequence, to crush all generous and charitable sentiments of the heart; because they left themselves no means to aid the deserving or to relieve the destitute. Those who to make a show constantly lived up to the very verge of their incomes, became oppressive landlords, harsh masters, and litigious customers. Instead of upholding national manners and feelings, many of our gentry and their imitators resided and spent vast sums in France and Italy; trained up their sons and daughters in the anti-British ideas so carefully instilled into all youthful minds in the virtuous convents and seminaries of those moral countries. Not only affable, but often cringing, abroad to the most despicable of foreigners, they were at home cold, haughty, and distant to their countrymen; seeking in exclusiveness the most wretched of all distinctions, because the easiest to be obtained, and never sought by those who have other means of attaining honest celebrity . . .

"Fashion thus aided," *Fraser's* concluded, "the progress of the Reform Bill."

4

Fraser's Magazine celebrated the beginning of its sixth year by a departure from custom. Instead of the usual single-page portrait sketch by Daniel Maclise in the magazine's popular "Gallery of

Literary Characters", the January 1835 issue displayed a proud double-page engraving of almost thirty gentlemen seated at a round table. They are, as the caption explains, "The Fraserians", a misleading phrase, since many of those represented never participated actively in the direction of the magazine, though all contributed something to its spirit. The scene is James Fraser's back room, the table *the* Round Table, and at the head Maginn himself rises to make a speech. Each man has a glass in his hand or before him on the table (Maginn has several decanters) and behind Maginn's shoulder stands the shadowy figure of "Jack Tapster" pouring whiskey. Across from Maginn sits his publisher, Fraser, at his left the Rev. Edward Irving, Carlyle's old friend, whose fervent faith had always found an organ in *Fraser's*. Farther to Maginn's left and right are the men who worked most closely with him in editing the magazine: "Father Prout", the Irish Jesuit who succeeded Maginn, Gleig, Jack Churchill, Percival Banks, Barry Cornwall. Then comes Thackeray—with the familiar screwed-up, round baby face, the dangling eye-glass, and the flattened nose. Further around the table to Maginn's right are Southey, Harrison Ainsworth, Coleridge, dead a year before but still the guiding spirit of *Fraser's* philosophy, James Hogg, the Scotch poet (in a plaid shawl), Crofton Croker, Lockhart (talking business with Fraser) and Theodore Hook. Then, between the serious Scotchman David Moir and the erudite scholar Sir Samuel Brydges, out peers the head of Carlyle, looking surprisingly youthful and appealing with serious eyes and unruly hair.

Just behind Carlyle (though neither man notices the existence of the other) sits an unexpected figure, the only "Fraserian" with his back to the sketcher. He is in the shadow, and his chair does not touch the rim of the table, but even from behind he is recognizable: the well-cut coat with wide collar and sloping shoulder, the tightly fitting sleeve flung negligently over the back of the chair, the elegant gauntlet glove, the curling hair and ruff of beard are all Count D'Orsay. But for the careful Gore House campaign to keep in touch with literary men—which at one point reached out to include Maginn—the thought of D'Orsay as a Fraserian would be ludicrous. There have been speculations as to what D'Orsay actually contributed to *Fraser's*; most probably he wrote nothing. But he charmed Maginn, whom he saw at Gore House (an extremely flattering sketch by Maginn of Lady Blessington had been included in the Gallery two years before) and at the home of Harrison Ainsworth (the elegant author of crime novels whose writings Maginn disapproved on principle but whose company Maginn enjoyed). The preceding issue of *Fraser's* had contained a Gallery portrait of D'Orsay, the accompanying text lauding his wit and citing Byron's praise of his talents; the Count was most cordially invited to become a contributor. And the final comment on D'Orsay by *Fraser's* (the magazine that vowed to destroy the dandy novel and went to work on Bulwer, D'Orsay's closest literary friend) would be, in the familiar words, that he was "the beloved of all who knew him."

D'Orsay's presence in Maclise's sketch of the Fraserians points to a Victorian paradox. The two decades that brought about a disintegration of Regency exclusivism were the twenty years of D'Orsay's "reign" in London. The very writers who created the Victorian reaction to dandyism were among D'Orsay's friends, and at least two of them, Dickens and Thackeray, owed to D'Orsay's influence much of their ambivalent attitude towards the dandy pose. D'Orsay reminded the Victorians of the attractions of another way of life.

Even Carlyle was sought out and reminded. He became worthy of D'Orsay's attentions when he delivered, in 1837, a successful lecture series in—of all places—the very Temple of the Dandiacal Body, the "new" Almack's known as Willis's Rooms. (Carlyle's audience was extremely select—"Marchionesses, Ambassadors, ah me! and what not," he wrote his mother; and to his brother "mere quality and notabilities"; and to John Sterling "mixtiform dandiacal of both sexes".) The next year, when Carlyle's position was reinforced by the publication of *The French Revolution*, "this Phoebus Apollo of Dandyism" (as Carlyle called D'Orsay) came to call.

He simply blew in ("whirling hither in a chariot that struck all Chelsea into mute dazzlement with its splendour," said Carlyle) and with his usual frank affability proceeded to make himself liked. He complimented Carlyle on "the fine epic", made a joke about Shelley and briskly invited the philosopher to come to Gore House, looking splendid all the while. The arrival of D'Orsay, without warning or introduction, Carlyle took as a

compliment and not as an impertinence—"the strangest compliment of all", he wrote.

> Jane laughed for two days at the contrast of my plaid dressing-gown,
> bilious iron countenance, and this Paphian apparition. I did not call
> till the other day . . . and left my card merely. I in fact do not see well
> what of good I can get by "meeting him" much, or Lady B. and Demi-
> repdom, tho I shall not object to see it once, and then oftener if
> agreeable.

This, from Carlyle, was an astonishing admission. He did indeed
leave his card, and he did go to dine at Gore House, and he was
again impressed with D'Orsay's "decided natural gifts". He
came away puzzled, and like the others tried to justify his enjoyment of D'Orsay by imagining him more than a *mere* dandy: "a
dashing man, who might some twenty years sooner born, have
become one of Bonaparte's marshals, and *is*, alas—Count
D'Orsay." The product of this incongruous relationship was one
of the best portraits of Carlyle in his forties, dashed off by D'Orsay
in twenty minutes after dinner, and catching admirably the set
jaw, the piercing eyes, and the wild hair of the Anti-Dandiacal
prophet.

CHAPTER IX

Thackeray

*O! me, we are wicked worldlings most of us, may God better us and
cleanse us . . .*

WILLIAM MAKEPEACE THACKERAY was born in
India in 1811—ten years too late, and in the wrong place.
One has only to compare his early career with that of Edward
Bulwer—a comparison often in Thackeray's mind—to sense the
penalties of date and place. In 1817–18–19, the last years of
Prince George's regency, Bulwer was growing into a precocious
but self-assured dandy, old enough to refuse to go to Eton, to
take part in the balls and *conversazioni* of the London season, to
flirt with Caroline Lamb. Thackei·y, only eight years younger
than Bulwer, was at this period merely a frightened little boy,
shipped home to England on board the Indiaman *Prince Regent,*
taken by his black servant to peer through the railings of Carlton
House, excited by his excursion to the Royal Yacht anchored in
Southampton Water, where he saw "the bed in wʰ his Rˡ Highness breaths his *royal snore.*" With lesser talents and greater
social aplomb, Bulwer was able to capitalize on the trivial success of his first novel *Falkland,* published in 1827. With false
starts, procrastinations and failures behind him, Thackeray would
not bring out his first novel, *Vanity Fair,* until 1847.

And Thackeray's circumstances were not, in fact, vastly less
than Bulwer's. His people had done great things in the England
of the Four Georges, winning position and prosperity in the
church, in the university, in the Indian army and civil service.
During his childhood and young manhood under the last George,
Thackeray looked forward to the comfortable, genteel existence
proper to his family for more than a century; but hardly had he
come of age, during the reign of William IV, when financial
disaster completely altered his prospects. He saw his queenly
mother and distinguished stepfather retreat from their creditors

to the Continent, and he found himself forced to push his way with his pen, sketching and writing for his life.

One mark left on Thackeray by this sudden downturn in his family's fortunes was his absorption with the past, not only with his own youth, but with the eighteenth and early nineteenth centuries when the Thackerays, Ritchies, Bechers and so on had been people of consequence. His best novels would be written about the past, without being true historical novels; the past had for him a presence he rarely found in contemporary life. "A man can be alive in 1860 and 1830 at the same time, don't you see?" he explained when he was an "oldster" (his own phrase) of forty-nine.

> Bodily I may be in 1860, inert, silent, torpid; but in the spirit I am walking about in 1828, let us say;—in a blue dress-coat and brass buttons, a sweet figured waistcoat (which I button round a slim waist with perfect ease), looking at beautiful beings with gigot sleeves and tea-tray hats under the golden chestnuts of the Tuileries . . .
> *(Roundabout Papers)*

Another result of the financial collapse was Thackeray's concern with the problem of status, which he put in the form of a nagging, persistent question: what is a gentleman? Was it true that "it takes three generations to make a gentleman", as he said on several occasions? Or was a gentleman the hard-working literary hack who wrote anything the publishers would buy in order to support his family? Was it gentlemanly to accept free passage from a steamship company, and write notices of their ship in your *Notes of a Journey from Cornhill to Grand Cairo*? (When the critics thought not, Thackeray said they were unfamiliar with "the customs of English gentlemen".) Was Bulwer a gentleman, was D'Orsay a gentleman, was Colonel Newcome (a character Thackeray conceived as the personification of gentlemanliness) a gentleman, or was Dickens's Dan'l Peggotty even more of a gentleman (for Thackeray was soon bored with Colonel Newcome)? All these questions came back to the same absorbing personal question: am *I* a gentleman?

2

Toward the end of 1830, the first year of *Fraser's*, Thackeray was engaged in the leisurely tour of the Continent proper to wealthy young Englishmen. At that time he looked forward to an inheritance that would assure him about £500 a year, not munificent but enough to allow him to take his time in the choice of a career, and to suit his own tastes. These tastes, in 1830, were gentlemanly in the Regency sense of the term. Thackeray had recently left Cambridge without taking his degree—for a variety of unsatisfactory reasons, of which laziness was the least discussed and the most important. He was inordinately fond of gambling and had already lost over £1500 at that diversion; he loved good food, spent far too much time at the theatre and the ballet, thrived on masculine company, cigars and doing nothing. In 1830 he was only nineteen, and he was enjoying the provincial airs and old-fashioned formalities of the sleepy court at Weimar, which received every young Englishman of good family with gratifying hospitality. He sent home to his bookseller for the back issues of *Fraser's* that he had missed and took them around to Goethe, with whom he had several flattering audiences, and he noted that Goethe was particularly delighted with the gallery portraits by Maclise.

Back in England the next year, and established in the Temple for the distasteful purpose of preparing for the bar, Thackeray was already thinking of a literary life and his thoughts turned to *Fraser's*. He submitted a few poems to the magazine which forthwith rejected them. In 1832, just before coming of age, collecting his inheritance, paying off his gambling debts and dashing off to Paris, he made the acquaintance of William Maginn. And when Thackeray took his first serious step toward a career by buying a newspaper, he hired Maginn's part-time editing services at an extravagant salary.

The letters and diaries Thackeray wrote during this period are despondent documents testifying to inadequacies, idleness, small sins and profitless remorse, and over all an air of indecision and lassitude curious in so young a man. His confusion was aggravated by the widely varying groups with which he travelled, fully at home in none of them. First in importance was his own family, the scattered but proud and clannish tribe of Thackerays—and Ritchies, Bechers, Shakespears, Dicks, Crawfords, Carmichael-Smyths—who turned out to welcome, fondle and scold him in every town he visited, in England or abroad. They gave him a sense of belonging and mattering and being someone of considerable importance, which was valid inside the family but often inconvenient outside it.

Then there were his friends from Cambridge, young men of good family and distinguished prospects, preparing for careers in parliament or the civil service by going into society and discussing issues of the day as if matters of national concern were their personal responsibility. Chief among them were the Buller brothers, their family, and their friends—Spedding, Milnes, Kinglake, the Procters—with whom Thackeray spent a good deal of time in his early twenties, accepted as one of their own and, while he was with them, sharing their concerns. These were the people who gave Carlyle his introduction to London society (to Carlyle's growling displeasure), a semi-fashionable, semi-intellectual circle Thackeray referred to as "The Set". He smoked, chatted and drank ale with them, observing their habits and trying to follow their purposeful steps to success. Young Charles Buller, Carlyle's former pupil, was writing creditable articles for several of the more serious and respected periodicals. After a day with his friend, Thackeray noted in his diary that Buller "makes money by magazine writing, in wh. I shd. much desire to follow his example." Thackeray also went along to help canvass for Buller's seat in parliament, and the experience delighted and impressed him. "I have certain Parliamentary visions in my own head," he jotted down again, "& am thinking of the best way of fulfilling them."

Unlike his Cambridge friends, Thackeray also had a fondness for what his family would have called "low" company—tipsy Irishmen, professional gamblers, seedy adventurers and literary hacks, a class including the brilliant Maginn and Francis Mahony (*Fraser's* "Father Prout"), two gentlemen with whom Thackeray's friendship was long and intimate. He was fascinated by Maginn from their first meeting at the Somerset Coffee House, liking him "for his wit & good feeling", and for a time in 1832 they saw each other constantly. A typical entry in Thackeray's diary for this period is "Idle all day dined with Maginn"—and the companionable Irishman seemed to his young friend "a very loveable man I think." One day Maginn took Thackeray to dine with his literary cronies at the Kean's Head ("a dull party of low literary men"); a few weeks later he spent Sunday morning in Thackeray's room reading Homer aloud and pointing out the beauties of the Greek; that afternoon he took Thackeray to a brothel. Thackeray was disgusted, not because brothels were new to him, but because it was a "common" brothel, and he was "sickened to see a clever & good man disgrace himself in that way." These friends from *Fraser's* were favourite companions for evenings at the taverns and "poor man's clubs" (like the famous Cider Cellars) where Thackeray went to relax—and to savour a sense of sinning.

Whatever condescension there may have been in Thackeray's relationship to Maginn vanished in 1834, the year which, in Thackeray's life, marked off the past from the present. The failure of a Calcutta bank completed the decimation of his inheritance, already dissipated by his extravagances and the failure of his paper, the *National Standard*. Thackeray beseeched Maginn for employment on *Fraser's* and he faced a reality from which he never wholly escaped: the necessity to earn his living, and to regain his social status, by literary hackwork.

The appearance of Thackeray in Maclise's portrait of the Round Table company of Fraserians in 1835 was visible evidence of the social group to which Thackeray perforce belonged. His acceptance as a Fraserian, later as a "Punch man", fixed his early career firmly in the world of London journalism, a less respectable world, in those days, than the Thackerays were in the habit of entering. There one quality marked him off from his "low" friends: "his *outer breeding*, which," in Carlyle's words, was "fixed enough, and *perfect* according to the modern English style." Thackeray's education, abortive as it had been, was a social distinction in this circle: few of his fellow-Fraserians were Oxford or Cambridge men, and when a friend recommended Thackeray to the more respectable *Blackwood's*, it was as "a gentleman, a Cambridge man". On the other hand, when Thackeray brought together friends from his two worlds, there were often protests from the genteel: Brookfield had to defend the raffish Father Prout to the proper Mrs Brookfield as "a clever scholar and pleasant companion and not indecorous."

Thackeray had constantly to weigh the merits of periodicals against his need for money, for some were respectable and some were not. When he contemplated working on *Punch* friends warned him against associating with the Fleet Street venture and Charles Lever, to whom Thackeray had the presumption to offer advice about the literary market, commented that Thackeray "would write for anything, and about anything, and his status in London is not good." From time to time he tried to break out of the bondage of hack journalism, and on one occasion he even proposed to the editors of *Punch* that he should edit a new "gentlemanlike" paper, which would make use of contributions from his Cambridge friends, and "should have a decided air of white kid gloves." The publishers decided that white kid gloves, in the new literary age, were too expensive and too easily soiled.

The problem of the literary man's social status troubled other, better established authors as well as Thackeray. In 1846 Sir Edward George Earle Lytton Bulwer Bulwer-Lytton, Bart., took the occasion of a charitable venture on behalf of the indigent family of a deceased literary man to apologize in print for literary poverty, and to bewail the waste of high talents on low journalism. It fell to Thackeray to review Bulwer's statement in *Fraser's*, and though he had often confided similar sentiments to his diary (where he had also noted his opinions of Bulwer's novels, and hopes to improve upon them), he bridled at Bulwer's well-meant condescension and airy idealizations. A writer was like a shoe-black, said Thackeray with more vigour than candour; bread was his main incentive, honest work and a clean conscience should alone be his concerns. For, "after all," he asked—perhaps of himself—"what is this Reputation, the cant of our trade . . . ? Why should we get it? Why can't we do without it? We only fancy we want it . . ."

3

When Thackeray came to the attack on fashionable values in the *Yellowplush Papers* in 1837, he was thoroughly familiar with *Fraser's* long-drawn-out campaign against Bulwer (he may even have contributed a line or two to Maginn's satires), and his own assault on Bulwer was cast in Maginn's mould. It was a departure from his "fixed, perfect outer breeding" that he was later sincerely to regret.

Thackeray's contribution to the anti-dandiacal campaign began officially in November 1837, when *Fraser's* assigned him to review a work on etiquette entitled *My Book; or, the Anatomy of Conduct*, by an ex-linen-draper convinced that he was Brummell's true successor as an arbiter of fashionable behaviour. The book aroused all Thackeray's prejudices: against *fashnablisms* and genteelisms, snobs and social climbers. To put down the book and the draper he invented Charles Yellowplush, self-satisfied footman, as author of the review, which he accurately entitled "Fashnable Fax and Polite Annygoats". The idea of a vulgar, uneducated snob of a servant pronouncing on matters of fashionable life was a stroke of minor but unquestionable genius. Yellowplush delighted *Fraser's* readers, and Thackeray was able to write in his name an extended satire of fashionable novels.

That servants were the probable authors of most anonymous fashionable novels (and the source of most high society gossip) was a commonplace of the time, and Maginn had often used it satirically. "Oliver Yorke" makes the point again at the conclusion of the first *Yellowplush* article. After praising the footman's "luxury of fashionable observation" and "intimacy with the first leaders of the *ton*" the editor points out that "he who stands behind a fashionable table knows more of society than the guests who sit at the board. It is from this source that our great novel-writers have drawn their experience . . ."

Yellowplush, as Thackeray draws his portrait in the continued stories of 1838 and 1839, is an upside-down Pelham. He boasts of his elegant *livry*, revels in titles and good society, knows how to be worldly and egotistical. With solemn impudence he explains the origin of his aristocratic name: Charles James Harrington Fitzroy Yellowplush. As coolly as Pelham had recounted his mother's *amours*, Yellowplush slanders his own mother and sets forth the possibility that he is *illygitimit*: "I've always had genlmnly tastes through life, and have no doubt that I come of a genlmnly origum." Like the heroes of other dandy novels, Yellowplush tells his own story, beginning with his family and a blithe outline of his shabby schooling and "jewvenile follies". The vulgarity of his style, studded with genteelisms and mis-spelled French tags, parodies the language of his betters in society and in their fashionable reading—for exclusive conversation is carried on, says Yellowplush, in the "kind of flumry style [which] comes, you see, of reading novvles . . . How much better is it to be puffickly ignorant of the hart of writing, and to trust to the writing of the heart. That is *my* style: arytfiz I despise and trust compleatly to natur."

By modern readers unfamiliar with the butt of Thackeray's parody, the Cockney misspellings of Yellowplushese are often discounted as dialect humour of the most obvious sort. In fact, spelling in the *Yellowplush Papers* is the tool of a bitter satire. For Thackeray's purpose is to underline the difference between what should be fashionable and what is widely considered fashnable; what should be honourable and what is, to the exclusive rabble, honrabble; what should be a gentleman and what, in Regency terms, *is* a genlmn.

Yellowplush's masters illustrate Thackeray's perception of the gap between the truly gentlemanly and the falsely genlmnly. The first of them, Mr Frederic Altamont, is a handsome, well-mannered young man who dresses like a dandy and drives "one of the neatest turnouts" in the Park. As a gentleman he is a fraud, for he earns his genlmnly luxuries as a crossing sweeper. The question of gentlemanly occupations was much in Thackeray's mind at this time, during his first year of full-time magazine work—work which, in Carlyle's memorable phrase, was "below street-sweeping as a trade."

Yellowplush's second and more famous master, the Honrabble Halgernon Percy Deuceace, provides a blunt commentary on the whole questionable morality of the Regency genlmn. His story is set two decades back into the heart of the Regency, and Deuceace is drawn as an out-and-out dandy, the youngest son of an Earl, who goes to "Holmax" and "Crockfud's", moves "in the most xquizzit suckles," lives on "clarrit", "shampang", and "patty defau graw", swings a gold-headed cane and dresses in highly varnished boots and coats by Stulz or Staub. He goes abroad in 1818 and displays his English insolence, abusing the French, swearing at the servants, and swaggering in his self-importance. "With his glas in his i," says Yellowplush, "he staired at every body . . . and he did wright. I've always found through life, that if you wish to be respected by English people, you must be insalent to them, especially if you are a sprig of nobiliaty."

As a genlmn, Deuceace is less a fraud than a scoundrel. His luxurious existence derives not from the mean (if honest) labour of street-sweeping, but from no labour at all. His father the Earl allows him two hundred a year: "it would have been a very comforable maintanants," as Yellowplush says, "only he knever paid him." Thackeray points the class moral in careful Yellow-

plushese: "The young genlmn was a genlmn, and no mistake;
he got his allowents of nothing a year, and spent it in the most
honrabble and fashnabble manner . . . These fashnabble gents
have ways of getten money, witch comman pipple doan't
understand."

Deuceace's "way of getten money" is the way of a gambler.
He cheats at cards, cheats innocent victims, cheats rogues, cheats
his creditors—and comes to grief only when he tries to cheat
his own father, who out-cheats him. Thackeray's hostility to
Deuceace had its roots in experience, for just such a gentlemanly
sharper had won £1500 from him at Cambridge. But Thackeray's
satire is based less on Deuceace's dishonesty than on his society's
willingness to accept a crooked gambler as a genlmn. Yellowplush moralizes:

> I do bleev it was because . . . he was the *Honrabble* Deuceace, that he
> manitched to live as he did. If he had been a common man, you'd have
> said he was no better than a swinler. It's only rank and buth that can
> warrant such singularities as my master show'd. For it's no use
> disgysing it—the Honrabble Halgernon was a GAMBLER. For a man
> of wulgar family, it's the wust trade that can be—for a man of common
> feelinx of honesty, this profession is quite imposibil; but for a real
> thoroughbred genlmn, it's the esiest and most prophetable line he
> can take.

Thackeray moved from a generalized attack on the Regency
genlmn to a specific assault on the literary dandy in the last instal-
ment of the *Yellowplush Papers* ("Mr Yellowplush's Ajew"). It
was of course against Bulwer, *Fraser's bête noire*, that his satire
turned, responding to the most recent episode in the novelist's
long run of good fortune (Bulwer had just been made a baronet).
Thackeray dubs him *Sawedwadgeorgeearllittnbulwig** and brings
him on stage to swagger and sway, to egotize and pontificate.
The announcement of this honour paid to a fashionable writer
convinces Yellowplush to throw up the life of a footman for a

---

* Thackeray's favourite distortion of Bulwer's elegant name as "Bulwig"
was in part a spoof at the absence of *r*'s in Bulwer's speech, a mannerism
belaboured in this sketch, where Bulwer calls for "clawet" and "bwandy-
and-water". It must also have been a snide reference to the fact that Bulwer's
grandfather—for family reasons—had changed his name from Wiggett to
Bulwer.

"littery career". Both the snobbish footman and the dandified novelist are, to Thackeray, genlmn. Yellowplush makes his *ajew* "hoping some day to set on that same bentch of barranites which is deckarated by the presnts of my honrabble friend."

> Why shooden I ? It's trew I ain't done anythink as *yet* to deserve such an honour; and it's very probable that I never shall. But what then ? —*quaw dong*, as our friends say ? I'd much rather have a coat-of-arms than a coat of livry . . .

Bulwer's genlmnly pretensions *as a literary man* antagonized Thackeray: his dandified way of life (in contrast to Thackeray's heavy domestic responsibilities) and his disdain for the bread-and-butter side of the literary market (as opposed to Thackeray's humiliating bondage as a penny-a-liner). Two years later Thackeray brought Yellowplush back to set upon Bulwer again in one of *Fraser's* "Epistles to the Literati". The footman ordered the novelist to stop "this canting about great motifs!"—the boast that he wrote for the glory of literature—in words that satirized the dandy as well as the author.

> The tailor who makes your coats (and very well they are made too, with the best of velvit collars)—I say Stulze or Nugee, might cry out that *their* motifs were but to assert the eturnle truth of tayloring, with just as much reazn; and who would believe them?

Dandy clothes and dandy habits seemed to Thackeray the root cause, almost more than the symptom, of Bulwer's intellectual failings. He used the appurtenances of the dandy life metaphorically and satirically, as *Fraser's* had always done, but with a new, Victorian intensity of feeling. In his recipe for the metamorphosis of Bulwer from a posturing genlmn to a real Man he revealed himself as disturbingly sensitive to surface effeminacies, and as willing to counter with a coarse and nasty Philistinism basically foreign to his own nature. If Bulwer "would but leave off scents for his handkerchief", Thackeray wrote in a *Fraser's* review (1838),

> and oil for his hair; if he would but confine himself to three clean shirts in a week, a couple of coats in a year, a beef-steak and onions for dinner . . . how much might be made of him yet! An occasional pot of porter too much—a black eye, in a tap-room fight with a carman—a night in the watchhouse—or a surfeit produced by Welsh rabbit and

gin and beer, might, perhaps, redden his fair face and swell his slim
waist; but . . . [he would attain] intellectual pluck and vigour . . .

In an 1841 piece for *Fraser's* called "Men and Coats",
Thackeray even blamed the defects of Bulwer's literary style on
Bulwer's dandy costume. Playfully of course, but in that distinctive half-cynical and half-apologetic tone Thackeray reserved for
all moral pronouncements, he announced that a certain "popular
writer is in the habit of composing his works in a large-flowered
damask dressing-gown, and morocco slippers." If he exchanged
the elaborate dressing-gown for the simple jacket he would write
in a different style: terse, uncomplicated, honest. Without the
dressing-gown there would be "no great, long, strealing tails of
periods, no staring peonies and hollyhocks of illustrations, no
flaring cords and tassels of episodes . . ." The rough, manly,
unadorned jacket was becoming a moral symbol to Thackeray;
it was the costume of a gentleman. The genlmn in a dressing-gown
could not possibly be a good writer. Scott wore a jacket; Napoleon
wore a jacket; Carlyle wears a jacket; only "a man IN A JACKET is
a man."

This simple-minded, even childish idea took hold of Thackeray;
indeed, it seized the Victorian imagination. Maginn and his
Fraserians had maintained that good kings and good writers did
not dress like dandies. Carlyle in *Sartor Resartus*, calling on the
great Quaker leader to stitch away at his suit of leather, had insisted that personal dandyism was incompatible with greatness,
and that the greatness of the nation's destiny was at stake.
Thackeray cared less for the nation than for the man, but he
echoed Carlyle's obstinacy on the subject. In their philosophy a
compromise between the good life and the decorative life was
impossible; total renunciation was required. The clothes themselves, the lovely rooms, the exquisite dinners, the wit and the
manner were somehow at fault. Only a man IN A JACKET was a
man.

Carlyle covered the thinness of his anti-dandical position with
the eloquence of rage—and what he knew of the exclusive
Regency justified his fury. Thackeray covered the silliness of his
position, which he was to maintain in novel, essay and sketch
throughout his career, by his consciousness of its stupidity, his
irony, his diffidence. Both men were led to denounce dandyism

for itself, rather than as a cause or a consequence of social evil, by the naïve intensity of their religious upbringing: in Carlyle's case, that of strict dissent from dissent; in Thackeray's, that of the convert's passionate Evangelicalism.

Certainly Thackeray's quest for the gentleman was in part a religious one. Hesitations, anxieties, doubts blocked the choosing of the way, and Thackeray had to shed many outward selves (genlmn, Bohemian, snob, fogy) before he could glimpse the soul of the Christian gentleman. In a thrown-off, scarcely considered paragraph he wrote for *Fraser's*, Thackeray drew a fantasy portrait of himself as hypocrite and hesitant, and he drew it in *Fraser's* favourite metaphor: clothing. The fantasy was part of a parody he wrote in the middle of his first tour of America (over a pseudonym), and it was directed at the inflated, inaccurate accounts of the visiting author then appearing in the American press. The burlesque is illuminating nonsense about Thackeray himself. The author's "daily costume", he wrote

> is a hanging chlamys, or frock coat, which he closely buttons, to avoid the incumbrance of a waistcoat . . . He wears no braces, but his nether garments are sustained by a suspensory belt or bandage of hemp, round his loins. Socks or stockings he despises as effeminate . . . A hair-shirt close to the skin . . . with a changeable linen front of the finest texture; a mortification, or penance, according to his cynical contempt and yet respect for human vanity, is a part of his ordinary apparel . . . With all his excessive simplicity, he is as elaborate in the arrangement of his dress as Count D'Orsay or Mr Brummell . . .

4

"I shall try and go for a fortnight to Spa when I can arrange matters so as to get myself free," Thackeray wrote his mother from Boulogne on July 18, 1848. "And if I like it perhaps I'll stop for six weeks there: and compose that book wh. is coming out. May God Almighty keep me honest and keep pride and vanity down. In spite of himself a man gets worldly and ambitious in this great place: with every body courting & flattering. I am frightened at it and my own infernal pride and arrogance—" The "book wh. is coming out" was *Pendennis*, in the writing during 1848 and 1849 and 1850, and Thackeray's fears of worldliness he explained in a postscript. "What I mean is that all of a sudden I am a great man. I am ashamed of it: but yet I can't help seeing it—being elated by it trying to keep it down—&c."

The brilliant success of *Vanity Fair,* which appeared in book form the day of this letter, had brought Thackeray a new status in his late thirties, and swept him into a society he feared, pooh-poohed and enjoyed. Throughout the years of the serial publication (and the writing) of *Pendennis,* he was dining out at Gore House and Holland House and Devonshire House and Lansdowne House, being accused by his literary friends, from Carlyle to FitzGerald, of absolute snobbery. This was the period of his friendship not only with D'Orsay, but with minor dandies of the D'Orsay set like the Hon. Spencer Cowper, the wealthy young gentleman who later married D'Orsay's widow, and who invited Thackeray to a "Sybaritic repast in a magnificent apartment." "We were all of us young voluptuaries of fashion," Thackeray wrote Mrs Brookfield, and "we young dogs" enjoyed the fine food and "most exquisite liquors", the soft armchairs and brilliant candlelight and sparkling conversation with "quite as pleasant companions as one deserves to meet." "As for your humble servant," he added, "he saw a chapter or two of Pendennis in some of them."

Like other early Victorians, Thackeray could attack the dandy pose in print and find it pleasant company in society. He valued his friendship with the elegant Ainsworth. He was fond of the society of ageing bucks, remnants of the Regency manner like Henry Luttrell and Charles Villiers, Foley Wilmot and "Poodle" Byng. One of his closest friends in France was Roger de Beauvoir; and there were anonymous gentlemen he kept up with for the brilliance of their manner. "I think my father had a certain weakness for dandies," wrote Annie Thackeray some years after his death, adding, with her gift of phrase, "those knights of the broadcloth and shining fronts. Magnificent apparitions used to dawn upon us in the hall, glorious beings ascended the stairs on their way to the study . . ."

The most glorious of them all, according to Thackeray's daughter, was Count D'Orsay, "the most splendid person I ever remember seeing." Recalling one of D'Orsay's visits to her father, she described the dandy as a pagan god, a great Apollo who "seemed to fill the bow-window with radiance." Thackeray may have met D'Orsay in the 'thirties, at one of the *Fraser* dinners or at Ainsworth's house, but their acquaintance officially began in 1848—*after* (D'Orsay took no chances in the literary market) the great success of *Vanity Fair*. Thackeray was taken off to dine at Gore House, where, on one unfortunate occasion, he was tactless enough to criticize Edward Bulwer to his brother Henry, a lapse for which he found himself apologizing to Lady Blessington the following morning. From Thackeray's description (to Mrs Brookfield) of an evening when D'Orsay came to dine, it is easy to see how the novelist was won. D'Orsay drank wine graciously with Thackeray's friends, radiated good humour, complimented a journalist present as "one of the handsomest men he had ever seen", exchanged gossip and news in amusing French-English, and ate vast quantities of roast beef: "He likes it just as well as the best of great dinners. He says it is the best and what is better." This was the authentic D'Orsay charm—smooth and adaptable.

Thackeray was also attached to Lady Blessington, and when the splendours of Gore House were at last auctioned off, he was the only person present, so a servant wrote her, with tears in his eyes. And he proved a good friend in adversity, writing Lady Blessington kind, farewell messages, paying several visits to the exiled D'Orsay, and helping to provide for the support of indigent members of the Blessington family. After the breakup of the Gore House establishment Thackeray made a special pilgrimage to Gore Lodge—a cottage adjoining the main house, which D'Orsay had for a time occupied—and astonished the friend with him by his extraordinary absorption: "Thackeray carefully examined every room from basement to garret, and peered into every nook and cranny, as if to memorize it." It must have given Thackeray a wry satisfaction to revisit Gore Lodge some time later in the company of "Father Prout", when it had become the home of Jack Sheehan, another of the old *Fraser* cronies and the probable model for the "low literary man" Captain Shandon in *Pendennis*.

5

The History of Pendennis is set in the last years of George IV and the first years of William IV—the period, that is, when Bulwer and Disraeli were publishing their dandy novels. *Pendennis* is Thackeray's serious imitation of and commentary on the fashionable novel as Bulwer and Disraeli had made it: the saga of a young man making his way in the world, adopting the dandy manner and moving into society to his profit and loss, especially to his instruction. The book is also autobiography, in a more complex sense than is generally realized. Into this novel Thackeray put not only his actual youth, but the youth he might have been and the middle-aged man he feared he was becoming.

At a small but fashionable college at Oxbridge ("it's *ton* is very good") Pen plays the absolute dandy, described by Thackeray with a wealth of accurate detail. His dress is extravagantly elegant in the late-Regency manner: gorgeous velvet waistcoats, richly embroidered cravats, rings over primrose gloves. His dressing case has the ritual silver mountings. Leader of the fashionable set, he sets the rules of Taste, choosing the correct colour for a satin cravat, the correct foods for a French dinner. "He and his polite friends would dress themselves out with as much care in order to go and dine at each other's rooms, as other folks would who were going to enslave a mistress."

Pen's fastidiousness is obviously modelled on Pelham's. He abandons the study of Mathematics, for example, because "one or two very vulgar young men, who did not even use straps to their trousers so as to cover the abominably thick and coarse shoes and stockings which they wore, beat him completely in the lecture room." And his defences are Pelhamite in their affectation: "That he took perfumed baths is a truth; and he used to say that he took them after meeting certain young men of a very low set in hall." Thackeray enlarges on the glories of Pen's dandyism to show that pride goes before a fall: he is amused and patronizing and very wise about the follies of youth. There is a strongly personal quality to his chastisement of young Pen, as though he were going over the faults of his own early days; but Thackeray had never been Pendennis, even at the height of his Cambridge career. His tastes had been rather luxurious, his habits idle, but he had set no fashions and led no coteries, and his letters and diaries of the period tell not of triumphs but of hesitations, timidity and guilt. He had *wanted*, however, to be Pendennis; what his mature self chastens in the novel is the dream world of his younger self, who read *Pelham*.

In London Pen, like Thackeray, moves into the Temple. But

unlike Thackeray he begins at once to publish fashionable nothings.

> He was by this time . . . pretty well introduced into London, and known both in literary and polite circles. Amongst the former his fashionable reputation stood him in no little stead; he was considered to be a gentleman of good present means and better expectations, who wrote for his pleasure, than which there can not be a greater recommendation to a young literary aspirant.

Fashionable connections had provided the passport to literary success for Bulwer, not for Thackeray, but Thackeray had certainly dreamed of just such an exclusive success on his return from the Continent in 1830.

Pendennis contributes feeble poetry to a fashionable Annual, and is hired to write *"a genuine West End article*—you understand —dashing, trenchant, and d—— aristocratic," for the *Pall Mall Gazette.* And his first novel is published at once, a fashionable success by virtue of its sensational nature, Pen's fashionable reputation and the sycophantic puffery of Bacon and/or Bungay —Thackeray's version of Colburn and Bentley. Begun by Pen in his university years, but put away and forgotten for a time, *Walter Lorraine* is described as being full of Byronic despair and German sentiments, and characters drawn from actual people but elevated in rank "at the request of the publisher". It is a book, then, like nothing Thackeray ever published but very like Bulwer's first *succès de scandale, Falkland.* Again, Pen's career seems to be drawn from Bulwer's, and Thackeray is ambivalent in his attitude toward it, expressing a mixture of disapproval and regret, the grown man's tender animosity toward what might have been himself when young.

Thackeray's early diary testifies to the closeness with which he followed Bulwer's exclusive rise to fame, and the care with which he read *Falkland, The Disowned, Pelham, Devereux* and so on. When he noted his opinion of *Eugene Aram* he was quick to add a hopeful comparison: "The book is in fact humbug, when my novel is written it will be something better I trust." When he judged *Pelham* as "rather dull & very impertinent" he added "—find my ideas verging toward a novel, the plot is not yet conceived—but still I think something witty is coming—Amen—". Thackeray was not to become a literary rival to Bulwer, was not indeed to publish a novel, until both men were middle-aged. But *Pendennis* stands to record Thackeray's shame at having once envied the career of a fashionable writer he morally disapproved. "Bulwer has a high reputation for talent," he had noted in his diary at twenty-one, "& yet I always find myself competing with him—This I suppose must be vanity—If it is truth why am I idle? Here is enough conceit for to night—".

With the brilliant creation of Major Pendennis, Pen's worldly-wise old uncle, Thackeray departs from the fashionable novel formula, which had endowed dandy heroes with social mentors in the form of cynical, ageing ladies—not men. The Major is of the vintage of Brummell, but his class is that of the multitudinous military dandies, like Captain Jesse and Major Chambre and Captain Gronow, who ornamented the Regency and perpetuated its traditions in a later age on the humiliating bounty of "half-pay". Thackeray did his work so well that no one can read Gronow's or Chambre's memoirs, or even Jesse's biography, without hearing the unmistakable accents of Major Pendennis. He is quintessentially the ageing Regency buck, full of anecdotes about the good old days of George III and the Regent, stigmatized by the younger generation of men about town as an "old fogy" and "old wigsby", and in his turn disdainful of the new dandyism, with its fast manner and brightly coloured clothes, its flamboyant whiskers and cigars. ("Confound these young men: how they poison everything with their smoke . . . Every fellow who smokes and wears mustachios is a low fellow.") Thackeray even permits old Pendennis the querulous grandeur of this admonition to the new butterfly dandy, in the person of his nephew Pen: "the old fogies, as you call them, at Bays's, are some of the first gentle-men in England, of whom you youngsters had best learn a little manners, and a little breeding, and a little modesty."

This was another kind of gentleman, that Thackeray, in the years of *Pendennis*, was meeting with increasing frequency now that *Vanity Fair* had made him a personage. He had already studied such a military gentleman of Brummell's period in the person of his wife's uncle, Colonel Shawe, whose anecdotes of the Regency great—particularly Lord Yarmouth—furnished material for Thackeray's novels. He had also read with care Captain Jesse's biography of Beau Brummell, whom Thackeray called, in an 1844 review of the book for the *Morning Chronicle*,

"the model of dandyhood for all time". Thackeray, like a true
Fraserian, had of course taken after Brummell: "Let us . . . not be
too hard upon him," he wrote, "because he was heartless, and a
swindler, a fool, a glutton, and a liar." But he showed more sympathy for the strong side ("simplicity, elegance, and neat impudence and presence of mind. There seems to have been a calmness
about him . . .") than the generality of Jesse's reviewers. And
the biography stayed in his mind: he drew on Jesse as a source for
The Four Georges, and at the end of his life he did a bitter study
of the exiled Brummell in the *Roundabout Papers*.

Much of "Poodle" Byng and Colonel Shawe, Captain Jesse and
Beau Brummell went into Thackeray's portrait of Major Pendennis, but there was also a great deal of Thackeray himself—
again, not so much the real middle-aged Thackeray as the middle-
aged self he wondered, he suspected, he feared he wanted to be.
"I perceive or think I perceive a great change in my character
lately," Thackeray had written remorsefully at twenty-one; "—I
have become much more worldly & far less open to enthusiasm
. . . If I live to fifty I dare say I shall be as cold-blooded & calculating as the worst of them." Now Thackeray was nearing forty
(it felt like sixty) and the old fears of worldliness returned to
plague him with increasing justification. "My vanity would be
to go through life as a gentleman," he wrote Mrs Brookfield,
"—as a Major Pendennis you have hit it—".

Thackeray put another of his ideal visions of himself into the
character of George Warrrington, Pen's manly friend, who em-
bodies his creator's high-minded, Victorian convictions about
gentlemanliness. Warrington's strong moral character, his manner and his appearance provide the antidote to Pen's reprehensible
dandyism. He first appears sitting astride a table and smoking a
pipe; he needs a haircut and wipes beer from his "bristly blue
beard"; he wears a "ragged old shooting-jacket"—that prescribed attire for the great, good man. "He was drinking beer-
like a coal-heaver," says Thackeray, "and yet you couldn't but
perceive that he was a gentleman."

Warrington's function as an antidote demonstrates the weakness of *Pendennis*. Warrington's crusty manliness is set against
Pen's selfish affectation, Laura Bell's solid worth against Blanche
Amory's superficial charms, and Helen Pendennis's motherly
sanctity against the Major's corrupting worldliness. Thackeray

began *Pendennis*, as he began all his novels, with the conviction that the rules of life could be set down in two opposing columns, good against bad—only to discover toward the end a saving confusion in his own sympathies. (Thus Pen's mother comes to irritate Thackeray, as his own mother did, with her rigid intolerance; and the wicked old Major wins him over by his easy-going acceptance of life as it is.) But the preconceived plan of the novel is to set decent provincial people against corrupted city people, country manners against town manners, and finally the morality of Regency London against the morality of the old-fashioned (but now again in fashion) English country life. The note of contrast is struck in the first scene of the novel, where Major Pendennis, eating breakfast at his London club, goes eagerly through his London correspondence, disdainfully leaving for the last a letter from his sister Helen, "which lay solitary and apart from all the fashionable London letters, with a country post-mark and a homely seal."

Helen Pendennis teaches her son to give love with a generous heart, to value self-sacrifice, to pray, to be honest and kind and sexually pure. The Major teaches his nephew to shun emotion, to look out for himself, to go to church only as a social gesture ("he said that every *comme-il-faut* person made a point of attending the English service abroad"), to be calculating and snobbish and arrogant—and to satisfy the desires of the flesh as long as they do not compromise worldly position. His is a consistent morality, as Thackeray points out: "It might not, perhaps, tend to a man's progress in another world, but it was pretty well calculated to advance his interest in this." The suggestion is that Helen's morality suits a man for another world, and that the alternative to worldliness is other-worldliness. Thackeray had wanted to prove with *Pendennis* that the necessary alternative to the dandy was the Christian gentleman.

Carlyle in *Sartor Resartus* had attacked dandyism as a monstrous social delinquency, a vicious, imbecile tendency of the upper class to waste precious time and energy on frivolities. Thackeray was far less concerned with social morality; he wished to find out why every man had something of the dandy in him, to discover the causes and consequences of dandyism in the little domestic world. His persistent habit of reducing issues to their smallest possible dimension irritated Carlyle, who felt that

Thackeray's "test of greatness in a man is whether he would like
to meet him at a tea-party." Thackeray, Carlyle said magis-
terially, "had no convictions, after all, except that a man ought
to be a gentleman, and ought not to be a snob."

In the course of describing his own youth as the history of
Pendennis, Thackeray came to the conclusion that dandyism was
nothing more nor less than selfishness raised to the nth degree,
and that it was a universal failing of the male sex. Men become
dandies, selfish beings convinced that the world revolves about
them, because their mothers make them so—and their wives
compound the error. In this elaborately autobiographical novel
Thackeray returns again and again to the point that the "unfortunate superstition and idol-worship" of Pen's mother are the
cause of Pen's departures from gentlemanliness. His conclusion
at the end of the novel is spoken by Laura Bell, the girl who loves
Pen in spite of herself.

> I often thought our dearest mother spoilt you at home, by worship-
> ping you . . . And as for the world, when men go out into it, I sup-
> pose they cannot be otherwise than selfish. You have to fight for
> yourself, and to get on for yourself, and to make a name for yourself.
> Mamma and your uncle both encouraged you in this ambition. If it
> is a vain thing, why pursue it?

Dandyism is then inescapable as the difference between the
sexes. "Women are pure, but not men. Women are unselfish,
but not men." The neat double columns of Thackeray's moral
ledger hold all the realm of judgment. On the one hand: "What
had made Pen at home such a dandy and such a despot? The
women had spoiled him, as we like them and as they like to do."
And on the other: "Pen was different. Pen was a man. It seemed
natural, somehow, that he should be self-willed and should have
his own way." Thackeray laughingly protests that he would not
"incite the women to revolt", a prospect far indeed from his
mind. The old way of the world is still the best way. In spite of
everything, the dandy Pen is to win success, happiness, the girl
he loves; as a man Thackeray could not bear to punish himself
through Pen. But as a novelist he used the most effective punish-
ment at his command. He withdrew from Pen the gift of heroism.
Let Pen think himself the centre of the universe, and let his women
encourage the deception; the reader will not find Pen at the centre

of his own novel. Thus Thackeray made of *Pendennis*, as he had of *Vanity Fair*, a novel-without-a-hero.

6

The central themes of *Yellowplush* and *Pendennis* absorbed Thackeray throughout his writing life. He dealt with the fashionable novel satirically in a character sketch of "The Fashionable Authoress", in *Vanity Fair*, in *Lords and Liveries* (his parody of Mrs Gore) and in *Codlingsby* (his parody of Disraeli); with fashionable snobbery in the *Snob Papers* and *The Great Hoggarty Diamond*; with dandyism and its gentlemanly alternatives in the *Fitz-Boodle Papers*, *Sketches and Travels in London*, *The Newcomes* and his last essays in the *Cornhill*, the *Roundabout Papers*. After further jibes at Bulwer in *Punch*, Thackeray learned to relax in the security of his own success, and to leave Bulwer alone. Though he always felt a private irritation at the affectations of the man he liked to call "the Knebworth Apollo", he was able to extend Bulwer a handsome, if tardy, public apology for the offences of "the days of hot youth."

There was one genlmn, however, whom Thackeray never ceased belabouring, whose reputation he damaged more permanently than Bulwer's, and to whom he never saw fit to tender an apology: George IV. From the first appearance of Yellowplush in *Fraser's* to Thackeray's last lecture series on *The Four Georges*, the unfortunate Regent was roundly abused. Thackeray's famous denunciation of him as the last and the worst of the Georges set the Victorian attitude to the Regent—and by extension to the Regency era—until the 'nineties. George IV, Thackeray said, was cowardly, extravagant, idle, drunken, debauched, foul-mouthed, gluttonous and fat. His only positive act was the invention of a shoe-buckle. He pretended to encourage the arts, but patronized cooks and ballet-dancers; he pretended to friendship with the Whigs ("That fribble the leader of such men as Pitt and Burke!"), but "his natural companions were dandies and parasites." And worst of all his follies was his fondness for clothes. The other Georges were, with all their own faults, men, and so was William IV, "but this George, what was he?"

> I try and take him to pieces, and find silk stockings, paddings, stays, a coat with frogs and a fur collar, a star and blue ribbon, a pocket-

handkerchief prodigiously scented, one of Truefitt's best nutty-brown wigs reeking with oil, a set of teeth and a huge black stock, under-waistcoats, more underwaistcoats, and then nothing.

The image of the empty heap of clothes came from Fraserian satire. Its relevance to the Regent was suggested to Thackeray by the long-remembered spectacle of the posthumous auction of the King's effects. In the notes made in preparation for this lecture, in fact, Thackeray jotted down a reminder of "the sale of his wondrous wardrobe at his death". And the relevant comment on the Regent's wardrobe came to Thackeray from the title given to George in his lifetime by contemporaries with Regency convictions about gentlemanliness, from Brummell to Byron. "*He* the first gentleman of Europe!" indeed, Thackeray sputtered. There were other candidates for that title, great writers like Scott and Southey, a naval hero like Cuthbert Collingwood: a "Christian soldier" full of "that old English feeling of what I should like to call Christian honour!" But the Regent, never. "There is no stronger satire on the proud English society of that day than that they admired George."

Using the device of the damning comparison, drawn again from *Fraser's*, Thackeray put side by side two scenes from the same year, 1784: the celebration of the opening of Carlton House, and George Washington's resignation of his military command. Thackeray's conclusion was a classic statement of the Victorian concept of the gentleman, and it came most obviously out of a reaction to Regency values.

> Which is the noble character for after ages to admire;—yon fribble dancing in lace and spangles, or yonder hero who sheaths his sword after a life of spotless honour . . . ? Which of these is the true gentleman? What is it to be a gentleman? Is it to have lofty aims, to lead a pure life, to keep your honour virgin; to have the esteem of your fellow-citizens, and the love of your fireside; to bear good fortune meekly; to suffer evil with constancy; and through evil or good to maintain truth always? Show me the happy man whose life exhibits these qualities, and him we will salute as a gentleman, whatever his rank may be . . .

CHAPTER X

Dickens

(1) CHARLES DICKENS, GENT.

Gents! Gents! ye are horrible things
With your slang-looking coats, and gaudy rings:
Where shall a gentleman wander or dwell,
Horrible Gents, but ye come there as well?
—Punch

THACKERAY liked to call the Regency dandy the *genlmn*, and to admire in his place the new Victorian "gentleman". Neither species is to be confused with *The Gent*, an obnoxious specimen of town life that flourished on the London streets in the eighteen-thirties and -forties, to the amusement and indignation of his contemporaries. "The Gent" was a label pasted on young men at the very bottom of the respectable class, the scrubby clerks, apprentices and medical students who scraped along in the backwaters of London on less than £50 a year, calling themselves (hopefully) "gents" and their betters (admiringly) "swells". The Gent was a creature of once-a-month sprees and splurges, of false fronts to calico shirts, of phony jewellery, half-price tickets to the theatre, greasy hair and dirty ears. He was a second-hand, shop-worn imitation of the dandy.

The Gents thrived on the disreputable new ready-to-wear clothing shops of early Victorian London. These shops provided their clothes and also, often, their livelihood: the most commonly caricatured breed of Gent was the haberdasher's or linen draper's clerk known as the "counter-jumper" of the "cheap shop". Clothes displayed in the windows of these shops were commonly ticketed *Gent's. Newest Fashion*, and the name for the Gent species probably originated from this derisive abbreviation. To flatter the Gent's snobbery the cheap tailors called their fashions after aristocrats and dandies: the "Chesterfield" great-coat; the

"Byron tie"; the "Gent's. Patent Alberts" (His Highness's favourite boot, with a shiny leather toe and mock-pearl false buttons down the side). An especially large variety of outlandish garments was named after D'Orsay, Patron Dandy of the Gent. "If the things are not dignified by these terms," wrote a contemporary authority, "the Gent does not think much of them."

The Gent's style borrowed heavily from the faded extravagances of the years of William IV. To discards of dandy fashion he added vulgarisms of his own: glaring patches of colour, pattern and ornament to atone for indifferent cut and shoddy materials. Peculiar to the Gent were the bright blue handkerchief with large white dots, trousers in gaudy checks, the "D'Orsay" blouse of puckered calico with braid round the pockets, rings of coloured glass, huge stick-pins made of something called "electro gold" and resembling, according to merciless *Punch*, "large white currants with gilt eels twisting around them" or "blanket-pins with water on the brain". The Gent could most easily be recognized—from a distance—by his waistcoats, of which he wore two or even three: shrieking tartan over damson-coloured silk over a false roll-collar in flowered satin.

Early Victorian satirists had a good deal of malicious pen and pencil fun with the Gent. The early volumes of *Punch* described him in detail with a technique borrowed from the French press: the short humorous sketch in mock-scientific style originally called the *physiologie*, and naturalized in England as the physiology or social zoology or natural history. The importation was sponsored by Albert Smith, a well-travelled lightweight journalist with a flair for publicity and showmanship. One of the original *"Punch* men", and one of the "low literary men" with whom Thackeray found amusement at the Cider Cellars, Smith had begun life in London as a poor medical student and must surely have been something of a Gent himself. In a fully illustrated miniature volume called *The Natural History of the Gent*, he set down the Gent class, with scientific accuracy, as the product of "our present condition of society—that constant wearing struggle to appear something more than we in reality are."

Gents are to be found, Smith writes, in the Park on Sundays (where they go to ogle the nobs), on the short steamers on holidays, in the tops of omnibuses in the early morning, and at billiard parlours, taverns, theatres and promenade concerts at night—particularly at night, "when Gents and cheap umbrellas chiefly flourish." The Gents live (very poorly) in lodgings. They form intimate friendships with young men just like themselves, with whom they loudly sing tavern songs as they walk down the street arm-in-arm—often as many as six abreast, to the disgust of other pedestrians. They like cigars and whiskey, neither of which agrees with them. They have their own characteristic slang, half outdated Tom-and-Jerryisms, half dateless Cockney: "the cheese", "the Stilton" and "the ticket" as synonyms for the fashion, and "nobby", "the right sort", "flash", "a downy cove", "up to everything", "doing the fast thing, and no mistake" to characterize the fashionable. They have a passion for all things theatrical, and their style of dress has much of the "light comedian" about it. They are very young, very gullible, very fresh and very vulgar, and they dream of falling into money.

The Gent appeared frequently in early Victorian fiction. Thackeray drew him in *The History of Samuel Titmarsh and the Great Hoggarty Diamond*, which appeared in *Fraser's* in 1841. Young Titmarsh is himself the "thirteenth clerk of twenty-four young gents who did the immense business of the Independent West Diddlesex Fire and Life Insurance Company." The aspirations of the group are represented by the open-mouthed Gus Hoskins, drawn in front of a shop on Coventry Street, with a cigar in his mouth ("to give himself as it were a *distingué* air") and his hands in his pockets:

> as Gus stretched out his pantaloons as wide as he could from his hips, and kept blowing away at his cheroot, and clamping with the iron heels of his boots, and had very large whiskers for so young a man, he really looked quite the genteel thing, and was taken by everybody to be a person of consideration.

A study of the Gent more depressing than Thackeray's, Samuel Warren's *Ten Thousand a-Year*, appeared (in book form) during the same year. Now neglected as a work of fiction, Warren's bulky novel is invaluable as a study in "social zoology". The subject is a verminous little Gent name Tittlebat Titmouse, a self-styled "tallow-faced counter-jumper" in a "cheap shop", who lives in lodgings on thirty-five pounds a year, spends his Sundays lounging in Hyde Park "to see the swells and the fashions", and dreams of money: "Say that somebody was to leave me lots of

cash—many thousands a-year, or something in that line! My
stars! wouldn't I go it with the best of them!" Warren's originality is to give the Gent his wish, in the form of a mysterious
inheritance amounting to the impressive figure in the title of the
novel, and to observe "how the reptile propensities of his mean
nature had thriven beneath the sudden sunshine of unexpected
prosperity."

The first chapters of the novel are devoted in their entirety to
Titmouse's toilette, a horrid operation carried forth in the spirit
of snobbery and sham amidst the realities of poverty and filth. As
Titmouse dresses he muses on a genuine, aristocratic dandy he
has seen in the Park on a Sunday. "What trousers!—they stuck
so natural to him, he might have been born in them. And his
waistcoat and satin stock—what an air!" Titmouse is most particular about the dressing of his hair, the crown and glory
peculiarly sacred to the Gent as a symbol of his strivings after
fashion—and maturity, and masculinity:

> Every hair of his spreading whiskers was sacred from the touch of
> steel; and a bushy crop of hair stretched underneath his chin, coming
> curled out on each side of it, above his stock, like two little horns
> or tusks. An imperial—*i.e.* a dirt-coloured tuft of hair, permitted to
> grow perpendicularly down the upper-lip of puppies—and a pair of
> promising moustaches . . .

It was D'Orsay who had established ornamental whiskers as
a sign of fashion, and it is the great D'Orsay who inspires Titmouse and points Warren's moralizing. Like most Victorians,
Warren found the Gent a revolting excrescence of the new era
and the new middle class. But with all that he was preferable,
Warren concluded, to the genuine dandy of the D'Orsay class.

> What was the real difference between Count Do-'em-all and Mr
> Tittlebat Titmouse? Only that the Count had dark hair and whiskers,
> and owed more money than Mr Titmouse's creditors could be per-
> suaded to allow *him* to owe! Would to Heaven—thought Titmouse
> —that any one tailor would patronize *him* as half a dozen had
> patronized the Count!

2

Among the young men who could have been mistaken for
Gents in the late 'twenties and early 'thirties (before the species

had a name) was Charles Dickens, then in his 'teens or barely out of them, working his way slowly up the social ladder as a lawyer's clerk, then as a reporter for the newspapers. Dickens had begun very early to fuss over his appearance, to conceal the awkwardness of a boy under the clothes of a man of fashionable pretensions, to comb his vanity into his hair. There were no whiskers yet, but he had a fine head of lustrous brown hair which he wore, in one of the romantic fashions of the day, parted on the side and long, almost billowing out over his temples and ears. This was the time when Dickens formed passionate friendships with fellow-clerks (with whom he walked two or three abreast in the approved manner), smoked his first cigars, drank his first whiskey-and-water and roamed the London streets till he knew them by heart. At this time he laid serious plans to become an actor and, as he confided to Forster many years later, "went to some theatre every night, with a very few exceptions, for at least three years; really studying the bills first, and going where there was the best acting."

In his first published volume, *Sketches by Boz*, Dickens suggested a portrait of the artist as a shrewd and observant young Cockney enjoying in the company of his fellow clerks the most modest pleasures of life-upon-town: "we keep no horse, but a clothes-horse; enjoy no saddle so much as a saddle of mutton . . ." Boz is familiar with the streets, the Sunday pleasure haunts and most of all the theatres. These are full of Gents, especially the so-called "private theatres" where the stage-struck young men pay money to play their favourite parts—"divers boys of from fifteen to twenty-one years of age, who throw back their coat and turn up their wristbands, after the portraits of Count D'Orsay, hum tunes and whistle when the curtain is down . . . and speak familiarly of the inferior performers . . ." "Dirty boys," Dickens calls them, "low copying-clerks in attorneys' offices . . ."

By 1836, the year of *Boz*, Dickens could safely look down on the lawyer's clerk. He was soaring upward like the pilot balloon to which, in his first preface, he compared the *Sketches*, "trusting it may catch favourable current, and devoutly and earnestly hoping it may *go off well*", as it carried along in its attached car "not only himself, but all his hopes of future fame, and all his chances of future success." Although only twenty-four, he had already achieved a position of respect on an important newspaper, seen his first writings in print, and been taken up by such personages as Thomas Noon Talfourd and Harrison Ainsworth.

The blazing triumph of *Pickwick* in 1837, reinforced by the extraordinary popularity of *Oliver Twist* the next year, brought Dickens in his mid-twenties the status of a literary lion. He began to be a frequent visitor at Samuel Rogers's pretty home, at Holland House and Gore House. Through Ainsworth and Talfourd Dickens came to know Bulwer and D'Orsay, and around this time, one of his friends recalled some years later, there could be observed "a great difference in Charles Dickens's appearance and dress, for he had bought a new hat and a very handsome blue cloak, with black velvet facings, the corner of which he threw over his shoulder *à l'Espagnol* . . ." The young Gent in *Boz*, to whom Count D'Orsay had meant only a name and a portrait, now became an unabashed follower of the D'Orsay style: the cut of the curve, brilliance of colour, ornament, materials. For the daytime Dickens affected a swallow-tail coat with a very high velvet collar, an enormous, billowing black satin stock with double breast-pin; a crimson or green velvet waistcoat (sometimes two under-waistcoats) with a very long gold chain "meandering over it", and tight or "Cossack" trousers; for evening, black pantaloons with buttons at the ankles, speckled black silk stockings and pumps, a puffed out shirt-frill and a white cravat ornamented with a bow "about eight inches wide!" Over all this, there was the pretty face, oval and girlish, with slightly protruding, half-open lips, brilliant eyes, and a glistening head of brown hair either falling into his eyes or curling (artificially) over his temples.

This was the Dickens of the famous "Nickleby" portrait by Maclise, and of the less well known but perhaps even more characteristic sketch by Cruikshank: young Dickens seated in an armchair in a very elegant pose, his tightly-trousered legs crossed, his head resting languidly on his right hand. This was also the "Pickwick" who met Carlyle for the first time in 1840, at a dinner for "lords and lions". Carlyle took away the impression of a strikingly mobile face set over "a small compact figure . . . dressed à la D'Orsay rather than well." And this was the Dickens who appeared backstage at St James's Theatre one night to dazzle George Augustus Sala, then only a boy, and to impress him as having been "next to Count D'Orsay, the choicest and most tastefully dressed dandy in London."

The bulk of contemporary opinion on Dickens's appearance veered more to Carlyle's view than Sala's: that Dickens dressed à la D'Orsay *rather than* well. His friends were struck mainly by his piercing eyes and his face, that always changing, lively, expressive actor's face of Dickens the Inimitable, the Man of Genius. ("What a face it is to meet in a drawing-room!" exclaimed Leigh Hunt. "It has the life and soul in it of fifty human beings.") Most people felt that the face alone expressed the true Dickens, and they refused to notice what he was wearing. But those who did notice his clothes were most often dismayed. Adolphus Trollope long remembered the shock of his first sight of Dickens in the 'forties. "We were at first disappointed," he recalled, "and disposed to imagine there must be some mistake! No! *that* is not the man who wrote 'Pickwick!' What we saw was a dandified, pretty-boy-looking sort of figure . . . with a slight flavour of the whipper-snapper genus of humanity." It was somehow disturbing that the novelist who gave humour and pathos with so generous a hand could appear in person to be devoted to a kind of dandyism—and a dandyism marred by a liberal dash of Cockney vulgarity.

The contrast between Dickens's appearance and Dickens's personality—at least as deduced from his novels—was particularly remarked when he went to America in 1842. Dickens had refurbished his wardrobe with special extravagance for the great tour; the Americans were eager to associate an unfamiliar man with a familiar author, and noticed everything. He came off the boat with his hair in corkscrew curls—and a debate broke out as to whether the great Boz took the trouble to curl his hair. For his evening lectures he appeared in conventional, black, formal dress, but his waistcoats—and this most shocked Boston—were velvet, in crimson or brilliant green. (Dickens had brought along one waistcoat in proper black satin, but it was richly embroidered with flowers, and with it he wore a black neckcloth traced with colour and fixed with two large diamond pins.) The press stigmatized these waistcoats in the Gent's language, as "somewhat on the flash order".

"Mr Dickens's vivid tints were very conspicuous," protested a young lady in Boston; another young lady in Cincinnati confessed to "considerable disappointment" in the appearance of her "idol": his manner was "easy, negligent, but not elegant. His dress was foppish; in fact, he was overdressed . . ." "Disappointed in Dickens's appearance," began Charles Henry Dana's diary notation of his first impressions. After sourly listing the details that distressed him (such as "a dissipated looking mouth with a vulgar draw to it", and "stubby fingers and a hand by no means patrician") Dana concluded with a regretful admission of the strong "Gent" air of the novelist he earnestly admired:

> He looks wide awake, "up to everything," full of cleverness, with quick feelings and great ardor. You must admire him and there is a fascination about him which keeps your eye on him, yet you cannot get over the impression that he is a low bred man . . .
> He has what I suppose to be the true Cockney cut . . .

3

To Dickens, as to the Gent, the art of dress meant nothing; but he took a naïve, almost childlike pleasure in dressing up. In one of his very rare comments about his own clothes, Dickens once confessed that he had "the fondness of a savage for finery". He could also, like Disraeli, further ambition with the drama of dress. Disraeli, however, had lived on the border of a society that recognized only the *ins* and the *outs* (ignoring vast reaches of the lower orders, which were nowhere), and clothes helped to get him *in*. Dickens hoped merely to push himself vaguely *up*, up and away from the poverty-, jail- and debt-ridden world of his childhood. Far from idealizing the aristocratic *ins*, the young Dickens viewed what he called the "nobs" as remote, mysterious, vaguely sinister creatures from a world apart. He would never be a snob or a tuft-hunter.

Early fame brought Dickens an introduction to the last remnants of exclusive Regency society; he was curious, momentarily flattered, never overwhelmed. Indeed his refusal to be patronized; his fierce self-confidence; his jaunty, careless, independent manner in the presence of those who considered themselves his betters, destroyed for ever the system of literary lionizing. Lady Holland tried to snub him, and he would not be snubbed. The Misses Berry, whose intimate relation with seventy years of the English past reduced Thackeray to nostalgic tears, called to invite Dickens to dinner, but he found himself too busy to accept. (They had to invoke the aid of Sydney Smith, who wrote Dickens, "Pray come, it is as much as my place is worth to send them a refusal.")

Sam Rogers cautiously opened the door of his house on the Green Park, and Dickens countered by asking Rogers to tea, and dedicating a book to him. Lady Blessington threw open the doors of Gore House to him, and Dickens promised her a contribution for the *Keepsake* which he delivered four years later, though, as he wrote another friend, "for scattered scraps of writing here and there I really have no leisure." D'Orsay exerted the famous D'Orsay charm, and Dickens responded with enthusiasm ("quel homme, quel ange . . .!" he wrote Forster); then he paid D'Orsay the astonishing compliment of asking him to stand as godfather to his sixth child. The other godfather was Tennyson, and the unfortunate boy was duly christened Alfred D'Orsay Tennyson Dickens, a name received in sophisticated circles with some amusement. Robert Browning observed to Elizabeth Barrett that "Alfred is common to both the godfather and the devil-father," and Edward FitzGerald thought the name reeked of "Snobbishness and Cockneyism". Snobbishness it was not, as Dickens was genuinely fond of D'Orsay; but it was a name for a Gent to be proud of.

Dickens named sons after his Regency friends and dedicated books to them, and when they were ill and penniless he got up subscriptions on their behalf. If there was condescension in the relationship, it was on Dickens's side. In a letter he wrote a friend after making a quick survey of London society on his return from America, he gave his image of them: it was jaunty, detached, irreverent.

Lady Holland has fitted up some of the lower rooms at Holland House, and there are dinners there, as of yore . . . Sydney Smith is in greater force than ever, though waxing gouty . . . Brougham is in good health and spirits. Lyndhurst has been ill, but is recovering. Jeffrey is much better, and sits in his court again. Rogers is a thought more deaf than he was eight months ago. Tom Moore ages. Mrs Norton and Lady Seymour are both sights for the Gods, as they always have been. Poor Southey's case is quite hopeless. Landor is confined at home by bailiffs, but is not an atom the worse in temper, health, looks, or spirits. Lady Blessington wears brilliantly, and has the

gloss upon her, yet. Bulwer is out of town, and I have not yet seen
him . . .

Bulwer was the closest to Dickens of the Regency literati, and
their relationship brought out all of Dickens's self-confidence.
He had his first glimpse of Bulwer in the House of Commons—
when he was a shorthand reporter and Bulwer, only nine years
his senior, an M.P. They were introduced in the late 'thirties by
Ainsworth and began to exchange dinners. Bulwer gave Dickens
all praise and encouragement, and introduced him to society
figures. (Once, to Bulwer's indignation, he had to assure Lady
Holland that "Boz was presentable.") This generosity came in
spite of the fact that "the great Boz" (as Bulwer wrote Forster)
". . . certainly never needed my good word . . .—yea, tho' I
foresaw that he of all men was the one that my jealousy might
best be aroused by." And when in a few years Dickens's fame did
pass Bulwer's, the acquaintance continued, bolstered by Forster,
who was an intimate friend of both men. Dickens and Bulwer
worked closely together in the 'fifties, when they were co-
founders of the ill-fated Guild for Art and Literature.

Dickens was one of the few Victorians to whom Bulwer's
lingering dandyism must have been impressive rather than distasteful. But a mutual, if very different concern with dress was
not the bond between the two novelists. Their friendship rested
on the fact that they were both successful, prosperous literary
men, the only two nineteenth-century English novelists to whom
fame, money and honour came early and stayed late. They exchanged books and criticisms, influenced each other's work (it
was Bulwer who told Dickens to give *Great Expectations* a happy
ending) and banded together to fight for the independent dignity
of the literary calling. Starting from opposite ends of the world,
the two lions met in the mid-century.

Dickens's contribution to the cause of literary dignity was far
greater than Bulwer's, because every achievement in his career
marked a defeat for the tyranny of exclusivism in the world of
letters. His unconscious blow against lionizing was only the
beginning. The success of his early novels about the poor and
lower middle class demonstrated that fashion was not necessarily
the formula for a popular book. His choice of the serial form of
publication for *Pickwick*, despite his friends' warnings that it was

10. Daniel Maclise: Bulwer (1832)

Alfred d'Orsay

AUTHOR OF "JOURNAL"

Published by James Fraser, 215 Regent Street, London.

11. Daniel Maclise: Count D'Orsay (1834)

"a low, cheap form of publication", fastened "parts" on the English novel for fifty years, and took away from an aristocratic coterie the power of determining literary fame. "Conversation turned on Boz, the new comic writer," wrote the darling of Almack's, Tom Moore, in his diary, one day in 1837. "Was sorry to hear Sydney Smith cry him down, and evidently without having given him a fair trial; whereas, to me it appears one of the few proofs of good taste that 'the masses', as they are called, have yet given, there being some as nice humour and fun in the Pickwick Papers as in any work I have seen in our day."

Dickens's arrogant, independent method of dealing with his publishers (his letters to Bentley and Chapman & Hall are a whole world—of time and temperament—away from Thackeray's letters to *Fraser's*) demonstrated that authors could get rich on literature, and that authors, not publishers, ruled the literary scene. It was the end of Colburn and his ways; and it is a wry comment on the passage of the puff that Colburn's fortune went to his widow, and Colburn's widow went to John Forster. They were married in 1855, when Forster was at the height of his Podsnap period.

4

In the 'forties Dickens put his youth behind him and drank in his success. Adolphus Trollope marked the passage from Dickens's face of that "look of delicacy, almost of effeminacy" that had puzzled him some years before. "In later life he lost this D'Orsay look completely . . . In fact, when I saw him subsequently in London, I think I should have passed him without recognizing him. I never saw a man so changed." His features, as well as his figure, had coarsened and broadened; his expression was now less ethereal, more hearty and open; his face became weather-bronzed and red from exertion and over-eating, and he grew moustaches. But his delight in dressing-up stayed with him.

In the later eighteen-forties and -fifties, men's clothes underwent a gloomy change. In place of the D'Orsay cut, which emphasized a slim, youthful figure with graceful, curving lines, the fashion was to look stiff, portly and middle-aged. Materials were heavier, trousers were baggy and shapeless, exuberant cravats gradually dwindled into narrow ties. Dickens followed all these fashions, but he kept his jewellery, his wide velvet collars—and his waistcoats. These last were, on occasion, brighter than ever, made of heavy patterned velours or staring tartans. For his trousers he chose loud tweeds, and he wore brighter colours than were customary for literary men: according to legend, he went to his first sitting for the Frith portrait wearing—to the painter's horror—a sky-blue overcoat with red cuffs.

And in the last years of his life—the years of the readings, of the dissolution of his marriage, of ill health and of the blackest of his novels—Dickens's clothes became stranger still. Everyday male dress in the 'sixties was probably the ugliest ever worn: black settled over the Victorians like a pall, cloth wrinkled into deep, greasy folds, and huge straggling beards turned men at the height of their powers into solemn patriarchs. But Dickens, despite the beard which he had dutifully, even gleefully grown, came to resemble an altogether different sort of Victorian figure—the raffish Heavy Swell, a remote and prosperous descendant of the Gent (via the Man About Town and the Swell) who took to the London streets in the 'sixties. The formal dress in which Dickens appeared for his readings was conventionally black-and-white, but as Sala wrote, "he was one of the few men whose individuality was not effaced by the mournful conventionality of evening dress." Part of the reason was the persistent magic of his personality, but equally important were the heavy gold chains that hung down his waistcoat, ending in a dangling bunch of seals and trinkets; his oddly combed, brilliantined earlocks; and the strange combination of flowers (violets and a camellia, for instance) that made up his ever-present boutonnière. To these embellishments, all beloved of the Heavy Swell, were added on occasion the Swell's stovepipe hat, out-size cuff-links and rings and tiepins, coloured waistcoats, slanting cloaks. His favourite costume of this period was the walking coat that ornaments the Gurney photograph from Dickens's final trip to America, and dominates the astonishingly irreverent caricature drawn by Spy in the year of Dickens's death, showing him as a crazy old man advancing tipsily down the street. Cut to swoop from shoulder to mid-thigh in great flaring diagonals, the coat was all jet black, decorated with out-size round buttons and deep cuffs of narrowly tucked silk, its silk lining, collar and reveres quilted in an elaborate scrolled pattern.

Dickens sat for the Gurney photograph with this coat thrown open on one side and his hand thrust jauntily in his trouser pocket —to display the braid and velvet of his jacket lapels against the gala lining of his favourite coat.

It was Dickens the actor, rather than Dickens the novelist, who dressed like the Heavy Swell. There had always been something vaguely theatrical about his style of dress. At the beginning of his career people who sensed his Gentism defined it regretfully as the air of young men who hung about stage doors. ("You frequently meet similar-looking young men," one reporter explained, "at the theatres and other public places." "Take the genius out of his face," suggested a disappointed admirer, "and there are a thousand London shopkeepers about the theatres and eating houses who look exactly like him . . .") In middle age, as Dickens began to look less like a stage-struck hanger-on and more like an actor, his dress came to be flatly described as "a gay costume—theatrical in style rather than literary." In fact, he was now attempting to find a second career in acting, amateur but quite in earnest: theatricals at home, charity performances and the final readings.

As his dandy friends died off or mellowed, Dickens found inspiration for his clothes in his theatrical friends. From Macready, the actor with whom Dickens was most intimate, he not only copied but borrowed, in the case of one glorious waistcoat worn by the actor on the stage and in private life. Dickens remembered it as "a remarkable and precious waistcoat, wherein certain broad stripes of purple disported themselves by a combination of extraordinary circumstances, too happy to occur again." He wanted the loan of it for a very special occasion, the marriage of Christiana Weller, with whom he had had one of his imaginary love affairs, and asked Macready to let him show it to his tailor ("my artist", Dickens called him) "as a sample of my tastes and wishes." He planned to "—ha, ha, ha, ha!—eclipse the bridegroom!" And his letter to Macready ended with bravado: "I will send a trusty messenger . . . He is sworn to secrecy. He durst not for his life betray us, or swells in ambuscade would have the waistcoat at the cost of his heart's blood."

Dickens was to play a part at the wedding, and the sublime waistcoat would be his costume. This playing of parts, which he did more and more as he grew older (on the stage, in the lecture hall, in his novels and letters), was a release for those superabundant energies which made him increasingly restless and dissatisfied. It was also an essential escape from the confining pattern of existence the Victorians insisted was proper for their great men. The very sights and smells of the theatre put Dickens in a state of magnificent excitement—"such a confusion of unaccountable shapes of beams, bulkheads, brick walls, ropes, and rollers, and such a mixing of gaslight and daylight, that . . . seemed . . . the wrong side of the pattern of the universe."

What dandyism Dickens had was the actor's dandyism. Where the actor's temperament touches on the dandy's temperament, there Dickens and dandyism touched. He had the actor's relish for the pose. He had the actor's vanity, evident in a passion for mirrors and a curious fetish of combing his hair "one hundred times a day". He had the actor's flair for disguise, for exaggeration, for effect. Unlike many Victorians, he felt neither shame nor guilt in getting up an appearance, rather a sense of release and of excitement. In this bastard theatrical dandyism Dickens approached most closely to Disraeli, a man with whom he had no personal sympathy and many political disagreements. Disraeli he referred to, borrowing Carlyle's words, as impostor and humbug. But it was part of Dickens's complexity to have something of the humbug in his own personality, and a hidden sympathy with the impostors—the dandies, the actors, the Micawbers—of this world.

(II) CHARLES DICKENS, GENTLEMAN

5

Conscious class judgments came late to Dickens, and the dandified aristocracy Thackeray attacked from the start of his writing career in *Fraser's* hardly figured in Dickens's early books. Although in the 'thirties and early 'forties, in the years of his first success, Dickens was going frequently "into society", the whole world of his early novels was middle class, and class hardly mattered.

The very few aristocratic characters in the early novels are aliens from stage melodrama and stage farce (seen nightly by the young Boz at the popular theatres). In *Nicholas Nickleby* (1838–9) for example, Sir Mulberry Hawk and Lord Frederick Verisopht are stock villains with stage names. The former is all black, a "systematic and calculating man of dissipation"; the latter is "not thoroughly irredeemable" for he conceals a bit of a tender heart beneath his irritatingly "dandified and listless air". The villain of *Barnaby Rudge* (1841) is almost equally theatrical and unreal. Selfish, hypocritical, totally corrupt, Sir John Chester exhibits the fine manners of the scoundrel nobleman of melodrama: he lounges, poses, takes snuff, uses scent—and dresses elegantly in a style anachronistic to the period of the novel (the seventeen-seventies.) But Sir John Chester, M.P., also arouses in Dickens rumblings of a naïve class radicalism. His name must be a reference to the Lord John Crewe for whom Dickens's grandmother had worked as housekeeper, and after whom Dickens's father had probably been named: Lord John had been M.P. for Chester before he was raised to the peerage.

A significantly more mature class attitude characterizes the books of Dickens's "middle period"—roughly from *Martin Chuzzlewit* (1843–4) to *David Copperfield* (1849–50). His unquestioned, almost unconscious allegiance to the middle class, right or wrong, then gave way to critical disillusionment. (The change resulted ostensibly from his first tour of America in 1842, which, besides being reward and proof of success, showed Dickens the disagreeable realities of a presumably "classless" but actually middle-class society.) The middle books are in large part devoted to vigorous denunciations of the self-righteous Pecksniffs, Murdstones and Dombeys of the moneyed bourgeoisie. In *Dombey and Son* (1846–8), the finest of this group, antagonism to the upper middle class makes room for a tentative sympathy with the standards of the higher orders of society, who (as Edith Dombey's aristocratic family) are extensively personified for the first time in Dickens's work. And in *Dombey's* successor *David Copperfield* (that unsatisfying transitional production which harks back to the sugary sentiment of the *Pickwick* period as it looks forward to the deeper themes of the late novels), Dickens for the first time draws a character whose 'aristocratic' temperament, manners and attitudes play a major part in the novel. Steerforth the wicked seducer is merely a repetition of immature melodrama; but Steerforth, the schoolboy hero of David

Copperfield, is Dickens's first attempt to deal with a problem that
would bedevil him in maturity.

Disillusionment with the middle class came late to Dickens,
and it implied disillusionment with himself, particularly with the
ideals his youthful ambition had unquestioningly strained after
and his early success had easily achieved. Thackeray, shocked by
an early loss of social status, had asked from the beginning, Am
I a gentleman? Only in his middle years, in the uneasy enjoyment
of success, did Dickens come to a similar question, and then he
phrased it indirectly, nervously, tentatively as: Should I be a
gentleman, after all? Steerforth is the first personification of that
question.

Some time around 1850, the year of the completion of *Copperfield*, the pilot balloon sent bravely aloft by the young Boz reached
its maximum altitude, and from then until the end of the journey
in 1870 would bobble aimlessly above the Victorian world. From
his exalted eminence Dickens faced the dilemma put into words
by the lovelorn Mr Venus of *Our Mutual Friend*:

> And so a man climbs to the top of the tree, Mr Wegg, only to see that
> there's no look-out when he's up there! I sit here of a night surrounded
> by the lovely trophies of my art, and what have they done for me?
> Ruined me . . .

In the decade that followed Dickens reached forty, felt middle
aged, looked middle-aged, and marked the change by growing
a moustache and then a beard. The terrifying memories of childhood, which he had stirred to the surface by writing *David
Copperfield*, came back to overwhelm him at the death of his father
in 1851 and, four years later, in the grotesque reunion with Maria
Beadnell, his childhood sweetheart. He bought Gad's Hill, the
house that had symbolized his youthful dreams of wealth. At the
same time his early love affair with the theatre exploded into an
obsession, and by 1853 he was already reading for the public.

Theatrical ventures led to relationships symptomatic of disillusionment: a new friendship with Wilkie Collins, a love affair
with Ellen Ternan. The too-faithful, too-earnest Forster felt
resentfully that he was being displaced in the Inimitable's affections by a new, unsavoury crowd: notably "Dickens's Young
Men", who wrote for *Household Words*, young men more untidy
and aimless in their way of life than Forster (Sala, Percy Fitz-

gerald, Edmund Yates, particularly Collins). In maudlin self-pity Dickens complained to Forster about the "sense" that "always comes crushing upon me now, when I fall into low spirits, as of one happiness I have missed in life, and one friend and companion I have never made"—a curious dissatisfaction to confide in Forster, who wished to be the all-in-all to each of his friends.

For Ellen Ternan's companionship Dickens destroyed his marriage and broke up his home. His brothers wore him out with their constant complaining and sponging; his wife's parents, of whose gentilities he had once boasted, grated on his nerves; his children, grown out of pretty infancy, were a source of anxiety and discomfort. Domesticity became little but an irritation to the man who had once advised young couples to believe "that round the household gods Contentment and Tranquillity cluster in their gentlest and most graceful forms; and that many weary hunters of happiness throughout the noisy world have learnt this truth too late, and found a cheerful spirit and a quiet mind only at home at last." Now, according to his daughter Kate, "he did not care a damn what happened to any of us. Nothing could surpass the misery and unhappiness of our home."

With the change in the man came a corresponding change in the novels. They grew gradually more complex—more atmospherically dense, as Edmund Wilson has put it—and more sombre, while Dickens's view of Victorian society grew more subtle and more harsh. From 1852, the year of *Bleak House*, to 1859, the year of *A Tale of Two Cities*, Dickens wrote what Lionel Stevenson has called the "dark novels"; the books of the 'sixties, still more despairing, might be called the black novels. In any case, all the late novels, beginning with *Bleak House*, abandoned Dickens's early optimism and showed evil forces triumphing meanly over good.

Also peculiar to these books of the 'fifties and 'sixties is the fact that they are, like Thackeray's fiction and for reasons not vastly dissimilar, novels-without-a-hero. Almost all of the earlier novels had been built around a central figure, some thin stock character who is, nevertheless, enough of a hero to give a name to the book in which he appears. Nicholas Nickleby, Martin Chuzzlewit, David Copperfield are all pretty much of a virtuous piece: sentimental young things, gentle and girlish, with a refinement of manner a bit above their class—ideal images, that is, of the young Dickens of blacking-house days. They are fond of domestic ties, clean, proper, chivalrous and tender-hearted—as well as courageous in their campaign against injustice and misery. For they have the energy and optimism of the young, and confidence that good intentions and hard work can right the wrongs of the world. "Youth is not prone to contemplate the darkest side of a picture it can shift at will," Dickens had commented on young Nickleby's momentary despondency over the evils of society. "By dint of reflecting on what he had to do . . ., Nicholas gradually summoned up his utmost energy, and when the morning was sufficiently advanced for his purpose, had no thought but that of using it to his best advantage . . ."

As Dickens's view of society became more sophisticated, this naïve heroism gradually disappeared from his novels. As he came to question his youthful ideals the Nicklebys and Copperfields vanished altogether. In their place, beginning in the books of the 'fifties and persisting up to his last finished work, came a fascination with an entirely different sort of male character, neither hero nor villain, but a complicated grey figure who in his first appearance fills Dickens with aversion, and in his last with a guilty sympathy. The shift in Dickens's attitude parallels his growing awareness of certain social attitudes which must be described as upper class—if only because they are above, beyond and inimical to those of the middle class. Dickens's "grey man" is patently a gentleman, and his habits of mind, his manner, his appearance bespeak a gentleman of a new dandy tradition—isolated in a middle-class society hostile to dandyism. None of Dickens's late books is without one of these characters (some have two versions of him): Steerforth in *David Copperfield* as a prefiguration; Richard Carstone and Harold Skimpole in *Bleak House*; James Harthouse in *Hard Times*; Henry Gowan in *Little Dorrit*; Sydney Carton in *A Tale of Two Cities*; Pip in *Great Expectations*; Eugene Wrayburn and Mortimer Lightwood in *Our Mutual Friend*. Dickens seems to offer a clue to the resemblance among them all: Carstone, Harthouse, Gowan, Carton, Wrayburn are names of one family.

The first bond among the grey men is a negative one: they are nothing like Dickens's early heroes—*not* good as gold, *not* energetic, *not* pure in heart, *not* domestic, *not* successful. They are

irresponsible, lazy, listless, worn out, indifferent, cold, dissatisfied. They live with failure, not with success. Almost all of them
are vaguely aristocratic in upbringing : they have at least been to
a "good" public school,* and they have left it with great, never-
to-be-fulfilled expectations. They have lost or are losing caste,
and they are all wracked with a sense of having come down in the
world. They are forced to work to live, but they hate the specific
work they do and they object to the prevailing ideal of work as a
good in itself. They are occasionally unscrupulous and always
careless in money matters, and they survive by sponging on
others or going into debt.

The prime vice of the grey men is the great dandy virtue :
selfishness. If they redeem themselves at all (few are, by middle-
class standards, redeemable) it is by one final, uncharacteristic
act of self-sacrifice which usually terminates in their destruction.
To their friends as well as their enemies they are arrogant or
condescending. Most of them travel in pairs ; that is, they win the
subservience and adoration of a masculine companion. (Harthouse is dogged by Tom Gradgrind, Pip by Herbert Pocket,
Eugene by Mortimer.) Their relations with women are unsatisfactory. Most of them are seducers by temperament, and if none
of them succeeds in seduction (in deference to the code of novels-
in-parts) they have made their plans. They desire the wrong
woman, usually fail to get her, and lose the one they get. (The
two notable exceptions merely illustrate the rule, for Pip would
have lost Estella but for Bulwer's insistence on a happy ending ;
and in the original plan for *Our Mutual Friend* Eugene was to die
at the end of the novel.)

These grey men are a very grey sort of dandy. Their manner,
which Dickens finds both irritating and attractive, is cool,
languid, insolent ; they lounge, they mumble, they talk in half sen-
tences. Some of them (the worst of them) dress with the effortless
ease and impeccable taste of the born dandy ; none with the flashy
theatricality of Dickens's own style. In the pursuit of their
prejudice against the middle class they occasionally form queer
alliances with the very poor, especially the criminal element. In
striking contrast to the idiot aristocrats of Dickens's early and

* Upper-class childhood in an upper-class family was beyond Dickens's
imagining ; but he knew, by bitter contrast to his own experience, that it
would include upper-class education.

middle novels, they are coldly acute, with an intelligence sharpened by cynicism and pessimism. They are the observers rather than the doers—and hostile observers, who do not belong. They are strangers, even outcasts in a middle-class world. Such characters would have been impossible in Dickens's early novels, but Dickens's world had changed. These grey men are finally—in a word that must appear singularly un-Dickensian—decadents. They predict the connection, drawn more and more tightly in the second half of the century, between decadence and dandyism.

6

Dickens's awareness of dandyism as a social force is a striking feature of *Bleak House*, the first novel into which he put a version —possibly two versions—of the grey man. *Bleak House* was written at the high point of Dickens's friendship with Carlyle, whose strong influence on the novelist's social theory here results in an interpolated diatribe against Dandyism as the Perpetual Stoppage (Chapter XII), which reads like an appendix to "The Dandiacal Body" in *Sartor Resartus*. Dickens had learned from Carlyle to use *dandyism* as a grave, insulting word pregnant with implications of social disaster. But while Carlyle had attacked the narrow Pelhamite dandyism that died out with the Reform Bill, Dickens is here concerned with a more persistent, more pervasive phenomenon: "Dandyism of a more mischievous sort, that has got below the surface." The evils grouped under the heading of the new Dandyism are the aristocratic tendencies to sneer at the Vulgar, to gloss over injustices with a snobbish sentimentality, to support the Boodle-Coodle-Doodle system of do-nothing government. Its underlying principle is want of earnestness, refusal to feel, to think, to believe, to act. Subscribers to the new Dandyism "have found out the perpetual stoppage."

Dickens's concurrence with Carlyle's anti-dandiacal dogma implies a Carlylean resolve to feel strongly and to be up and doing, like the "good boy" heroes of the early novels. But *Bleak House* has no hero, and no substitute for a hero; the whole novel is weighed down by the lassitude of the "perpetual stoppage". Situated in the plot-structure where a hero ought to be is Richard Carstone, the young man whose fortunes are inextricably involved in the interminable Jarndyce lawsuit, and whose resolve has been worn away by the meanderings of Chancery law. Carstone is a victim and a failure, not a defender of the right. Though sharing many of the sweet qualities of Dickens's early heroes, he is guilty of an unshakable selfishness and a serious want of energy. He cannot bring himself to choose a profession; he cannot work at anything with determination; he prefers to live on his expectations and to complain: "Ah, cousin, cousin, it's a weary word this Chancery." He is a drifter, "one of the most restless creatures in the world." By somewhat underhanded means—a secret and forbidden marriage—he "gets" the girl he loves, but he dies soon afterward. Dickens's attitude to Richard Carstone is pity mixed with irritation: pity for the victim of a social system (*and* a public school education); irritation particularly with Carstone's carelessness ("something of the careless spirit of a gamester") with money. He is heedlessly extravagant, and goes into debt by "buying the oddest little ornaments and luxuries," and by taking "rather too much to billiards, and that sort of thing."

A tentative alliance is formed between Carstone and Harold Skimpole mainly on the basis of their mutual carelessness in money matters: want of worldliness, they both call it. Skimpole, the shiftless literary man who lives parasitically off anyone who will permit him to sponge, is recognized as a rather harsh caricature of the Regency-Victorian poet Leigh Hunt. His annoying sentimentalism, his lazy, amateurish attitude to literature, his financial irresponsibility reflect actual traits in Hunt's personality. Portrait or not, however, Skimpole is a match for Carstone, the aimless drifter. Skimpole's wonderment at the purposeful activity of people around him is the key to his character. "You are ready at all times to go anywhere, and do anything," he says to Mr Jarndyce and Esther Summerson, the only resolute inhabitants of *Bleak House*. "Such is Will! I have no Will at all—and no Won't—simple Can't."

Skimpole phrases the credo of the grey man of failure in a memorable tirade upon the "overweening assumptions of Bees", those industrious insects sanctified by popular Victorian verse. "He didn't at all see why the busy Bee should be proposed as a model to him"; he preferred to imitate the drone.

It was not necessary for the Bee to make such a merit of his tastes. If every confectioner went buzzing about the world, banging against

everything that came in his way, and egotistically calling upon everybody to take notice that he was going to his work and must not be
interrupted, the world would be quite an insupportable place.

The Dickens of *Bleak House* actively disapproves of Skimpole's
tirade against the Bees, of his whole lackadaisical, irresponsible
way of life; but an older Dickens would return to the parable of
the Bees with different sympathies.

Neither Carstone nor Skimpole looks like a dandy, but the
grey man of the next novel, *Hard Times* (1854), adds a thorough-
going dandyism of dress and manner to the qualities he shares
with his predecessors. James Harthouse is presented by Dickens
as a dangerous man, particularly dangerous because of his dandy
polish—"a conscious polishing," as Dickens puts it, "of but an
ugly surface." He carries his fine clothes with a careless air; he
is languidly indifferent, ritually bored. Harthouse personifies the
aristocrat for the middle-class world of the novel: "good-looking,
good figure, good teeth, good voice, good breeding, well-
dressed, dark hair, bold eyes." It is his polish which attracts
young Tom Gradgrind, the "whelp" who rebels against the
gritty bourgeois qualities of his father and finds in the aristocratic
dandy an insidious ideal. " 'He don't seem to care about his
dress,' thought Tom, 'and yet how capitally he does it. What an
easy swell he is!' "

> There was something so very agreeable in being so intimate with
> such a waistcoat; in being called Tom, in such an intimate way, by
> such a voice; in being on such offhand terms so soon, with such a pair
> of whiskers . . .

Harthouse's influence on Tom is wholly pernicious: the young
man turns criminal and is vigorously punished. But Harthouse's
own destiny is ambiguous. Like Carstone a wayward aristocrat
unable to settle on a profession, he attaches himself parasitically
to the rich middle class; he is, he says, "as ready to 'go in' for
statistics as for anything else." His major role in the novel is that
of the near-seducer of Louisa Gradgrind: he drifts into a desire
to seduce her and, at her one show of moral strength, drifts
aimlessly away and drops out of the novel.

Harthouse has been described by T. A. Jackson* as "a parasite

* One of the first critics to maintain at length that Dickens was a radical
in the Marxist sense.

upon the Bounderby–Gradgrind class," who, "in his dandiacal boredom, and unprincipled heartlessness," rounds out Dickens's "scornful repudiation of everything aristocratic." But, in fact, Dickens is relatively lenient with Harthouse. Dickens's principal animus in *Hard Times* is directed against the ruthless maker of money and destroyer of men. His "scornful repudiation" of the dandy is qualified by a recognition that the Harthouse type despises the new bourgeoisie as much as Dickens; and this concurrence places Harthouse, despite all his vices, on his author's side. He is an observer, a critic, from the outside. Harthouse strolls anonymously on to the scene midway in the course of the novel, characterized as a visitor and a stranger from the gentleman's world.

> The visitor having strolled to the window, and being then engaged in looking carelessly out, was as unmoved by this impressive entry as man could possibly be. He stood whistling to himself with all imaginable coolness, with his hat still on, and a certain air of exhaustion upon him, in part arising . . . from excessive gentility. For it was to be seen with half an eye that he was a thorough gentleman, made to the model of the time; weary of everything, and putting no more faith in anything than Lucifer.

Dickens later amplifies the portrait of Harthouse as a dandy-devil figure: the Devil at his most dangerous, "when he is trimmed, smoothed, and varnished, according to the mode: when he is aweary of vice, and aweary of virtue, used up as to brimstone, and used up as to bliss . . ." Harthouse is incapable of acting upon good or evil principles, even of distinguishing between the two: "no energetic wickedness ruffled his lassitude." To an appeal to his better nature Dickens has Harthouse express his scepticism about the existence of such a thing: "I cannot say that I have any sanguine expectations of ever becoming a moral sort of fellow, or that I have any belief in any moral sort of fellow whatever."

There is pathos as well as outrage in Dickens's presentation of Harthouse, whose essential loneliness is dramatized by a poignant image drawn from the water symbolism that figured increasingly in Dickens's late novels. Harthouse is standing in an "easy attitude" beside "a piece of ornamental water" on the Bounderby grounds, idly throwing rosebuds over a stone parapet. They float on the water like "a little surface-island . . . which was always drifting to the wall as if it wanted to become a part of the mainland." When Harthouse drifts off at the end—unchanged, and ashamed rather than proud of the one moral act of his existence—his summation of the story has a lyrical quality reflecting Dickens's guarded sympathy. "Only a poor girl—" (he thinks) "only a stroller—only James Harthouse made nothing of—only James Harthouse a Great Pyramid of failure."

7

The man of failure returns again in *Little Dorrit* in the person of Henry Gowan, the lazy descendant of the Barnacle clan who takes amateurishly to the career of a painter and marries the unfortunate Pet Meagles. Gowan's first appearance in the novel recalls Harthouse at the water's edge, languidly throwing rosebuds: a well-dressed gentlemanly lounger, Gowan stands by the river "idly tossing stones into the water with his foot." Like Harthouse he is public-school trained, aristocratic in his manner, impudent in his bearing, disappointed in his expectations. Like Harthouse he is cynically convinced that "there is much less difference than you are inclined to suppose between an honest man and a scoundrel." Like Harthouse he plays the role of nearseducer, as the mysterious Miss Wade reveals in her autobiography, the curiously clinical "History of a Self Tormentor". (Gowan's temperament also includes a sadistic strain merely latent in his predecessors.) Gowan, too, is caught in the "perpetual stoppage". Dickens describes his situation as a "halting state": "to have left one of two Powers in disgust, to want the necessary qualifications for finding promotion with another, and to be loitering moodily about on neutral ground . . ." Defiant and unscrupulous in his consciousness of failure, Gowan is the most disagreeable of Dickens's grey men. And his "habit . . . of seeking some sort of recompense in the discontented boast of being disappointed" elicits Dickens's disapproval in the strongest words: it "is a habit fraught with degeneracy."

Certain aspects of Gowan's career as an artist have led commentators to suggest that this character is, like Skimpole in *Bleak House*, a portrait of one of Dickens's literary rivals. In the case of Gowan there is no evidence, merely speculation. (Hesketh Pearson has suggested that Thackeray is the original of what was not meant as an exact portrait.) But it would seem most likely that Dickens used Gowan to dramatize not an individual but a state of mind prevalent among his literary and artistic friends, especially his *new* friends. And the man who had most stimulated his interest in such a state of mind was Wilkie Collins. Throughout the writing of *Little Dorrit* (1855–7) Dickens was very close to Collins. Much of the book was done in Paris, where, as Dickens wrote Macready, Collins "dines with us every day". During these years the two men collaborated on several pieces, Dickens had Collins appointed associate editor of *Household Words*, and Collins wrote a play in which Dickens was to act one hero and himself the other. Their intimacy, which has distressed many of Dickens's critics, dated from 1851 and would persist until Dickens's death.

That Dickens consciously sat down to do a portrait of Collins in Gowan is impossible, for he and Collins were on the best of terms. They met on the common ground of their shared passions for the theatre, for *gourmandise*, for travel on the Continent in general and France in particular. The relationship prospered because Collins was a decent, kindly man, capable of generosity in friendship. But there were qualities in Collins that disturbed as they fascinated Dickens, because they were foreign to his own nature—qualities which drew from Dickens's daughter Kate (who married Collins's brother and appreciated Collins's virtues) the comment that he was "as bad as he could be."

In contrast to Dickens's keyed-up, driving energy, Collins was a man of relaxation—relaxed in his moral code (his irregular liaisons were notorious), in his attitudes to his work, in his whole manner of being. Where Dickens was scrupulously punctual, tidy and regimented, where Dickens was a high-powered, pushing machine, Collins was lazy, sceptical, epicurean, languid. What Jack Lindsay has called Collins's "careless hedonism" charmed Dickens and repelled him and gave rise to a complicated jealousy which Lindsay defines as "an impersonal sense of displacement by the younger generation, a keen but not altogether unpleasant feeling of regret for not being able to take life and love so easily."

The tensions latent in the Dickens–Collins relationship are strikingly reflected in Dickens's letters to Collins in the *Little Dorrit* years, and most dramatically in *The Lazy Tour of Two Idle Apprentices*, a collaborative work they undertook in the fall

of 1857. The two men had been together through the months
preceding the tour, producing and starring in Collins's play, *The
Frozen Deep*; and early in August Dickens had made the acquaintance of Ellen Ternan, her sister and her mother, the "Professional Ladies" who were to take over three parts in the play. At
the end of August, the thrilling final performances in Manchester
concluded, Dickens sent Collins an appeal, proposing that they
should "go anywhere—take any tour—see anything—whereon
we could write something together." "Will you rattle your head
and see if there is any pebble in it which we could wander away
and play at marbles with?" he asked. "We want something for
Household Words, and I want to escape from myself. For when I
do start up and stare myself seedily in the face . . . my blankness
is inconceivable—indescribable—my misery amazing."

This project, a tour through Cumberland, was typical of
Dickens: it was to be at once a release from work and a source
of more work. Indeed Dickens's inability to *stop* working, to be
relaxed and careless and indifferent like his friend Collins, was
the theme of the resulting travel piece in *Household Words*, which
Dickens called *The Lazy Tour of Two Idle Apprentices*.

The two gentlemen setting out on a walking tour together are
apprentices in the sense that they are "bound to a highly mere-
torious lady (named Literature)"; both are idle in the sense that
they are bent on "shirking their duty". But the essential temperamental differences between the two "apprentices" are summed
up by the names Dickens gives them: Francis Goodchild (himself) and Thomas Idle (Collins).

> Goodchild was laboriously idle, and would take upon himself any
> amount of pains and labour to assure himself that he was idle; in
> short, had no better idea of idleness than that it was useless industry.
> Thomas Idle, on the other hand, was an idler of the unmixed Irish
> or Neapolitan type; a passive idler, a born-and-bred idler, a con-
> sistent idler, who practised what he would have preached if he had
> not been too idle to preach; a one entire and perfect chrysolite of
> idleness.

A constant interplay between the two temperaments provides
all the interest in *The Lazy Tour* (otherwise a foolish piece of
hackwork.) Goodchild runs about, plans, manages and runs about
again, while Idle drifts, yawns, lounges, waves his hand languidly
and goes to sleep in protest. Goodchild fumes and frets about the

12. George Cruikshank: Charles Dickens (*c*. 1836-37)

13. Constantin Guys: Second Empire Dandy

anguish of being in love (he is "always in love with somebody, and not unfrequently with several objects at once"); while Idle drawls his opinion that it is not worth the trouble to fall in love "so I keep out of it altogether." Goodchild soars up mountains and plunges down them, while Idle, who "was always the last, and was always the man who had to be looked after and waited for," lags behind, sprains his ankle and must be half-carried home —leaning on his undaunted friend.

This last episode, the "rescue" of the weak man by the strong, is insisted upon as symbolic of the whole Idle–Goodchild relationship. The scene actually took place during the Cumberland tour, and Dickens wrote home to friends about it with a kind of superstitious glee. For, in one of those dramatic coincidences by which Dickens felt his destiny was marked, Collins had (*before* the tour) written just such an episode into *The Frozen Deep*, the play he had conceived with Dickens and himself as joint heroes. On stage, therefore, as well as in life, Dickens/Goodchild had rescued Collins/Idle. On another occasion in *The Lazy Tour*, but this time for no apparent reason, Goodchild falls to carrying Idle around again, and Idle petulantly protests: "What are you doing? Idiotically plunging at your own sex, and rescuing them or perishing in the attempt?" The contrast between Idle and Goodchild, which draws them together as it forces them apart, is that of the idle as against the busy, the weak as against the strong, the drifting as against the purposeful—and also the vaguely effeminate as against the aggressively virile.

It is Idle who summarizes Dickens's dissatisfaction with himself. Goodchild, he says, "goes systematically tearing himself to pieces, and putting himself through an incessant course of training, as if he were always under articles to fight a match for the champion's belt, and," Idle protests, "he calls it Play!"

> Play . . . You *can't* play. You don't know what it is. You make work of everything . . . To me you are an absolutely terrible fellow. You do nothing like another man. Where another fellow would fall into a footbath of action or emotion, you fall into a mine. Where any other fellow would be a painted butterfly, you are a fiery dragon . . .

Of the two men, it was Collins—ugly, slightly misshapen, eternally ailing, and a slovenly dresser in the Bohemian manner —who knew about painted butterflies. Conversant with the

Pre-Raphaelite group, Collins set a high value on the plastic arts, talked a theory of aestheticism and idealized the practice of dilettantism, or what he once called the "dandy-dilettante sort of life". The connection between aestheticism and dandyism, that came to England from mid-century France to preoccupy the 'nineties, is prefigured in one of Collins's best villains, Miserrimus Dexter, the horrible effeminate dwarf of *The Law and The Lady* (1875). Dexter (who is also a projection of Collins's obsession with deformity) is a magnificent torso without legs; what there is of him is elegant, vain, acutely sensitive, sadistic and sensual. He has hair like a woman's which must constantly be combed, he uses perfumes and wears a great deal of jewellery, his house is conceived as a "monument to the picturesque and the beautiful", he plays the harp and does needle-work, he is an epicure and prides himself on his cooking. He is a painter, a poet and a story-teller who, in one of the many touches which relate him to Collins, excels in hair-raising melodrama. In Dexter's defence of his gorgeous clothes, Continental aestheticism is more prominent than native English dandyism:

> Except in this ignorant and material nineteenth century, men have always worn precious stuffs and beautiful colours as well as women. A hundred years ago the patricians of the classic times wore bracelets exactly like mine. I despise the brutish contempt for beauty and the mean dread of expense which degrade a gentleman's costume to black cloth, and limit a gentleman's ornaments to a finger-ring, in the age I live in. I like to be bright and beautiful . . .

8

If Carlyle's influence led to the choice of the French Revolution as the subject of Dickens's next novel, Collins's influence helped to shape the book's characters and plot. In his preface to *A Tale of Two Cities* (1859) Dickens confusingly confessed his debt to Collins: he wrote that he "first conceived the main idea" of the story while acting in *The Frozen Deep*, a devious allusion to the fact that the novel's plot-spring can be found in Collins's play, where a man sacrifices his life to save his successful rival in love. What Dickens goes on to admit is even more strangely phrased:

> A strong desire was upon me then, to embody it [*i.e.* this main idea] in my own person; and I traced out in my fancy, the state of mind of

which it would necessitate the presentation to an observant spectator, with particular care and interest.

As the idea became familiar to me, it gradually shaped itself into its present form. Throughout its execution, it has had complete possession of me; I have so far verified what is done and suffered in these pages, as that I have certainly done and suffered it all myself.

Behind the wordiness and the peculiar grammar of this preface lie confused references to the role Dickens played in *The Frozen Deep*, dying in the last scene to the accompaniment ("the presentation to an observant spectator") of genuine tears from the Ternan sisters—and also, to some of the events of the lazy tour.

The strains of Dickens's friendship with Collins (of the strong man's support of, along with dependence upon the weak) inspired the unhistorical human situation of *A Tale of Two Cities*. Dickens made illuminating alterations in the plot he borrowed from Collins's play. In *The Frozen Deep* Dickens had played Richard Wardour, a character Collins obviously tailored to his friend's personality: a strong, energetic, dark man of fiery passions, christened "the Bear" by his companions but still the most resourceful member of the expedition to "the frozen deep". The part Collins wrote for himself is that of Frank Aldersley, an amiable, handsome, fair young man whose weakness leads him eventually to rely on the strength of his older friend. Wardour calls Frank "young one", and tells him he has "what the women call a lucky face". Frank wins the lady Wardour loves, and lives to possess her because of his friend's sacrificial death. In *A Tale of Two Cities* the roles are reversed. Charles Darnay, the successful suitor, has Wardour's strength and resourcefulness. Sydney Carton, the unsuccessful martyr, is a return once again to the idle, drifting, disappointed man, Aldersley–Collins—or Carstone–Harthouse–Gowan. Through this reversal Dickens is able to sympathize with the man of weakness: to pity him, to punish him, essentially to identify with him ("I have certainly done and suffered it all myself . . .").

Charles Darnay rejects the aristocratic traditions of his French family to throw in his lot with the forces of progress. "I must do, to live," he tells his villainous uncle the Marquis, "what others of my countrymen, even with nobility at their backs, may have to do some day—work." To this estimable determination Darnay adds the virtues of quiet manliness, simple clothes, an admiration for George Washington and a social conscience. He was a hero to make Carlyle proud—and had certainly been drawn up by Dickens with the Carlylean gospel in mind.

But Sydney Carton, the hero's unsuccessful rival in love, who resembles Darnay so closely that he can at last be guillotined in Darnay's place, is morally more complicated. He is certainly no villain: Dickens treats Carton's intelligence as a positive virtue, and his moral laziness as pitiable failing rather than reprehensible vice. Carton is the first genuinely sympathetic version of Dickens's grey man. Once a boy of promise at "old Shrewsbury School", Carton begins at an early age to waste his talents, refusing from some central weakness in his character to work and fight for himself. He goes off to Paris as a young man (like Wilkie Collins) ostensibly to study, also to pick up "other French crumbs that we didn't get much good of." Now he has settled uneasily (as Collins did) into the legal profession.* He has a sharp mind and a retentive memory, always devoted to the profit of anyone but himself; but he is the "idlest and most unpromising of men", a disappointed and disappointing figure. There is "no sadder sight", says Dickens, "than the man of good abilities and good emotions, incapable of their directed exercise, incapable of his own help and his own happiness, sensible of the blight on him, and resigning himself to let it eat him away."

Carton's habits and appearance are in keeping with his irresolution. He is the first of the grey men to be a heavy drinker, but the vice is appropriate. Though he does not dress with the dandified elegance of Harthouse, his style contrasts sharply with the conventional sobriety of Charles Darnay. He is a slovenly man (again like Collins) and his slovenliness has a studied air: he is insolent in his unconcern. "Something especially reckless in his demeanour . . . gave him a disreputable look." At the moment of Carton's self-sacrifice, Dickens calls his pose "not a reckless manner . . . [but] the settled manner of a tired man, who had wandered and struggled and got lost, but who at length struck into his road and saw its end." Its end, in this case, is Carton's approaching execution.

In his next novel Dickens put a tired, grey figure at the very

* Referring to Thomas Idle's choice of a profession in *The Lazy Tour*, Dickens had called the Bar, after the Church, "the next best profession for a lazy man in England".

centre of his story, as the "I" of a semi-autobiographical book. Except for Pip and his weaknesses, *Great Expectations* (1860–1) is unlike the other books of its period : its tone is less harsh, shading from a sunny lyricism to a gentle, nostalgic melancholy, and it has a relatively unified plot.* Consciously venturing again into autobiographical fiction as he had in *David Copperfield* (he re-read the earlier novel to make sure there were no "unconscious repetitions") Dickens made *Great Expectations* wholly different from its predecessor—for David Copperfield shares the idealism of Dickens's youth, while Pip feels the anguished perplexity of the successful Dickens, now identifying himself with young men of great expectations going down in the world. *Great Expectations* clearly marks the shift in Dickens's sympathies to what Bernard Shaw, always a Dickens enthusiast, called the *downstart*.

The problem that bedevils Carstone, Harthouse and Carton is also Pip's : like them he rejects work and determination and energy, choosing to stumble along uneasily on the neutral ground between two social worlds. Unlike them, however, he is no born aristocrat. Dickens has reconciled the Carstone–Harthouse–Gowan situation with his own life pattern by giving Pip a lowly origin, and by grafting on to Pip's position in early youth the mysterious promise that he is a young gentleman of great expectations. This promise spreads out over Pip's career like a giant web; just as Richard Carstone's will and energy were sapped by the great expectations of his Chancery suit, so Pip's expectations cramp him, warp him, turn him into an unsettled drifter. Pip's selfishness, snobbery and dandyism are merely aspects of his drifting state. Like his predecessors he is drawn to the melancholy symbolism of the water: "It was pleasant and quiet," Pip reflects, "out there with the sails on the river passing beyond the earthwork, and sometimes, when the tide was low, looking as if they belonged to sunken ships that were still sailing on at the bottom of the water."

Between 1861, the year of the completion of *Great Expectations,*

---

* The influence of *Pendennis* was suspected at the time; and Dickens and Thackeray come more closely together in these two books than in any others. Considering the difference in origin and childhood between the two men, the similarities between Pip and Pen are remarkable. Both "heroes" of these novels-without-a-hero are reflections of a double self, the young and the middle-aged.

and 1870, the year of Dickens's death, he finished only one novel. These years were the most unsettled of his life, witnessing the dissolution of his family, the liaison with Ellen Ternan (which seems to have brought him more anxiety than satisfaction), ill health, the disastrous readings—the most eccentric clothes. And *Our Mutual Friend*, the one complete novel Dickens wrote in his fifties, is the blackest of all his novels.

The sweet lucidity of *Great Expectations* has disappeared. In its place are half a dozen densely interwoven plots, an atmosphere compounded of crime, melodrama and passion, and a complicated symbolism of dust and water, parched dryness against muddy damp. At the same time, something striking has happened to the hero-structure of Dickens's novel. The figure around whom the central plot revolves (John Rokesmith) is a cipher, of no interest to author or reader; instead, Dickens identifies himself intimately and passionately with two other characters: Bradley Headstone, the parvenu schoomaster; and Eugene Wrayburn, the decadent aristocrat. The two men are rivals in a guilty passion; they are also rivals for Dickens's approval. That Bradley should be handled almost with loathing and Eugene almost with adoration is significant of Dickens's despair—for Bradley, rather than Eugene, is modelled on his creator. A man of fierce passions and strong will, Bradley, like Dickens, has risen from poverty to respectability through hard work; he takes pride in the struggle and is suspicious of those above him, notably Eugene. "I have worked my way onward, out of both [origin and bringing-up] and in spite of both," he tells Eugene, "and have a right to be considered a better man than you, with better reasons for being proud." Yet Bradley's pride comes before a horrible fall, death in circumstances combining accident, murder and suicide. For the triumphant bourgeois saga of Bradley Headstone has produced a warped and hypocritical personality: respected citizen by day and criminal outcast by night, outwardly decent and inwardly guilty. Like the Dickens who had torn apart his family for Ellen Ternan, he is a moral failure.

In the character of Eugene Wrayburn Dickens fashioned the last of his grey men, and the only one to come close to heroic stature. In *Our Mutual Friend* Dickens was at last able to display warm and open sympathy toward the dandy-decadent figure who stands on the periphery of the novel, observing and commenting, rarely doing. Like Carstone and Pip Eugene is weighed down by great expectations: the small income left him by an aristocratic grandfather "has been an effective Something, in the way of preventing me from turning to at Anything." Like Harthouse he has the gifts of manner and good looks, the art of wearing clothes gracefully, and a fine set of whiskers. Like Gowan he is capable of insolence and cruelty, and disavows all moral judgments. Like Pip and Harthouse he is followed about by an adoring, imitating friend. Like Carton, he has taken to the law unwillingly and despises his profession. "I have been 'called' [to the Bar] seven years," says Eugene, "and have had no business at all, and never shall have any. And if I had, I shouldn't know how to do it." Like Skimpole he is indolent, and mocks those who sing the praises of Energy.

"Then idiots talk," said Eugene, leaning back, folding his arms, smoking with his eyes shut, and speaking slightly through his nose, "of Energy. If there is a word in the dictionary under any letter from A to Z that I abominate, it is energy. It is such a conventional superstition, such parrot gabble!"

Exactly like Skimpole—and it is illuminating that Dickens returned to this conceit eleven years after *Bleak House*—Eugene puts his distaste for the energetic in terms of a refusal to emulate the busy bees. But where Dickens had treated Skimpole's rejection of The Bee as a foolish, even repellent aberration, it is his own voice that speaks Eugene's protest. Eugene's words are here, as often in the novel, almost lyrical in quality, and full of a quiet irony unusual in Dickens. He backs Mr Boffin humorously into a corner until that respectable gentleman can only protest, about his idols the bees, that "at all events, they work."

"Ye-es," returned Eugene disparagingly, "they work; but don't you think they overdo it? They work so much more than they need— they make so much more than they can eat—they are so incessantly boring and buzzing at their one idea till Death comes upon them— that don't you think they overdo it? And are human labourers to have no holidays, because of the bees? And am I never to have change of air, because the bees don't? Mr Boffin, I think honey excellent at breakfast; but regarded in the light of my conventional schoolmaster and moralist, I protest against the tyrannical humbug of your friend the bee . . ."

Dickens rarely describes Eugene directly. But with every word he speaks, in his drawling abbreviated way, with every cigar he smokes, every lazy gesture he makes, he is the most convincing of Dickens's dandified loungers. He appears to be entombed in boredom, making his first appearance (unwillingly) at one of the Veneerings' dinner parties "buried alive in the back of his chair, behind a shoulder—with powder-epaulette on it—of the mature young lady, and gloomily resorting to the champagne chalice." Boredom is his favourite theme, and the root of his protest to matrimony: "Could I possibly support it? I, so soon bored, so constantly, so fatally?" Revulsion, too, is part of his dandyism. He makes gestures of physical disgust toward creatures beneath his notice, airily fumigating his room, for example, to protect himself from the shabby, drunken Mr Dolls. ("He took the shovel from the grate, sprinkled a few live ashes on it, and from a box on the chimney-piece took a few pastiles, which he set upon them; then, with great composure, began placidly waving the shovel in front of Mr Dolls, to cut him off from his company.")

More serious, even sinister aspects in Eugene's character are also rounded out, where they were only suggested in his predecessors. His friendship with his copy, Mortimer Lightwood, is painfully intimate. It culminates in the passionate exchange between them as Eugene lies bruised and mutilated on what, in Dickens's original scheme, was to have been his deathbed. Mortimer, whose final act of friendship is to be the arrangement of a deathbed marriage, says to Eugene:

> My poor dear fellow, you wanted to say something to your old friend —to the friend who has always loved you, admired you, imitated you, founded himself upon you, been nothing without you, and who, God knows, would be here in your place if he could.

And Eugene, facing marriage-in-death, speaks with even greater tenderness:

> Touch my face with yours, in case I should not hold out till you come back. I love you, Mortimer. Don't be uneasy for me while you are gone . . .

Eugene's curious attraction to crime is also essential to the portrait. He is drawn in spite of himself to the criminal, he can put himself in the mind of the criminal; and he associates this forbidden sympathy with his guilty feelings toward the lower-class girl he desires. When he thinks of Lizzie Hexam he feels "like a dark combination of traitor and pickpocket". His role in the novel is that of tracker and detector of criminals, but his very success fills him with guilt—and he dryly calls on Mortimer to resolve that "next time . . . we'll commit the crime, instead of taking the criminal."

These dark sides of Eugene, together with his laziness, his irresponsibility, his hatred of energy and the busy bees, place him in alliance with the people of the river banks. He belongs with the world of sluggish, drifting, muddy waters, in Dickens's sombre water-symbolism. Lizzie Hexam, daughter of the water-man, rejects Bradley Headstone, whose gritty respectability would make her "quit of the river-side and the old disagreeables belonging to it" (as her brother says). Yet she is drawn to Eugene, whose class, whose whole world are alien to her own. Eugene does not fight and push and press, as Bradley does. He can be quiet and relaxed and idle, able, as he thinks, to "float with the stream".

9

"Upon my soul," says Eugene Wrayburn, "don't know. I know less about myself than about most people in the world, and I don't know." Vague and shadowy dissatisfactions, of which Dickens himself was only partly conscious, lay behind the heroic treatment of unheroic qualities in *Our Mutual Friend*. Dickens put more of his anguish into this book than into any other: each character speaks some phrase that might come from the letters of Dickens's last years, and they speak despairing words. Mr Venus describes the bleak lookout from "the top of the tree"; Mortimer Lightwood asks "Is Anything satisfactory, Mr Boffin?" Mr Twemlow, the lonely old gentleman left over from the age of the Regent, says what Dickens said so often to Forster: "No Adorable to bear me company here! . . . A waste, a waste, a waste . . .!" John Rokesmith evokes Dickens's love affair when he defends his bondage to the mercenary, selfish Bella: "I cannot help it; reason has nothing to do with it; I love her against reason." And Bradley Headstone gives thanks that he has never married, "for if I had, and if the same spell had come upon me for my ruin, I know I should have broken that tie asunder as if it had been thread."

Despite success and fame and honour Dickens came at the end to be obsessed with a kind of personality, half dandy, half decadent, to which his world offered only failure. ("I am a ridiculous fellow," says Eugene Wrayburn. "Everything is ridiculous.") No one did more than Dickens to admit the literary man to the world of middle-class respectability. No one showed more dramatically than he that literary men were entitled to the good things of middle-class success: plump wives and large families; cosy houses and nine-course dinners; public speeches and parlour games. But no one came more surely than Dickens to discover that the literary man of genius (or the artist, as he would in another decade call himself) could not remain at peace with the bourgeois world.

Many of Dickens's contemporaries in France, of whose existence he was hardly aware, were already declaring open war. His personal solution was to take refuge in a clandestine existence that was not, by any definition, middle-class respectability. In the imaginative world of his novels Dickens found release by worrying, by pitying, at last by idealizing the anti-bourgeois aristocrat, the irresponsible drifter, the alien dandy—a figure his society rejected, and with whom Dickens had nothing in common, save unspoken thoughts. "Realities and idealities are always comparing themselves before me," he said, "and I don't like the realities except when they are unattainable—*then*, I like them of all things."

Part Five

FRANCE: THE MID-CENTURY

CHAPTER XI

Barbey d'Aurevilly

*Malheureusement je ne suis ni Montesquieu ni Beyle, ni aigle ni lynx ;
mais j'ai tâché pourtant de voir clair dans ce que beaucoup de gens, sans
doute, n'eussent pas daigné expliquer.*
—Barbey: *Du Dandysme*

THE news of Brummell's death in Caen, three years after
Victoria came to the throne, was in England no news at all.
Nor could the early-Victorian world be bothered with the publication in 1844 of Captain William Jesse's biography, still the one
indispensable memorial to Regency dandyism. Ten years passed
before a second edition was required. Reviews of Jesse's book
were few (even *Fraser's* ignored it) and the few there were
treated Brummell as a disreputable or ludicrous oddity from a
distant age. "Folly will have its victims to the end of time—"
intoned the *Athenaeum*, "—though few will be so heartless, so
mean, so guiltless of the qualities which fascinate." Thackeray,
Jesse's one important reviewer, was alone in his tentative separation of Brummell from the Regency attitude for which he stood:
"the model of dandyhood for all time." The biography seemed to
the Victorians a morality book, not a memorial, for Brummell's
end was horrible enough to punish all his sins. Jesse's readers
opened his two heavy volumes "under the impression", as another reviewer put it, "that nothing satisfactory could be made
of their empty and frivolous, if not worthless subject". But they
found that there was "matter of grave instruction, as well as
warning, in the life and death of poor Beau Brummell."

The patronizing tone, and the emphasis on Brummell's decline
rather than his glory, were not merely read into the biography
by hostile reviewers. Captain Jesse devoted more than half the
work to the agonizing decay of the dandy; he was himself of two
minds about his subject. Though consumed with an admiring
curiosity about Brummell, Jesse felt compelled to confess (to the

"community of Utilitarians") that the great dandy had every quality to make him "agreeable, amusing, and ornamental, but not one that tended, in the most remote degree, to make him useful." He could find no defence for concerning himself (at such length) with so much frivolity. "Posterity," he concluded apologetically, "will hardly accord to George Bryan Brummell one line in the annals of history."

Despite their predestined cool reception, other sets of dandy memoirs appeared throughout the mid-century. There was material on Brummell and other dandy exiles in Thomas Raikes's *France, since 1830* (1841) and further comments in Raikes's lengthy *Journal*, which came out in 1856–7. The invaluable Captain Gronow (who, like Raikes, spent many of his last years in France) brought out his *Reminiscences and Recollections,* in four rambling, nostalgic instalments, from 1861 to 1866. It is significant that Gronow's memoirs were not collected into one convenient edition until the 'eighties, when they were brought together by J. C. Nimmo. The same publisher also then reissued Jesse's biography of Brummell, perhaps in response to the complaint by Percy Fitzgerald, the 'eighties biographer of George IV, that this "curious account of the Beau" was "so exceedingly scarce as to be worth guineas."

Another memorialist deserves a place beside Jesse, Raikes and Gronow for the wealth of his information about the Regency dandy: Cecil, the fictional hero of an anonymous "autobiographical" novel. *Cecil; or the Adventures of a Coxcomb*, and its successor, *Cecil, a Peer* (six volumes in all) appeared in 1841, and gave a big, splashy, perceptive portrait of the dandy's Regency from one man's viewpoint. Though popular as a work of fiction, these volumes were studied by the few Victorians mindful of the Regency (Jesse among them) as social history.

Cecil was the creation of a lady, Mrs Catherine Gore, about whom little is known beyond the fact that she did live on the fringes of that society which provided her with subjects for two hundred volumes spread over a writing career of thirty-five years. The last, but far from the least, of Regency-inspired fashionable novelists, Mrs Gore could simultaneously catch the surface gaiety and mark the underlying rottenness of her period. From this formidable, hard-headed literary lady (Disraeli once described her as a "very sumptuous personage, looking like a full-blown rose") come the best of the tags that stick to the Regency. She called it "the gilded not the golden age"; she summarized the Brummell saga as the rise of a man who "was a nobody, who had made himself somebody, and gave the law to everybody"; she defined the Regency doctrine as "promoting the greatest happiness of the smallest number."

Of all the society novelists to succeed Mrs Gore, only one responded to her influence: Thackeray. He read her books in the 'thirties (finding at least one "a sensible book enough"); he duly satirized them in the 'forties for *Punch*, in his *Novels by Eminent Hands*. So close to Mrs Gore's was Thackeray's critical-nostalgic attitude to the Regency that he was rumoured to have written *Cecil*. ("How I wish I had written it," he said, "not for the book's sake, but for the filthy money.")And his *Fitz-Boodle Papers*, which came out the following year in *Fraser's*, was unmistakably influenced by the lucrative *Cecil*. Mrs Gore's was one of the homes Thackeray visited during the writing of *Pendennis*; from her daughter he took some touches for the characterization of Blanche Amory.

Society novels continued to be written and read throughout the Victorian period; then as now, they were usually by and for ladies but about gentlemen. After Mrs Gore, however, the Regency-style dandy was no longer the hero of fashionable fiction. It took time to devise a substitute. The first important new style in fashionable heroes was set by Guy Livingstone, which heroic name was also the title of G. A. Lawrence's novel of 1857. The formidable Guy, as drawn in Bret Harte's satire of the novel, represented in part a carry-over of Regency ideals:

> His broad, deep chest, his sinewy and quivering flank, his straight pastern, showed him to be a thoroughbred. Perhaps he was a trifle heavy in the fetlock, but he held his head haughtily erect. His eyes were glittering but pitiless. There was a sternness about the lower part of his face . . . heightened, perhaps, by the snaffle-bit which, in one of his strange freaks, he wore in his mouth to curb his occasional ferocity . . .

Harte was correct: the new ideals applied less to manhood than to horse-flesh. Guy Livingstone is four parts Byronic hero, three parts Etonian, two parts muscle and only one part dandy. By setting the fashion for force and ferocity he left a long progeny of

heroes, and most of his successors were, not surprisingly, military
gentlemen. The Victorians could take a modest admixture of
dandyism in military men, whose surface effeminacy, elegance and
irresponsibility (in peace-time) could be excused by the supposi-
tion that (in war-time) they would die for their country like
brave Englishmen and true Christians. Captain Gronow and
Captain Jesse were real counterparts, after all, of splendid heroes
like Rhoda Broughton's Major Dick M'Gregor (*Cometh Up Like
a Flower*, 1867) and Ouida's Bertie Cecil (*Under Two Flags*, also
1867), the most popular of this lady's dandified guardsmen.
There is far more of Lawrence's nonsense than Mrs Gore's good
sense in this second Cecil, half fierce, ascetic legionnaire and half
"gay, indolent, indulgent, *pococurante* Guardsman, whose most
serious anxiety [was] the set of a lace tie, the fashion of his
hunting dress, or the choice of the gold arabesques for his smoking
slippers."

2

Dandy biographies, Regency memoirs, fashionable novels
were not reading matter for serious people in mid-century
England. But mid-century France was different. In 1845, the year
the celebrated Bulwer–Tennyson battle began (culminating in
the righteous denunciation of Bulwer as "the padded man—that
wears the stays", a "little would-be Brummell"), Jules Amédée
Barbey d'Aurevilly laid the foundations of his literary career in
France with a slender volume in praise of Brummell's dandyism.
Barbey's book is the pivotal work upon which the history of the
dandy tradition turns. Little that came after it (the intellectual
dandyism of Baudelaire, the "negative dandyism" of Huysmans,
the aesthetic dandyism of the English 'eighties and 'nineties)
cannot somehow be traced to Barbey's *Du Dandysme et de Georges
Brummell*. Little that had come before it (the memoirs, the novels,
the legends of the original Regency tradition) had escaped
Barbey's attention. That Barbey could preserve as well as renew
was the result of a curious series of literary, psychological and
geographical coincidences, tracing back to the early eighteen-
thirties, when four ill-assorted gentlemen found themselves in
Caen, the modest and inaccessible "Athens of Normandy".

Barbey d'Aurevilley arrived late in 1829 to take up the study
of law at the University of Caen. (His conservative Norman

family was confident that there he would outgrow the anti-clerical and republican opinions he had absorbed during his school years in Paris.) Brummell appeared in the summer of 1830 to assume his duties as the English consul. William Jesse, a twenty-five-year-old lieutenant in the English army with nine years as an officer already behind him, came early in 1832 to recuperate from six years of service in India. A slim, sweet-faced young man, handsome in regimentals, he was taken up by local Society and at one evening party he met the Beau, of whose "superlative taste and unquestionable authority" he had heard and read even in India. Barbey met neither Jesse nor Brummell (though he later claimed to have *seen* Brummell at this time) but he began an intimate and lasting friendship with Guillaume-Stanislas Trébutien, a native of Caen whose semi-invalidism had obliged him to lead a scholar's life far from the excitements of the capital. Trébutien would serve Barbey throughout his writing career as good listener, patient researcher and loyal ally. His first important service to his friend, though at the time neither realized it, was to bridge the gap between French and English dandyism: some time in the early 'thirties he made the acquaintance of Lieutenant Jesse. A decade later, through Trébutien, Brummell's French biographer would be able to draw on the knowledge of Brummell's English biographer.

Barbey left Caen to return to Paris in 1833, when the rage of Anglomania was at its height. For a decade he lived on the fringes of two literary worlds: too shy and unproductive, too little a poet to join the Romantics, too poor and provincial to join the dandy journalists (though he was intimate with such dandies of the press as Roger de Beauvoir and Arsène Houssaye). Among his points of contact with both groups was a firmly established and highly personal anglomania. Born in 1808 in the heart of the Cotentin peninsula of Normandy, which pokes up inquisitively into the English Channel, Barbey had grown up in a country of English colonies and Norman families proud of their ancestors' role in English history. His descriptions of his beloved province would always emphasize the resemblance between the two countries:

> There are in certain parts of lower Normandy—and notably in the Cotentin peninsula—landscapes so similar to English landscapes that the Normans who cast their anchor from one to another of these lands

could think . . . they had not changed country . . . Even the sky, the so often grey and rainy sky of our West . . . adds in Normandy to this illusion of England, and seems sometimes to push the resemblance between the two countries even to identity.*

For a few years a small inheritance enabled Barbey to maintain an elegant Paris apartment, to keep a mistress, to wear clothes made by the best tailors, to cut the figure of a dandy at the Café de Paris and the Café Anglais. But there was never enough money to give him his own carriage and horses or a box at the races. This limitation was oddly important to the development of French dandyism. Circumstance as well as taste cut Barbey off from the sport-mad, Jockey-Club dandy that fascinated Sue and Musset; his dandyism was perforce restricted to the spirit.

The prosperity and fame that came to many of his journalist friends during the July Monarchy eluded Barbey. He participated in a short-lived intellectual review, wrote a prose poem, and two novels reflecting what Barbey called "le high-life de Paris", none of which found a publisher. By 1837 his inheritance had virtually disappeared and he was forced to take to journalism for a living. It was something of an admission of defeat, though also a source of amusement for the intellectual dandy Barbey had become, when in 1843 he agreed to supply articles on fashion for *Le Moniteur de la mode*. "Ma vie d'aventurier . . . m'a poussé à écrire des légèretés," he wrote to Trébutien gaily; ". . . devinez-où? dans un journal de modes, mon cher ami!"

Barbey's connection with *Le Moniteur de la mode* was brief and produced only two articles, both of them supercilious analyses of the distinction between beauty and elegance, containing unpopular pronouncements on the higher issues of fashion. (Writing of the fashionable display that centred round the races at Longchamp, for example, Barbey sneered at "cette stupide prome-

---

* Barbey's confidence in the Normandy–England identification was never troubled by any contrary experience: he never set foot in England. His highly exotic view of England ("ce pays des grotesques," he called Victoria's kingdom, "où le spleen, l'excentricité, la richesse et le gin, travaillent perpétuellement à faire un carnaval . . .") was the product of an active imagination fed on legend and literature. His own novels would further the tradition of Scott, and he was Byron's most faithful French disciple.

nade" which, he said, would soon be abandoned by "les gens vraiment élégants".) All this the proprietors of the magazine (Barbey referred to them airily as "les industriels") found too "metaphysical" for their readers, and Barbey took his talents elsewhere. But the project of a biographical article on Brummell, which had first occurred to Barbey as perfect material for a fashion-minded audience, survived his break with the magazine and expanded rapidly in his mind. It was to be a lengthy article devoted primarily to an exegesis of dandyism, and only second-arily to Brummell's life; its title would be *Essai sur le Dandysme, avec une biographie de Brummell*; and it should appear, not in a fashion magazine, but in the dignified *Revue des Deux Mondes*.

Barbey's first step in planning his essay on dandyism was to write the reliable and studious Trébutien for information. His questions indicate that he began almost as ignorant about Brummell's life as, say, Balzac; he wanted to know, for example, if Brummell was married. In addition to supplying the little infor-mation he had, Trébutien told Barbey about the amiable Captain Jesse. It was the beginning of a productive three-way correspon-dence: letters passed between Barbey and Jesse, Barbey and Trébutien, and Trébutien and Jesse, all on the subject of Brum-mell, who had died three years before. Apparently delighted to find another admirer of the Beau, Jesse sent Barbey in June of 1843 an answer to all his questions and, even more valuable, a suggested reading list. "Il a fait les choses," Barbey wrote to Trébutien approvingly, "avec beaucoup de bon goût et d'élé-gance." Barbey set himself conscientiously to his reading and, by February 29, 1844, he could inform Trébutien that he had finished "mon *Brummell*". But Jesse's part in Barbey's study was not over. With a show of uncommon literary altruism he wrote to Barbey in March promising to send his own completed bio-graphy, then in the press, when it appeared. Barbey read through Jesse's biography and benefited by its lavish details. Jesse's book did not modify in any essentials Barbey's conception of dandyism, but it turned his account of Brummell into a genuine and percep-tive biography, which eventually gave the essay a far wider audience, especially in England, than might otherwise have been expected.

From the extant letters between Barbey and Trébutien, and also from many references in *Du Dandysme*, it is clear that Barbey read, or at least looked at, virtually everything then available on dandyism. Some of the material he had been familiar with for years; some he would not have read without Jesse's insistence. The rash of Regency books in France during the 'thirties had been published for just such anglomaniacs as Barbey. Into the making of his essay went such fashionable novels as Lister's *Granby*, Mrs Gore's *Cecil*, Lord Normanby's *Yes and No* and, of course, Bulwer's *Pelham*, which Barbey had read in French, and now reread in the original. (Barbey much admired Bulwer's novel, and later sent a copy of his *Dandysme* to Bulwer with the neat but sadly outdated inscription: "Hommage d'un admirateur inconnu au plus spirituel des fashionables et au plus fashionable des auteurs spirituels.") For information about Regency society, Barbey drew on Harriette Wilson's *Memoirs*, Bulwer's *England and the English* and every conceivable scrap of Byroniana. He once boasted to Trébutien that he knew by memory ("à une virgule près") every line Byron wrote, even the most negligible and the least literary.

Barbey also had a useful knowledge (rare in a Frenchman) of the non-dandy side of the Regency world: he was familiar with the major and minor English Romantics, the radicals and utilitarians. He knew enough of the history of the Restoration, of the careers and attitudes of eighteenth-century beaux, statesmen, novelists and dramatists to trace intelligently the background of English dandyism. He knew virtually every paragraph on dandyism written in France in the 'thirties, even to fashion articles in magazines like *La Mode*, and a recently published piece on Brummell in the *Revue de Paris*. He was not familiar at this time with Balzac's *Traité de la vie élégante* but he had read and appreciated, with a warmth not then universal, all of Balzac's novels, and had remarked their dandy portraits. Stendhal, too, had caught his wide appreciation: it was the spirit of the author of *De l'amour* that Barbey invoked when undertaking his study of Brummell.

Barbey had read his "sources" over a period of thirty years as a dilettante anglophile, and there is nothing of pedantry about *Du Dandysme et de Georges Brummell*. On occasion he passed over fact to reinforce the French fantasy-portrait of the English (he says, for instance, that Brummell was like all Englishmen, a drunkard), but on the whole his account of Brummell gained depth and accuracy from his wide reading of English sources in general and of Jesse's biography in particular.* But he had no intention of accepting Jesse's book as a model. In *Du Dandysme* he refers to the biography as "une chronique timorée, sans le dessous des cartes de l'histoire"; to Trébutien he criticized it more vigorously as a "coup d'eau tiède", "un insipide breuvage". In contrast to the heavy-handed massing of detail that characterized Jesse's two-volume portrait of Brummell, Barbey drew a subtle, delicate silhouette suggestive of dandyism. He wished to produce something brief, light, elegant, dandified in form as well as in matter.

The final form of *Du Dandysme* was influenced by the circumstances of its publication. Barbey had conceived it as a magazine article, and had hoped that its appearance in a major review would bring him the reputation he felt was long overdue. But when the *Revue des Deux Mondes* and the *Débats* rejected it, he consigned the manuscript to Trébutien for printing in book-form in Caen. Both friends were enthusiastic bibliophiles, and Barbey wrote Trébutien many letters about the physical appearance of the volume: its size, its title page, the colour and quality of its binding. The principle guiding Barbey (and hardly lost on his successors of the *fin de siècle*) was that a book on a dandy subject should be, physically, eccentric, rare, precious: "Il faut qu'il soit aussi Dandy à sa façon." The book's cover bore an unusual design; the epigraph on its title page was an unknown quotation from a forgotten book; decorating the bottom of the pages was an overlay of digressive notes, which Barbey delighted in, regarding them as an embroidered fringe of commentary "dans le genre de celles dont Stendhal (c'est un esprit que j'aime!) a bariolé son charmant livre *De l'Amour*". And the style itself was compressed, finicky, precious—the kind of style which, Barbey suggested, "sent les *mille fleurs* du Dandy . . ."

3

Barbey approached Brummell with absolute respect, even with awe, as no one before him had and as everyone who followed him would. His Brummell is twice as large as life, far more indistinct, essentially inexplicable. He was a significant figure in the history

---

* "Il faut croire et copier M. Jesse," wrote Barbey resignedly, when correcting his spelling of the Beau's name from Brummel to Brummell.

of his times; he is now a legend; he compels analysis. Barbey wryly explains why such an analysis has not so far been attempted: "Pour cela," he writes, "les esprits profonds n'avaient pas assez de finesse; les esprits fins, de profondeur."

The essential fascination, the greatness of the man lie solely in his dandyism.

> En effet, il ne fut qu'un Dandy . . . ôtez le Dandy, que reste-t-il de Brummell? Il n'était propre à être rien de plus, mais aussi rien de moins que le plus grand Dandy de son temps et de tous les temps.

Barbey does away with apologies: to be *merely* a dandy, pure and exclusive in dedication to a pose, is for the first time a distinction. To Barbey, dandyism is a spiritual achievement of considerable dimensions. He minimizes the place of clothes in Brummell's dandyism, not because he considers the art of dress negligible (on the contrary) but because he wishes to emphasize what he calls the *intellectual* quality of Brummell's irony, wit, impudence and poise. What he does say about Brummell's style of dress (and here Barbey benefits particularly from careful attention to Jesse) is that it was so restrained and so natural as to be a triumph of mind rather than of body. "On l'a considéré comme un être purement physique, et il était au contraire intellectuel jusque dans le genre de beauté qu'il possédait."

Originally assuming that Brummell was a wit in the French (and in Barbey's own) manner, Barbey had hoped to quote Brummell epigrams at length. He wrote asking both Trébutien and Jesse for a sample of Brummell's "aphorismes précieux". But when Jesse at last convinced him that in place of pithy statements on life in general there was only a disdainful silence, Barbey turned this very absence of words into a compliment to Brummell's mind. "Cet homme, trop superficiellement jugé," he writes, "fut une puissance si intellectuelle qu'il régna encore plus par les airs que par les mots." His power over others derived from subtleties of manner so fine they cannot be reproduced: "Il la produisit par l'intonation, le regard, le geste, l'intention transparente, le silence même." This was uncommon deference from a man of Barbey's volubility, already proud of his reputation as a brilliant talker.

In the same way, Barbey (whose life was an unending series of love affairs) made it a corner stone of Brummell's dandyism that he had never become involved with a woman. By avoiding love, Barbey explained, Brummell had kept his vanity intact— for "Aimer, même dans le sens le moins élevé du mot, désirer, c'est toujours dépendre, c'est être esclave de son désir."

In selecting details to round out his account of Brummell's career, Barbey deviates in one essential way from Jesse: he ignores the dandy in decline. For he is concerned with Brummell the dandy and without the greatness of absolute success, he implies, there is no dandy. Barbey's fiction proves what delight he took in melodrama, horrors, pathos; but in *Du Dandysme* he disdained to dwell on the tragic finale of the dandy story, elaborated with such relish by Jesse, "cet admirable chroniqueur qui n'oublie pas assez". "C'est du Dandy qu'il est question," he writes, in a conversational and moving aside:

> Qu'importe le reste? Quand on meurt de faim, on sort des affectations d'une société quelconque, on rentre dans la vie humaine: on cesse d'être Dandy. Laissons cela.

The single point that Barbey seizes on as significant in Brummell's miserable exile is the fact that, for at least a time, several of his noble acquaintances came forward with money for Brummell's support. In Barbey's view, this assistance was merely payment for services rendered: Brummell had served his society as critic, entertainer, artist. "On était reconnaissant au nom d'un service rendu, et l'on avait raison; car le plus grand service à rendre au sociétés qui s'ennuient, n'est-ce pas de leur donner un peu de plaisir?"

Barbey's originality is to make dandyism available as an intellectual pose. The dandy is equated with the artist; society thus ought to pay him tribute. Brummell is indeed the archetype of all artists, for his art was one with his life. His achievements in costume and manner were living masterpieces: "Il plaisait avec sa personne, comme d'autres plaisent avec leurs œuvres." And Brummell is a very special kind of artist, not a creature of small charms and pretty graces; not, Barbey insists, a D'Orsay. Brummell was born to rule, and he ruled with insulting wit and cruel irony. The Beau *shocked* the haughty Regency world, and "il aimait encore mieux étonner que plaire".

Art must shock rather than please: this was the new aesthetic. For Barbey the art of dandyism was particularly significant in the social atmosphere of mid-century France. He had defined dandyism to Trébutien simply as *Anti-Vulgarité*, and the essay is to show dandyism as an attitude of protest against the vulgarized, materialistic civilization of the bourgeois century. Barbey points out that the dandy's distinction, almost his responsibility, is his abhorrence of uniformity, mediocrity and vulgarity: "Un Dandy qui marque tout de son cachet, qui n'existe pas en dehors d'une *certaine exquise originalité* (Lord Byron), doit nécessairement haïr l'uniforme." In a note explaining Byron's word, originality, Barbey clarifies his protest. Originality, he says, has no home in contemporary France; the reigning spirit of mediocrity forbids it and hates it "comme une distinction nobiliaire". In its place there is the universal dictum, "*Etre comme tout le monde*".

Dandyism is relevant to the artist and intellectual, therefore, because it is essentially an anti-bourgeois attitude. The dandy is independent of the values and pressures of a society in pursuit of money. He does not work; he exists. And his existence is itself a lesson in elegance to the vulgar mind. To prepare the dandy for his apotheosis as the mid-century artist, Barbey first presents him carefully as an exotic. Brummell, he insists, could have been born only in England (a country as exotic as Arabia); he was a phenomenon wholly alien to French society and the French temperament. "Le mot *Dandysme* n'est pas français. Il restera étranger comme la chose qu'il exprime." And the very fact that dandyism is an alien phenomenon makes it attractive to the artist in rebellion against his society.

In temperament Barbey's Brummell is akin to the mid-century intellectual. His supposed alcoholism, for example, which Barbey insists on despite all Jesse's evidence to the contrary, is hardly the coarse drunkenness of the ordinary English *milord*. "Lymphatique et nerveux", as Barbey with a certain poetic licence describes him, Brummell drank to escape from the state of mind Barbey, as well as Baudelaire, called *le spleen*: a mixture of boredom, lethargy and despair. "Il recherchait l'émotion de cette autre vie que l'on trouve au fond des breuvages, qui bat plus fort, qui tinte et qui éblouit."

Finally, the dandy's sexual ambivalence is not a weakness but a strength. In the dandy's mysterious blend of feminine elegance with masculine power Barbey sees the archetypal decadence;

there the *fin de siècle* would also see a reflection of its ideals. The dandies are for Barbey the *androgynes* of history:

> natures doubles et multiples, d'un sexe intellectuel indécis, où la grâce est plus grâce encore dans la force et où la force se retrouve encore dans la grâce . . .

How indecently lyrical would this tribute have sounded to Victorian ears! And how far from the anti-dandiacal position, how far from the Regency position, how far indeed from George Bryan Brummell is Barbey's definition of the Dandy as a holy man:

> un homme qui porte en lui quelque chose de supérieur au monde visible.

4

The quest for "something superior to the visible world" was Barbey's own; that too he brought to the dandy tradition. After *Du Dandysme* his life shifted in a direction most of his acquaintances could not have predicted. It is a shift to be placed beside the change in Eugène Sue, for as Sue became the dandy-revolutionary, so Barbey would exhibit the anomaly of the dandy-priest.

Barbey d'Aurevilly was a contemporary of Eugène Sue, not of Baudelaire, whose concept of dandyism he so strongly influenced. He was born only four years after Sue and almost twenty years before Baudelaire; he outlived them both by more than two decades. Barbey's not insignificant position in French letters derived partly from the sheer expanse of his life, from 1808 to 1889, partly from the fact that, like Sue, he underwent a conversion in the middle of his career. He responded, as Sue responded, to each of the socio-political shocks that deflected the course of French literature in the nineteenth century—but in an exactly opposite direction. Brought up to Catholicism, monarchism and the aristocratic tradition, Barbey became a radical during his two years of study in Paris in the late 'twenties; thus he rejoiced at the advent of the Revolution in 1830—when Sue was at the height of his fashionable career. In the late 'thirties, when Sue turned away from the aristocracy of the Faubourg, Barbey ended his brief flirtation with radicalism, developed a distaste for democrats and jacobins, and became a dandy of the salons, the cafés and the boulevards. The radical young Barbey began to call himself Jules Amédée Barbey *d'Aurevilly*.*

Barbey began to write his *Dandysme* only a year after Sue started on his *Mystères de Paris*; Sue's book ingratiated its author with the socialists and brought him a mass audience, while *Du Dandysme* strengthened Barbey's connection with the aristocratic world. (Disappointingly few reviews greeted the appearance of the pretty volume, but Barbey made sure that copies circulated to those among the intellectuals and the aristocrats who would be interested in dandyism.) The book enjoyed a limited but enthusiastic word-of-mouth popularity and made Barbey the lion of the season. ("Les blondes et les impertinents du faubourg Saint-Germain m'appellent *Brummell II* . . .", he wrote to Trébutien; "les invitations à dîner me pleuvent".) Three years later the Revolution of 1848 gave Sue's new-found "socialism" a political as well as a literary significance; the same events confirmed Barbey in his hatred of liberalism. And the advent of Louis-Napoléon, which sent Sue into exile and brought him the threat of excommunication, found Barbey a spokesman of the Jesuits and a staunch supporter of the new régime, which he respected as the incarnation of force and stability.

Barbey's "conversion" to Catholicism was neither so sudden nor so superficial as his enemies maintained: his brother Léon, a priest, had designated him years before as a "future Christian". His early journals reveal the temperament of a man groping after religious faith, and the actual conversion was quietly in the making through the 'forties. It became a matter of public record when, in 1846, the year after *Du Dandysme*, Barbey joined the *Société Catholique*, a lay organization devoted to the aim of refurbishing the liturgy and the aesthetic of the Church. Barbey's role in the movement was as guiding spirit of the *Revue du Monde Catholique*, founded in 1847.

Throughout the Second Empire Barbey exerted a growing influence in the intellectual community, less as a novelist (though most of his best fiction was written in this period) than as a critic

---

* The aristocratic name of d'Aurevilly had been in the family since 1756, when Vincent Barbey, the author's bourgeois grandfather, purchased a patent of *nobilité de fonctions*. Worship of the nobility and the Bourbons was a Barbey failing: family tradition had it that his mother was descended from Louis XVI.

for and of the Jesuit faction. As a distinguished journalist he wrote excited polemics on political and Church affairs, and vigorous, eccentric literary criticism for many influential reviews. In 1868, as the Empire ebbed toward its end, he became a regular contributor to the *Constitutionnel,* where his bi-weekly *Chronique littéraire* alternated with that of Sainte-Beuve.

Changes in his political and religious convictions did not alter Barbey's essential character: he was always to be the Byronic rebel, the romantic eccentric or, as D. B. Wyndham-Lewis has called him, the Cyrano de Bergerac (Rostand's Cyrano) of nineteenth-century letters. In theory a faithful devotee of the Jesuits, in practice he was a radical and independent Catholic, liable to many arguments with the Church. Of his numerous novels and stories devoted to Catholic subjects none is characterized by humility, by pietism or by doctrinal orthodoxy. His theme was the prevalence of evil, particularly the sins of adultery and murder, and his central preoccupation was diabolism. His novels and stories were meant to shock, as their melodramatic titles attest (*Une Veille Maîtresse, L'Ensorcelée, Un Prêtre marié, Les Diaboliques,*" Le Bonheur dans le crime"), and when they did shock Barbey's more timid contemporaries, such as the pious Trébutien, he was ready with a defence that has since been echoed, in one form or another, by all French Catholic writers. "Mon catholicisme est tranquille," he wrote in answer to one of Trébutien's increasingly frequent protests.

> Ce qu'il y a de magnifique dans le catholicisme, cher ami, c'est qu'il est large, compréhensif, immense; c'est qu'il embrasse la nature humaine tout entière . . . et que par-dessus ce qu'il embrasse, il a déployé la grande maxime : Malheur à celui qui se scandalise! Il n'a rien de prude, de bégueule, de pédant, d'*inquiet.* C'est bon cela, pour les vertus fausses, pour les puritanismes tondus . . . Le catholicisme aime les Arts, et accepte, sans trembler, leurs audaces.

This confident manifesto was another flourish of Barbey's literary *panache.* He was increasingly attacked by the clerics—and applauded by poets in trouble with both Church and state. It was not the Church but Huysmans, another novelist drawn to Catholicism through diabolism, who claimed Barbey as a major Catholic writer: "le seul artiste, au pur sens du mot, que produisit le catholicisme de ce temps." It was Paul Verlaine who called

Barbey a *formidable* Catholic, one of the few serious and clear-sighted thinkers on religious matters among his contemporaries. Verlaine also pointed out that the major sphere of Barbey's influence was the literary world. "Les poètes l'apprécient hautement," he wrote, "les poètes le lisent avec ferveur, et c'est encore le plus beau fleuron de sa couronne."

Barbey repaid the homage of poets with an essential service. Provided with a critical chair, he was in a position to comment on the appearance of successive generations of the young writers from the symbolist or aesthetic or decadent confraternity, to whom he felt temperamentally akin. He could find merit in the work of Baudelaire in the 'fifties or Huysmans in the 'seventies where others found ground for scandal and mockery. And that merit he defined in Catholic terms. It was Barbey who held out to the author of *Les Fleurs du mal* the choice between two alternatives: either to blow out his brains or to embrace the feet of the Cross. And he repeated the same directive (now famous, because Huysmans quoted it in his 1903 preface) to the author of *A Rebours*. Barbey's distinction was to see potential Catholics where his contemporaries saw perverse celebrants of evil things; to point out that a poet like Baudelaire "was primarily occupied" (as T. S. Eliot remarked in the 'twenties) "with religious values."

In those writers he called Christians Barbey also found elements of the dandy pose. He used the two terms with enthusiastic vagueness (in his writings it sometimes seems that both *dandy* and *Christian* are meaningless synonyms for admirable.) But the association was more legitimate than Barbey at times made it appear. In its hostility to the bourgeois ethic and to romantic liberalism, dandyism was in part a complement and in part an alternative to the Catholic revival. In its insistence on order and ritual and discipline, in its disdain for enthusiasms and entanglements the dandy pose had much to commend it to the intellectual Catholic.

Barbey's long career as novelist and critic guaranteed that dandies and dandyism came repeatedly before the French reading public. In fact, as a persistent admirer of English literature, he found dandies prevalent even in the Victorian climate. Although familiar with *Sartor Resartus*, he made the ingenuous suggestion in his notes to the second edition (1861) of *Du Dandysme* that

Carlyle's *Heroes and Hero-Worship* might well have included a portrait of *le Héros Dandy* alongside *le Héros Roi, le Héros Poète, le Héros Prêtre*. When G. A. Lawrence's *Guy Livingstone* was translated into French (also in 1861) Barbey hailed the book as a return to the tradition of the "roman de high life, ni plus ni moins que *Pelham*", and seized on Guy as a realization of the "dandy héroique". (Lawrence himself, furthermore, showed promise as a "grand romancier chrétien".) More interesting, when Balzac's *Traité de la vie élégante* appeared for the first time in book form (in a posthumous collection of the novelist's early writings), Barbey wrote a long, appreciative review of what he rightly took for a precursor of his own *Du Dandysme*.

In Barbey's late fiction the dandy figure was absorbed into the perfumed atmosphere of "flowers of evil", and juxtaposed with devil-obsessed female antagonists. *Les Diaboliques* (1874), his finest work, is a collection of short stories about these devil-women and dandy men. It contains a whole catalogue of the dandy species—French dandies, military dandies, libertine dandies, especially old dandies, for Barbey was now well over sixty. In "Le Bonheur dans le crime", for example, the villainous, cold-blooded Count de Savigny is a consummate dandy, dressing in a style "simple et *dandy* comme l'entendait Brummell, c'est-à-dire *irrémarquable*." Only one "détail *ridicule*" mars the perfection of his dandyism, and that has a special significance for the ageing Barbey: a pair of brilliant sapphire earrings, worn proudly to display "assez de dédain pour le goût et les idées du jour."

Barbey's own costume, as an old man in the eighteen-seventies and 'eighties, was also a reminder of dandyism, though it certainly owed nothing to Brummell. His garish wardrobe of props and disguises, like de Savigny's sapphire earrings, proclaimed the essential doctrine of *Du Dandysme et de Georges Brummell*: disdain for the ideas and taste of the day. He affected tight black satin trousers, blood-red gloves, full-skirted frock coats, shirts with lace frills, gaudily striped capes, towering broad-brimmed hats, white linen trousers strapped under the foot and trimmed with a band of mauve silk. The extraordinary feature of this costume was not so much that it was flamboyant as that it was resolutely old-fashioned. These were the clothes of the 'thirties, and the younger men of Barbey's old age, knowing him as the prophet of *le dandysme*, saw him (with some justice) as a survivor from the first generation of French *lions*.

In his eccentric clothes, in his eccentric way of life,* the old Barbey demonstrated to the last that in temperament he was more the romantic than the dandy. Yet, largely through his influence, French dandyism achieved intellectual maturity, forgetting its origins as a horse-ridden, anglomaniac fad of the 'thirties. Barbey had proved that there could be a distinction between aristocratic dandies and literary dandies, and his distinction went into the making of the poet Charles Baudelaire. It was perhaps the major contribution of the eccentric, romantic, Bohemian, *chouan*, Catholic and dandy that, enthusiastically mixed together, were Barbey d'Aurevilly. Of this *bouillabaisse* of poses he was wholly conscious and rather proud. "C'est que le Dandy commence à être las de sa défroque," he wrote in the middle of his career, "et plutôt qu'on ne croit peut-être abaissera le capuchon du moine sur son orgueilleux front de Giaour."

* In his seventies and eighties he still ran after women, or at least talked about doing so; he drank too much, went into society too much, argued, gesticulated too much. He was often seen surrounded by a circle of ardent young disciples; this gave rise to the rumour (it was part of the legend of Barbey's eccentricity) that he was an ageing homosexual, to which Barbey's rumoured, characteristic defence was that "mes goûts m'y portent, mes principes me le permettent, mais la laideur de mes contemporains me dégoûte."

CHAPTER XII

Baudelaire

Eternelle supériorité du Dandy.
Qu'est-ce que le Dandy?
    —Mon Cœur mis à nu

THE legend of Baudelaire the Dandy began with the reminiscences of his friends—Asselineau, Nadar, Cousin, Banville, Gautier, Champfleury—who, after Baudelaire's death, turned away from the tragic spectacle of his last years to recall the young poet of the early eighteen-forties. In place of the haggard face with deep lines around the mouth, thinning hair and haunted eyes (the face of the Carjat and Nadar photographs from the 'sixties, which have become the permanent image of Baudelaire), they saw the strikingly handsome head of a young man in his early twenties, radiating confidence and vitality. He then wore his hair long and waving, with full moustache and a dark, curling beard encircling his chin in the D'Orsay style; "une barbe," Théodore de Banville called it, "enfantine, rare, idéale de jeune dieu." Banville insisted with lyrical emphasis on the appearance of the young Baudelaire, who in his twenties was, he said, rich, happy, beloved, already famous. "O rare exemple d'un visage réellement divin," wrote Banville, "réunissant toutes les élégances, toutes les forces et les séductions les plus irrésistibles!"

In 1842, Baudelaire came of age, took an elaborate apartment in the Hôtel Pimodan, began his liaison with Jeanne Duval and chose his friends from the Right Bank worlds of café and boulevard. In 1844, distress over his mounting debts led his family to restrict his expenditures legally through the appointment of a *conseil judiciaire*. In the brief time between these two events, Baudelaire had unquestionably the appearance of a dandy: he dressed with elegance, with distinction, with subtle originality. Those were the years of affluence. It is no accident that a panegyric on wealth introduces Baudelaire's famous portrait of *le dandy* . . .

What most impressed Baudelaire's friends in those years was his insistence on black—overwhelming, gleaming black from his lustrous high hat to his impeccably polished shoes. At that time black was hardly the obligatory colour for either day or evening wear; when, later in the century, it became the mark of respectability, devotees of costume like Dickens or Barbey d'Aurevilly resented its tyranny. But Baudelaire always relished black, at once as a colour and as a negation of all colour. In the 'forties world of *lions* and *incroyables* this unity of tone was a consciously dramatic gesture of separation. "Aussi quelle merveille que ce costume noir," remarked one of Baudelaire's friends, "toujours le même, à toute heure, en toute saison . . ." Commenting on this sombre blackness, on Baudelaire's forbidding formality of manner, on his obvious obsession with dandyism, Catulle Mendès gave the poet a witty nickname: His Eminence Monsignor Brummell (*S. Em. Mgr Brummel*).

His clothes were then cut according to his own minute instructions, and in a manner slightly different from the prevailing fashion: trousers slim and buttoned under his shoes, coat unusually long and straight. As a very young man he would use a dash of colour to set off the blackness of his clothes. Nadar remembered a cravat of red (*sang de bœuf*) and pale rose gloves; Asselineau a white cravat and neutral gloves. Somewhat later, however, according to Le Vavasseur, the poet appeared completely in black, including waistcoat and cravat, out of a desire to appear more *grave*. He knew the symbolic possibilities of costume. Black was appropriate, he felt, to an age in mourning; the century moved down in a declining path, not upwards toward progress; "nous célébrons tous quelque enterrement." And austerity of line, restraint in colour and ornament symbolized a spiritual aloofness. So he came to shave his beard, to clip his hair close to his head and at last to abandon his moustache, finding, according to Théophile Gautier, "que c'était un reste de vieux chic pittoresque qu'il était puéril et bourgeois de conserver." These were sacrifices to a conscious dandyism. The perfect dandy, Baudelaire wrote in the 'sixties, valued costume merely as a symbol of spiritual aristocracy. "Aussi, à ses yeux . . ., la perfection de la toilette consiste-t-elle dans la simplicité absolue, qui est, en effet, la meilleure manière de se distinguer."

Beau Brummell's refinements of costume had been a means of

marking his superiority to the aristocratic world in which he moved; his disciples, from Bulwer to Barbey, looked for a fashionable audience. Baudelaire was a different dandy. He spent scarcely any time in the Paris salons; he had no close friends among the aristocrats; and, for all his scorn of the bourgeois, he did not identify himself with the aristocracy as a class. For him, as for his English contemporary, Matthew Arnold, the aristocrats were not champions of civilization but barbarians. The Jockey-Club in particular, once the temple of French dandyism, incurred Baudelaire's wrath. When its members opposed the introduction of opera without ballet (that is, without their mistresses among the ballet girls) and thereby contributed to the failure of *Tannhäuser* in Paris, Baudelaire wrote a diatribe against them all. "Keep your harem," he told the Jockey-Club dandies, "and conserve its traditions religiously; but let us have a theatre where those who think differently from you can find other pleasures better adapted to their taste. Thus," he concludes with a gesture of dismissal, "we shall be quit of you and you of us, and each will be content."

The "we" of Baudelaire's proclamation are the aristocracy of the future, the idle, *déclassé* intelligentsia on whom sensitivity to the new and powerful in art confers a special distinction:

> une espèce nouvelle d'aristocratie, d'autant plus difficile à rompre qu'elle sera basée sur les facultés les plus précieuses, les plus indestructibles, et sur les dons célestes que le travail et l'argent ne peuvent conférer.

Baudelaire posed as a dandy, then, not for the fashionable world but for the community of artists. The austerity of his style was a protest against the adolescent dramatics of his own circle: the *joyeux enfants de la Bohème*. In the Bohemian world the very cleanliness of his linen, the presence of a rug on the floor of his apartment, the formality of his speech and the old-fashioned politeness of his manner were conscious anomalies. They expressed his belief in an aristocracy of spirit, which disassociated itself equally from extravagant affectations and negligent disarray. "One might say of him that he was a dandy lost in Bohemia," Gautier commented, "but preserving his rank and his manners and that cult of self which characterizes the man imbued with the principles of Brummell."

2

Brummell's principles meant a great deal to Baudelaire; Brummell the man, nothing. He took no interest in the Regency origins of dandyism, and he was by no means a votary of anglomania. For him the dandy was a permanent but also immediate essence to be superimposed on his conception of the artist. For this view of the dandy he was indebted to Barbey d'Aurevilly. "Rereading the book *Du Dandysme*," he wrote in the *Salon de 1846*,* ". . . the reader will clearly see that dandyism is a modern thing, springing from causes completely new."

Barbey's contribution to Baudelaire's mind was important, not because it added anything to the content of his thoughts but because it provided a shape within which these thoughts could be organized. To Baudelaire, organization was vital. His profoundest convictions—on life, on art, on the role of the poet— were always intimately related to the sum of petty habits and superficial gestures with which he lived: black clothes, white hands, clean boots. Like so many men of the nineteenth century, Baudelaire organized the profound with the trivial by means of a construct that was both ideal and pose. Barbey provided the Dandy.

No detail of Baudelaire's existence was too trivial to be scrutinized in the light of principle; no principle too profound to be expressed in habit and gesture. In this sense, for him as for his numerous followers among the "aesthetes", life and art were one. His solitary existence and his refusal to accept the homage of disciples related to his concept of poetic genius. (*La plus belle destinée: avoir du génie et être obscur.*) His exaggerated politeness, even to his closest friends, implied an intellectual misanthropy. (*La politesse . . . C'est le meilleur bâton de longueur qu'il y ait entre soi et les sots.*)

His passion for the woman of colour (*brune, dorée, parfumée comme le vin de son pays*) with fluid movements suggesting the animal grace of the cat (*le plus voluptueux animal qui fût jamais*) grew out of his view of woman as pure body—and that the body of an animal (*l'animal inférieur se retrouve toujours*). His experiments with opium (*cette drogue enivrante et maudite*), his quest for release through drinking (*cette autre vie que l'on trouve au fond*

* One year after the publication of Barbey's study.

des breuvages) were justified by the elevation of Boredom to the status of an all-powerful divinity (*l'ennui, qui est bien le dieu de ma vie*). And Boredom itself inhabited a persistent climate (*un temps gris, pluvieux, spleenétique*). Disgust with the commonness of a middle-class world (*J'ai tellement la haine du commun que la vérité m'ennuie*) was at the root of his aesthetic of control; this principle in turn regulated both the form of his poetry and the form of his life: a mask of indifference concealing inner despair. (*Sous un dédain léger je voile ma torture . . .*)

The quotations interpolated above, so apposite to Baudelaire, are drawn of course from the writings of Barbey d'Aurevilly. They illustrate the temperamental similarities which guaranteed their mutual attraction to dandyism. Yet the differences between the two men were greater than their resemblances. Barbey, outspoken Catholic, polemicist, naïve romantic, saw that the bond between them consisted less in what they admired than in what they detested. "Il n'a pas notre foi ni nos respects, "he wrote Trébutien of Baudelaire, "mais il a nos haines et nos mépris."

Barbey and Baudelaire knew each other in the 'fifties and 'sixties. They exchanged letters, books, expressions of encouragement and sympathy. Considerably older and already established, Barbey was for the poet, as Porché puts it, "un soutien moral en ces dures années". Barbey insisted on the publication of Baudelaire's Poe translations in *Le Pays* (1854) when they had been rejected everywhere else. He wrote laudatory reviews of *Les Fleurs du mal*, at the time the state condemned the book and the great Sainte-Beuve, supposedly sympathetic to Baudelaire, refused to write a line in its defence. Baudelaire referred to Barbey. as *le vieux mauvais sujet*; Barbey called Baudelaire, with equal affection, *chère horreur de ma vie*, and hoped to convert him.

Like Barbey, Baudelaire repeatedly used the word *dandy* as a value term, a kind of personal, suggestive, imprecise shorthand. Artists and writers in whom he found fellow feelings, and whom he therefore admired, he would call dandies for reasons often difficult to decipher; the rest he could then dismiss as non-dandies. Proudhon, for example, he wrote, "la plume à la main, c'était un bon bougre; mais pas dandy du tout . . ." He was able to find elements of dandyism in Delacroix and Poe, in Emma Bovary and in Valmont (the hero of *Les Liaisons dangereuses*).

He once planned to do a study of his contemporary "dandys-littéraires" that would include, besides Barbey d'Aurevilly, the Marquis de Custine and Chateaubriand!

Scattered references to dandies and dandyism occur in Baudelaire's journals, in his letters and critical essays—never, directly, in his poetry. They are on the whole as mysterious, if as pregnant with feeling, as the citation at the head of this chapter. In only one work, *Le Peintre de la vie moderne*, did Baudelaire expound a full perception of dandyism. But this solitary examination, though it grew out of Barbey's work, brought new power and new depth to the dandy tradition. Because of its intensity, its luminous language and the greatness of its criticism, this essay alone made *dandysme* a necessary commonplace of Baudelaire criticism. Critics of the poet have labelled as dandyism his passions for artificiality, for perfection, for refinement, and his antipathies to vulgarity, to sentimentalism and to extravagance. One critic has called Baudelaire's thought a "philosophy of dandyism"; another has found his aesthetics to be the faith of a *"dandy intérieur"*; another has studied his *"religion du dandysme"*; and latterly Jean-Paul Sartre has contrived to claim Baudelaire as an existentialist precursor by redefining his dandyism.

Barbey had glorified Beau Brummell for the post-romantic generation by means of his own, wholly romantic enthusiasm. His admiration was essentially for a Life, for a kind of life not his own yet, in the best of worlds, possible. And his *Du Dandysme*, though serious in its implications and assumptions, was essentially a clever *tour de force* which created, through the careful amassing of biographical detail, an awesome symbolic figure. Given Barbey's work, Baudelaire could reach for the Dandy whole, as a symbol in the poetic sense. In *Le Peintre de la vie moderne, le dandy* is not a man but a concept rich in linguistic—rather than specifically historical—associations. *Du Dandysme* provided Baudelaire with a kind of poet's anthology. Barbey had offered up the dandy figure for the pleasure of the intellectuals; Baudelaire, by sheer strength of language, forced it on succeeding generations of poets.

3

Le Peintre de la vie moderne appeared in *Le Figaro* in 1863, eighteen years after the publication of Barbey's *Du Dandysme*. It presents Baudelaire in three roles, by turns the professional art critic, speaking dryly on his subject; the analyst of modern society, evoking with a fine sweep of words the mid-century and Second Empire France; and, finally, the poet, propounding in a poet's prose a credo for the modern artist.

The essay begins (Section 1: *Le beau, la mode et le bonheur*) in a brisk and professional manner: the art critic rustles his notes and calls his audience to attention. There are those, says the critic, who think they have *done* their museums when they admire Titians and Raphaels; I shall speak today of the *minor* artists whose work is a portrait of their age. I have before me several costume prints from the last century . . . And this is an excellent occasion to establish a "rational and historical" theory of beauty: that Beauty is two beauties, the eternal and the transitory, inseparable even in the highest art.

A short second section lauds the revival of engraving and touches on its best known practitioners.

The third section, too (*L'artiste, homme du monde, homme des foules et enfant*), opens in the style of a lecture: I shall speak today of a man . . . But here the poet enters, to speak less of one man, a specific artist, than of The Artist: man of the world, man of crowds, child.

The actual person of whom the critic speaks, and on whom he bestows the title of "the painter of modern life", is never referred to by name but merely by initials: as *Monsieur G.* or *Monsieur C. G.* For so unorthodox a procedure the art critic offers an explanation: the artist in question has a *bizarre désir*; he wants to remain anonymous, indeed he insists that preservation of his anonymity is a condition for preservation of friendship between himself and the critic. For the poet this explanation is merely a pretext. Baudelaire's "painter of modern life" is an ideal transcending the unnamed *G.* He insists that the reader *and the critic* are to pretend that *G.* does not exist. And he offers his reconstruction of the artist's personality as a purely "poetic hypothesis, conjecture, work of imagination."

There was, however, a real *G.*: the brilliant draughtsman and illustrator, Constantin Guys, for many years known personally to Baudelaire but at the time almost unknown to the general public. Guys's desire for anonymity was both sincere and consistent. He did not sign his drawings, and he once quarrelled with Thackeray when the novelist mentioned Guys by name in a piece of *his* art criticism. What may have puzzled Thackeray delighted Baudelaire.

Love of self-concealment was only one of the bonds between artist and poet. Théophile Gautier (who may have brought about their acquaintance) later wrote extensively of the sympathy between Baudelaire and Guys. They shared, he said, a passion for "le haut dandysme" and an instinct for "les corruptions modernes".

Born into a distinguished French family living in southern Holland, Constantin Guys spent his early years as a traveller, a cosmopolitan, man of means and man of action. He followed Byron to Missolonghi, enlisted in a French regiment, and then drifted to England, where, his money apparently running out, he supported himself as a tutor. (Gavarni ran across him in the Blessington–D'Orsay salon.) Some years earlier he had begun to draw, simply as a pastime. In 1848 (he was then forty-six) he found a position on the *Illustrated London News*, which he served as a Paris art correspondent, sending drawings of the opera and ballet; as a correspondent from the Balkans, the Near East and North Africa, where he travelled extensively; and then as a war correspondent sending daily drawn dispatches from the Crimea. Finally he returned to Paris, establishing it as his permanent base between travels (while he had the money and health to travel) and continuing to sketch almost compulsively.

Guys led a solitary life, resolutely apart from the artistic and literary Bohemias of the capital. But the small circle of writers and painters to whom his work was known (Delacroix, Félicien Rops, Manet, Garvarni, Nadar, Champfleury and the Goncourts were among his admirers) recognized Guys as the unofficial historiographer of Second Empire Paris. He haunted the theatres, the streets, the parks, storing up impressions for countless sketches which, when a small pension from his family was exhausted, he would gather into bundles and sell for a few francs —the bundle. On the evidence of his drawings, Guys spent his time admiring from a distance those appurtenances of a rich man's life which he had once known intimately: women and horses.

Little more is known about Guys today; Baudelaire probably knew less. From this meagre silhouette of an anonymous life Baudelaire built the almost mythological figure of the artist-dandy. *G.*'s mania for anonymity is, for Baudelaire, the dandy's imperious aloofness. To the insensitive and the uninitiated, the form of *G.*'s life may appear to be absolute idleness. As the apparently idle man, however, *G.* again approaches dandyism : he is the stroller and onlooker, the dandy as *observateur passionné* and *parfait flâneur*. His place is not in the studio but out on the boulevards, among the crowds of a modern city. "L'observateur est un *prince* qui jouit partout de son incognito"—a Prince Rodolphe, perhaps, whose destiny among the crowds is not to rule but to observe. To this role he brings a deep curiosity and a sensibility Baudelaire likens to that of the convalescent (recalling Poe's story, "The Man of the Crowd") and to that of the child.

Through his refusal to sketch for money *G.* escapes the stigma of *specialist*, which for Baudelaire is comprised in the word *artist*. Rather let us call him a *man of the world*, "c'est-à-dire homme du monde entier, homme qui comprend le monde et les raisons mystérieuses et légitimes de tous ses usages." Better still, let us call him a *dandy*, for—and here Baudelaire brings a new dimension to that already weighted term—"car le mot *dandy* implique une quintessence de caractère et une intelligence subtile de tout le mécanisme moral de ce monde." The artist-dandy exercises this subtle moral sense in portraying that elusive something Baudelaire calls modernity.

> Ainsi il va, il court, il cherche. Que cherche-t-il? A coup sûr, cet homme, tel que je l'ai dépeint, ce solitaire doué d'une imagination active . . ., a un but plus général, autre que le plaisir fugitif de la circonstance. Il cherche ce quelque chose qu'on nous permettra d'appeler la *modernité*; car il ne se présente pas de meilleur mot pour exprimer l'idée en question . . .

Guys's first claim to be "the painter of modern life" lies in his sensitivity to the nuances of modern dress, his concern with the costume, the pose and the gesture even before the individuality of his model. In the simplest sense Baudelaire's definition of modernity implies nothing more than modern dress, and his plea for the modern in art is merely a demand that painters forget classic draperies and portray men and women of today as they are and as they dress. The costume of every period is in its way beautiful, says Baudelaire, even our poor modern clothes—"our poor clothes (which have their own grace, it is true, but of rather a moral and spiritual nature) . . ."

Clothes, then, can be said to have a *moral* grace, just as the dandy has a *moral* intelligence and just as beauty, Baudelaire goes on to explain, assumes a *moral* aspect. The recurring word has both theological and aesthetic implications. In Baudelaire's view the duality of beauty corresponds to the duality of man, a permanent soul in a transitory body. The transitory or *modern* elements in beauty are related to corporeal man, the clothed body knowing sin and corruption. The artist who attempts to suppress the transitory, the modern or the *moral* is thus left with only "the emptiness of an abstract and indefinable beauty", like the beauty of (and here Baudelaire's metaphor is carefully chosen) "woman before the first sin".

In choice of subject, G. also reveals himself as the painter of modernity. Avoiding the quiet beauties of nature, he pursues the moral drama in the noisy splendour of great modern cities.

> Il admire l'éternelle beauté et l'étonnante harmonie de la vie dans les capitales . . . Il jouit des beaux équipages, des fiers chevaux, de la propreté éclatante des grooms, de la dextérité des valets, de la démarche des femmes onduleuses, des beaux enfants, heureux de vivre et d'être bien habillés ; en un mot, de la vie universelle.

These parks and boulevards, these men of wealth and women of leisure, these horses and carriages and parades evoke in the beholder deep and impetuous desires; in that sense they are, "en un mot, de la vie universelle". These sketches speak eloquently to Baudelaire of intoxicating happiness and sinister misfortune, of pleasure for the flesh and corruption in the soul.

Baudelaire is familiar with the sinister women of Guys's world. Their hard faces and slanting eyes, their impudent white shoulders and swelling breasts, their attitudes of abandon as they sway their huge crinolines gracefully about their graceless legs, evoke all the horror and corruption of what Baudelaire called the animal sex. Woman, he writes here, as he examines G.'s sketches, is a terrible divinity with nothing to say, stupid as an idol. But she must fascinate poet and artist as the incarnation of beauty, not the pure beauty of the classic sculptors but, once again, that fugitive modern beauty with its moral consequences. Her crinolines, her scarves, her heavy jewels, her rouge—all are part of this beauty. Indeed, artifice is the one sublimity of her animal nature.

In his praise of cosmetics (Section XI: *Eloge du maquillage*) Baudelaire outlines the metaphysics of modernity. Artifice is not a denial of true beauty but an improvement on nature—"une déformation sublime de la nature". The naïve and mediocre thinkers of my day, Baudelaire insists, perpetuate the major error of the eighteenth century in believing nature pure and good. On the contrary, all evil comes from nature, and all good—art, beauty, virtue—from artifice, a triumph of reason and calculation over instinct. Contemporary thought is most stupid and most blind when it idealizes nature, pretending thus to reaffirm a superficial optimism and to deny the existence of original sin. And woman can be said to bring the most significant beauty to modern life precisely because her beauty derives from evil—the actual, living beauty, that is, of woman *after* the first sin.

Baudelaire lingers over G.'s carefully differentiated portraits of the beautiful sex. With the artist he descends from the superficial decency of the young girls of the aristocracy to the sinister degradation of the lowest level of prostitute. There particularly he finds that *beauté qui vient du Mal* which is for him the essence of modernity. It is G.'s genius, it is the genius of the artist-dandy, Baudelaire concludes, to extract beauty from corruption. There is nothing in his art to excite the lascivious or shock the prude, nothing but "le vice inévitable, c'est-à-dire le regard du démon embusqué dans les ténèbres."

4

Baudelaire has now made over his *Monsieur G.* as the artist-dandy, dandy in his independence of money, dandy in his self-control, dandy in his observant idleness, dandy most of all in his sensitivity to the modern and the moral in beauty, in his acceptance of evil. But he also wishes to establish G. as the artist *of* the dandy, and here *Le Peintre de la vie moderne* departs most from art criticism. In the great majority of Guys's sketches of Paris his women take the foreground. Only in the corner of the sketches, half-hidden by a spreading crinoline or dwarfed by a towering coiffure, are the men for whom these women exist. They are Second Empire dandies who, slouching against the door of a café, top hat tilted and long cigar brandished in the night air, recall the Jockey-Club barbarians who aroused Baudelaire's antagonism. But Baudelaire's eloquent and passionate portrait of the ideal dandy is almost independent of Guys's sketches. *Le dandy*, the ninth section of *Le Peintre de la vie moderne*, is a poetic distillation of Barbey's *Du Dandysme* (with only a passing reference to Brummell). This is Baudelaire's perception of the pure dandy, superior to the mere artist and the very incarnation of modernity, available to the artist as a modern ideal.

Inviolable and apart but not irrelevant, Baudelaire's dandy rules over the corrupt civilization of the modern century. He is a creature of wealth but unconcerned with money ("un crédit indéfini pourrait lui suffire"); an adept at love ("l'occupation naturelle des oisifs") but not its dupe; a votary of elegance, but never a slave.

Baudelaire's dandy detests vulgarity above all else: it is more than a crime. The dandy could, says the poet, commit a crime without remorse, "mais si ce crime naissait d'une source triviale, le déshonneur serait irréparable." Revelation of his sufferings to the world would also mean dishonour; they must be hidden under a mask of indifference or disdain. Thus the dandy's ritual of the toilette, even his addiction to the rigours and dangers of sport, can be seen as a form of dedication to control: "une gymnastique propre à fortifier la volonté et à discipliner l'âme." The dandy doctrine of elegance and originality is as demanding as the most rigorous monastic rule.

Approaching the religious position through self-discipline, Baudelaire's dandy approaches the aesthetic position through an insistence on self-beautification. Outlasting all the illusions of life, outlasting especially, the poet writes, the search for that happiness which derives from the love of a woman, is the dandy's passion for distinction, that "culte de soi-même" which is the essence of the dandy pose. The dandy recognizes before all else "le besoin ardent de se faire une originalité": not, that is, the need to be original (with the naïveté of a romantic or the extravagance of a Bohemian) but the need *to make of oneself something original*—as the artist creates an original work out of his own being . . .

"Dandyism is the last burst of heroism in the midst of decadence." Against the rising tide of triviality and mediocrity the dandy stands in brief revolt. He is superb, without warmth and full of melancholy, like the setting sun.

Le dandysme est un soleil couchant; comme l'astre qui décline, il est superbe, sans chaleur et plein de mélancolie. Mais, hélas! la marée montante de la démocratie, qui envahit tout et qui nivelle tout, noie jour à jour ces derniers représentants de l'orgueil humain et verse des flots d'oubli sur les traces de ces prodigieux myrmidons.

5

With *Le Peintre de la vie moderne* the dandy tradition reached its apogee. Baudelaire brought out all the capacity of the dandy figure for rebellion: for scornful, silent, unsuccessful rebellion against the mediocre materialism of a democratic era. Dickens had suggested a dandyism of failure; Barbey had expounded a dandyism of dissatisfaction; Baudelaire finally posited a dandyism of despair. Precisely because the dandy was, for Baudelaire, a figure apart from life, irresponsible, idle, absorbed with self, he could serve as a moral consciousness for the contemporary world. Defiant in a bourgeois society, Baudelaire's dandy admitted the originality and permanence of sin; he observed and acquiesced in the modernity of evil.

What Baudelaire began in all seriousness, Oscar Wilde would finish off in all folly. When dandyism at last re-emerged in English letters, it had absorbed Baudelaire's attitude of despair, his praise of artificiality, his recognition of evil. But Baudelaire's thought was transmitted to the *fin de siècle* through the feverish imagination of J.-K. Huysmans and the juvenile imagination of Algernon Swinburne. Dandies and corruption, dandies and sin, dandies and *les fleurs du mal* would in the 'nineties become partners in cliché. Baudelaire's ideal dandy took ridiculous shape in the posturings of Dorian Gray, who, a yellow-bound copy of *A Rebours* in hand, "looked on evil simply as a mode through which he could realize his conception of the beautiful."

Baudelaire's vision of the dandy as the last representative of human pride drowning in a rising sea of democracy would find ironic confirmation in the last chapter of the dandy's history. For the dandy was to go down to defeat at the hands not of decadence but of vulgarity. The *fin de siècle* made him over for a mass audience.

Part Six

ENGLAND: FIN DE SIÈCLE

CHAPTER XIII

Fin de Siècle:
The Decadence of Dandyism

(I) MEN

It may be, indeed, that we ourselves are beginning to appreciate that the new era of letters is not so much decadent as vulgar.
—Arthur Waugh in the *Yellow Book*

WHEN John Ruskin accused James McNeill Whistler of "ill-educated conceit", "wilful imposture", "cockney impudence" and the effrontery of a "coxcomb", he brought to an inglorious end the grand Victorian tradition of anti-dandiacal invective. Whistler took Ruskin to court for libel in the following year, 1878. Though he won only a contemptuous farthing in damages, and went bankrupt paying the costs of the trial, he succeeded in making the ageing prophet seem out of date, if not ridiculous. Ruskin was mentally ill and would soon disappear from the public eye; Whistler's star was slowly rising. The trial gave him his first opportunity to display before a large public the flamboyant personality which was to influence largely the last two decades of the century.

Between this suit for libel and the even more famous action Oscar Wilde brought against the Marquess of Queensberry in 1895 lies the history of the *fin de siècle* movement in England. The weakening of Victorian values and vitality, the strengthening of Continental influences, the revival of Regency attitudes, all combined to produce a favourable atmosphere for what Holbrook Jackson called the New Dandyism—the atmosphere of the Yellow 'Nineties. Yellow, the yellow of the Yellow Book, was the appropriate colour, for it was equally the décor of the Regency and the mark of the wicked French novel. Aestheticism and decadence became poses of fashion; a newly elegant and irresponsible aristocracy began once again to concern itself seriously with fashion, and to be taken seriously for that reason. The middle class appeared to lose its hold on the imagination (perhaps because so much of the community had become in fact middle class) and the upper class came forth openly at the theatre, opera and court to glamorize what looked like Regency ideals. The fashionable novel thrived. Masculine dress improved. Sex was mentioned.

The New Dandies of the era, Wilde, Beardsley, Beerbohm, the Rhymers' Club poets, built a literature around themes from the dandy tradition: worship of the town and the artificial; grace, elegance, the art of the pose; sophistication and the mask. The wit of epigram and paradox was called upon to confound the bourgeois. Such different figures as Wilde and Yeats glamorized the aristocracy as a breeding-ground for art and charming people, for "the fine life", as Yeats said, "which we look at with affectionate eyes out of our garret windows." All this appears, to the literary historian, a reversal of the Victorian position.

> The wit, the charm, the easy grace of the later Georgians, which had hidden away throughout the early and mid-Victorian years in tightly closed circles, emerged at last from long concealment to become the most conspicuous inheritance of Arnold's "Barbarians" . . . For among such people . . . there lingered, if not a creative art, surely a true abundance of artistic materials. . . . From their world . . ., Oscar Wilde and his "aesthetic" friends drew an idiom, a gesture, and a pose.

In youth, under the Regency, the dandy mirrored the tone of English aristocracy; he did so again, in old age, under Albert Edward, Prince of Wales. Queen Victoria had ceded to her son the leadership of High Society (it had never much interested her); he insisted on calling himself Edward and on behaving more like the Englishman about town than the scion of German sobriety. From his first visit to Paris at the age of fourteen Edward adored that city and the French, and his serious interest was the diplomatic groundwork for the *entente cordiale*. Edward turned away from his father's intellectual and domestic sources of amusement: he preferred cigar-smoking, club-going, marked attention to the ladies, sports of all varieties, gambling above all. In his early manhood all such pursuits were suspect, and the Prince had a bad press. It was commonly feared that he took after his great-uncle, George IV.

Most significant, however, to the passage of Victorian ways was Edward's unprecedented sociability. Immediately after his marriage in 1863 he took to dining or staying for protracted visits at the homes of dozens of his Society favourites, something Victoria and Albert had hardly ever done. People he liked, who amused or entertained him, were drawn into a society within Society, which became known as the Marlborough House set, a *smart*, a *swagger*, a *fast* set, reputedly (to the dismay of a group of titled matrons who protested formally to the Archbishop of Canterbury) loose in domestic morals and addicted to high-stake gambling. Edward even took a serious interest in clothes and set a few new fashions in male dress—this despite his mother's early warning against any *extravagance* or *slang* in attire "because it would prove . . . an offence against decency, leading—as it has often done before in others—to an indifference to what is morally wrong."

By the mid-'eighties male costume was again open to the influence of taste, which dictated a return to the Regency ideals of grace, youthfulness and elegance. By the 'nineties every fashionable novel (and in that decade every other novel on the circulating library shelf was fashionable) had its chorus of showy dandies. On the stage the plays of Pinero and Wilde and even Shaw demanded (as they still demand) from their producers super-fine, even fantastical costumes for the hero and his young male supporters. An exchange in the pages of *Vanity Fair* (the London weekly famous for its full-page caricatures by "Spy" or "Ape", filled out with a little of everything and a lot of Society chit-chat) marked the peaceful revolution. A new column, "The Fashion for Men" by "the Man in the Mall", was instituted on February 23, 1889, with detailed recommendations for stiff collars, velvet bands, true and false waistcoats, peg-top trousers, yellow gloves, gilded sticks, violet boutonnières—and against the "very objectionable custom" of paying tailors, which "we must set down to the ignorance and bluster of the age." A subsequent issue brought heartfelt praise from a fashion-minded reader, hailing the signs of change from the "dreariness", "mediocrity", and "priggishness" of the recent past.

Fashionable London still centred round the display of elegance in Hyde Park. There, "in the mornings", remembered Consuelo Vanderbilt, sometime Duchess of Marlborough, "we rode thoroughbred hacks and looked our best in classic riding habits, and . . . again in the evening, elaborately bedecked in ruffles and lace we drove slowly back and forth in stately barouches." The high point of the day was the moment when the lovely Princess of Wales drove by before the marshalled lines of well-dressed Society. In the fashionable novels London skies were invariably blue and brilliant (just as they were heavy with fog and black with soot in the contemporary unfashionable novels of Gissing and Wells). The season rolled inevitably round during what E. F. Benson, one of the more pretentious of the fashionable novelists (his father was the Archbishop of Canterbury), called London's "annual golden days":

> days to be associated with cool, early rides in the crumbly Row, with sitting on small, green chairs beneath the trees at the corner of the park; with a general disinclination to exert oneself, or to stop smoking cigarettes; with a temper distinctly above its normal level, and a corresponding absence of moods.

This might be Disraeli's distant London, except for the cigarettes; though indeed, without the ubiquitous cigarette, gold-tipped and opium-scented, the 'nineties could hardly be recognized.

2

Edward's long apprenticeship as Prince of Wales was, however, no Regency. Although invisible, Victoria was still very much in command of her enormous international family and the destiny of England's ruling house. Max Beerbohm's famous, malicious cartoon labelled *"The rare, the rather awful visits of Albert Edward, Prince of Wales, to Windsor Castle"* fixes Edward VII for all time as the prince who became king when he was over sixty, having grown older, fatter and naughtier without losing a healthy fear of his mother. In the cartoon he stands plump, middle-aged and ridiculously contrite with his face in the corner; in the foreground sits the old queen, his mother, tiny and formidable. Beerbohm, incidentally, was one of the many who found the Prince antipathetic. Undeniably charming and amiable, perhaps too amiable, Edward gave the impression of being mad for amusement but unimaginative in his pleasures, cordial to authors and painters but devoid of taste. Though restless, *fin de siècle* England secretly applauded Edward's escape from his mother's narrow morality, it was unable to take him wholly seriously. Outside the Marlborough House set, his was a small and not very influential personality.

The similarities between Regency and *fin de siècle* Society were in fact all on the surface—more obvious than important. For if Edward did set a fashion in high life, it was the reverse of exclusivism. By giving an enthusiastic welcome to the two pariahs of Victorian aristocracy, Jews and Americans, he signed an "open door policy" through which fresh winds could blow into late-Victorian and Edwardian society. The rule of fashion by Regency salon, club and subscription, and by Victorian country house and family circle gave way to a new proliferation of "sets" advertised in a venal press. In an article entitled "The New Society and its Sets" (1889), *Vanity Fair* bewailed the subsidized publicity given to *nobody's* parties in the *suburbs*! And when Edward's reign was over, the *Nineteenth Century* regretfully summed up the overwhelming testimony of twenty years' worth of fashionable fiction:

> The painting of society manners is for the moment somewhat out of date, for in the first place, there is no Society with a big S in the old sense, and there are no manners. There are groups and coteries.

How people were got into Society, not how they were kept out, became the chosen theme of fashionable novels from Benson's *Mammon and Co.* to Ouida's *The Massarenes*. Light-headed, long-winded Marie Corelli, one of Edward's very favourite novelists, let the devil outline the process (and emphasize the Prince's role in it) in *The Sorrows of Satan*, one of Edward's very favourite books. Satan supplies his protégé, a young nobody, with the first, the only essential requirement for social success: wealth. Then, he explains, "you must be presented at the first Levée of the season, and later on, I will get you an invitation to some great lady's house, where you will meet the Prince of Wales privately at dinner." A seat in Parliament can be dispensed with —"that is no longer necessary to the career of a gentleman"— but you are to purchase a "fine country seat", win the Derby, enter for a yacht race at Cowes, allowing "the Prince of Wales to

beat you just narrowly. Then you will give a grand dinner,
arranged by a perfect *chef*—and you will entertain His Royal
Highness to the strains of 'Britannia rules the waves', which will
serve as a pretty compliment." By means of judicious disburse-
ments, all these events will be well-paragraphed in the press.
"Then," in no time at all, "your name in society may be considered as made, and you can marry whatever fair lady happens
to be in the market!"

Essentially, it was not the breeze of fashion but the chill blast
of economic reality which blew down social barriers. W. H.
Mallock, vocal conservative and able apologist for the aristocracy, argued against the new Socialist propaganda with statistics
proving the decline of landed wealth and the rise of commercial
fortunes. Most of the 'seventies and 'eighties (the decades of
Henry George and of Marx in English translation, of William
Morris, Hyndman, the budding Shaw and the Webbs) were
depression years; if Society's children were to carry on Society,
they had to marry money from whatever source—Americans,
Jews, suburbanites, stock-brokers, colonials or (newest of all)
advertising magnates. When self-preservation was in question,
the aristocracy of England had always been careless about antiquity of title and origin of wealth. Now it found no difficulty in
absorbing families enriched and, as often as not, ennobled by
nineteenth-century industrialism. Thus the 'nineties made an
easy truce to the battle the Regency exclusives had so nastily
fought in the days of the dandies.

3

As we come further off in time from the literary and artistic
movements of the 'nineties, there is less and less to be seen of
Yeats's "tragic generation", wasted by poverty, disease and
public neglect, or Holbrook Jackson's age of experiment, vitality,
curiosity and high spirits—both images elaborated in the first
quarter of this century. Instead, the dominant note of the decade
appears to be its commercialism: the *tragic* spectacle of literature
and personality thrown open on the market place, the great
experiment of selling talent by advertising, publicity and showmanship. Little of the posing of the time makes sense unless we
remember the enormous public before which it was performed.

Never before had so many literary men taken their squabbles into court: it was the fashion to sue for libel or plagiarism on the slightest provocation. ("One really can't live in London," said Whistler, "without a lawyer.") It was also the fashion to communicate by postal card or telegram, to carry on a literary dispute in the "letters to the editor" column of a newspaper with a large circulation, to advertise literary or artistic events in gossip columns, to exploit artistic temperament through booking agents. Perhaps the type figure of the decade was neither Oscar Wilde nor Aubrey Beardsley but Frank Harris, the journalist with loud mouth and lucrative pen, bred in Ireland and seasoned in America (the pure *fin de siècle* combination), returning to England to make copy—or, as the age put it, letterpress—of the literary mind.

The *Yellow Book*, the decade's most glamorous monument, has often been confused with the "little magazine" of this century or the coterie review essential to literary innovation in France. But it was neither passionate nor poor. How heavy and solid and self-conscious of excellence it now appears, with its board covers, yellow though they may be, its thick paper, its wide margins and the evidence of elaborate commercial organization at the foot of its title page: *London: Elkin Mathews & John Lane; Boston; Copeland & Day; Agents for the Colonies; Robert A. Thompson & Co.* The *Yellow Book* was founded, after all, not by a coterie with a Message, but by a publisher with an eye for value.

John Lane was certainly the Colburn of the day. From the official (if unflattering) biography, written by a one-time associate and published by the firm he founded, he emerges as an entrepreneur of genius, a man of little culture but of great sensitivity to contemporary tastes. He founded "The Bodley Head" as a bookshop in 1887, published his first book in 1889 (by 1892 the firm was subtitled *Publishers, and Vendors of Choice and Rare Editions in Belles Lettres*), founded the *Yellow Book* in 1894, opened an American branch in 1896. During those years Lane established and made the most of a reputation for publishing rather daring literature in exquisite format, for championing the cause of poetry—especially "minor poetry"—and for gathering in new talent. His publishing methods were brilliant. He sold in advance the bulk of his elegant first printings by subscription: where Colburn had exploited the snobbery of the *nouveau riche*, Lane made the most of the aesthetic rage then belatedly sweeping the suburbs—and of the "collector's" (*i.e.* resale) value of his distinctive volumes. For his books were pre-eminently limited *first* editions—even when they were reprintings palmed off on the public as the genuine article.

John Lane never fancied himself as the publisher of decadence, but he did fancy the reputation of wickedness that helped sell his books. Far from emulating the bold Vizetelly, who had gone to prison in the 'eighties for publishing Zola, he exhibited the greatest prudence when necessary: he scrapped a Laurence Housman frontispiece design for fear of indecency, advertised an "improved" translation of Sudermann with moral testimonials from the eminent, and, terrified by the furor over what he called "the Oscar trial", hastily withdrew Wilde from his catalogue and Beardsley from his magazine. At the same time, subtle suggestions of the *risqué* often figured in his advertisements, and he welcomed jibes at his decadent poets, even satires on his own methods, as good publicity.

The publisher of the *Yellow Book* was prosperous and respectable. The publisher of the *Savoy*, which took over Beardsley and decadence in 1896, eluded the police just long enough to die at liberty, penniless and disgraced: Leonard Smithers made a career of publishing erotica and Beardsley forgeries as well as poetry and art. Yeats has described the distaste with which this "scandalous person" was regarded by his contributors and the efforts they made to keep out of his company. He has recorded one evening when the talented young "decadents" of the *Savoy* foregathered reluctantly at Smithers's ostentatious Bedford Square mansion:

> Our publisher, perspiration pouring from his face, was turning the handle of a hurdy-gurdy piano—it worked by electricity, I was told, when the company did not cut off the supply—and very plainly had had enough of it, but Beardsley pressed him to labour on, " The tone is so beautiful," " It gives me such deep pleasure," etc., etc. It was his method of keeping our publisher at a distance.

4

Decadence was in the air. It appeared not so much in salacious writings, strenuous iconoclasm, perverse poses and foreign influences as in the thinning out of talent, the nervousness and timidity of innovators and the complicated, perilous awe of Woman as the stronger sex. Weakened by *fin de siècle* aestheticism, coarsened by *fin de siècle* commercialism, dandyism made its return to English life and letters with no less a publicist than Oscar Wilde.

Wilde's resources were few when he left Oxford for London in 1878, resolved to make himself famous. He had an intellectual but Irish and eccentric family background; the Newdigate Prize for poetry and a few poems; a small inheritance from his father, largely spent on a trip to Greece; a modest reputation for good talk and individuality; and a brother in London whose position on a Society paper, the *World*, enabled him to tout the witty sayings and clever antics of the young Oscar.

Like Benjamin Disraeli at the outset of his career half a century before, Wilde began to prepare his way with his clothes. But in 1878 there was no single fashionable male set delimited by membership in a few select clubs, no single style of dress conceived to express the quintessence of gentlemanliness, and therefore no premium on subtle deviations from the norm. When an undergraduate at Oxford, Wilde had dressed in the prevailing style: tiny bowler hats with curled brims tipped squarely over the eyes in the Swell manner, bright tweeds and loud checks patterned uniformly over coat, trousers and waistcoat, all cut along heavy lines. Now he styled himself Professor of Aesthetics and adopted a costume for the part—the knee breeches, drooping lily, flowing green tie, velvet coat and wide, turned-down collar which first made him famous. This style was not calculated to impress the aristocracy, nor, from all accounts, was that Wilde's aim. His company seems to have been in demand from the beginning at many of the best houses, and certainly it is characteristic of the age that (as Alfred Douglas put it) "Oscar had the entrée to the best society from the first moment of his appearance in London." But that entrée (not so complete, of course, as Douglas claimed) was no longer a young man's guarantee of fame and fortune. The coin had been cheapened. The fact that Wilde dined at a friend's home across the table from the Prince of Wales, and that he entertained the Prince in his own rooms, was of only limited utility.

Whatever degree of sincerity lay behind Wilde's support of aestheticism, he wore the knee-breeches and the lily to impress the worlds of theatre and press and, through them, the larger, paying public. When first in London he laid determined siege to such notables as Lily Langtry, Ellen Terry, Henry Irving and Sarah Bernhardt, writing them verses, sending them flowers and requests for photographs, inviting them to his rooms in Salisbury Street and having them write their names across the panels of his white walls. These celebrities and their friends were news; news was what Willie Wilde made of Oscar's early adventures. By 1880, two years after Wilde came down from Oxford, *Punch* had taken up his foibles, and the large public was secured.

George Du Maurier's famous black-and-whites called *Nincompoopiana* and directed against the aesthetes began in *Punch* while Wilde was still at Oxford. It is illuminating to watch Du Maurier's caricature of the affected nincompoop change its shape through the months until it is fixed as an unmistakable jibe at Wilde. His languid poets and conceited painters resemble in appearance and manner Swinburne, Whistler or nobody recognizable until, around the middle of 1880, both Jellaby Postlethwaite the Great Poet and Maudle the painter take on the least attractive physical and psychological characteristics of Oscar Wilde. Whistler, at whose home and studio Wilde had been an eager student of the aesthetic pose, was angry at the substitution and upbraided both Du Maurier (an old acquaintance from Paris and student days) and Wilde (who had of course made friends with Du Maurier). For, in the *fin de siècle*, caricature, however insulting, was counted good publicity.

In 1881 Wilde reached the stage: Beerbohm Tree played a caricature of the aesthete as charlatan in a play written by the editor of *Punch*, and Gilbert and Sullivan's *Patience* fixed Wilde's position as the most affected man in London. Gilbert, incidentally, had begun the play as a satire of languid curates, turned to the aesthetic craze in the person of Swinburne, and ended with two poets compounded equally of Whistler and Wilde. But Wilde insisted to the world and his wife that Gilbert had had only Wilde in mind when he wrote of walking "down Piccadilly with a poppy or a lily in your mediaeval hand". Oscar further maintained that he had never actually made such a fool of himself, that his greatness lay in making people *believe* he had—and he contributed to the success of *Patience* by ostentatiously attending several of the performances. His eagerness to exploit caricature, much of it malicious, became part of his legend and was in turn spoofed by *Punch*. The magazine ran a cartoon entitled "Frustrated Social Ambition", illustrating the

> Collapse of Postlethwaite, Maudle, and Mrs Cimabue Brown [a lady aesthete] on reading in a widely circulated Contemporary Journal that they only exist in *Mr Punch's* vivid Imagination. They had fondly flattered themselves that Universal Fame was theirs at last.

Walking down the street with a friend, Wilde heard a passer-by say, "There goes that bloody fool, Oscar Wilde." Wilde's comment was: "It's extraordinary how soon one gets known in London."

The path to fortune was even broader. Wilde's first published volume, a book of poems, came out in 1881 and sold well, thanks to the publicity surrounding his name and energetic praise from his theatrical friends, some of whom figured in the book as recipients of sonnets. The reviews were generally bad, though satirical notices in *Punch* ("Aesthete of Aesthetes! . . . What's in a name? . . . The poet is Wilde, . . . But his poetry's tame") did the sales no harm. Then Wilde had his brother Willie insert a paragraph in his paper to the effect that, because of the excellence of his verse, Oscar had been invited to go to America—the great back door of the *fin de siècle* literary market place. Reality followed on advertisement. Wilde did go to America in the following year, to lecture on aesthetics; his trip was arranged and sponsored by the D'Oyly Carte interests, seeking to publicize the current New York production of *Patience*. Asked, in effect, to sell his notoriety, his aesthetic clothes and mannerisms, his resemblance to a comic character in a light opera and his appeal to public curiosity of the lowest sort, Wilde replied by cable, "Yes, if offer good". Surely the American press was justified in parodying the key-note of the tour:

> A lily by the river's brim,
>   An advertising dodge to him
> It was, and nothing more.

Between his return from America and his marriage in 1884 (which considerably eased financial pressures) Wilde wrote some plays and poems, but the major source of his income was a

series of lecture tours in the English provinces. The latest
advertising techniques yielded bigger and better posters:

HE IS COMING!!!
WHO IS COMING???
OSCAR WILDE!!!
THE GREAT AESTHETE!!!

It was a sign of the times that the success of these lectures, partly
bolstered by a Whistler–Wilde fight over plagiarism (following
the standard course of an exchange of witty telegrams reprinted
in the *World* and parodied in *Punch*), gave Whistler the idea of
his famous lecture, "The Ten O'Clock". He delivered it in 1885
under, once again, D'Oyly Carte management.

What was there of dandyism in all this? A concern with clothes,
surely, but clothes worn openly (not secretly, in the Dickens way)
as a theatrical costume. These clothes, and the accompanying
mannerisms, were neither mask nor embellishment to Wilde's
individuality, and they had nothing to say about his social
superiority or his "gentlemanliness". They were an expression
of his willingness to sell his privacy and to let himself be laughed
at for the achievement of (as Alfred Douglas put it) notoriety
before fame. Douglas, who met Wilde many years after he had
abandoned his "aesthetic costume", wrote with all the candour
of absolute egotism that "it would probably have repelled me if
he had been wearing it when I first met him. I was, with all my
unusualness in certain respects . . . a typical product of the
English Public School system. I doubt whether I would have
'swallowed' the aesthetic Oscar."

Wilde's friends, who always protested that in *their* company
Oscar was the most natural of companions, were never confused
about his motives: Douglas, along with Robert Sherard, blandly
ascribed his affectations to an insistence "at all costs to attract
attention to himself." The cost was that for many years he was
merely a figure of fun to the larger public. "His 'serio-comic'
position as High Priest of Aestheticism," wrote Graham
Robertson, "was won in drawing-rooms by means of persistently
making a fool of himself."

If Frank Harris is for once to be believed, Wilde was always
ready to discuss his scramble after fame. He would compare himself to the best-selling Pears' soap and enumerate the qualities

on which self-advertisement rested. Harris agreed: "singularity of appearance, wit, rudeness," he wrote, "count doubly in a democracy." The years in which Wilde and Whistler, Shaw and George Moore made names for themselves as eccentrics were years in which, Harris said, "the personality school of success was just beginning to assert itself. In America they called them 'go-getters'. I suspect I was one myself." Surely the youthful personality of Oscar Wilde had less to do with the old-fashioned dandy than with this new-fangled *go-getter*—or, as Arnold Bennett would have translated the term into English, the *card*.

The week before his marriage in 1884, *Vanity Fair* presented Wilde with a handsome wedding present: that cachet of *fin de siècle* fame, a full-page caricature by "Ape". The accompanying letter-press treated him with friendly condescension. Wilde had "got brilliantly laughed at, and good-naturedly accepted", said *Vanity Fair*. "He has lived through much laughter, in which he has always joined . . ." A few years later Wilde had found himself, both as a homosexual and as a writer. In 1895, when the storm of the Wilde–Queensberry trial broke in London, it must have seemed incredible that Oscar Wilde had ever been dealt with so casually. Ridicule had by then given way to suspicion and hatred, farce to tragedy.

5

Wilde's style of dress changed as he achieved the double status of financial security and creative accomplishment. Despite his foolery he genuinely cared about costume, writing and lecturing on the subject with heavy sincerity; success permitted him to demand less of it. In the mid-'eighties he consciously replaced the get-up of the "professor of Aesthetics" with that of the florid out-of-date dandy. English observers deduced an imitation of Brummell and D'Orsay, French observers with greater accuracy recalled the extravagances of Balzac. In the 'nineties, when the success of his plays brought him a wide and deserved fame in place of a trivial notoriety, Wilde's dress became coldly and formally correct. He was content to express individuality (aside from his enormous and oddly proportioned bulk) with a single detail: a green boutonnière, a bright red waistcoat or a turquoise and diamond stud.

In his literary work Wilde dealt constantly with dandyism, approaching it in two ways. As novelist and playwright he found aristocratic society the only suitable material for his talent. As critic and "aesthete" he turned inward upon himself in search of a dandy-artist figure. In neither preoccupation was he an innovator. Extraordinarily well read in the literature and criticism of his century, both in France and in England, Wilde drew upon minds as disparate as Arnold and Gautier, Ruskin and Baudelaire to fashion his aestheticism. "It was precisely because he was not of [the movement] by birth and by early association," wrote Yeats of Wilde the 'provincial', "that he caught up phrases and adjectives for their own sake, and not because they were a natural part of his design, and spoke them to others as though it were his duty to pass on some password, sign or countersign." As a popularizer, however, Wilde was brilliant. He wrote his own justification: "It is style that makes us believe in a thing—nothing but style."

"Unless one is wealthy there is no use in being a charming fellow. Romance is the privilege of the rich. . . . The poor should be practical and prosaic." Wilde's snobbery took individual form: naïve delight in the prettiness of aristocratic life, and simple unconcern with the habits of the lower orders, a lack of interest based on boredom rather than disgust. His stories and plays, his one novel, even his criticism—often conceived as a dialogue between two young aristocrats—used high society backgrounds. In a review of a fashionable novel by a titled lady, Wilde openly regretted that the "novel of high life" had ever fallen into disrepute—and that "the fashionable and brilliant young dandies, in whom Disraeli and Bulwer Lytton took such delight, have been entirely wiped out as heroes of fiction by hard-working curates in the East End."

What Wilde the aesthete admired in high society was the artificiality, the decorous surface, the mannered ritual. "The canons of good society," he wrote, "are . . . the same as the canons of art. Form is absolutely essential to it." This *rapprochement* of Art and Society was a commonplace of the period; it had been formulated before Wilde left Oxford. In his brilliant satire of 1877, *The New Republic*, W. H. Mallock had demanded of the aristocracy the same "practical skill in life as a fine art." He posited *tone* as the sine qua non of good society, redefining that

Regency word to include aesthetic and Pater-esque shadings. "Tone," he said, is

> that special and indescribable way of looking at things, and speaking of things, which characterizes good society, and distinguishes it from the rest of the world so completely, and yet by marks so subtle that they would utterly escape the notice of those who don't know their meaning—that little extra stroke of polishing that brings to light such countless new delicate veins in the marble of life—the little extra stroke of the brush that puts a new refinement, and self-possession into the face. . . .

As early as 1882 *Punch* had summoned Mr Grigsby ("a briefless Barrister who writes Comic Songs") to spoof the aesthete's re-evaluation of the social classes:

> "Well, *first* of all, I put those who live by the exercise of an Intellectual *Profession*, like myself . . . *Next* to these, I place the *Aristocracy*, on account of their 'pooty manners.' *Then* comes the *Working-Man*, who earns his bread by the Sweat of his Brow. *After* him (a good long way, of course), the *Criminal Classes*; and last of all, the *Middle Class* . . ."

When Wilde proclaimed that "we can forgive a man for making a useful thing as long as he does not admire it. . . . All art is quite useless," he demonstrated that his way to dandyism lay along the aesthetic path. If art was useless, so was dandyism; if the artist did nothing, neither did the dandy; if the aesthetic existence was the most graceful form of inactivity, then the graces of dandyism were to gild the artist in his daily life. A stream of paradoxes followed: "The first duty of life is to be as artificial as possible." "A really well-made buttonhole is the only link between Art and Nature." "Style. not sincerity, is the essential." "No crime is vulgar, but vulgarity is crime." "One should either be a work of Art, or wear a work of Art." "The condition of perfection is idleness . . ." Dandyism itself, he asserted in a celebrated definition which echoes Baudelaire, was "an attempt to assert the absolute modernity of beauty."

Wilde brought one element of novelty to Baudelaire's artist-dandy figure: his substitution of the critic for the artist. In his long essay, "The Critic as Artist", written before he knew he could make a good play or even a successful, bad novel, Wilde apologized brilliantly for his own shortcomings by elevating the passive (if talkative) critic over the creative artist. The portrait Wilde draws of himself as critic bears little resemblance to the workaday professional he actually was, turning out monthly reviews for the *Woman's World* or the *Nineteenth Century*. Instead the Critic appears as the ideal aesthete, the arch-dilettante, concerned less with sharpening his judgments than with refining his way of life. "The influence of the critic will be the mere fact of his own existence. He will represent the flawless type. . . . You must not ask of him to have any aim other than the perfecting of himself."

Wilde placed the critic, as elsewhere he placed the dandy, among the elect who exist to be somebody but to do nothing. Art is his refuge against action, for it is "through Art, and through Art only, that we can shield ourselves from the sordid perils of actual existence." So, with a gentle revision of the ideas of Pater and Arnold, Wilde finds that the end-result of the critical spirit is a kind of hedonistic dandyism.

> Calm and self-centred, and complete, the aesthetic critic contemplates life, and no arrow drawn at a venture can pierce between the joints of his harness. He at least is safe. He has discovered how to live.

6

The Picture of Dorian Gray, Wilde's only novel (1890–1), is an incoherent amalgam of three different books. First it is a fashionable novel of the recognized school, full of idle young men decorating elegant little houses in Mayfair, luncheon parties, select dinners, shooting weekends—and a dandy hero. Surrounded by all the familiar accessories (a silver Louis-Quinze toilet set, an embroidered cashmere dressing-gown, an onyx-paved bathroom and a large collection of dinner invitations) Dorian Gray directs the tastes of the young men of his class. "Fashion . . . and Dandyism . . . had, of course, their fascination for him."

> His mode of dressing, and the particular styles that from time to time he affected, had their marked influence on the young exquisites of the Mayfair balls and Pall Mall Club windows, who copied him in everything that he did, and tried to reproduce the accidental charm of his graceful, though to him only half-serious, fopperies.

Then it is a novel of supernatural melodrama, "after the manner of Poe", as Pater pointed out in a rather embarrassed review. In this context—the portrait which ages hideously while its subject remains beautifully young, the sinister opium dens, the murder concealed by cunning and chemistry, the sailor plotting vengeance and the climactic suicide—Dorian Gray is less a character than a plot-device.

Finally, it is a novel of decadence, in which Wilde "airs his cheap research among the garbage of the French decadents like any drivelling pedant", as the indignant *St James's Gazette* intoned with unnecessary vehemence. Essentially, however, the review was correct: the novel's decadence was all too plainly the end result of Wilde's industrious (and not very well digested) reading, especially in Huysmans. Wilde gives *A Rebours* a place in his novel as the sinister yellow book that casts a spell over Dorian Gray, and he obviously tries to cast his hero as a fashionable English version of Des Esseintes. But in this final role Dorian lacks conviction. Wilde never succeeds in reconciling the exquisite "young Adonis . . . made out of ivory and rose leaves", the "brainless, beautiful creature" who seems incapable of thought, with the world-weary decadent who experiments ruthlessly on his sensations. Not all the paradoxical chatter of Lord Henry Wotton or all the yellow-backed novels in France could work such a transformation.

In *A Rebours* (1884), which Mario Praz has called "the pivot upon which the whole psychology of the Decadent Movement turns", J.-K. Huysmans carried Baudelaire's figure of the dandy one step further—into negation. For Huysmans the man of the crowds became a complete solitary, the artist became a sterile sensualist, the convalescent relapsed into disease. Des Esseintes, the single figure whose mental aberrations are the novel itself, retreats from the world into a hermetic, barely vital existence, and experiments with sights, smells, tastes and silences in an effort to soothe the irritated fibres of his nerves. There is nothing here left of dandyism, except its rejection. Among the *extravagances* Des Esseintes has put behind him for ever, at the beginning of the novel, is the desire to astonish his contemporaries (somewhat, one imagines, in the manner of the young Eugène Sue) by inventing fantastic furnishings and costumes and by preaching what he calls "le sermon sur le dandysme".

. . . Aujourd'hui le mépris lui était venu de ces ostentations puériles et surannées, de ces vêtements anormaux, de ces embellies de loge- ments bizarres. Il songeait simplement à se composer, pour son plaisir personnel et non plus pour l'étonnement des autres, un intérieur confortable et paré néanmoins d'une façon rare, à se façonner une installation curieuse et calme, appropriée aux besoins de sa future solitude.

Although Huysmans recognized Baudelaire as his predecessor in "la psychologie morbide", he emphasized as Baudelaire had not the diseased nature behind the mental states of *ennui* and disgust. This almost clinical aspect of *A Rebours*—the most im- portant and the most influential—seems to have made no im- pression on Wilde. Though he may have known that something of Des Esseintes's character was derived from the legend of Robert de Montesquiou, the dandy-homosexual-poet who later sat for Proust's Charlus, Wilde gleaned from Huysmans only a superficial acquaintance with the literary paraphernalia of deca- dence. Dorian, Lord Henry and Basil Hallward, the central characters of *The Picture of Dorian Gray*, may have been Wilde's pictures of the homosexual, but homosexuality to Wilde was anything rather than a disease. He thought of it as an ideal love, a part of the glorified New Hedonism, with perhaps a tantalizing touch of evil to mark it off from the humdrum.

After the novel first appeared in *Lippincott's Magazine*, Wilde wrote a letter of elucidation to the *Scots Observer* with the follow- ing statement: "Each man sees his own sin in Dorian Gray. What Dorian Gray's sins are no one knows. He who finds them has brought them." He had no intention of being explicit about homosexuality,* yet he reserved the right—and, one feels, the pleasure—of talking endlessly about mysterious sins and un- named evils. "Sin," says Lord Henry Wotton, the cynical ripe dandy who is Dorian's mentor, "sin is the only real colour-

---

* In contemporary homosexual circles, however, the name of Dorian Gray soon became a familiar by-word. It appears frequently in clinical cases reported by Havelock Ellis. Ellis, whose researches into inversion began during Wilde's lifetime, observed significant effects of the publicity sur- rounding Oscar Wilde: greater self-awareness for the individual homo- sexual, greater solidarity and courage for the homosexual community. Speculations follow: how much of the mannerisms of to-day's overt homo- sexual, including his dandyism, can be traced back to the *fin de siècle*, and how much of that can be credited simply to Wilde's legend?

element left in modern life." Such statements were clichés of the *fin de siècle*, which amused itself with what had been for Baudelaire a solemn recognition. Wilde's plays lean heavily on this affectation. His dandies (Lord Darlington in *Lady Windermere's Fan*, Lord Illingworth in *A Woman of No Importance*, Lord Goring in *An Ideal Husband*) come prettily on stage boasting of their reputation for wickedness. But Lord Darlington speaks for them all: "As a wicked man I am a complete failure. Why, there are lots of people who say I have never really done anything wrong in the whole course of my life. Of course they only say it behind my back."

Wilde's constant chatter about sinning reflected naïve confusion rather than self-awareness. Yet the fact that he was a homosexual did present him with a theme which occasionally lends depth to his creative work: an obsession with youth, Youth terrible in its beauty, fatal in its attraction. "Youth! Youth! There is absolutely nothing in the world but youth!" shrills Lord Henry Wotton. The refrain is echoed by all the other "elderly" (*i.e.* around thirty-five, or Wilde's age) dandies in the plays. These gentlemen assume a half-professorial, half-seductive attitude before the enchanting young, and entreat them to follow the new hedonism to moral ruin. "Ah! realize your youth while you have it," cries Lord Henry to Dorian. "Don't squander the gold of your days, listening to the tedious, trying to improve the hopeless failure, or giving away your life to the ignorant, the common, and the vulgar . . ." In *A Woman of No Importance*, Lord Illingworth, a more actively evil version of the same character, tries to seduce his rediscovered bastard son away from the moral tutelage of the boy's mother by drumming on the same note: Youth, "the most wonderful thing in the world," "the Lord of Life".

The most convincing dandy and one of the most successful characters Wilde created is Lord Goring in *An Ideal Husband*, whose more complicated attitude to "the most wonderful thing in the world" brings a note of pathos to the play. Over thirty (therefore, in Wilde's view, no longer young) and unmarried (thus sharing in the delightful aimlessness of the young), Goring can both analyse and demonstrate the fascination of youth. His is not the brainless beauty of Dorian Gray but the consciously cultivated pose of the "flawless dandy", "the result

of Boddle's Club", "the idlest man in London". And his epigrams on fashion, vulgarity, egotism, pleasure and idleness are
in Wilde's most spontaneous manner. Yet there is one chink in
his dandy armour: his slowly loosening grasp on youth.
Goring's father, Lord Caversham, is always at him with the
proddings of common sense, urging him to abandon his idle
conceit, to marry and choose a career, especially to give up the
detestable affectation of being young. ("Youth isn't an affectation," says the dandy. "Youth is an art.") Goring parries all
this sound advice with graceful impudence until the moment
when his father reminds him he is getting on in years ("thirty-
four years of age, sir"), and his dandyism falters.

> "Yes, father, but I only admit to thirty-two—thirty-one and a half
> when I have a really good buttonhole. This buttonhole is not [*pause*]
> trivial enough."

Shortly thereafter the father, and then the son, feel a draught
in the room, "a dreadful draught". It is one of Wilde's nicest
dramatic touches.

Out of the fact of Wilde's homosexuality, then, came a
division of the *genus* dandy into two classes, the old and the
young, who travelled together in perilous familiarity. With
the Lord Gorings and the Lord Henry Wottons, cynical, domineering, intellectual, essentially aristocratic, Wilde tried to
identify himself. They are the Brummells of his world. Toward
the Dorian Grays, the beautiful Narcissus boys, his attitude
was distantly adoring, and fearful. Though Dorian may set a
few fashions and mouth a few borrowed witticisms, he is less
a dandy than a golden boy with a perfumed handkerchief,
worshipping his own beauty in a mirror carved round with
laughing Cupids (a gift of Lord Henry) and coldly accepting
the homage of others. He exhibits the petulance, the stubborn-
ness, the cruelty of spoiled youth with the heedlessness of a
D'Orsay; but the fascination he inspires is more destructive
than anything D'Orsay's contemporaries would have cared to
discuss publicly. Basil Hallward, the painter, talks openly of the
love he bears Dorian, which first terrified, then enslaved him,
and now has come to dominate his art.

> I worshipped you. I grew jealous of every one to whom you spoke. I
> wanted to have you all to myself. I was only happy when I was with

you. When you were away from me you were still present in my art. . . . You are made to be worshipped.

And the "idolatrous words" of the "mad letter" written to Dorian by "some one who had terribly loved him" ("You are made of ivory and gold. The curves of your lips rewrite history") are scarcely less guarded than the language of the letters Wilde himself addressed to young Alfred Douglas ("those red-leaf lips of yours . . . made . . . for the madness of music and song . . . for the madness of kissing . . .").

These letters were entered as evidence against Wilde at the '95 trial, when he spoke at length and somewhat embarrassingly of the inspirational magic of youth and of the "Love that dare not speak its name." That love he described as intellectual, fine, noble and natural: "it repeatedly exists between an elder and a younger man, when the elder man has intellect, and the younger man has all the joy, hope and glamour of life before him."

Youth-worship did serve Wilde as an inspiration. The spirit animating the whole joyous farce of *The Importance of Being Earnest*, the single work which erases from the mind all the tedious nastiness of the Wilde story, is effervescent, sparkling youth. The play is essentially about children, who act their age in their sublime unconcern for realities. Witness their delightful gluttony, which consumes mounds of tea-cakes, cucumber sandwiches, muffins and bread-and-butter through the play: it belongs to the charmed world of the nursery.

Wilde's haunting fairy tales display a real sympathy with children, as well as an obsession with youth as the centre of life. In almost all the tales the heroes are children, gifted with divine beauty and an immense power for cruelty or love. There is the aesthetic Young King, who adores his own body in a mirror borne by a bronze Narcissus; the young Fisherman, "bronze-limbed . . . like a statue wrought by a Grecian"; the exquisite and cruel Star-Child, "his body like the narcissus of a field where the mower comes not"; the Happy Prince; and the young Student with lips "as red as the rose of his desire", for whom the Nightingale dyes a blood-red rose. Even Wilde's lasting preoccupation with the Christ figure, which inspired many of his tales and parables, took the form of adoration of the

divine Child in whose gift is salvation—once he has abandoned
the cruel heartlessness of youth.

"The condition of perfection is idleness," runs Wilde's
dandy maxim; "the aim of perfection," it concludes, "is youth."

(II) WOMEN

*The home seems to me to be the proper sphere for the man. And certainly
once a man begins to neglect his domestic duties he becomes painfully
effeminate, does he not? And I don't like that. It makes men so very
attractive.*
—Gwendolen Fairfax in *The Importance of Being Earnest*

7

What a decaying Brummell, a senile George IV, an irate Carlyle,
a guilt-ridden Thackeray, even an intellectual French poet like
Baudelaire had been unable to do to the ideal of the Dandy, a
lady did effortlessly with a cigarette, a bicycle and a will of her
own. A figure which had survived so much succumbed in the
fin de siècle to the domination of the New Woman—not because
she fought against him (she had her own uses for the dandified
male) but because she pushed him from the centre of the stage.
Without centrality the dandy could only retreat into nostalgia;
he languished in the midst of his revival. It was the vogue to
laugh at the Victorian "'idea of a Christian gentleman', than
which," said Tubby (the absurd hero of G. S. Street's *Autobiography of a Boy*), "I can imagine nothing more pompous and
tiresome and ridiculous." But for the *fin de siècle*, the nature
of the gentleman was a minor question. Wilde's era asked
instead, and with a new urgency, what it meant merely to be
a man.

Under the political agitation for women's rights seethed a
genuine revolution of thought and custom regarding the relative positions of male and female. This battle of the sexes,
rather than aesthetic principles and foreign thought, was the
central issue of the 'nineties, reflected in changing legislation,
in shifting fashions of costume and even furniture, and of
course in the literature of the period. For the most serious of
the last Victorians—Hardy, Meredith, Shaw, Butler and

Gissing—sex, marriage and family life were the absorbing themes. It was, indeed, time for a change. As Richard Le Gallienne pointed out in an article on the subject in the *Yellow Book*, no one had ever set up more arbitrary barriers between the sexes than the mid-Victorians. Le Gallienne cited two dictionary definitions from the 'fifties ("when everything on earth and in heaven was settled . . . in penny encyclopedias") which established *manly* as firm; brave; undaunted; dignified; noble; stately; and *womanly* as soft; mild; pitiful; kind; civil; obliging; humane; tender; timorous; flexible; modest. Such nonsense was a legitimate target for the *Yellow Book*'s scorn, but that publication had only *fin de siècle* nonsense to put in its place. "To ask the sex of a beautiful person," Le Gallienne lamely concluded, "is as absurd as it would be to ask the publisher the sex of a beautiful book."

Whatever was genuine in English decadence of the 'nineties rested on a fear of the decay of one sex beside the looming dominance of the other. The blurring of the sexes had long been the preoccupation of the decadent movement in France. First, and tentatively, in the work of Gautier and Balzac, then decisively in Baudelaire, at last frenetically in Gustave Moreau and Josephin Péladan, its exalted figure had been the hermaphrodite. Mario Praz cites a pronouncement by Péladan (occultist, eroticist, Rosicrucian, aspiring dandy and arch-decadent) as typical of the French attitude:

L'androgyne est le sexe artistique par excellence, il confond les deux principes, le féminin et le masculin, et les équilibre l'un par l'autre. Toute figure exclusivement masculine manque de grâce, toute autre exclusivement féminine manque de force.

Indeed, much of the serious attention paid to the dandy figure in Second Empire France derived from its seemingly triumphant fusion of the masculine and feminine principles. It was no accident that Barbey d'Aurevilly (whose disciple Péladan considered himself) had written of George Brummell as the ideal *androgyne*—and of the dandies as "natures doubles et multiples, d'une sexe intellectuel indécis . . ."

English decadence had its own poet of the hermaphrodite in Aubrey Beardsley, who boasted that his suspiciously erotic drawings of flat-chested harpies and bosomy eunuchs were "quite a new world of my own creation". Beardsley himself was as puzzling a creature as anything he drew. Absorbed above all in perverse sexuality—with the encouragement of Leonard Smithers he collected and illustrated many volumes of erotica, and his one long literary work, the privately printed *Under the Hill*, evoked a purgatory of perversions—Beardsley had all the mannerisms of the homosexual without, apparently, any of the substance. Wilde baited him incessantly ("Don't sit on the same chair as Aubrey," he would tell the ladies. "It's not compromising") and Beardsley's reciprocal distaste undoubtedly accounted for Wilde's absence from the *Yellow Book*. Words, images and attitudes seemed to satisfy Beardsley's craving for the perverse. "He affected an extreme cynicism," as Rothenstein observed; ". . . he *spoke* enormities; *mots* were the mode, and provided they were sufficiently witty, anything might be said. Didn't someone say of Aubrey that even his lungs were affected?"

Elegantly dressed and traditionally languid, Beardsley was just a bit too precious or too childlike or too effeminate—and withal too middle-class—to be a dandy of the recognizable nineteenth-century breed. Brummell might have recognized the Beardsley who declared he caught a bad cold by leaving a tassel off his cane. But what could anyone before Firbank have made of Beardsley's letters, written with the feverish fussiness of the consumptive, in which London is described as "adorably bright and busy", Paris as "looking perfectly sweet", the Brompton Oratory is regretted as "such a loveable church" and thanks are given for "an adorable little manual of Catholic belief . . ."?

8

The fashionable novels of the 'nineties abound in dandies; yet there was no return to the dandy novel of the Regency. Elegant young men served as the background for these books, not the reason for their existence. To the foreground came instead the artist, possibly dandified and aristocratic but essentially a creature of the aesthetic movement. The most disparate books boast artist heroes: a novelist in Marie Corelli's *Sorrows of Satan*, a tenor in Ouida's *Moths*, a painter in Du Maurier's *Trilby*, a man of letters and an actor in W. J. Locke's *Stella Maris*. Most amusing is H. G. Wells's *Ann Veronica*, a fictional tract about a New Woman who takes a biologist as her lover—only to be rewarded at the end by marrying the gentleman, who has somehow been transformed into a successful playwright. *Ann Veronica*, however, like all the rest of these popular novels, does not *centre* around its artist hero: these are books about Woman, the newer the better.

For the amusement and gratification of the New Woman, the best-selling novelists created a new kind of masculine foil which combined the aesthete, the decadent and the dandy. The resulting species was disturbingly rather than gracefully effeminate. More playthings than heroes, these gentlemen are actually "kept men". One example is *The Limit*, a novel by Ada Leverson (the "Sphinx" of the 'nineties), in which the repellently *fast* heroine openly "deceives" her husband with her cousin Harry de Freyne, a fashionable painter. A wholly decorative being, gifted with grace, charm and the art of wearing beautiful clothes that are just on the acceptable side of foppery, Harry is bored by women but coldly calculates the financial value of his attractiveness. The plot turns on his decision to marry—for money—an athletic, sexless heiress who talks like a guardsman; and the long-suffering husband's intervention to spare his wife the pain of separation from her lover.

An even more unsavoury example of the kept man appears in *Mammon and Co.*, an 1899 novel by E. F. Benson. Ted Comber's objectionable effeminancy is briskly summed up by one of the more virile characters: "He ain't a man." He doesn't shoot, ride or play games; he "sits on chairs and looks beautiful." He wears perfume, does embroidery, plays the mandolin, interests himself in the making of women's clothes. His own clothes are extremely dandified—and "to be a sort of arbiter elegantiarum in town" is one of his "nasty little ideals". To this overdrawn dandyism he adds the failings of the amateur aesthete and the inveterate snob, as well as a neurotic concern about ageing: at thirty, he rouges to look twenty-five Yet his role in the novel is neither that of the Regency's cold perfectionist nor that of a later day's homosexual sport; he is the true *fin de siècle* ladies' man. The fast young wife of *Mammon and Co.* is seduced by Comber's effeminacies; and she betrays her husband doubly by becoming pregnant, for the first time, during their affair. "Isn't it funny!" exclaims one of the more old-fashioned ladies of the novel. "So many women don't seem to know a man when they see him."

The dandy as effeminate seducer (or rather, seducee) could be swallowed by the writers of the 'nineties, but not the dandy as homosexual. That waited on the new century, on Proust and Firbank. Science, in the person of Havelock Ellis, and historical criticism, in the person of John Addington Symonds, addressed themselves to the systematic analysis of homosexuality. But the subject entered *fin de siècle* literature directly in only one instance: satires of Wilde himself. Well in advance of the 1895 trials, caricatures in *Punch* expressed the Philistine antipathy to suspicions of sexual abnormality attached to the arch-aesthete. The most urbane parody of Wilde appeared in 1894, causing a furor among the sophisticates by its acute sketch of the Wilde–Douglas relationship. This was *The Green Carnation* by Robert Hichens, a clever young man of the 'nineties who consciously planned the parody—his first success —as a book to set everyone talking.

Hichens solicited an introduction to Wilde from young Lord Alfred Douglas, whom he met while both were travelling in Egypt. Then Hichens carefully studied Wilde during four or five casual encounters in London, the extent of their relationship. The novel was brought out anonymously at Heinemann's insistence, and the portrait of Wilde as the over-blown "Esme Amarinth" was so skilfully drawn that Wilde was forced to deny he had done it himself. Many years later Hichens wrote of having seen Wilde in his heyday make a dramatic entrance at a fashionable first night in a London theatre. Ten minutes after the curtain rose, Wilde arrived to take possession of the big empty stage box. He was, Hichens remembered, "of course immaculately dressed, and wearing in his buttonhole a large carnation dyed a violent green. Behind him came I think five ultra-smart youths, all decorated with similar green carnations. This startling procession strolled slowly across the front of the stalls . . ." In the novel, which derived its title from this episode, a lady of little sophistication but considerable common sense describes this scene in a manner that underlines Wilde's dubious sexuality:

> I only saw about a dozen [green carnations] in the Opera House tonight, and all the men who wore them looked the same. They had the same walk, or rather waggle, the same coyly conscious expression, the same wavy motion of the head. When they spoke to each other, they called each other by Christian names. Is it a badge of some club or some society, and is Mr Amarinth their high priest? They all spoke to him, and seemed to revolve round him like satellites around the sun.

Hichens's caricature of Wilde is inevitably less flattering than the idealized self-portraits Wilde created in Lord Henry Wotton or Lord Goring. Esme Amarinth is neither a Lord nor an artist, but a mere tame social lion who has given up a shallow aestheticism for "the art of preposterous conversation". Nor does he have the chilling wit, the aloof poise or the controlled elegance of Wilde's mature dandies. Amarinth is a flabby, flamboyant creature who feeds on the admiration of idle young men and the astonishment of silly society women; his wit is more titillating than alarming. "I am intensely and strangely refined," he boasts; "I am absurd . . ."

Lord Reggie Hastings, the Lord Alfred Douglas of the parody, is much the sort of Narcissus-dandy figure Wilde had made of Dorian Gray. Young, beautiful and aristocratic, he is weakly disposed to imitate the older man's every mannerism, and unpleasantly given to fits of vanity, petulance and selfishness. Hichens also allows him enough of the homosexual's attitude toward women and sex to make credible his deference to Amarinth's disapproval of his proposed marriage.

> Lord Reggie . . . didn't in the least wish to be married, and he felt that he never should. But he also felt that marriage did not matter much either way. . . . To him it simply meant that a good-natured woman, who liked to kiss him, would open an account for him at her banker's, and let him live with her when he felt so disposed. He considered that such an arrangement would not be a bad one, especially as the good-natured woman would in course of time cease to like kissing him, and so free him from the one awkwardness that walked in the train of matrimony.

"The future," Wilde had incorrectly prophesied, "belongs to the dandy. It is the exquisites who are going to rule." How much shrewder was the perception behind his analysis of London Society as "entirely made up of dowdies and dandies . . . The men," he went on, "are all dowdies and the women are all dandies."

In the uneasy relationship between the Dorian Grays and the Lord Henry Wottons, Lord Reggies and Esme Amarinths, the history of nineteenth-century dandyism dwindles to a close. Mere shadows of the arrogant heroes of the Regency, the *fin de siècle* dandies survived on the bounty of good-natured women or (more often) the sufferance of ill-natured women. Their effeminancy was a weakness, not an embellishment; their allegiance turned to the aesthetic fringe, not the ruling aristocracy; their sphere reduced itself to the problematic domain of pathology, leaving the glory of an ideal far behind. In the final analysis, their dandyism was a handful of mannerisms retrieved from the past. "On est bien changé," as the great Beau would put it; "voilà tout."

CHAPTER XIV

Epilogue: Sir Max Beerbohm

I may be old-fashioned, but I am right.

—Beerbohm

RAPALLO is a modest, pleasant resort town on Italy's Mediterranean coast. It has a fine curving promenade along the sea, a few first-class hotels high above the water, innumerable crowded *pensioni* and sprawling cafés along the promenade. Back from the water, in the town itself, are busy shops, service stations, moving picture theatres, apartment houses bristling with terraces. These contrasts remind the traveller of the changes in fashion and fortune to which such places are liable. A quiet fishing town at the turn of the century, Rapallo was "discovered" by the Italophile English just before and after the first War and built its best hotels for their enjoyment. Americans and Brazilians and Scandinavians commandeered the best rooms after the second War; and today the middle-class Italian takes his bride to Rapallo for her honeymoon, returning some years later with his large family and his dogs to enjoy the donkey-cart rides on the promenade, the hot chocolate at the cafés, and by night the soccer games on the *televisione*, which stands behind a beaded curtain in the dining-room of his hotel. Fashion has moved westward, in which direction are to be found the elaborate villas and rock-carved swimming-pools of film stars, popular novelists and retired millionaires, where the tardy admirers of E. M. Forster's Italy search out the more artfully preserved fishing village atmosphere of Santa Margherita Ligure and Portofino.

A modest, pleasant house fronting on the coast-road that leads up into the hills in the south-easterly, or unfashionable, direction was until 1956 the home of Sir Max Beerbohm. He had lived here, with few interruptions, for nearly half a century. Here he received his infrequent but persistent visitors with the same mannered politeness that once alarmed Oscar Wilde and William Rothenstein, and spoke politely (if the visitor was an American) of Henry James and Chicago in '95. He spoke of himself, of course, with the greatest reluctance, but the landmarks of the unchanging fashion in Max were unmistakable. There was the old man himself, fragile and dapper and elegant in artful tweeds, smoking MAX cigarettes with an air, looking still like an "obviously precious" museum piece, as he did to Rebecca West in the 'twenties. There were the caricatures of pre-Raphaelite and decadent frescoed on the walls; there, to be spied through an open door, was the gentleman's dressing-room, with the patchwork dressing-gown, the commonplace objects laid out with precision and, on the dressing-table, a Dighton dandy-portrait.

"I am," Beerbohm told a B.B.C. audience twenty years ago, "what the writers of obituary notices call 'an interesting link with the past'." He hardly went anywhere, even to Rapallo; he lived modestly on slight financial resources; he quietly turned his back on his contemporaries. Serene in exile, he preserved the last of the dandies.

2

From Bulwer to Wilde every writer on dandyism took the dandy seriously as a present ideal or pleasure or nuisance or threat. Beerbohm was the first to take him, possibly with greater seriousness, as a remnant of the past. When all about him in the 'nineties (Beerbohm included) pretended to become dandies in their own right, his was the voice that announced that an era had passed for good. He was, albeit loosely, the historical conscience of his period.

Beerbohm's first essay on dandyism appeared in an undergraduate magazine (edited by Lord Alfred Douglas) at Oxford in 1893. Entitled "The Incomparable Beauty of Modern Dress", it was very much what was to be expected of a clever young man of twenty-one, at that time and place. Steeped in Wildesque aesthetics and Oscarian afflatus (*Intentions* was one of the three books Beerbohm admitted to reading while at the University *) the young Oxonian prated of "our artistic

* The other two were Lear's *Nonsense* and Thackeray's *Four Georges*.

duty to the community". "As in Life our first duty is to realise the soul," he wrote, "so in Art it should be to idealise the body." So much for Oxford. In 1895 Beerbohm travelled to the United States with his much older half-brother, Herbert Beerbohm Tree, the famous actor-manager, and the year after that he wrote the essay "Dandies and Dandies" which was to open his first book. While it incorporated ideas and phrases from the Oxford piece, along with material from three articles printed in New York, Chicago and London periodicals, "Dandies and Dandies" was mature Beerbohm and something new and necessary for the 'nineties. Here was an approach to dandyism, long overdue, through the great original dandies; here was a snub to pretentious modernity through an ironic glorification of the Regency.

"How very delightful Grego's drawings are!" the essay begins. "For all their mad perspective and crude colour, they have indeed the sentiment of style, and they reveal, with surer delicacy than does any other record, the spirit of Mr Brummell's day." As an opening sentence, this is an illuminating index to Beerbohm's concern with the Regency—in two ways. It shows the sort of reading and looking that, by 1896, had tied his interest in dandyism to the historical past. And it demonstrates that he was no historian. For the sentence is, of course, completely inaccurate. These were no "Grego drawings", but re-engravings from authentic prints of "Mr Brummell's day"; thus their crude perspective and sense of style. "I started off with a howler," Beerbohm said a few years ago, with the pained air of one who has not been allowed to forget. "It sounded like a very good way for a young man to start."

The most readable and informative memoirs about the Regency, for those interested in its fashionable and dandy side, were those of our old friend and gossip Captain Gronow. They were not published until the 'sixties, when they were issued in four instalments illustrated with a few prints the Captain had collected in the course of his career. Some of the prints (including two Beerbohm particularly noted) were re-engraved by Joseph Grego, along with many others of the same nature, for the first collected edition of Gronow, in 1889. Other "sources" available by the mid-'nineties were Jesse's biography of Brummell (reissued in 1886), Grace and Philip Wharton's silly and inaccurate survey of the *Wits and Beaux of Society*, John and Hunter Robinson's life of Romeo Coates (1891), Percy Fitzgerald's *Life of George the Fourth* (1881). All these contributed something to Beerbohm's Regency pieces, along with other material he invented or blithely altered for his own purposes. "To give an accurate and exhaustive account of that period," he wrote later of another decade of the nineteenth century, "would need a far less brilliant pen than mine."

Whatever Beerbohm may have known, at first hand, of Regency memoirs and Regency gossip, the legend of the *ur*-dandies came to him shaped by the intelligence and the wit of Barbey d'Aurevilly. "Dandies and Dandies" is first of all an irreverent answer to *Du Dandysme et de Georges Brummell,** and to all the intellectual posing that followed on Barbey. Beerbohm took it upon himself to provide a corrective to the Gallic intensity and Norman airs that Barbey had brought to the tradition. He looked at dandyism with the impudence and detachment and absence of melodrama proper to the native English dandy. The point of his essay is that the art of costume itself is the essence of Brummell's dandyism. Costume is not a mere outward show of some profound spiritual achievement. "Dandyism," Beerbohm writes, "is ever the outcome of a carefully cultivated temperament, not part of the temperament itself." The "oblique attitude toward life" that distinguished Brummell and attracted the aesthetes and the decadents after him, was not, in Beerbohm's view, an accomplishment peculiar to dandies; it was the sort of thing cultivated by *all delicate spirits* . . . To Brummell's mastery of this attitude Beerbohm pays a full sentence of tribute:

> Like the single-minded artist that he was, he turned full and square towards his art and looked life straight in the face out of the corners of his eyes.

What set Brummell apart, however, was the cut of his clothes. "Those are true words," says Beerbohm of Carlyle's famous angry definition of the dandy as the clothes-wearing man; "they are, perhaps, the only true words in *Sartor Resartus*."

---

* Beerbohm read and quoted from Barbey in the original French; *Du Dandysme* was not translated until 1897, a year after *The Works*.

Beerbohm laughs at Carlyle; he laughs at Barbey; and of course he has his laugh at Brummell, though all in the most polite manner. (Brummell is invariably "Mr Brummell" in the essay; while Count D'Orsay, of whom Beerbohm thinks less, is D'Orsay). But the last laugh, somehow, is on Beerbohm's own contemporaries. By indirection, by sly comparisons, by careless asides and by irony, always irony ("I wish, Ladies and Gentlemen, I could cure myself of the habit of speaking ironically," Beerbohm told a B.B.C. audience in the 'forties. "I should so like to express myself in a quite straightforward manner"), he rubs the sheen from the pretensions of the 'nineties. To all the *delicate spirits* of his day he opposes the cool dandies of the Regency, never troubling to say which group his reader shall find wanting. The aesthetic posing, the strenuous straining after Art with a capital letter he dismisses in a scornful reference to D'Orsay as a portraitist:

> It is the process of painting which is repellent; to force from little tubes of lead a glutinous flamboyance and to defile, with the hair of a camel therein steeped, taut canvas, is hardly the diversion for a gentleman. . . .

Here, after seventy years, is the quintessential Regency position (made as clear as it is made ridiculous): "The aesthetic vision of a dandy should be bounded by his own mirror."

Something had come over the young Max of Merton, who talked of Art and Life and the soul—something beside Gronow and Jesse, Regency prints and Barbey d'Aurevilly. He had learned to laugh at Oscar Wilde. There is amusing documentary proof of his growing detachment from the patron aesthete of the generation coming to maturity in the 'nineties. In 1894, two years before the "Dandies and Dandies" essay, one year after "The Incomparable Beauty of Modern Dress" (which had paid tribute to Wilde as a "poet" and the author of "that splendid, sinister work, *Dorian Gray*"), Beerbohm wrote a piece which would probably have annoyed Wilde more than anything else written about him, had it appeared during his lifetime. "A Peep into the Past" (what a title for a piece on Wilde!) was designed as Beerbohm's début in the first number of the *Yellow Book*. One can only imagine the circumstances of

its rejection:* the hearty laughter of Will Rothenstein, the
malicious pleasure of Beardsley (both Beerbohm's friends at
Oxford), the alarmed timidity of John Lane (to whom they
had introduced Beerbohm). For this was no anonymous satire
of Wilde transformed to Esme Amarinth, as in the *Green
Carnation* of the same year, but a cool bit of open condescension
from the younger generation to the older. And Wilde as
homosexual was part of the fun.

"Oscar Wilde!" the essay opens. "I wonder to how many
of my readers the jingle of this name suggests anything at all?
Yet, at one time, it was familiar to many and if we search back
among the old volumes of Punch, we shall find many a quip
and crank out at its owner's expense." Beerbohm presents
himself as a student of Early Victoriana who ("knowing that
Mr Sala was out of town") hunts up the forgotten Mr Wilde,
now living in obscure retirement in Chelsea, as "the survivor
of a bygone day". There he finds the old gentleman is a neighbourhood fixture, known for his old-fashioned clothes (though
"evidently cut by a good tailor"), greeted on his daily walk
up the King's Road ("the trades people . . . often waylay him
as he attempts to pass on"), his well-ordered domestic life
(which includes reading Ruskin to his children after an early
dinner) and his insistence upon punctuality ("perhaps this
accounts for the constant succession of page-boys, which so
startles the neighbourhood . . ."). "As I was ushered into the
little study, I fancied that I heard the quickly receding *frou-frou*
of tweed trousers, but my host I found reclining, hale and
hearty, though a little dishevelled upon the sofa."

Beerbohm makes fun of Wilde's sexual habits, his flashy
Bohemianism, his peculiar family life, his Irish wit, his superficial scholarship and his imitative works (among them "a
volume of essays, which Mr Pater is often obliged blushingly
to repudiate"). All this is stronger criticism than Wilde was
used to from Philistia, yet the piece is not offensive. The young

---

* "A Peep into the Past" was first "privately" printed in New York in
1923. Beerbohm's mature attitude to Wilde was consistently one of admiration for his talents coupled with reservations about his sincerity. His 1905
review of *De Profundis* in *Vanity Fair* hails its author as a "Lord of
Language" while marking his fondness for playing with emotions, and
"his old peculiar arrogance".

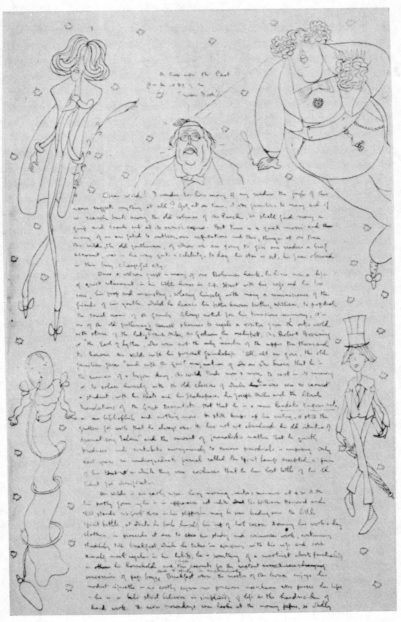

14. Beerbohm: "A Peep into the Past".
(Oscar Wilde) (1894)

15. Max Beerbohm: Self-Caricature (1899)

Max had already mastered an art which would serve him for the rest of his career: the art of satirizing, lambasting, insulting with impeccable decorum; the art of getting away with it. Here the specific stings of the satire are overshadowed by the general conceit: that Wilde (then at the height of his career) belonged to the forgotten past. And the pose of the author, patronizing, maddeningly tolerant and excessively deferential on the grounds of age alone, never of talent, is so outrageous that the reader thinks of Max, not of his victim.

The present-as-past conceit was far from fortuitous. Wilde's own career made it wickedly apt. For there were two Oscar Wildes, the "young self" of the long hair and the lily who, although he did not discover Beauty, as Beerbohm wrote elsewhere, managed her *début* in the 'eighties; and the "old self" of the 'nineties, now triumphing more solidly as an undeniably clever and fashionable playwright. It was Beerbohm's role to keep the old self from forgetting the young. "After all," he wrote maliciously, "it is not so much as a literary man that Posterity will forget Mr Wilde, as in his old capacity of journalist."

In Beerbohm's individual perception, the old had a way of becoming the young, the young the old; and the *fin de siècle* seemed to change places with the Regency. As for himself, he was amused to think of his precocious career as ending before it had fairly begun. The public applauds me, he wrote in 1899, simply because "it knows me to be a child author, and likes to picture me at my desk, dressed in black velveteen, with legs dangling towards the floor." Three years before that, however, he had already declared himself dated and had said farewell, half-seriously, to an alien world.

3

Caricatures always show the young Max Beerbohm with a high stiff collar, gloves, a carefully tilted silk hat, a cane, a boutonnière, an artfully bulging frock-coat, tapering trousers. These were basic equipment for the 'nineties dandy of the most correct school. Certain eccentricities have been recorded. Frank Harris noted "a strangeness in floating tie or primrose gloves or flowered buttonhole, lending a touch of the exotic

to the conventional—a sort of symbol of unique personality."
And Robert Hichens particularly remembered a "marvellous
overcoat . . . held together by only one tiny button, attached
to it in an unexpected place thought out by himself." But it
was the young dandy's manner that most impressed his contemporaries, and what struck them was less manner than
manners, awesomely good manners.

Beerbohm's speech was formal, his gestures quiet, his
round, babyish face expressive of that cool, worldly, faintly
satirical wisdom sensed in new-born infants. "Though we were
the same age, and in some ways I had more experience of life
than he," wrote Will Rothenstein of his meeting with Max at
Oxford, "his seemed to have crystallized into a more finished
form than my own. So had his manners, which were perfect."
Although free from snobbishness and rather inclined than not
to make friends, the young Beerbohm was noted—even feared
—for his passionless self-control. "When you are alone with
him, Sphinx," Wilde once asked Ada Leverson, "does he take
off his face and reveal his mask?"

To his contemporaries of the 'nineties, this very young man
was a successful dandy. The absolute achievement of poise was
behind him from the start; no one ever saw him strain after an
effect. He seems to have had always (Holbrook Jackson suggests, from birth) that which young men envy more than
anything else: a finished personality. But his widely recognized
dandyism was, considering the tradition, of a new and peculiar
variety. It went nowhere.

Not, certainly, into society. Max Beerbohm was resolutely
middle class. The youngest of a large, affectionate, prosperous
London family, he was neither pressed to follow his father into
trade nor driven to fight for a place in the sun of the aristocracy.
Indeed, he always wrote of high society with the gentle irony
he reserved for attractive fossils. Beerbohm was even less
English in origin than Disraeli (his father had immigrated from
Baltic Germany in the 'thirties), and while his foreign background undoubtedly played a part in shaping his personality,
it could not be deduced from a single line of his literary work.
What can be sensed, and what obviously mattered more, was
the fact that his father was sixty-two when Max was born.
Julius Beerbohm had known Paris in the 'twenties and London

in the 'thirties—and had fathered previous sons old enough to give Max, born in 1872, a quite illegitimate sense of familiarity with what he affectionately called the Medio-Victorian Age. The dandy in young Beerbohm was neither scrambling up nor sliding down the ladder of the classes; instead he ambled, slowly and serenely, backwards into time. Oval portraits of his grandparents, in eighteenth-century dress, adorned his mother's drawing-room, and caused Will Rothenstein to marvel "that anyone's grandparents could have flourished so long ago."

After a happy, quiet childhood and his schooling at Charterhouse, Beerbohm entered Merton College, where he set about meeting the only set with which he wished to be friendly, and for which the cultured atmosphere of his home had fitted him: the leading literary and artistic talents of the 'nineties. Many of them he came to know as the half-brother of Herbert Beerbohm Tree, who, three years before Max entered Oxford in 1890, had attained the distinction of actor-manager and knew most of the people worth knowing. (Tree was friendly with Wilde, for example, and produced *A Woman of No Importance* in 1893.) But on his own merits Beerbohm at once became known as a unique personality, and his talent won him a place of honour in the first number of the *Yellow Book*, when he was still an undergraduate and only twenty-two.

Dandyism, the Regency, and the worship of Fashion loomed large in all Beerbohm's writings of the 'nineties. In fact, it was as prophet and popularizer of these subjects that his early reputation was made. Mindful of Wilde's slight but lasting interest in the Regency, of Beardsley's delight in the décor of the Brighton Pavilion, of G. S. Street's nostalgic essays on Regency London, of theatrical versions of the lives of early dandies (like Clyde Fitch's *The Last of the Dandies*, in which Beerbohm Tree played D'Orsay), of reprinted Regency memoirs and biographies that appeared in increasing numbers through the 'eighties and 'nineties, a visitor asked Sir Max in his Rapallo parlour about the *fin de siècle* revival of interest in the Regency. He replied with a polite sniff. A widespread Regency revival? "I think it was m'self." For the budding essayist, drawn to that rare literary form as none had been since Thackeray, and as none has been since Beerbohm, the discovery of fresh subject matter was the essential luck; and

the young-old Max could be most freshly original with material
from the past. "To treat history as a means of showing one's
own cleverness may be rather rough on history," he told Ada
Leverson when she interviewed him in 1895, "but it has been
done by the best historians, from Herodotus to Froude and
myself."

Besides "Dandies and Dandies", *The Works of Max Beerbohm*
(Beerbohm's first book) contained a long essay entitled "King
George the Fourth". It is a rambling, conversational, absolutely irresponsible reconstruction of the Regent's life story
and the age he ornamented. Beerbohm takes as his thesis a
statement that George was, "in the practical sense of the word,
a fine king", and works out the argument as a reply to
Thackeray, whose lecture on George IV he follows rather
closely, with queries and quibbles. Thackeray, according to
Beerbohm, had "applied to his subject the wrong method, in
the wrong manner, and at the wrong time." Now that Victorian values themselves are in question, the moment has come
for a sprig of the *fin de siècle* to redress old wrongs and admire
in the last of the Georges the decorative virtues (intelligence,
wit, sensitivity, taste and style, especially style) once again
in fashion.

What was new, and essentially *Max* about the piece, was
that the reader could never be sure exactly where Beerbohm
stood: with the Regency, the medio-Victorians or the 'nineties.
The mincing play of his irony made the footing slippery indeed.
Punch was sure that the memory of its sacred Thackeray had
been insulted and printed an angry parody ("A Phalse Note
on George the Fourth") in Yellowplushese. "I meant all I
said about George," was Beerbohm's answer; "but I did not
choose to express myself quite seriously."

"A Good Prince", a little *tour de force* about the royal infant
in his perambulator, appeared in the same volume and is
generally considered a pendant to the essay on George IV.
For here Beerbohm mocked the ideal of royal angelic imbecility
erected by the Victorians in horrified reaction against the
unmourned Regent. In "Dessein's", one of the *Roundabout
Papers*, Thackeray had raised the ghost of Sterne to senti-
mentalize about his glimpse of a royal infant "in his cradle at St
James's, a lovely little babe; a gilt Chinese railing was before

him, and I dropped the tear of sensibility as I gazed on the sleeping cherub." At the heart of Thackeray's irony was his knowledge that this prince had grown up to be George IV. Beerbohm lived to relish the fact that *his* prince turned out to be the Duke of Windsor.

"Poor Romeo!", further on in *The Works*, was another step in Beerbohm's private Regency revival. A wistful tribute to the pseudo-dandy of Bath, Romeo Coates, it introduced a new satiric technique for the chastisement of the present by the past. Whimsy, fantasy and all the paraphernalia of the fairy tale were beloved of the literary 'nineties; Beerbohm spoofed the devices and, through them, the more grievous affectations of the age. On a larger scale, and in a work of fiction, he used the same technique to make fun of the pretension to wickedness, the presentation of evil shallowly understood which had made a book like *Dorian Gray* ridiculous. In *The Happy Hypocrite*, a long fairy tale written for the *Yellow Book* in the year that *The Works* appeared, Beerbohm clearly parodied Wilde's novel, and he used a Regency fantasy for his pleasant purpose.

"None, it is said, of all who revelled with the Regent," (the story begins) "was half so wicked as Lord George Hell." For the benefit of "my little readers" Beerbohm reveals that his hero-villain "often sat up at Carlton House until long after bed-time, playing at games, and that he generally ate and drank far more than was good for him. His fondness for fine clothes was such that he used to dress on weekdays quite as gorgeously as good people dress on Sundays . . ." (For the benefit of bigger readers, there are invented sources—like "Captain Tarleton's *Contemporary Bucks*"—which provide footnotes, and evoke a host of Regency memorialists.) The story of Lord George Hell owes something to the Regency legend of "Golden" Ball Hughes's elopement with a ballet girl. But the device of the saintly mask to cover an evil face and the dénouement of the mask's removal—to reveal a face grown saintly through the years of good behaviour—reverse the point and tone of Wilde's melodrama. Like Dorian, Lord George is "proud of being horrid", but Beerbohm destines him to play the *happy* hypocrite.

Zuleika Dobson, too, owes something to a novelist whose works were taken seriously in the *fin de siècle*: to Disraeli, who provided the 'nineties with a living tradition of dandy fiction. His early novels were little read, but his last two books, *Lothair* (1870) and *Endymion* (1880), had won him readers among the new literary generation. Wilde, for example, was "most impressed" by Disraeli's works, and Beerbohm himself placed Disraeli (along with Byron and Rossetti!) among the three most interesting Englishmen of the nineteenth century.

In *Lothair* and *Endymion* the ageing Disraeli had intensified the aura of romance that transfigured *The Young Duke*. Disraeli's own experience, moving from triumph to greater triumph, conjuring up an Empire and hypnotizing a Queen, had fully satisfied the wild imagination that bedevilled him as a young man. "It is a privilege to live in this age of rapid and brilliant events," he had written in the 'sixties when the Greek throne was going begging among the English aristocracy. "What an error to consider it an utilitarian age! It is one of infinite romance. Thrones tumble down and crowns are offered like a fairy-tale."

Lothair, a more sober version of the young duke, and Endymion, a gentle idealization of the young Disraeli himself, are both representatives of the English ruling class that Disraeli found as rich, as beautiful, as graceful in manner as heroes of romance. Their ideal of life envisions perpetual spring passed in a whirl of enchantments.

> "But we cannot always be dancing," said Lothair.
> "Then we would sing," said Euphrosyne.
> "But the time comes when one can neither dance nor sing," said Lothair.
> "Oh! then we become part of the audience," said Madame Phoebus, "the people for whose amusement everybody labours."

These young men stroll coolly through a maze of the burning issues of the day—issues like imperialism and English Catholicism and political reform, which absorbed Disraeli in his parliamentary career—miraculously escaping the dangers of entanglement like fairy princes in a magic thicket.

The dreamlike, all-is-gold-that-glitters quality of the late Disraeli novels is echoed in *Zuleika Dobson*, Beerbohm's famous full-length dandy novel. Its hero, John Albert Edward Claude Orde Angus Tankerton Tanville-Tankerton, fourteenth Duke of Dorset (and so on),* is one more version of the nineteenth century's ideal young duke, caught as he steps across the fatal boundary of the past into the new era. (*Zuleika* was published in 1911.) Fabulously wealthy, miraculously gifted, consummately dandified, he is also—and this is the point which makes *Zuleika* the very last of the dandy novels—wholly insufferable. Like Disraeli, Beerbohm saw in the dandy hero a natural subject for romance; unlike Disraeli, whose lasting respect for the English aristocracy approached adoration, Beerbohm used the gilding of fantasy primarily to evoke laughter. *Zuleika Dobson* was written both as a devoted return to the tradition of full-fledged dandy fiction, and as an outrageous farce with a noodle of a dandy for its hero. "Better be vulgar with Byron than a noodle with Dorset!" reflects Beerbohm's dandy duke at the bitter crisis of his love affair. "Still, noodledom was nearer than vulgarity to dandyism."

Had Beerbohm ever been gravely presented with a choice between the old-fashioned gentleman, willing to die for his standards of class honour and personal dignity, and the New-fangled Woman, crass and overbearing in the freshness of her independence, he would unquestionably have opted for the dandy. He often expressed strong prejudices for the one and against the other. ("Women," he once said sourly, "are becoming nearly as rare as ladies.") But for Beerbohm the satirist there was no choice. Zuleika must triumph in all her vulgarity, and the Duke must sink to a watery grave, propelled to the final plunge by a few warning drops of rain. The dandy's last thoughts are for the fading magnificence of his finery. Thus the demands of caricature were satisfied, and the dandy was reduced in scale to fit a small, absurd, fantasy world where pearls turn pink or black to blush or mourn, and young men drown themselves, *en masse*, for love.

4

So the twentieth century came to England, with the horrid present tucked up its horrid sleeve, and found Beerbohm pre-

---

* The name, if nothing else, is a reminder of Disraeli's idol, Count D'Orsay. Dorset is pronounced D'Orsay by Zuleika's French maid, and Tankerville was the name of the English family connected by marriage with D'Orsay's sister.

paring to disappear. By 1910 he was safely out of harm's way
in his house above Rapallo, avoiding not the minor dangers of
war (he returned to England during both World Wars) but
the major horrors of Compulsory Education, central heating,
fast cars, quick lunches, the skyscraper, the advertiser
("greatest of all modern pests") and, in general, a modern
London "cosmopolitanised, democratised, commercialised,
mechanised, standardised, vulgarised . . ."

In *The Works* Beerbohm had announced his discovery, while
an undergraduate at Oxford, that he "could have no part in
Modern Life." "To unswitch myself from my surroundings, to
guard my soul from contact with the unlovely things that com-
passed it about, therein lay my hope." Younger men pressed
forward, he was already out of date, he belonged "to the
Beardsley period". He planned a retreat out of reach of the
modern madness of London, where he would make himself
"master of some small area of physical life, a life of quiet,
monotonous simplicity, exempt from all outer disturbance."
This had all been a superlative joke, a dandy's impudence at
play, but truth was only fifteen years behind it. When Beerbohm
left London, and took his new wife to Italy, it was for much the
purpose prophesied in *The Works*; his intention, it seemed to
Logan Pearsall Smith, was simply to loaf and invite his soul.
"As to the loafing," Smith wrote, "there could be no question;
I have never known a more wisely idle person . . . He was
quite content, so far as I could see, to live on the most modest
of incomes and do nothing all day long."

Beerbohm preserved his personal shadow of the dandy
tradition by retreating into isolation; his self-imposed exile
was to be the last word in dandyism. He looked back not to
the flamboyant dandyism of homosexuality and decadence,
which found its way into the twentieth century without his
help; not to the intellectual dandyism of Baudelaire, with its
appeal to the critical temper; but to the oldest form of the
tradition, the dandyism of pose and poise and a hedge against
the world. Beerbohm's dandyism was one from which all
heroic qualities had been stripped away: arrogance, class
superiority, exclusivism. In space and in time, quite simply
and without vulgar assertion, he kept his distance. Relinquish-
ing the dandy position at the centre of the stage, finally relin-

quishing the stage itself for mastery of "some small area of physical life", Beerbohm in his work also rejected the heroic for a modest alternative: perfection in small sizes.

He held his place in the intellectual world of the twentieth century, when bold experiments, profound thoughts and weighty trilogies have been the fashion, by an elegant output of little things. The essay and the portrait caricature, both outdated forms, both handled in as unpretentious a manner as possible, were the playthings of a talent whose limits he often marked with the disdain of the dandy. "My gifts are small," he wrote an aspiring biographer. "I've used them very well and discreetly, never straining them; and the result is that I've made a charming little reputation." Keeping within the range of the self-styled "dilettante" and "*petit maître*", however, Beerbohm never permitted himself wispiness of thought or sloppiness of execution. Shape of word and meaning of drawn line were plotted with the greatest care—with that "fastidiousness" and "daintiness" he applauded in Whistler's prose as "dandyishness" of style.

Beerbohm's dandyism reduced at last, in his life and writings, to the simple fact of a well-ordered existence made up of little things which gentlemen once took wholly for granted. Politeness, personal dignity, care in the choice of spoken and written word, formality of dress: the artificial props of the civilized life were the handful of Beerbohm's principles. "I take my stand shoulder to shoulder with the Graces. On the banner that I wave is embroidered a device of prunes and prisms."

The tone of mild regret and wistful nostalgia that enters into all of Beerbohm's pleas for the Graces was itself part of his dandyism—and part of his certainty that dandyism was irrevocably of the past. "The love of by-gone things is a quite recent growth—," he said, "—due mainly to the fact that we have fallen on evil times." He himself looked without apology into the past for one figure, the recollection of which never failed to charm, amuse, delight and refresh him: the man-about-town, the exquisite, the dandy, the simple gentleman—

a now extinct species, a lost relic of the eighteenth century and of the days before the great Reform Bill of 1832; a leisurely personage, attired with great elaboration, on his way to one of his many clubs; not necessarily interesting in himself; but fraught with external character and point: very satisfactory to those for whom the visible world exists. From a sociological standpoint perhaps he was all wrong, and perhaps his successor—the earnest fellow . . . hurrying along to his job—or in quest of some job—is all right. But one does rather wish the successor looked as if he felt himself to be all right.

Acknowledgments

I AM grateful for the kindness encountered at an appallingly large number of libraries and museums: the New York Public, Morgan, Columbia University and New York Society Libraries, the Berg Collection, and the Metropolitan and Cooper Union Museums in New York; the British Museum Reading and Print Rooms and the Victoria and Albert Museum in London; the Bibliothèque Nationale, the Musée Carnavalet and the Petit Palais in Paris; the Widener and Houghton Libraries and the Fogg Museum of Harvard University; the Bodleian Library of Oxford University; and the Boston Athenaeum. I also thank David Thayer Hersey, Robert Hodes, John Kinnaird and Margherita Repetto for special assistance.

It is with particular pleasure that I acknowledge the encouragement, advice and precious time given with generosity by James L. Clifford, Susanne Howe Nobbe, Justin O'Brien and Lionel Trilling of Columbia University.

Notes on the Illustrations

1. "The DANDY I'm sure" (1816)   *frontispiece*

Unsigned, undated and uncatalogued by the British Museum. Probably, in the artist's original intention, a personal caricature—subject unknown. My date is from the watermark.

2. Robert Dighton: Beau Brummell (1805)   *facing p. 32*
Courtesy *Sir Owen Morshead*

Robert Dighton (1752–1814) made his living, as he advertised in the *Morning Chronicle*, by taking "correct elegant likenesses in miniature for half a guinea, in half an hour in a manner peculiar to himself" —in other words, he was the contemporary equivalent of the portrait photographer. He worked in London, Bath, Oxford, Cambridge and Brighton and is best remembered for his caricatures of late-eighteenth-century personages from the theatrical, professional, university, City and fashionable worlds. His "likeness" of Brummell is the only satisfactory full-length portrait of the man in his prime.

3. George Cruikshank: "The Dandies *Coat* of *Arms*" (1819)
facing p. 33

"*Coat of Arms*. Azure. The *Sexes impaled improper* between two Butterflies. . . . On the [sinister] flanch three pair of Stays, argent, . . . charged with Rouge Pomat^m & smell^s bottle, . . . a frill rampant . . . a false collar rampant—small cloaths *passive* in *oils* supported by *pins*—Supporters—Two Monkies—*proper*—
"Order of Puppyism suspended . . .
"Crest, a p^r of Stays full padded—supporting a Cravat & Collar Rampant proper, holding a *blockhead argent* & *gules*, winged with *asses ears proper* the whole under cover of a *Sable Bever*."

4. George Cruikshank: "His Most Gracious Majesty George the Fourth" (1821)   *facing p. 48*
Courtesy the *Victoria and Albert Museum*

George Cruikshank (1797–1851) made his first reputation as the most successful political and social caricaturist of the Regency, in the coarse and vigorous manner of Rowlandson and Gilray. His innumerable insulting caricatures of the dandies showed them as "Monstrosities": boned, padded, stretched and straining insects of the fashionable world. Again and again he drew the Regent as a dissolute, lecherous, obese degenerate, but this portrait, drawn for the post-Coronation market, celebrates the "First Gentleman of Europe", dressed with great simplicity in Brummell's style, adorned only by the Order of the Garter. Brighton Pavilion is in the background.

5. Richard Dighton: "A Welch Castle" (Lord Gwydyr) (1818)
facing p. 49

Richard Dighton (1795–1880) was the second son of the Robert Dighton who drew Brummell (the first son, Denis, was appointed military draughtsman to the Regent in 1815). Like his father he did miniature portraits and caricatures of fashionable and City people, and from about 1817 to 1828 he produced an extraordinary gallery of the dandies as they must really have appeared: among others, Alvanley, Raikes, Romeo Coates, Kangaroo Cooke, Wellington, Poodle Byng, Bessborough, Hertford, Golden Ball Hughes, Worcester.

Peter Robert Drummond-Burrell, 2nd Baron Gwydyr, was one of Brummell's successors as dandy-favourite of the Regent. He served as deputy Chamberlain at the Coronation, and arranged the dandy breakfast by which the Regent placated the exclusives. His wife was one of the patronesses of Almack's.

6. Daniel Maclise: Disraeli (1833) *facing p. 96*
Courtesy the *Metropolitan Museum of Art*

This exquisite portrait of the young dandy-aspirant, complete with all the ungentlemanly and unfashionable affectations long held against Disraeli (ringlets, frilled cuffs, rings, velvets, bows and general air of Oriental languor) made *Fraser's* wax lyrical: "O Reader dear! do pray look here, and you will spy the curly hair, and forehead fair, and nose so high, and gleaming eye, of Benjamin D'Is-ra-e-li, the wondrous boy who wrote *Alroy* in rhyme and prose, only to shew how long ago victorious Judah's lion-banner rose. . . . etc."

7. Isaac Robert Cruikshank: "A Dandy fainting or—An Exquisite in Fits" (1818) *facing p. 97*

Less famous than George, Isaac Robert (1794–1843) followed after his younger brother in choice of subject and style of caricature. He is best remembered for having finished the illustrations to Pierce Egan's *Life in London* (Tom and Jerry) begun by George. Here three dandies of the effeminate Monstrosity variety minister to their companion, who has fainted at the Opera.

"I am so frighten'd I can hardly stand!"—"Mind you don't soil the Dear's linnen"—"I dread the consequence! that last Air of Signeur *Nonballenas* has thrown him in such raptures, we must call [a] Doctor immediately"—"You have no fello feeling my dear fellos, pray unlace the dear loves Stays, and lay him on the couch."

8. Horace Vernet: *Incroyable* (1814) *facing p. 112*
Courtesy the *Bibliothèque Nationale*

Vernet, in addition to being one of the most popular painters of the century (specializing in Arabs and battle scenes), was the finest *graveur de modes* of nineteenth-century France. Like Richard Dighton he inherited an eye for fashion: his grandfather had worked for Louis XV; his father, Carle, had also been a court favourite, and had done the first *incroyables* series in the year V. Born in 1789, Horace enjoyed court patronage during the Empire, the Restoration, the July Monarchy and the Second Empire. He is said to have begun his career, while still a boy, by designing the vignette at the head of the letter paper on which the Imperial court sent invitations to the races. He received the Cross of the Legion of Honour in the year of the publication of his *Incroyables et Merveilleuses de 1814*, of which this dandy, dressed probably for the races (with parasol and spy-glass) is Plate 14.

9. "L'Egoïsme personnifié": *Le Bon Genre* (1814)   *facing p. 113*

Courtesy the *Houghton Library*

One of over a hundred "Observations sur les modes et les usages de Paris" engraved by various hands (including Horace Vernet) for La Mésangère, editor of the *Journal des Dames et des Modes*. He published them in 1817 and in 1827 as the *Bon Genre* series, the most precious fashion documents of the century in France. The anonymous caricaturist here, in the first year of the dandy invasion of Paris, documents the behaviour of the anglophile *incroyables*, which old-fashioned Frenchmen found obnoxious. "Le *dandy* doit avoir un air conquérant, léger, insolent," wrote Chateaubriand; ". . . il décèle la fière indépendance de son caractère en gardant son chapeau sur la tête, en se roulant sur les sofas, en allongeant ses bottes au nez des ladies assises en admiration sur des chaises devant lui. . . ."

10. Daniel Maclise: Bulwer (1832)   *facing p. 224*

Courtesy the *Metropolitan Museum of Art*

Over the signature Alfred Croquis, Maclise (1806–70) sketched for *Fraser's Magazine* a brilliant series of portraits of distinguished men of the 'thirties. To accompany this "Gallery of Literary Characters", *Fraser's* printed a text, usually by William Maginn, which gave impertinent, unpalatable but usually sound advice to successful authors. "If he would but give up his 'affectations'", Bulwer was told here, "—and learn to believe, that to be a Garrick Club dandy is not one of the highest objects of human ambition . . ." Thackeray never forgot this portrait of Bulwer in a dressing gown: twelve years later he was still blaming Bulwer's defects of style on his "habit of composing his works in a large-flowered dressing-gown, and morocco slippers". Only "a man IN A JACKET", Thackeray said, "is a man."

11. Daniel Maclise: Count D'Orsay (1834)   *facing p. 225*

The best full-length portrait of D'Orsay at the height of his "presidency of fashion's court", as *Fraser's* described it. The magazine was unusually flattering, invited D'Orsay to become a contributor and inquired after D'Orsay's Journal over which Byron was said to have waxed enthusiastic.

12. George Cruikshank: Charles Dickens (*c.* 1836–7) *facing p. 240*
     Courtesy the *Victoria and Albert Museum*

Cruikshank the dandy caricaturist became, in the period of his greatest fame, Cruikshank the friend of Dickens and illustrator of *Boz*. This pencil sketch is probably the one F. G. Kitton described as having been drawn at a meeting of the Hook & Eye, a literary club to which both men belonged ("Sit still, Charley, while I take your portrait!"). It shows the dandified young Dickens before he was enough of a celebrity to be portrayed as a proper Victorian. The elegant pose, tight trousers, black cravat and curving lapels *à la* Count D'Orsay form the young Dickens who made Adolphus Trollope exclaim, "No! *that* is not the man who wrote 'Pickwick'!"

13. Constantin Guys: Second Empire Dandy   *facing p. 241*
     Courtesy the *Musée Carnavalet*

A very unusual Guys drawing: ordinarily his dandies come in groups, surrounded by women and horses. Undated and untitled.

14. Max Beerbohm: "A Peep into the Past" (Oscar Wilde) (1894)
                                                    facing p. 320
     Courtesy the *Berg Collection*

The first page of Beerbohm's impudent satire of Wilde discussed in Chapter XIV. As if a study for Beerbohm's later caricatures of the "Young Self" and "Old Self" of notable Edwardians confronting each other, this early sketch gives the four stages of Wilde's life: infant, schoolboy, young aesthete with lily and flowing collar, and puffy man-about-town.

15. Max Beerbohm: Self-caricature (1899)   *facing p. 321*
     Courtesy the *Bodleian Library*

Notes

O N its first appearance in these notes, each source is given in full in CAPITAL LETTERS. Thereafter, within that chapter, the source is given in abbreviated form (ordinarily only author's surname) in lower-case letters). Where the note refers to a source given in full as part of the notes to another chapter, the *abbreviated* form appears in CAPITALS. Bracketed italic numbers following the abbreviated form indicate the chapter and chapter-section in which fuller bibliographical information may be found. Thus, for example:

Jesse, I, p. 100: page 100 of Volume One of the work by Jesse, the full title of which is to be found in capital letters earlier in the notes to this chapter.

JESSE [*I–1*], I, p. 100: page 100 of Volume One of the work by Jesse, the full title of which is to be found in capital letters in the notes to section 1 of Chapter I.

INTRODUCTION

"La rébellion humaine . . .": ALBERT CAMUS, *L'HOMME RÉVOLTÉ* (1951), p. 41.

"Yankee Doodle": O. G. T. SONNECK, *REPORT ON . . . "YANKEE DOODLE"* (Library of Congress, 1909); JOHN TASKER HOWARD, *OUR AMERICAN MUSIC* (1946), pp. 113–17; GROVE'S *DICTIONARY OF MUSIC AND MUSICIANS* (1889).

"Encore un livre . . .": JULES LAFORGUE, "LOCUTIONS DES PIERROTS, xii".

CHAPTER I. Brummell

1

BARBEY D'AUREVILLY, *DU DANDYSME ET DE GEORGES BRUMMELL* [*XI–2*], p. 227.

Brummell on his father: LADY HESTER STANHOPE, *MEMOIRS IN CONVERSATIONS WITH HER PHYSICIAN C. L. MERYON* (1845), I, p. 281; on lakes: CAPTAIN WILLIAM JESSE, *BEAU BRUMMELL* (Grolier Society, 19—), I, p. 107. *Hereafter, facts, anecdotes and contemporary opinions otherwise unsupported can be assumed to derive from Jesse. Every effort has been made to substantiate Jesse's account, and especially to find his own source for Brummelliana.*

Brummell's silent snub of Prince: letter from anonymous contemporary to Jesse, II, pp. 352–3; his wit: HAZLITT, "BRUMMELLIANA", Vol. XXV of *COMPLETE WORKS* (ed. P. P. Howe, 1934).

Brummell's "fineness": THOMAS HENRY LISTER, *GRANBY*

(New York, 1826), I, p. 40; his taste: CAPTAIN REES HOWELL GRONOW, *REMINISCENCES AND RECOLLECTIONS* (1900), I, p. 45; THOMAS RAIKES, *JOURNAL* (1858), I, pp. 325–6; THOMAS RAIKES, *FRANCE SINCE 1830* (1841), I, pp. 375–6; HARRIETTE WILSON, *MEMOIRS* (1929), pp. 598–9.

Brummell and costume: BEERBOHM, "DANDIES AND DANDIES", *THE WORKS*; "fine linen . . .": Wilson, p. 40.

2

Byron on Brummell: *BYRON A SELF-PORTRAIT* (ed. Peter Quennell, 1950), II, p. 504; cf. Hazlitt, "Brummelliana".

"Ring the bell": "PERSONAL REMINISCENCES OF BEAU BRUMMELL", *CHAMBERS'S JOURNAL* (Edinburgh, 4/21–28/ 1866); WILLIAM PITT LORD LENNOX, *CELEBRITIES I HAVE KNOWN* (1876), I, p. 299.

The Trebeck portrait in *Granby*: *ELIZABETH LADY HOLLAND TO HER SON* (ed. the Earl of Ilchester, 1946), p. 41; Barbey, p. 235; Brummell in Jesse, I, p. ix; Lister I, p. 77.

3

Brummell's origins: LEWIS MELVILLE, *BEAU BRUMMELL* (1924), pp. 21–7; KATHLEEN CAMPBELL, *BEAU BRUMMELL* (1948), p. 16; JOANNA RICHARDSON, *FANNY BRAWNE* (1952), pp. 2–3, 172; Wilson, pp. 43–4.

Contemporary estimates of his inheritance: JOHN CAM HOBHOUSE LORD BROUGHTON, *RECOLLECTIONS OF A LONG LIFE* (1910), II, p. 1; CHARLES MACFARLANE, *REMINISCENCES OF A LITERARY LIFE* (1917), p. 272; Jesse, I, p. 27.

"I'll chase her from society . . .": *TOM MOORE'S DIARY* (ed. J. B. Priestley, 1925), pp. 133–4.

Brummell-figure in novels: DISRAELI, *THE YOUNG DUKE* [*IV–5*], p. 17; MRS CATHERINE GORE, *CECIL; OR, THE ADVENTURES OF A COXCOMB* (New York, F. A. Brady, 18—), I, p. 9.

Break with the Regent: Mrs Fitzherbert later commented, on hearing a rumour that George IV planned to appoint Brummell to the Calais consulate: "Some people are more partial to their enemies than kind to their friends!" (W. H. WILKINS, *MRS FITZHERBERT AND GEORGE IV* (1905), II, pp 198–9). And Brummell wrote Raikes, on hearing of George's accession to the throne in 1820, that he was hoping for "an indulgent amnesty of former peccadilloes" (Raikes, *Journal*, I, p. 323).

Brummell on Watier's: "Personal Reminiscences", p. 245; lucky sixpence: Raikes, *Journal*, I, p. 321.

"Rivalry" with the Regent: THOMAS MOORE, *INTERCEPTED LETTERS; OR, THE TWOPENNY POST-BAG*

(1813), p. 53; HENRY LUTTRELL, *ADVICE TO JULIA: A LETTER IN RHYME* (1820), pp. 117–18; Byron, *Self-Portrait*, I, p. 139.

Brummell's debts: Raikes, *Journal*, I, p. 321; Davies in Jesse, I, p. 311; Davies in Broughton, I, p. 215; Alvanley in Gronow, I, pp. 136–7; Wilson, p. 309; Hobhouse in Broughton, II, p. 1. Important new evidence about Brummell's financial entanglements (Campbell, pp. 118–21) indicates, though inconclusively, that he engaged in transactions unsavoury even by the standards of his own day. The exact details were probably known only to his intimates (Lords Robert and Charles Manners, perhaps also Lord Alvanley and Lord Worcester) who kept loyally silent; thus the Brummell legend was not affected (cf. vague allusions in Jesse, I, pp. 304–6). Miss Campbell's evidence goes far to explain a number of guarded contemporary references to the disreputable "Dandy Affair": Charles Bagot in a letter to Lord Binning: "the Dandy affair is a *very very* bad one, get out of it how they will. I hate the idea of Alvanley being tarnished, because he is wanted—as to Brummell—*tempus abire est*" (JOSCELINE BAGOT, *GEORGE CANNING AND HIS FRIENDS* (1909), II, pp. 19–20); and Peel's satisfaction over "the discomfiture of the dandies": "Mr. Brummell has decamped", he wrote Lord Whitworth, "to the confusion of his collaterals and his creditors. . . . What has become of Lord Alvanley, and how far he is implicated in Mr Brummell's misdeeds, I know not. . . . I believe some private good, as far as the rising generation is concerned, will result from the downfall of such heroes" (*SIR ROBERT PEEL FROM HIS PRIVATE CORRESPONDENCE* (ed. C. S. Parker, 1891–9), I, pp. 226–7). Harriette Wilson (pp. 602–4) tells the related story of Brummell's exposure at White's by a certain Richard Meyler; and Byron (*Self Portrait*, II, p. 618) refers to "that affair of poor Meyler, who thence acquired the name of 'Dick the Dandy-Killer'—it was about money and debt and all that." Less than a week after his flight to Calais, Brummell wrote Raikes (*Journal*, I, p. 322) alluding to "a worm that will not sleep called conscience".

Brummell's visitors in Calais: list in Jesse, I, pp. 338–41; Broughton, II, p. 1; cf. Wilson, p. 609; Lennox, I, pp. 297–9; Moore, *Diary*, p. 42; MAJOR CHAMBRE, *RECOLLECTIONS OF WEST-END LIFE* (1858), I, pp. 282–93; JAMES POPE-HENNESSY, *MONCKTON MILNES: THE YEARS OF PROMISE* (1949), p. 28.

His collapse: VIRGINIA WOOLF, "BEAU BRUMMELL", *THE COMMON READER*; cf. "BRUMMELL: THE STORY OF A BEAU", *ALL THE YEAR ROUND* (11/20/1880); PETER QUENNELL, "GEORGE BRYAN BRUMMELL", *THE SINGULAR PREFERENCE* (1952); his consulate: CHARLES GREVILLE, *DIARY* (ed. P. W. Wilson, 1927), I, p. 35; Brummell in MacFarlane, pp. 270–1.

4

Brummell's toilette: Gronow, I, p. 52; EDWARD GOULBURN, *PURSUITS OF FASHION* (1810), p. 53; late rising: MacFarlane, p. 268; observers: Raikes, *Journal*, I, p. 319 & *France*, I, pp. 376–7; teeth: Stanhope, I, p. 283; shaving: Jesse II, pp. 72–3.

Brummell on avoiding notice: see paraphrases in EDWARD BULWER, *GREVILLE* (unfinished novel printed in LYTTON SON [*III–1*]), p. 349; BALZAC, *TRAITÉ DE LA VIE ÉLÉ-GANTE* [*VI–2*], pp. 183–4.

Influence on the Regent: Melville, *Brummell*, pp. 42–4; Gronow, I, pp. 44–5; cf. WILLARD CONNELY, *THE REIGN OF BEAU BRUMMELL* (1940), p. 41.

Brummell and starching: Lennox, I, p. 292; "not a fop": anonymous correspondent to Jesse, II, p. 356.

5

Brummell and the sex: Raikes, *Journal*, I, p. 318; Wilson, p. 533; Lister, I, p. 91; Gouburn, p. 54. Jesse (I, pp. 113–15, 121) says Brummell proposed to "every pretty woman of rank" as a formal compliment, and was once furious at being taken at his word; he also prints many of Brummell's "love letters"—they are flowery exercises —and explains that the Beau "could write hundreds by his fireside at all seasons".

Brummell's conversation: GEORGE CRABBE, *THE LIFE OF THE REV. GEORGE CRABBE* (1837), p. 199; his "scrutinizing eye": "Personal Reminiscences"; his wit: Hazlitt, "Brummelliana"; his ambition: W. MASSIE, *SYDENHAM; OR, MEMOIRS OF A MAN OF THE WORLD* (Philadelphia, 1833), I, pp. 18–20; his contempt: Jesse, I, p. 135.

CHAPTER II. The Regency

1

Fashion: DISRAELI, *THE DUNCIAD OF TO-DAY* (ed. Michael Sadleir, 1928), p. 34; "It was dull . . .": DISRAELI, *VIVIAN GREY* [*IV–2*], I, p. 70.

The social Regency: some sources not elsewhere cited are: ALICE ACLAND, *CAROLINE NORTON* (1948); JOHN ASHTON, *THE DAWN OF THE XIXth CENTURY IN ENGLAND* (1922), (largely material from contemporary newspapers, as in the other Ashton books cited below); GRANTLEY BERKELEY, *ANECDOTES OF THE UPPER TEN THOUSAND* (1867); ROGER BOUTET DE MONVEL, *BEAU BRUMMELL AND HIS TIMES* (1908); ARTHUR BRYANT, *THE AGE OF ELEGANCE* (1950); E. M. BUTLER, *THE TEMPESTUOUS*

PRINCE (1929) (Hermann Pückler-Muskau); *CREEVEY* (1948)
& *CREEVEY'S LIFE AND TIMES* (1934) (both ed. John Gore);
PAUL H. EMDEN, *REGENCY PAGEANT* (1936); THEODORE
HOOK, *THE CHOICE HUMOUROUS WORKS WITH A LIFE
OF THE AUTHOR* (1889) & *SAYINGS AND DOINGS* (1836-9);
ROBERT HUISH, *MEMOIRS OF GEORGE THE FOURTH*
(1830) (scandal-mongering); CLARE JERROLD, *THE BEAUX
AND THE DANDIES* (1910); WILLIAM MAGINN, *WHITE-
HALL; OR, THE DAYS OF GEORGE IV* (1827) (novel by the
future editor of *Fraser's Magazine*); HARRIET MARTINEAU,
HISTORY OF THE THIRTY YEARS' PEACE (1878);
ETHEL COLBURN MAYNE, *A REGENCY CHAPTER* (1939)
(Lady Bessborough); LEWIS MELVILLE, *THE BEAUX OF
THE REGENCY* (1908) & *THE FIRST GENTLEMAN OF
EUROPE* (1906) (George IV) & *SOME ECCENTRICS AND A
WOMAN* (1911); DAVID L. MURRAY, *REGENCY: A
QUADRUPLE PORTRAIT* (1936); PETER QUENNELL,
BYRON: THE YEARS OF FAME (1935); STUART J. REID,
THE LIFE AND TIMES OF SYDNEY SMITH (1896);
SAMUEL ROGERS, *RECOLLECTIONS OF THE TABLE-
TALK* (ed. Morchard Bishop, 1952); ANGELA THIRKELL, *THE
FORTUNES OF HARRIETTE* (1936) (Harriette Wilson);
WILLIAM TOYNBEE, *GLIMPSES OF THE TWENTIES*
(1909); LEON HENRY VINCENT, *DANDIES AND MEN OF
LETTERS* (1913); GRACE AND PHILIP WHARTON, *THE
WITS AND BEAUX OF SOCIETY* (1890).

2

Jacobinism: *A MIRROR FOR PRINCES, IN A LETTER TO
H.R.H. THE PRINCE OF WALES* (1797), p. 53; cf. *ADVICE
HUMBLY OFFERED TO THE PRINCE OF WALES* (1789).

"Les modes des mots . . .": CHATEAUBRIAND, *MÉMOIRES
D'OUTRE-TOMBE* (Flammarion, 1950), III, p. 201.

Clubs: CATHERINE GORE, *SKETCHES OF ENGLISH
CHARACTER* (1848), II, p. 20; E. BERESFORD CHANCELLOR,
*MEMORIALS OF ST JAMES'S STREET TOGETHER
WITH THE ANNALS OF ALMACK'S* (1922); GRONOW
[*I-1*], I, pp. 55-8 & II, pp. 82-6; ALGERNON BOURKE, *HIS-
TORY OF WHITE'S* (1891); PERCY COLSON, *WHITE'S*
(1951); H. B. WHEATLEY, *LONDON PAST AND PRESENT*
(1891), I, p. 287; BYRON, *LETTERS AND JOURNALS* (ed.
Thomas Moore, 1830), I, p. 666; ALEXANDER BAILLIE-
COCHRANE LORD LAMINGTON, *IN THE DAYS OF THE
DANDIES* (1890), p. 12.

Almack's: in general: Chancellor; LEWIS MELVILLE,
REGENCY LADIES (1927), pp. 202-3; *ALMACK'S: A NOVEL*
(1826); refreshments: GORE, *CECIL* [*I-3*], p. 160; BULWER,
GODOLPHIN (Philadelphia, 1833), I, p. 127; patronesses:

Gronow, I, pp. 31–2 & II, pp. 221–2; Gore, *Sketches*, II, pp. 13–14; exclusivism: Melbourne in DAVID LORD CECIL, *LORD M.* (1947), p. 23; MRS CATHERINE GORE, *CECIL, A PEER* (1841), I, p. 17; Moore in Chancellor, p. 219; clothes: JOHN ASHTON, *SOCIAL ENGLAND UNDER THE REGENCY* (1899), p. 394; waltz: BYRON, *DON JUAN*, canto xi; deadline: GEORGE TICKNOR, *LIFE, LETTERS AND JOURNALS* (ed. G. S. Hillard, Boston, 1876), I, pp. 296–7; market-place: Bulwer, *Godolphin*, I, p. 82.

3

Fashion: STENDHAL, *SOUVENIRS D'ÉGOTISME* [*VI–4*], p. 102; Wellington in Gronow, II, p. 7; BYRON, *BEPPO*, Stanzas 75–6 & *Letters*, I, p. 666; cf. G. WILSON KNIGHT, *LORD BYRON: CHRISTIAN VIRTUES* (1952), pp. 227–8.

Fashions in money-lenders: Gronow, I, pp. 132–4; in fraternal coolness: Gore, *Cecil*, p. 15; in weddings: *THE EXCLUSIVES* (New York, 1830), I, pp. 115–16 [this extraordinary novel, the most bitter and violent attack on exclusivism produced by the Regency, is attributed by Michael Sadleir to LADY CHARLOTTE BURY].

Coronation of George IV: cf. E. M. FORSTER, *MARIANNE THORNTON: A DOMESTIC BIOGRAPHY* (New York, 1956), p. 89, for the account of Sir Robert Inglis, assigned the role of meeting the Queen and informing her "that it was her husband's good pleasure that she should not see the show".

4

Family libraries: BULWER, *ENGLAND AND THE ENGLISH* (1833), II, p. 115.

Poets: MacCarthy in *New Statesman* (12/1/1928); LADY BLESSINGTON, *JOURNAL OF THE CONVERSATIONS OF LORD BYRON* (1893), pp. 140–1.

Literature of *ton*: Bulwer, *England*, II, p. 12; G. F. BARWICK, "THE MAGAZINES OF THE NINETEENTH CENTURY", *TRANSACTIONS OF THE BIBLIOGRAPHICAL SOCIETY* (1912); FELIX SPER, *THE PERIODICAL PRESS OF LONDON 1800–1830* (1937); THACKERAY, "THE ANNUALS", *WORKS* [*IX–3*], XXV; DISRAELI, *THE VOYAGE OF CAPTAIN POPANILLA* (1828), pp. 149–57.

Colburn: MATTHEW WHITING ROSA, *THE SILVER-FORK SCHOOL* (1936); Ward: *D.N.B.*; P. G. PATMORE, *MY FRIENDS AND ACQUAINTANCES* (1854), I, pp. 250–1, 287–91; Jane Austen: WILLIAM AND RICHARD A. AUSTEN-LEIGH, *JANE AUSTEN* (1913), pp. 311–23.

Ward in society, and his letters: EDMUND PHIPPS, *MEMOIRS OF THE POLITICAL AND LITERARY LIFE OF ROBERT PLUMER WARD* (1850).

5

Exclusivism at opera: Gronow, I, pp. 35–6; "DRAMATIC TASTE", *FRASER'S MAGAZINE* (February 1830).

Dandy day: diary in Ashton, *Regency*, pp. 398–9; dress: Byron, *Don Juan*, Canto xiii; MILLIA DAVENPORT, *THE BOOK OF COSTUME* (1948); JAMES LAVER, *CLOTHES* (1953) & *TASTE AND FASHION* (1945); HERBERT NORRIS AND OSWALD CURTIS, *COSTUME AND FASHION* (1933); D. C. CALTHROP, "ROBERT AND RICHARD DIGHTON, PORTRAIT ETCHERS", *THE CONNOISSEUR* (1906); HENRY M. HAKE, "DIGHTON CARICATURES", *PRINT COLLECTOR'S QUAR-TERLY* (1926); racing: ROBERT BLACK, *THE JOCKEY CLUB* (1891); DORIS LESLIE, *THE GREAT CORINTHIAN: A PORTRAIT OF THE PRINCE REGENT* (1952), pp. 97–8; Hyde Park: *The Exclusives*, I, pp. 62–3.

6

Regency London: DISRAELI, *HENRIETTA TEMPLE* [*IV–6*], III, p. 193; Gronow, I, p. 53; DONALD PILCHER, *THE REGENCY STYLE* (1947), p. 104; P. G. PATMORE, *LETTERS ON ENGLAND* ("by Victoire, Count de Soligny", Colburn, 1823), I, pp. 63–9; AMÉDÉE DE TISSOT, *PARIS ET LONDRES COMPARÉS* (1830), pp. 172–3; Ashton, *Regency*, pp. 357–9; ARTHUR DASENT, *THE HISTORY OF ST JAMES'S SQUARE* (1895).

Regency architecture: Bulwer, *England*, II, pp. 230–1; Pilcher, pp. 41–59; *THE PRINCE REGENT'S STYLE* (New York, Cooper Union Museum, 1953); Ashton, *Regency*, pp. 118, 361–3; the architect C. A. Busby in Pilcher, p. 46; Gore, *Cecil*, p. 163.

The Regency style: Not only architecture, but all the minor domestic arts were ruled by a fashionable neo-classicism. Contemporary writers on costume approved the "common dress of gentlemen, the looser drapery of the trowsers, the tunic and the cloak" as exhibiting "regular and steady approaches to the refined and elegant taste of antiquity". They agreed "with the Athenians, that the dress and decoration of the human figure is not less a fine art, than the construction of houses or the arrangement of gardens". See *MALE AND FEMALE COSTUME* (ed. Eleanor Parker, who attributes this 1822 manuscript, first published in 1932, to Beau Brummell, and describes the work as largely a compilation of contemporary writings on costume).

CHAPTER III. Bulwer

1

Bulwer's name: THACKERAY, *YELLOWPLUSH* [*IX–3*], p. 127; his mother: EDWARD ROBERT LORD LYTTON, *THE LIFE LETTERS AND LITERARY REMAINS OF EDWARD*

BULWER, LORD LYTTON, BY HIS SON (1883; hereafter
LYTTON SON), I, p. 29; his school: VICTOR ALEXANDER
LORD LYTTON, *THE LIFE OF EDWARD BULWER FIRST
LORD LYTTON, BY HIS GRANDSON* (1913; hereafter
LYTTON GRANDSON), I, pp. 40–1; his tutor: Lytton Son, I,
p. 134; his satiety: Lytton Grandson, I, p. 59.

Preparation for *Pelham*: Cambridge: Lytton Grandson, I, pp.
74–5; watering-place (Broadstairs): *Ibid.*, I, p. 118; dress: Macaulay
in MICHAEL SADLEIR, *BULWER: A PANORAMA* (Boston,
1933), p. 325; Paris: Lytton Grandson, I, p. 134; writing-desk (italics
mine): *Ibid.*, I, p. 146.

2

Bulwer on *Falkland*: 1840 Preface to *Pelham*; letter to Rosina in
Lytton Grandson, I, pp. 185–6; in *FALKLAND* (New York, 1830),
p. 61.

Bulwer's memorandum on Rosina: "I married my wife against all
my interests and prospects—not from passion, but from a sense of
honour. She had given herself to me nearly a year before, and from
that moment I considered myself bound to her" (1846) (Lytton
Grandson, I, p. 184); marriage: *Ibid.*, I, pp. 206–48.

3

Restoration tradition: DISRAELI, *YOUNG DUKE [IV–5]*, p. 17;
Gore in ROSA *[II–4]*, p. 11. (The Regent described Charles II
as his only gentlemanly ancestor; Colburn brought out the first
editions of Pepys and Evelyn; Scott edited the memoirs of the Comte
de Grammont, the dashing forbear—as the Regency liked to remember
—of the Anglophile French family which intermarried with the
D'Orsays.)

PELHAM: all quotations, unless otherwise noted, are from the
first edition, which I have collated with an 1877 edition containing
Bulwer's revisions and all his prefaces; as a novel in the apprenticeship tradition: SUSANNE HOWE, *WILHELM MEISTER AND
HIS ENGLISH KINSMEN* (1930).

4

Self-love: Disraeli (discussing Greville) in CECIL, *LORD M.
[II–2]*, p. 53; HAZLITT, "THE DANDY SCHOOL", Vol. XXV
of *WORKS [I–1]*.

Brummell on *Pelham*: JESSE *[I–1]*, II, p. 72.

5

Colburn and *GREVILLE [I–4]*: Rosa, p. 200.

MILL on *England and the English* ("a work . . . greatly in advance
of the public mind"): *AUTOBIOGRAPHY* (New York, 1944),
pp. 138–9.

Brummell on *Pompeii*: Jesse, II, p. 198.

CHAPTER IV. Disraeli

1

DISRAELI on Imagination: *THE REVOLUTIONARY EPICK* (Moxon, 1834), pp. 72–3; *CONTARINI FLEMING* (Murray, 1832), II, p. 175.

Reception of *Vivian Grey*: Ward in PHIPPS [*II–4*], II, pp. 147–8; *Literary Magnet* (1826) reviews in DONALD BARR, *DISRAELI'S "VIVIAN GREY"* (unpublished Thesis, Columbia University, 1951), pp. 267–72. (*I am indebted to Mr Barr for information on many perplexing aspects of Disraeli's early career.*)

Disraeli's share in *THE STAR-CHAMBER* (William Marsh: April 9–June 7, 1826) and the *"Key to Vivian Grey"*: MICHAEL SADLEIR, "INTRODUCTION", DISRAELI'S *DUNCIAD* [*II–1*]; Barr, pp. 193–258.

Ward on Disraeli's "acquisitions": Phipps, II, p. 152.

2

Disraeli on his father: his "VIEW OF THE LIFE AND WRITINGS OF THE AUTHOR" in ISAAC D'ISRAELI, *CURIOSITIES OF LITERATURE* (1859); cf. SARAH KOPSTEIN, *ISAAC D'ISRAELI* (Jerusalem, 1939); LUCIEN WOLF, "THE DISRAELI FAMILY", *TRANSACTIONS OF THE JEWISH HISTORICAL SOCIETY OF ENGLAND* (Ballantyne, 1908).

D'Israeli-Ward relations: via Sarah Austen: WILLIAM FLAVELLE MONYPENNY, *LIFE OF BENJAMIN DISRAELI* (New York, 1911), I, pp. 79–81 (*hereafter, all biographical material— letters, journals, contemporary opinions—otherwise unsupported can be assumed to derive from Monypenny*); Barr, pp. 174–6; Ward a half-Jew: Phipps, I, pp. 1–2; letters: Phipps, II, pp. 136, 152, 165; "very close": Sadleir, p. 11.

All *VIVIAN GREY* quotations are from the "Centenary Biographical Edition" (ed. Lucien Wolf; De La More Press, 1904): the only modern reprint of the first edition, and conveniently collated with the 1853 edition revised by Disraeli. These revisions were less ruthless, and therefore less interesting, than those Bulwer made in *Pelham*.

4

Composition of *Vivian Grey*: LUCIEN WOLF, "INTRODUCTION" to *Vivian Grey*.

Disraeli in society: in addition to Monypenny, see RICHARD ALDINGTON, *FOUR ENGLISH PORTRAITS 1801–1851* (1948), p. 74; J. A. FROUDE, *LIFE OF THE EARL OF BEACONSFIELD* (Everyman), p. 53; ANDRÉ MAUROIS, *DISRAELI* (New York, 1936), pp. 208–9.

5

Social knowledge behind *The Young Duke*: a more complex problem than in the case of *Vivian Grey*, partly because of gaps in our knowledge of Disraeli's activities from 1827 to 1829, partly because of the strikingly confident tone of the later novel. LUCIEN WOLF states in his "INTRODUCTION" to *THE YOUNG DUKE* ("Centenary Biographical Edition", 1905; cf. *Vivian Grey* above) that before writing the book Disraeli gathered material at White's, Almack's and Crockford's, that *Vivian Grey* itself gave him his entrée to the great world, that he was already friendly with Bulwer, Viscount Mahon, Lord Petersham and "the Regency dandies" in general: an extreme statement of a common confusion. Disraeli was not a member of Crockford's till 1840, did not go to Almack's till 1834, was never a member of White's. Years later Disraeli noted down that he first met Bulwer, and first dined at his house in Hertford Street "just at the commencement of the spring of 1830"; by which time, according to Monypenny (I, pp. 123–8), *The Young Duke* was "nearly finished". Disraeli certainly did not become conversant with the exalted *Young Duke* circles until 1833, when he wrote in his diary (in August): "I have become this year very popular with the dandies. D'Orsay [whom he had met in February, 1832] took a fondness to me, and they take their tone from him." Disraeli therefore, though he may have spent more time in London before 1830 than Monypenny knew, had very little knowledge of high society before *The Young Duke*; but he had more second-hand information and his imagination was, characteristically, inspired by his sense of being close to the first-hand knowledge he craved.

"Oh! England! . . .": Imagination again. Disraeli's shadow was certainly not falling "upon a foreign strand", as he wrote the novel in England.   But it was written, with prophetic confidence, to finance his longed-for trip to the East.

6

Identification of Lady Sykes: Barr, p. 47.

HENRIETTA TEMPLE (Colburn, 1837): on the English nobility: II, p. 252; for the portrait of D'Orsay, see below, Ch. VII.

CHAPTER V. The Dandy Goes to France

1

BRIEF REMARKS ON ENGLISH MANNERS: published anonymously by John Booth, 1816.

Arrival of Dandy: SYDNEY OWEN LADY MORGAN, *FRANCE* (Colburn, 1817; better known, from later editions, as *France in 1816*), I, pp. 146–7.

"Je nourissais toujours . . .": CHATEAUBRIAND [*II–2*], II, p. 15.

English prisoners in France: CONSTANTIA MAXWELL, *THE ENGLISH TRAVELLER IN FRANCE* (1932), pp. 246–256; ROGER BOUTET DE MONVEL, *EMINENT ENGLISH MEN AND WOMEN IN PARIS 1800–1850* (trans. G. Herring, New York, 1913), Ch. i; "Young Englishmen . . .": George Call's diary, in JOHN G. ALGER, *NAPOLÉON'S BRITISH VISITORS AND CAPTIVES 1801–1805* (New York, 1904), pp. 196–7.

English soldiers: GRONOW [*I–1*], I, pp. 1, 68–86 & II, p. 11; PHILIP GUEDALLA, *THE DUKE* (1931), pp. 277–91; MARGERY E. ELKINGTON, *LES RELATIONS DE SOCIÉTÉ ENTRE L'ANGLETERRE ET LA FRANCE SOUS LA RESTAURATION* (1929), pp. 16, 30; JULES BERTAUT, "L'ANGLICISME EN FRANCE SOUS LA RESTAURATION", *REVUE DE PARIS* (1918), p. 154.

Dandy amusements: Gronow, *passim*; Boutet de Monvel, pp. 137–64; JACQUES BOULENGER, *SOUS LOUIS-PHILIPPE: LES DANDYS* (Ollendorf, 1907; hereafter BOULENGER 1907), pp. 97–125; MARGUERITE LADY BLESSINGTON, *THE IDLER IN FRANCE* (Colburn, 1841), II, pp. 79–80.

Faubourg society: Boutet de Monvel, pp. 206–28; JULES BERTAUT, *LE FAUBOURG SAINT-GERMAIN SOUS LA RESTAURATION* (1935), pp. 19–49.

2

Anglomania and dandy fashions: Béranger in GUSTAV KOEHLER, "DER DANDYSMUS IM FRANZÖSICHEN ROMAN DES XIX. JAHRHUNDERTS", *ZEITSCHRIFT FÜR ROMANISCHE PHILOLOGIE* (1911), p. 8; LADY MORGAN, *FRANCE IN 1829–1830* (2nd ed., 1831), I, pp. 12–13, 102–16; *HUIT SIÈCLES DE VIE BRITTANIQUE À PARIS* (Musée Galliera, 1948), pp. 44–51; Boutet de Monvel, pp. 221–3, 367–88; Boulenger 1907, pp. 112–15; JACQUES BOULENGER, *SOUS LOUIS-PHILIPPE: LES DANDYS* (Calmann-Lévy, 1932; hereafter BOULENGER 1932), pp. 35–44, 161–5; *La Mode* on cock-fighting in Bertaut, "L'Anglicisme", p. 171; Gronow *passim*; LÉON SÉCHÉ, *LA JEUNESSE DORÉE SOUS LOUIS-PHILIPPE* (1910), pp. 123–38; FÉLIX DERIÉGE, *PHYSIOLOGIE DU LION* (1841; illustrated by Gavarni and Daumier), pp. 10–11, 84–7.

Paris clubs: Elkington, pp. 96–7; Boulenger 1907, p. 126; HIPPOLYTE DE VILLEMESSANT, *MÉMOIRES D'UN JOURNALISTE*, (1867), I, pp. 277–92.

3

Driving and racing: Boulenger 1932, pp. 129–40; GÉRARD DE CONTADES, *LE DRIVING EN FRANCE* (1898) & *LES COURSES DE CHEVAUX EN FRANCE* (1892).

Lord Seymour: Alger, pp. 218–22; Gronow, I, pp. 171–3; Boulenger 1932, pp. 109–60; Villemessant, I, pp. 207–88; *Huit Siècles,* p. 51.

Jockey-Club: Deriége, pp. 69–71; Longchamp: JULES JANIN, *L'ÉTÉ À PARIS* (1844), p. 134; Blessington, II, p. 35.

4

Symbolism of costume: LOUIS MAIGRON, *LE ROMANTISME ET LA MODE* (1911), pp. 51–93, 139–77; HELEN T. GARRETT, *CLOTHES AND CHARACTER: THE FUNCTION OF DRESS IN BALZAC* (Philadelphia, 1941), pp. 18–29; Villemessant, I, pp. 68–9; *Huit Siècles,* pp. 45–7; Bertaut, "L'Anglicisme", pp. 159 ff.; Gautier in Maigron, p. 57.

Fashionable novels in France: M. G. DEVONSHIRE, "FASHIONABLE NOVELS AND DANDYISM", *FRENCH QUARTERLY* (Manchester, 1920) & *THE ENGLISH NOVEL IN FRANCE* (1929) (valuable throughout for background, reviews and the statistical appendix, "Index to Authors and Works".)

Brummell in France: Boulenger 1932, pp. 26–7; JESSE [*I–1*], II, pp. 28–9, 83.

CHAPTER VI. The Dandy Goes to Press

1

London dandy: CHATEAUBRIAND [*II–2*], III, pp. 101–2.

Girardin and the new press: PIERRE SINMARRE, "LA PRESSE SOUS LE RÈGNE DE LOUIS-PHILIPPE", *LES ŒUVRES LIBRES* (August 1934); ODYSSE-BAROT, *ÉMILE DE GIRARDIN* (1866), pp. 102–17; L.-J. ARRIGON, *LES ANNÉES ROMANTIQUES DE BALZAC* (1927), pp. 12–52.

La Jeunesse dorée: BOULENGER 1907 [*V–1*], pp. 130–63; SÉCHÉ [*V–2*], pp. 136–7, 231–2; VILLEMESSANT [*V–2*], I, pp. 161–206; STARKIE [*XII–1*], pp. 57–8.

2

Balzac's dress: GARRETT [*V–4*], pp. 10–13; H. CLOUZOT AND R.-H. VALENSI, *LE PARIS DE LA COMÉDIE HUMAINE: BALZAC ET SES FOURNISSEURS* (1926), pp. 39–52, 178–9; ANDRÉ LE BRETON, *BALZAC* (Boivin: "Collection des classiques populaires"), pp. 20–2; GRONOW [*I–1*], I, pp. 257–8.

His view of *la toilette: LE TRAITÉ DE LA VIE ÉLÉGANTE*, in *ŒUVRES DIVERSES* (early journalism), Vols. XXXVIII and XXXIX of *ŒUVRES COMPLÈTES* (ed. Marcel Bouteron and Henri Longon, 1938).

Gautier on the centaur: CONTADES, *COURSES* [*V–3*], p. xix.

3

Sue and the journalists: PAUL GINISTY, *EUGÈNE SUE* (1929), pp. 23–4, 50–8, 69–74; Boulenger 1907, pp. 130–1; EUGÈNE DE MIRECOURT, *EUGÈNE SUE* ("Les Contemporains", 1855), pp. 69–70; ANDRÉ BELLESSORT, "LE ROMANCIER POPULAIRE EUGÈNE SUE", *REVUE DE PARIS* (1937), pp. 41–2.

His relations with Balzac: Arrigon, pp. 80–4; Balzac, *Traité*, p. 169 & editors' note.

Sue and the salons: NORA ATKINSON, *EUGÈNE SUE ET LE ROMAN-FEUILLETON* (Nemours, 1920), pp. 82–6; Ginisty, p. 68; BOULENGER 1932 [*V–2*], pp. 190–204; CONNELY, *D'ORSAY* [*VII–2*], p. 506; his establishments: Mirecourt, pp. 90–7; Atkinson, pp. 87–8; Ginisty, pp. 80 ff.; Gronow, I, pp. 258–61; on the gentleman: *ARTHUR* (1845), I, p. 188.

Les Mystères de Paris: Considérant in Atkinson, pp. 99–107; Bellessort, pp. 50–62; and the legend of "milord Arsouille": Boulenger 1932, p. 114; Sue's masquerade: Ginisty, pp. 9–13.

4

STENDHAL's writings: unless otherwise noted, all references are to his *ŒUVRES* (ed. Henri Martineau, 1927).

His criticisms of the English, especially the dandies: *ROME NAPLES ET FLORENCE*, I, pp. 272 & II, pp. 22–3; *DE L'AMOUR*, I, p. 24 & II, pp. 34–8; *SOUVENIRS D'ÉGOTISME*, p. 102; "Rien ne peut égaler . . .": *Rome*, III, p. 204; his relations with England and English magazines: DORIS GUNNELL, *STENDHAL ET L'ANGLETERRE* (1908), pp. 5–40, 250–274.

Stendhal's hypersensitivity: *Souvenirs*, pp. 93, 110; *VIE DE HENRI BRULARD*, I, p. 215 & II, p. 291; his aristocratic liberalism: PROSPER MÉRIMÉE, *DEUX PORTRAITS DE STENDHAL* (Editions du Stendhal-Club, 1928), p. 4; *Henri Brulard*, I, pp. 204, 214–15; his love of mystification: *Souvenirs*, p. 48; his self-control: *Souvenirs*, p. 12; *De l'amour*, I, p. 57; his "grâces lilliputiennes": *Souvenirs*, p. 47. For all this as Stendhal's "dandyism", see KOEHLER [*V–2*], pp. 41–5; Boulenger 1932, pp. 45–6; EDWARD ROD, *STENDHAL* (1911), pp. 61–2; Gunnell, pp. 35–6.

Society background of *Le Rouge et le noir*: ten years after publication Stendhal ruffled through the opening chapters of the second part of *Le Rouge et le noir* (Julien's encounter with the society surrounding the Marquis de La Mole) and scribbled this marginal memorandum: "Il manque la description physique des personnages à la scène du salon. . . . Faute de trois ou quatre mots descriptifs par page pour empêcher le style de ressembler à Tacite, plusiers pages qui précèdent ont l'air d'un traité moral. . . .—Ajouter la partie pittoresque, s'il y a une seconde édition." These additions were never made. See

LE ROUGE ET LE NOIR (ed. Pierre Jourda, 1931), II, pp. 60, 355.

Dandy illustration in first edition: JULES MARSAN, *STENDHAL* (1932), p. 222.

Prince Korasoff's dandy maxims: "*Faites toujours le contraire de ce qu'on attend de vous,*" he tells Julien in England. "Voilà, d'honneur, la seule religion de l'époque." And in Strasbourg: "L'air triste ne peut être de bon ton; c'est l'air ennuyé qu'il faut. Si vous êtres triste, c'est donc quelque chose qui vous manque, qui ne vous a pas réussi. *C'est montrer soi inférieur . . .*"

Symbolism of mourning: ALFRED DE MUSSET, *LA CONFESSION D'UN ENFANT DU SIÈCLE* (1880), p. 11.

CHAPTER VII. D'Orsay

1

The New Yorker cover: Mr Rea Irvin of *The New Yorker* has kindly supplied me with the following information: that he drew the dandy without any specific person in mind, but after making a study of pictures of the period 1830–40. "Mr Ross wanted a character who would suggest light sophistication and gayety. Hence the dandy and the butterfly."

D'Orsay "cruelly spoiled": HENRY F. CHORLEY, *AUTOBIOGRAPHY, MEMOIR AND LETTERS* (ed. H. G. Hewlett, 1873), I, pp. 182–3; in Paris: BLESSINGTON, *IDLER* [*V–1*], II, pp. 132–5, 224; riding to Richmond: LAMINGTON [*II–2*], pp. 6–7.

2

D'Orsay's triumph in England: Count Marcellus in GÉRARD DE CONTADES, *LE COMTE D'ORSAY: PHYSIOLOGIE D'UN ROI DE LA MODE* (1890), p. 10; CHATEAUBRIAND [*II–2*], III, pp. 102–3.

His dress: BENJAMIN HAYDON, *AUTOBIOGRAPHY AND MEMOIRS* (ed. Tom Taylor, 1929), II, p. 655; JANE CARLYLE, *NEW LETTERS AND MEMORIALS* (1903), I, p. 76; LADY HOLLAND [*I–2*], p. 93 (letter from London, 1/5/1829, relaying rumours of D'O. in Paris); as "divinity of dandies": Charles Sumner in WILLARD CONNELY, *COUNT D'ORSAY: THE DANDY OF DANDIES* (1952), p. 282; his bedroom: Connely, p. 147.

Praise of D'Orsay: THACKERAY, *LETTERS* [*IX–1*], II, pp. 389–90; THOMAS CARLYLE, *NEW LETTERS* (ed. Alexander Carlyle, 1904), I, p. 158; P. G. PATMORE, *MY FRIENDS* [*II–4*], I, p. 194; Tennyson in W. TEIGNMOUTH SHORE, *D'ORSAY OR THE COMPLETE DANDY* (1911), p. 266; Fonblanque in Connely, p. 171; GRONOW [*I–1*], I, p. 162; Disraeli in MONYPENNY (*IV–2*], II, p. 50; Sue in R. R. MADDEN, *THE LITERARY LIFE AND CORRESPONDENCE OF THE*

COUNTESS OF BLESSINGTON (New York, 1855), I, p. 451;
W. C. MACREADY, REMINISCENCES (New York, 1875), p. 681;
"Lounging Through Kensington", *Household Words* (8/6/1853):
(I can find no reason to attribute this article, as Shore and Connely
do, to Dickens); *The Globe* in Madden, I, p. 292; Wellington in
Madden, I, p. 284; BYRON, *PORTRAIT* [*I–2*], II, pp. 721–5;
D'O. and Disraeli's finances: Monypenny, I, pp. 351, 357.

D'Orsay's circle: Connely's invaluable biography, *passim*.

4

D'Orsay's marriage: Connely, pp. 106, 183 ff.; MICHAEL
SADLEIR, *BLESSINGTON-D'ORSAY: A MASQUERADE*
(1933), pp. 157–61. Lady Harriet Gardiner, before leaving D'Orsay,
had begun her career as an open flirt; afterwards she divided
her time between going into society and writing novels, and her
person among many lovers—including, according to common gossip,
the Dauphin of France. Upon D'Orsay's death she settled down to
marriage and then a pious, charitable middle age, *à la* Becky Sharpe.

D'Orsay and Lady Blessington: Sadleir, p. 356; Bulwer in
LYTTON GRANDSON [*III–1*], I, p. 182.

His sexuality: HORACE DE VIEL-CASTEL, *MÉMOIRES SUR
LE RÈGNE DE NAPOLÉON III* (1883), II, p. 91 (cf. II, pp.
43–4, 83 for his open hostility to D'O.); Sadleir, pp. 45–8; Comtesse
de Flahaut in Connely, p. 139; CAMILLA TOULMIN CROSLAND,
LANDMARKS OF A LITERARY LIFE (1893), p. 115 ("his
teeth had gaps between them, which caused his smile to degenerate
into something approaching a sneer"); Jane Carlyle, I, pp. 76–7;
Byron in BOULENGER 1932 [*V–2*], p. 71; Cobden in POPE-
HENNESSY [*I–3*], p. 250; Madden, I, p. 281; for another view of
D'O.'s "effeminacy", see SAMUEL CARTER HALL, *RETRO-
SPECT OF A LONG LIFE* (1883), p. 369.

CHAPTER VIII. England in 1830

1

Fraserians: portraits in *Pendennis*: MIRIAM M. H. THRALL,
REBELLIOUS FRASER'S (1934), pp. 208–11; cf. AUGUSTINE
BIRRELL, "LIFE, 'LITERATURE' AND 'LITERARY' JOURN-
ALISM DURING THE FIRST HALF OF THE LAST CEN-
TURY", *LONDON MERCURY* (1920).

Maginn's career and temperament: Thrall, pp. 165–207. Miss
Thrall argues persuasively against the common assumption that
Maginn was the original of Thackeray's n'er-do-well Captain Shandon
in *Pendennis*; she proposes another Fraserian, Jack Sheehan.

Bulwer and *Fraser's*; SADLEIR, *BULWER* [*III–1*], p. 234 (only the first edition of *Paul Clifford* contains the "great unwashed" Preface); Bulwer on "that magazine" in LYTTON GRANDSON [*III–1*], I, p. 81.

2

Preparation for *Sartor*: CARLYLE, *LETTERS 1826–36* (ed. C. E. Norton, 1888), I, pp. 225–43; EMERY NEFF, *CARLYLE* (1932), p. 123; DAVID ALEC WILSON, *CARLYLE TO "THE FRENCH REVOLUTION" 1826–37* (1924), pp. 175, 200; C. F. HARROLD, "INTRODUCTION" to *SARTOR RESARTUS* (New York, 1937), p. xxv; W. H. MALLOCK, *MEMOIRS OF LIFE AND LITERATURE* (1920), p. 48.

Carlyle and the fashionables: "I see something of fashionable people . . .": DAVID ALEC WILSON, *CARLYLE TILL MARRIAGE 1795–1826* (1923), pp. 289–90; youthful glimpses of dandies: *Ibid.*, pp. 90, 112, 151, 206, 363; Neff, pp. 26–7, 52, 59, 71, 90, 94; MONCURE D. CONWAY, *THOMAS CARLYLE* (1881), pp. 161–2, 238; CARLYLE, *EARLY LETTERS 1814–26* (ed. C. E. Norton, 1886), p. 59; "High Life below Stairs": CARLYLE, "JOHN PAUL FRIEDRICH RICHTER AGAIN", p. 131, in *CRITICAL AND MISCELLANEOUS ESSAYS*, Vols. XXVI–XXX of *WORKS* ("Centenary Edition", New York, 1900–1).

Jane Welsh and the fashionables: J. W. CARLYLE, *EARLY LETTERS* (ed. D. G. Ritchie, 1889), pp. 34, 89; "When I compare . . .": Wilson, *Carlyle Till Marriage*, p. 412; see her *NEW LETTERS* [*VII–2*], I, p. 182, for her later (1845) thoughts of Captain Baillie as "once the reigning Dandy of London".

Carlyle and fiction: "Professor Sauerteig" in "BIOGRAPHY", *Essays*, III; CARLISLE MOORE, "THOMAS CARLYLE AND FICTION, 1822–34", *NINETEENTH CENTURY STUDIES* (Cornell, 1940). It should be remembered, however, that at the outset of his career Carlyle had thought of writing a novel.

3

Death of George IV: *FRASER'S*, I, pp. 762 & X, p. 106; BULWER, *GODOLPHIN* [*II–2*], II, p. 126; sale of wardrobe: JOHN ASHTON, *WHEN WILLIAM IV. WAS KING* (1896), pp. 3–5; coronation of William IV: Wilson, *Carlyle to "French Revolution"*, p. 251; see also MARY HOPKIRK, *QUEEN ADELAIDE* (1946); G. M. TREVELYAN, *THE SEVEN YEARS OF WILLIAM IV* (1952).

Reform Bill: Lytton Grandson, I, pp. 409–10, 419; *CREEVEY'S LIFE AND TIMES* [*II–1*], p. 339; RAIKES, *JOURNAL* [*I–1*], II, p. 91; DISRAELI, *"WHAT IS HE?"* (Ridgway, 1833), p. 10; GORE, *CECIL A PEER* [*II–2*], I, p. 41.

Portents of change: railways: DISRAELI, *ENDYMION* (1880), I, pp. 45–8; cholera: GREVILLE [*I–3*], II, p. 210; Gore, *Cecil Peer*, II, pp. 88–9; Lords' fire: Wilson, *Carlyle to "Fr. Rev."*, p. 375.

Success of Bulwer's *Pompeii*: Sadleir, p. 332; Blessington in CONNELY, *D'ORSAY* [*VII–2*], p. 224.

Regency London "Pompeiified": GORE, *CECIL* [*I–3*], p. 152; Thackeray at Gore House: Connely, p. 499; Soyer: G. M. YOUNG ed., *EARLY VICTORIAN ENGLAND* (1934), II, pp. 123–4; DICKENS on cholera: "SANITARY REFORM", *SPEECHES LITERARY AND SOCIAL* (1870); Albert Hall: CLAUDE DE LA ROCHE FRANCIS, *LONDON HISTORICAL AND SOCIAL* (1902), II, pp. 384–5; see also BERNARD DARWIN, *BRITISH CLUBS* (1947), pp. 24–31; *Fraser's*, X, p. 230; T. H. S. ESCOTT, *SOCIAL TRANSFORMATION OF THE VICTORIAN AGE* (1897).

4

D'Orsay and *Fraser's*: Thrall, pp. 33, 282; Connely, pp. 214–15, 259.

Carlyle on lecture audience: J. A. FROUDE, *THOMAS CAR-LYLE: A HISTORY OF HIS LIFE IN LONDON* (1884), I, pp. 84–93; relations with D'Orsay: CARLYLE, *NEW LETTERS* [*VII–2*], I, pp. 158–9; Jane Carlyle, *New Letters*, I, pp. 75–7; Connely, p. 297; D. A. WILSON, *CARLYLE ON CROMWELL AND OTHERS 1837–48* (1925), pp. 63–4.

CHAPTER IX. Thackeray

1

"O! me, we are . . .": THACKERAY, *LETTERS AND PRI-VATE PAPERS* (ed. Gordon N. Ray, 1945), IV, p. 425. (*Unless otherwise noted, all personal statements by Thackeray can hereafter be assumed to derive from letters and diaries printed in this edition.*)

2

Thackeray's status: Carlyle on his breeding in LIONEL STEVEN-SON, *THE SHOWMAN OF VANITY FAIR* (New York, 1947), p. 277; "a Cambridge man": GORDON N. RAY, *THACKERAY* (1955–8), I, pp. 195–6; Brookfield on Prout in Stevenson, p. 135; Lever in *Ibid.*, p. 113; reply to Bulwer: "A Brother of the Press on the History of a Literary Man, Laman Blanchard, and the Chances of the Literary Profession", by Michael Angelo Titmarsh, *FRASER'S* (March 1846).

3

Thackeray and *Fraser's*: CHARLES PLUMPTRE JOHNSON, *THE EARLY WRITINGS OF WILLIAM MAKEPEACE THACKERAY* (1888), pp. 37–47; HAROLD STRONG GULLI-VER, *THACKERAY'S LITERARY APPRENTICESHIP* (1934), pp. 66–89; cf. THRALL [*VIII–1*].

Other jibes at fashionable novels as deriving from servants: *Fraser's*, I (1830), p. 509 & IV (1831), p. 520.

The original of Deuceace: Ray, "How Thackeray Lost His Patrimony", Appendix IV to *Letters*, I.

All quotations from THACKERAY'S *WORKS* are from the "Centenary Biographical Edition" (1900–1), with Introductions by Lady Ritchie.

Thackeray and Bulwer: for the resemblance between the two men as a source of Thackeray's antagonism, see J. Y. T. GREIG, *THACKERAY: A RECONSIDERATION* (1950), p. 40; SADLEIR, *BULWER* [*III–1*], pp. 232–3.

Thackeray on his own dress: "MR. THACKERAY IN THE UNITED STATES", *Works*, XXV.

4

Thackeray and dandy set: Annie Thackeray in HESTER THACKERAY FULLER AND VIOLET HAMMERSLEY, *THACKERAY'S DAUGHTER: SOME RECOLLECTIONS OF ANNE THACKERAY RITCHIE* (1951), pp. 55–6; Henry Vizetelly in CONNELY, *D'ORSAY* [*VII–2*], p. 507; see also, besides *Letters*, Stevenson, pp. 231, 279; Thrall, pp. 208–11.

5

Original of Major Pendennis: GORDON N. RAY, *THE BURIED LIFE* (1952), Ch. vi; LEWIS MELVILLE, *THE THACKERAY COUNTRY* (1905), pp. 106–8.

Jesse's *Brummell*: THACKERAY'S review (5/6/1844) in *CONTRIBUTIONS TO THE MORNING CHRONICLE* (ed. G. N. Ray, 1955); as source for *Four Georges*: Notebooks, Introduction to *Works*, XXVI, p. xliii; Brummell in "DESSEIN'S", *ROUNDABOUT PAPERS*: "a shabby old man, in a wig, and such a dirty, ragged, disreputable dressing-gown. . . ." Thackeray makes Brummell talk like an ignorant, thick-skinned country squire.

Thackeray's "test of greatness"; Carlyle in Ray's "Biographical Memoranda", *Letters*, I, p. cix.

6

Clothes-image in *Fraser's*, I, pp. 566–9: "The Bard of Hope" (on Campbell and the *New Monthly*), no. 2 in *Fraser's* series of "Literary Characters by Pierce Pungent", a pen-name identified by M. M. H. Thrall (see her appendix on anonymity) as Maginn and/or Lockhart.

Thackeray's note on George's wardrobe: Introduction to *Works*, XXVI, pp. xliii–xliv.

CHAPTER X. Dickens

1

"Gents.": *PUNCH*, IV & V (1843); ALBERT SMITH, *THE NATURAL HISTORY OF THE GENT* (1847), pp. 3, 17, 33;

MARK EDWARD PERUGINI, *VICTORIAN DAYS AND WAYS*
(1946), pp. 102–4; THOMAS BURKE, *THE STREETS OF
LONDON THROUGH THE CENTURIES* (1940), p. 113.

Albert Smith and Thackeray: JAMES MONROE THORING-
TON, *MONT BLANC SIDESHOW: THE LIFE AND TIMES
OF ALBERT SMITH* (1934), p. 70; STEVENSON [*IX–2*],
p. 157.

Tittlebat Titmouse: compared to Count Do-'em-all: SAMUEL
WARREN, *TEN THOUSAND A-YEAR* (New York, 1889), pp.
16–17; his name: *Ten Thousand* appeared in *Blackwood's* in 1839 and
in book form in 1841, the year of *Titmarsh* in *Fraser's*. Thackeray's
work was not published as a book until 1849; but he had used "Titmarsh" as a pen-name before 1839.

2

Dickens to Forster on theatre-going: *LETTERS* (ed. Walter
Dexter; Vols. X–XII of *THE NONESUCH DICKENS*, 1937–8),
I, p. 681.

Life of "Gent" in *BOZ*: see esp. "Making a Night of It", "Hackney-
Coach Stands", "Private Theatres" (for Dickens' early patronage of
these theatres, see JOHN FORSTER, *LIFE OF CHARLES
DICKENS* (1904), I, p. 293.

Dickens' appearance in 1830s and 1840s: "a great difference . . .":
John Payne Collier in FREDERIC G. KITTON, *CHARLES
DICKENS BY PEN AND PENCIL* (1890), p. 14; Cruikshank
sketch: EDGAR JOHNSON, *CHARLES DICKENS: HIS TRA-
GEDY AND TRIUMPH* (1952), p. 214; R. J. CRUIKSHANK,
CHARLES DICKENS AND EARLY VICTORIAN ENGLAND
(1949), p. 2; Kitton, p. 17 & Supplement, p. 1; Carlyle in FROUDE
[*VIII–4*], I, p. 152; G. A. SALA, *CHARLES DICKENS* (1870),
p. 15; Leigh Hunt in Forster, I, p. 76; Adolphus Trollope in Kitton,
p. 53.

American observations: EDWARD F. PAYNE, *DICKENS
DAYS IN BOSTON* (1927), pp. 9, 42–8, 60; WILLIAM G.
WILKINS, *CHARLES DICKENS IN AMERICA* (1911), pp.
89–115; Forster, I, pp. 271–3.

3

Dickens on his "finery": Kitton, p. 173.

His relations with "Regency" society: Misses Berry: Johnson,
pp. 231–2; Lady Blessington: *Letters*, I, pp. 527–8, 566; D'Orsay:
Letters, II, p. 74; Johnson, p. 573; "Lady Holland has fitted up . . .":
Letters, I, pp. 468–9; Bulwer: LYTTON GRANDSON [*III–1*],
II, pp. 13–14, 74.

Serial publication and a new literature: Johnson, pp. 117–18,
154–5; MOORE, *DIARY* [*I–3*], p. 198; JOHN BUTT AND KATH-
LEEN TILLOTSON, *DICKENS AT WORK* (1957), pp. 35–8.

4

Changing appearance: Ad. Trollope in Kitton, pp. 53–4; Victorian fashions: D. C. CALTHROP, *ENGLISH DRESS FROM VICTORIA TO GEORGE V* (1934), p. 456; Perugini, pp. 51–2, 104–7; BARBARA WORSLEY-GOUGH, *FASHIONS IN LONDON* (1952), pp. 18–20, 70–3; in Dickens' last years: Sala, p. 14; Johnson, pp. 1075, 1089.

Dickens' theatricality: Wilkins, p. 90; Payne, pp. 10, 43; Kitton, p. 188; Macready's waistcoat: *Letters*, I, p. 708; "such a confusion . . .": *Little Dorrit*, Bk. I, Ch. xx; hair-combing: JACK LINDSAY, *CHARLES DICKENS* (New York, 1950), p. 294; see also Johnson, p. 1151; EDMUND WILSON, "DICKENS: THE TWO SCROOGES", *THE WOUND AND THE BOW* (1941), p. 68.

Micawber: it should be recalled that Uriah Heep predicted a circus career for that gentleman. Heep observed, as Micawber tells it, that "I should probably be a mountebank upon the country, swallowing a sword-blade and eating the devouring element. For anything that I can perceive to the contrary, it is still probable that my children may be reduced to seek a livelihood by personal contortion, while Mrs Micawber abets their unnatural feats, by playing the barrel-organ" (*David Copperfield*, Ch. xlix).

5

All quotations from DICKENS' writings are from *THE NONE-SUCH DICKENS* (1937–8) unless otherwise noted.

Domesticity: Dickens to Forster in Johnson, p. 830; early advice to young: *SKETCHES OF YOUNG COUPLES* (1840), pp. 90–1; Kate's view: GLADYS STOREY, *DICKENS AND DAUGHTER* (1939), p. 94; cf. ADA NISBET, *DICKENS AND ELLEN TERNAN* (1952).

"Dark novels": LIONEL STEVENSON, "DICKENS'S DARK NOVELS, 1851–7", *SEWANEE REVIEW* (Summer 1943); ROBERT MORSE, "OUR MUTUAL FRIEND", *PARTISAN REVIEW* (March 1949); GEORGE ORWELL, "CHARLES DICKENS", *DICKENS DALI & OTHERS* (1946).

Original ending of *Our Mutual Friend*: Marcus Stone, the illustrator, was instructed by Dickens with "special stress" to include the scene of Eugene's *death* in his design for the monthly cover. Dickens said that "one of the strongest features of the story will be the death of Eugene Wrayburn after the assault of the schoolmaster. I think it will be one of the best things I have ever done" (FREDERIC G. KITTON, *DICKENS AND HIS ILLUSTRATORS* (1899), pp. 195–7).

6

Bleak House: see Butt & Tillotson, pp. 187–8 for the suggestion that Dickens did the "new dandyism" scenes "with evident mockery of Disraeli's manner".

James Harthouse in *Hard Times*: T. A. JACKSON, *CHARLES DICKENS: THE PROGRESS OF A RADICAL* (1938), p. 146.

7

Gowan in *Little Dorrit*: as inspired by Thackeray: HESKETH PEARSON, *DICKENS: HIS CHARACTER, COMEDY AND CAREER* (New York, 1949), p. 220; Johnson, p. 892.

Wilkie Collins: closeness to Dickens: Pearson, pp. 207–24; ROBERT ASHLEY, *WILKIE COLLINS* (1952), Sec. II, Chs. ii–iii; EARLE DAVIS, "CHARLES DICKENS AND WILKIE COLLINS", *MUNICIPAL UNIVERSITY OF WICHITA BULLETIN* (Kansas, June 1945); viewed by Kate: Storey, p. 214; his "careless hedonism": Lindsay, p. 323; cf. MAMIE DICKENS, *MY FATHER AS I RECALL HIM* (1896), pp. 15–18 ("There never existed . . . a more tidy or methodical creature than was my father").

Collins' aestheticism: KENNETH ROBINSON, *WILKIE COLLINS* (1951), p. 83; Miserrimus Dexter in *THE LAW AND THE LADY*, Vol. V of COLLINS' *WORKS* (New York, Collier), p. 311.

8

Sydney Carton in *A Tale*: cf. the non-dramatic version of *THE FROZEN DEEP*, Vol. IV of Collins' *Works*. Note also that Carton is contrasted with his energetic legal patron Mr Stryver in terms reminiscent of the Idle-Goodchild opposition in the *Lazy Tour*. Here, when Stryver recommends "energy and purpose", Dickens's sympathies are obviously with Carton, who replies: "Oh! botheration! . . . don't *you* be moral! . . . You were always driving and riving and shouldering and pressing, to that restless degree that I had no chance for my life but in rust and repose."

Eugene Wrayburn in *Our Mutual Friend*: compare his tirade on the Bees (Bk. III, Ch. ii) with Skimpole's in *Bleak House* (Ch. viii). For another index to Dickens's development, compare Turveydrop, the "Regency" dancing-master caricatured in *Bleak House*, with Twemlow, who dresses and poses as a survivor from the days of George IV but, like all the characters in *OMF* who have come down in the world, is handled very sympathetically.

9

Personal statements in *OMF*: note also how apposite to his own situation as novelist and public reader is Dickens's description of Bradley Headstone's position as schoolmaster, torn between daytime respectability and night-time crime: "Tied up all day with his disciplined show upon him, subdued to the performance of his routine of educational tricks, encircled by a gabbling crowd, he broke loose at night like an ill-tamed wild animal."

"Realities and idealities . . .": Johnson, p. 911.

CHAPTER XI. Barbey d'Aurevilly

1

Reviews of JESSE's *BRUMMELL* [*I–1*]: *Athenaeum*, XVII; "under the impression . . .": *Tait's Edinburgh Magazine*, XI. The review in *Blackwood's*, LV, was slightly more sympathetic but concluded with the opinion that Brummell had been "magnanimously mean, ridiculously wise, and contemptibly clever". There was no review in *Fraser's*, the *Examiner*, the *Quarterly*, the *Gentleman's Magazine* or *The Times*.

Mrs Gore: Disraeli in MONYPENNY [*IV–2*], I, p. 203; ROSA [*II–4*], Ch. vi; THACKERAY, *LETTERS* [*IX–1*].

Fitz-Boodle Papers: Fitz-Boodle, like Cecil, is a lonely, well-meaning bachelor considered a dangerous rake by all the ladies. His personal tragedy is the same as Cecil's: his brother's wife keeps him away from her children in the belief that he would be a sinister influence. Thackeray appears to have taken one episode directly from Mrs Gore: Fitz-Boodle's German amours. Making the common comparison between the two novelists, Bulwer not surprisingly decided that Mrs Gore was superior: "She preceded Thackeray, and as she knew good society infinitely better than he did, her satire makes his like caricature" (SADLEIR [*III–1*], p. 277).

Guy Livingstone: parodied as "GUY HEAVYSTONE; OR, 'ENTIRE'. A MUSCULAR NOVEL", Vol. I (*CONDENSED NOVELS*) of HARTE'S *WRITINGS* (1902).

2

Bulwer-Tennyson quarrel: THOMAS R. LOUNSBURY, *LIFE AND TIMES OF TENNYSON* (1951), pp. 497–529.

Jesse's first encounter with Brummell: Jesse, II, pp. 67 ff.; RENÉ MARTINEAU, "LE PREMIER BIOGRAPHE DE BRUMMELL", *ASPECTS MÉCONNUS DE BARBEY D'AUREVILLY* (1938).

All quotations from BARBEY's writings are from *LES ŒUVRES COMPLÉTES* (François Bernouard, 1926) unless otherwise noted.

Barbey on England: *Ce qui ne meurt pas*, I, pp. 11–12; *Le Chevalier des Touches*, p. 18.

All references to BARBEY's correspondence—and all personal statements not otherwise justified in text or notes—can hereafter be assumed to derive from his *LETTRES À TRÉBUTIEN*, Vols. XIV–XV of *Les Œuvres complètes*.

Barbey-Jesse correspondence: this must be reconstructed from Barbey's letters to Trébutien, except for two extant letters printed in MÉLVILLE, *BRUMMELL* [*I–3*], pp. viii–x.

Preparation for *Du Dandysme*: articles in *Le Moniteur de la Mode*: ELIZABETH CREED, *LE DANDYSME DE JULES BARBEY D'AUREVILLY* (1938), pp. 40–1; evidence of reading: besides *Du Dandysme* and the *Lettres à Trébutien*, see his *Mémorandum* I & II.

4

Barbey and the aristocratic tradition: JEAN CANU, *BARBEY D'AUREVILLY* (1945), pp. 9–28, 100; and the Société Catholique: EUGÈNE GRELÉ, *JULES BARBEY D'AUREVILLY: SA VIE ET SON ŒUVRE* (1909), I, pp. 183–6.

His Catholicism in the literary scene: D. B. WYNDHAM-LEWIS, "INTRODUCTION" to his translation of Barbey's *ANATOMY OF DANDYISM* (1928); ALBERT LÉON GUÉRARD, *FRENCH PROPHETS OF YESTERDAY: A STUDY OF RELIGIOUS THOUGHT UNDER THE SECOND EMPIRE* (1913), Bk. I, Chs. ii–iii; J.-K. HUYSMANS, "PRÉFACE ÉCRITE VINGT ANS APRÈS LE ROMAN", *À REBOURS* (1922); PAUL VERLAINE, "JULES BARBEY D'AUREVILLY", Vol. V (*LES HOMMES D'AUJOURD'HUI*) of *ŒUVRES* (1920); BARBEY, "J.-K. HUYSMANS", *LE ROMAN CONTEMPORAIN* (1902), Vol. XVIII of *LES ŒUVRES ET LES HOMMES* (Lemerre).

Barbey on dandyism: "G.-A. LAWRENCE", *LITTÉRATURE ÉTRANGÈRE* (1891) & "BALZAC", *ROMANCIERS D'HIER ET D'AVANT-HIER* (1904), Vols. XII & XIX of *Les Œuvres et les hommes*; cf. ERNEST SEILLIÈRE, "LE DANDYSME ROMANTIQUE", *BARBEY D'AUREVILLY* (1910).

Barbey in old age: his clothes: Creed, pp. 76–80; Canu, pp. 230, 342-3, 424; EDMUND GOSSE, "BARBEY D'AUREVILLY", *FRENCH PROFILES* (1905); on homosexuality: JEAN DE BEAULIEU, "BOURGET ET BARBEY D'AUREVILLY", *MERCURE DE FRANCE* (3/1/1936).

CHAPTER XII. Baudelaire

1

All quotations from BAUDELAIRE's works are from the one volume *ŒUVRES COMPLÈTES* (ed. Y.-G. Le Dantec, "la Pléiade", 1951), unless otherwise noted.

"Eternelle supériorité . . .": Baudelaire jotted these words down at the head of an otherwise blank sheet of paper; see CHARLES ASSELINEAU, *CHARLES BAUDELAIRE: SA VIE ET SON ŒUVRE* (1869), pp. 45–6. For other random, vague and pregnant allusions to dandyism in Baudelaire's *Journaux intimes*, see *Fusées*, p. 1188; *Mon cœur mis à nu*, pp. 1199 ("La femme est le contraire du dandy . . ."), 1200 ("Le Dandy . . doit vivre et dormir devant un miroir"), 1204, 1205 ("Un Dandy ne fait rien . . ."), 1209 ("Dandysme.—Qu'est-ce que l'homme supérieur?"), 1216.

Baudelaire's appearance: THÉODORE DE BANVILLE, *CONTES, SOUVENIRS ET PORTRAITS* (1923), pp. 169–70; EUGÈNE

CRÉPET, *CHARLES BAUDELAIRE: ÉTUDE BIOGRA-PHIQUE SUIVIE DES BAUDELAIRIANA D'ASSELINEAU* (1919), p. 44; Mendès in FRANÇOIS PORCHÉ, *BAUDELAIRE: HISTOIRE D'UNE ÂME* (1944), p. 313; NADAR, *CHARLES BAUDELAIRE INTIME* (1911), pp. 36–7; Asselineau, pp. 10–11; Le Vavasseur in Crépet, pp. 44–5; THÉOPHILE GAUTIER, "CHARLES BAUDELAIRE LE POÈTE VIERGE", *PORTRAITS ET SOUVENIRS LITTÉRAIRES* (1892), p. 135.

Baudelaire on century in mourning: *Salon de 1846*; on perfect dandy: *Le Peintre de la vie moderne*; on Jockey-Club: "Richard Wagner et Tannhäuser", *L'Art romantique*; on a new kind of aristocracy: *Le Peintre de la vie moderne*.

Baudelaire as the dandy in Bohemia: Gautier, p. 141; ENID STARKIE, *BAUDELAIRE* (New York, 1933), pp. 140–5.

2

Baudelaire on dandyism: Proudhon "pas dandy": Porché, p. 134; "L'Œuvre et la vie d'Eugène Delacroix", *Curiosités esthétiques*; "Edgar Poe, sa vie et ses œuvres", in Vol. IX of *Œuvres complètes* (N.R.F., 1928); "Madame Bovary" & "Les Liaisons dangereuses", *L'Art romantique*; in "dandys-littéraires": Asselineau, pp. 45–6; see also Starkie, p. 413; MARGARET GILMAN, *BAUDELAIRE THE CRITIC* (1943), pp. 157–8.

Critics on dandyism in Baudelaire: S. A. RHODES, *THE CULT OF BEAUTY IN BAUDELAIRE* (1929), II, Ch. viii; ANDRÉ FERRAN, *L'ESTHÉTIQUE DE BAUDELAIRE* (1933), Pt. I, Ch. ii; ERNEST RAYNAUD, "BAUDELAIRE ET LA RELIGION DU DANDYSME", *MERCURE DE FRANCE* (July–August 1917); JEAN PAUL SARTRE, *BAUDELAIRE* (1942), pp. 153–83; see also RENÉ LAFORGUE, *L'ÉCHEC DE BAUDELAIRE: ÉTUDE PSYCHANALYTIQUE* (1931), pp. 70–1, 216–17; PHILIPPE SOUPAULT, *BAUDELAIRE* (1931), pp. 9–11.

3

Constantin Guys: Gautier, pp. 256–60; GUSTAVE GEFFROY, *CONSTANTIN GUYS: L'HISTORIEN DU SECOND EMPIRE* (1920); P. G. KONODY, *THE PAINTER OF VICTORIAN LIFE: A STUDY OF CONSTANTIN GUYS* (1930); CLIFFORD HALL, "INTRODUCTION" to *CONSTANTIN GUYS* (ed. L. Browse, 1945); ANNE D'EUGNY AND RENÉ COURSAGET eds., *AU TEMPS DE BAUDELAIRE GUYS ET NADAR* (1945).

CHAPTER XIII. Fin de Siècle

1

Ruskin-Whistler case: HESKETH PEARSON, *THE MAN WHISTLER* (New York, 1952), pp. 100–20; J. M. WHISTLER,

THE GENTLE ART OF MAKING ENEMIES (1936), "Prologue".

Aristocracy and fashion: W. B. YEATS, *AUTOBIOGRAPHY* (New York, 1938), pp. 396–7; "the wit, the charm . . .": JEROME H. BUCKLEY, *THE VICTORIAN TEMPER* (1951) p. 213; Queen Victoria in E. F. BENSON, *KING EDWARD VII* (1933), pp. 25–6; CONSUELO VANDERBILT BALSAN, *THE GLITTER AND THE GOLD* (1952), pp. 93–4; E. F. BENSON, *DODO* (1921), p. 2; MARGOT ASQUITH, *AUTOBIOGRAPHY* (1920); HOLBROOK JACKSON, *THE EIGHTEEN NINETIES* (Penguin), pp. 21–2.

2

Beerbohm on Prince: *THINGS NEW AND OLD* (1923), Plate 10; RIEWALD [*XIV–3*], pp. 25–6.

Decline of exclusivism: AMY CRUSE, *AFTER THE VICTORIANS* (1938), p. 246; MALLOCK, *MEMOIRS* [*VIII–2*], pp. 69–70; HELEN MERRELL LYND, *ENGLAND IN THE EIGHTEEN-EIGHTIES* (1945).

3

Whistler on lawyer: WILLIAM GAUNT, *THE AESTHETIC ADVENTURE* (1945), p. 173.

Yellow Book: J. LEWIS MAY, "THE TRUTH ABOUT THE YELLOW BOOK", *THE BERMONDSEY BOOK* (1927–8); E. F. BENSON, *AS WE WERE: A VICTORIAN PEEP-SHOW* (1930), pp. 313–18.

John Lane: his reprinted "first" editions: J. LEWIS MAY, *JOHN LANE AND THE 'NINETIES* (John Lane, 1936), pp. 33–4, 39–40. A "later generation" at the Bodley Head avows that reprinted volumes of the *Yellow Book* itself "were circulated by what can only be described as irregular methods and passed off as first editions" ("Bibliographic Note", *The Yellow Book: A Selection* (ed. Norman Denny, Bodley Head, 1950)).

Leonard Smithers: Yeats, pp. 275–80; R. A. WALKER, "PREFACE", *BEARDSLEY'S LETTERS TO LEONARD SMITHERS* (1947); WILLIAM ROTHENSTEIN, *MEN AND MEMORIES* (New York, 1931–9), I, pp. 244–5; VINCENT O'SULLIVAN, *ASPECTS OF WILDE* (1937), pp. 109–37.

4

Wilde's clothes: ROBERT SHERARD, *THE LIFE OF OSCAR WILDE* (1906), pp. 136–7 & *THE REAL OSCAR WILDE* (1915), facing p. 186; HESKETH PEARSON, *OSCAR WILDE: HIS LIFE AND WIT* (New York, 1946), facing p. 186.

His "entrée" to society: ALFRED LORD DOUGLAS, *OSCAR WILDE: A SUMMING-UP* (1940), pp. 71–2; to Prince and theatre: Pearson, *Wilde*, pp. 40–9; FRANK HARRIS, *OSCAR WILDE: HIS LIFE AND CONFESSIONS* (1930), pp. 42–3.

Wilde in America: Harris, *Wilde*, p. 51; FRANCES WINWAR, *OSCAR WILDE AND THE YELLOW 'NINETIES* (1940), pp. 71–87; ST JOHN ERVINE, *OSCAR WILDE* (1951), p. 103; Pearson, *Wilde*, pp. 52–8; LLOYD LEWIS AND HENRY J. SMITH, *OSCAR WILDE DISCOVERS AMERICA* (1936).

Wilde, advertising and the ridiculous: Sherard, *Life*, p. 247; Pearson, *Whistler*, pp. 165–77; Douglas, pp. 51–2; GRAHAM ROBERTSON, *LIFE WAS WORTH LIVING: REMINISCENCES* (New York, 1931), p. 137; Harris, *Wilde*, pp. 45, 72–3; FRANK HARRIS, *BERNARD SHAW* (New York, 1931), pp. 1, 91.

5

Wilde and the aesthetic movement: GEORGE WOODCOCK, *THE PARADOX OF OSCAR WILDE* (1950), pp. 28–65; KELVER HARTLEY, *OSCAR WILDE: L'INFLUENCE FRANÇAISE DANS SON ŒUVRE* (1935); ALBERT J. FARMER, *LE MOUVEMENT ESTHÉTIQUE ET DÉCADENT EN ANGLETERRE* (1931); G. R. TURQUET-MILNES, *THE INFLUENCE OF BAUDELAIRE IN FRANCE AND ENGLAND* (1913); Yeats, "Introduction", Wilde's *Works*, III, pp. xv–xvi.

All quotations from WILDE's writings are from *THE COMPLETE WORKS* (Garden City, 1923) unless otherwise noted.

Wilde on style: "Decay of Lying", *Intentions*, p. 55; on romantic rich: "The Model Millionaire", p. 155; on novel of high life: a review of Lady Munster's *Dorinda*, *Criticisms*, pp. 110–13; on form in good society: *Dorian Gray*, p. 260.

Art and Society: W. H. MALLOCK, *THE NEW REPUBLIC* (1877), I, pp. 58, 232.

Wilde's aesthetic dandyism: uselessness of art: "Preface", *Dorian*; paradoxes: *Phrases for the Use of the Young*; definitions of dandyism: *Dorian*, p. 236.

6

Des Esseintes and Montesquiou: ERNEST SEILLIÈRE, *J.-K. HUYSMANS* (1931), p. 76; JAMES LAVER, *THE FIRST DECADENT* (1954), pp. 75–7. Des Esseintes, is essentially a greatly idealized portrait of Huysmans himself—who barely knew Montesquiou. But it is certain that contemporary legend about the aristocrat's way of life entered into *à Rebours*. ROBERT DE MONTESQUIOU boasted of his influence on Huysmans—and complained bitterly of his portrait as Des Esseintes (*LES PAS EFFACÉS: MÉMOIRES* (1923), II, pp. 108–27 & III, pp. 270–1).

Homosexuality in *Dorian Gray*: *Scots Observer* (7/12/1890); HAVELOCK ELLIS, *STUDIES IN THE PSYCHOLOGY OF SEX* (New York, 1936), pp. 63 ff.

Youth-worship: Pearson, *Wilde*, p. 243; *OSCAR WILDE: THREE TIMES TRIED* (1928), p. 271.

7

Péladan: MARIO PRAZ, *THE ROMANTIC AGONY* (trans. A. Davidson, 1933), pp. 291, 318–20; Laver, pp. 127–33.

Beardsley: May, *Lane*, pp. 46–7; WILDE, *LETTERS TO THE SPHINX WITH REMINISCENCES BY ADA LEVERSON* (1930), p. 34; Rothenstein, I, p. 134; BEARDSLEY, *LAST LETTERS* (1904).

8

Satire of Wilde as homosexual: *Punch* (6/5/1880): in the cartoon "A Love-Agony", Postlethwaite the poet-aesthete, with Wilde's thick lips and heavy eyes, lies half-nude by a pond, displaying a grossly effeminate torso; the accompanying love poem inquires, "Shepherd art thou, or nymph, that smilest there?"; *Punch* (2/12/ 1881): Wilde again, appearing at an aesthetic soirée as the painter Maudle. He compliments Mrs Brown ("a Philistine from the country") on her "consummately lovely" son. "What?" answers the startled lady; "He's a *nice, manly* boy, if you mean *that*, Mr Maudle." And she resolves that he is not to study with Maudle. See also *ARISTOPHANES AT OXFORD* by "Y. T. O." (1894), an anonymous verse satire published at Oxford; for Beerbohm's satire, see below, Ch. xiv.

ROBERT S. HICHENS on Wilde: *YESTERDAY* (1947), pp. 69–70; *THE GREEN CARNATION* (1894), pp. 17, 140, 195–7.

Wilde on the future of the dandies: *A Woman of No Importance*, p. 259; on dowdies and dandies: *An Ideal Husband*, p. 184.

CHAPTER XIV. Beerbohm

1

Beerbohm and the past: "I may be old-fashioned . . .": "The Older and Better Music Hall", *AROUND THEATRES* (1953); a museum piece: REBECCA WEST, *ENDING IN EARNEST: A LITERARY LOG* (1931), pp. 66–7; an "interesting link": "A Small Boy Seeing Giants", *MAINLY ON THE AIR*. (A variety of editions of BEERBOHM's essays has been used.)

2

Beerbohm as undergraduate: his reading: ROTHENSTEIN [*XIII–3*], I, p. 146; *The Spirit Lamp* (ed. Douglas, Oxford, June 1893).

As historian: "a howler": Interview, 1954; "To give an accurate . . .": "1880", *WORKS*; irony: "Advertisements", *Mainly on the Air*.

D'Orsay as a painter: beside Beerbohm's view of the "repellent process" of painting should be placed Haydon's famous description of D'Orsay's visit to his studio in 1839, when the painter was doing a portrait of Wellington on his horse Copenhagen. "He took my brush in his dandy gloves, which made my heart ache. . . . In this prime of dandyism he took up a nasty, oily, dirty, hog-tool, and immortalised Copenhagen by touching the sky." But Haydon rubbed out D'Orsay's work: "This won't do—a Frenchman touch Copenhagen!" (HAYDON [*VII–2*], II–655).

Beerbohm as child author: "A Cloud of Pinafores", *MORE*.

3

Personal dandyism: J. G. RIEWALD, *SIR MAX BEERBOHM: MAN AND WRITER* (The Hague, 1953), pp. 34–5, 41–4; FRANK HARRIS, *CONTEMPORARY PORTRAITS: SERIES 4* (1924), p. 127; HICHENS, *YESTERDAY* [*XIII–8*], pp. 85–9; Rothenstein, I, p. 144; WILDE, *LETTERS TO SPHINX* [*XIII–7*], p. 42; see also VYVYAN HOLLAND, *SON OF OSCAR WILDE* (New York, 1954), p. 170; JACKSON [*XIII–1*], p. 117.

Beerbohm and the Regency: Interview, 1954; ADA LEVERSON, "A FEW WORDS WITH MR MAX BEERBOHM", *THE SKETCH* (1/2/1895); *Punch* (10/27/1894): "We never find *Thackeray* searching for the *mot juste* as for a wisp of hay in a packet of needles."

The ageing Disraeli: HARRIS, *WILDE* [*XIII–4*], p. 19; BEERBOHM, "Note" (1922), *ROSSETTI AND HIS CIRCLE* and "Whistler's Writing", *YET AGAIN*; Disraeli letter (1862) to Mrs Bridges Williams in MRS HUMPHRY WARD, *A WRITER'S RECOLLECTIONS* (1918), II, p. 140.

"Women are becoming . . .": "George IV", *Works*.

4

Beerbohm and the twentieth century: "London Revisited", *Mainly on the Air*; "The Fire", *Yet Again*; "Diminuendo", *Works*; LOGAN PEARSALL SMITH, "SIR MAX BEERBOHM", *ATLANTIC MONTHLY* (November 1942).

Self-imposed limits and style: Beerbohm's introductory letter to BOHUN LYNCH, *MAX BEERBOHM IN PERSPECTIVE* (1921); "Ouida", *More*; "Whistler's Writing", *Yet Again*.

His principles: "The Decline of the Graces", *Yet Again*; "A Small Boy Seeing Giants", *Mainly on the Air*.

"A now extinct species . . .": "London Revisited". *Mainly on the Air*.

Index

NOTE: *The most important sources used have been indexed below, either under the author or, in the case of a biography, the subject. Page numbers, in these cases, are italicized, and refer to the page of the notes in which the first full reference to a source is given.*